U0813701

教育部人文社会科学重点研究基地刊物
中文社会科学引文索引（CSSCI）来源集刊

藏学学刊

བོད་རིག་པའི་དུས་དེབ།

JOURNAL OF TIBETOLOGY

总第21辑
2019（2）

四川大学中国藏学研究所 编

中国藏学出版社

བོད་རིག་པའི་དུས་དེབ།
藏　学　学　刊
Journal of Tibetology

主编　霍巍　石硕

常务副主编　张长虹

编辑委员会

（以姓氏拼音为序）

主席　巴桑旺堆（西藏自治区社会科学院）

委员　才让太（中央民族大学）

霍　巍（四川大学）

石　硕（四川大学）

沈卫荣（清华大学）

熊文彬（四川大学）

张　云（中国藏学研究中心）

多吉旺秋（德国汉堡大学）

范德康（美国哈佛大学）

马休·凯普斯坦（法国巴黎高等研究实践学院、美国芝加哥大学）

滕华睿（美国纽约哥伦比亚大学）

谢　萧（法国巴黎高等研究实践学院）

编辑　陈　波　嘎尔让　华青道尔杰（张延清）

许渊钦　杨清凡　玉珠措姆（金红梅）

张长虹

编务　孙昭亮

བོད་རིག་པའི་དུས་དེབ།
藏 学 学 刊
Journal of Tibetology

Editors-in-chief Huo Wei, Shi Shuo

Deputy Editor-in-chief Zhang Changhong

Editorial Board

Pasang Wangdu (*Chair, Tibetan Academy of Social Science, China*)
Tsering Thar (*Minzu University of China*)
Huo Wei (*Sichuan University, China*)
Shi Shuo (*Sichuan University, China*)
Shen Weirong (*Tsinghua University, China*)
Xiong Wenbin (*Sichuan University, China*)
Zhang Yun (*China Tibetology Research Center*)

Dorji Wangchuk (*Hamburg University, Germany*)
van der Kuijp, Leonard W. J. (*Harvard University, U.S.A.*)
Kapstein, Matthew T. (*École Pratique des Hautes Études, France; University of Chicago, U.S.A.*)
Tuttle, Gray (*Columbia University, U.S.A*)
Scherrer-Schaub, Cristina A. (*École Pratique des Hautes Études, France*)

Editors Chen Bo, Gaerrang,
Pelchan Dorje (*Zhang Yanqing*),
Xu Yuanqin, Yang Qingfan,
Yudru Tsomu (*Jin Hongmei*), Zhang Changhong

Editorial Assistant Sun Zhaoliang

目　录

Table of Contents

Archaeological Evidence for the Bon *Mdos rgyab* Ritual at Samdzong, Upper Mustang, Nepal

Mark Aldenderfer

Abstract: It is not common that archaeologists discover clear and unambiguous traces of historically known ritual practices in their excavations. One exception to this is the discovery of artifacts at the Samdzong site in Upper Mustang, Nepal, that may be part of the so-called Bon *Mdos rgyab* ritual. A set of artifacts — an iron tripod, copper vessels, and wooden and bamboo cups — recovered from Samdzong 5, which is dated to the late 5th C. CE, are strikingly similar to ethnographically described artifacts that are key components of this ritual. This manuscript explains the Bon *Mdos rgyab* ritual, describes the context at Samdzong 5 and the key artifacts, and reflects on the presence of Bon in Upper Mustang at this time.

Introduction

Although rituals, be they religious in nature or secular, form a part of daily life, they often leave few material traces of their practice. This poses a challenge to archaeologists who seek to understand how rituals, especially those tied to the exercise of power, maintain and sometimes transform the cultures of the past.[1] In cultures with a written historical record, rituals may be described in some detail, and in some cases these accounts can be used to interpret materials

1 See Aldenderfer 2010.

found in the archaeological record. Oral tradition recovered through ethnography may provide similar records of ritual practices. Although these records must be used with caution because the details of such practices often change as new traditions and concepts are added and others subtracted, they nevertheless may offer unique insights into the ritual life of the past.

Charles Ramble has published an ethnographic study of the Bon *Mdos rgyab* ritual as he observed it in the community of Lubra (Klu brag)[2], a small village in southern Mustang, Nepal. His research, along with archaeometric data obtained from some of the artifacts at Samdzong, provides the foundation for the argument presented in this manuscript.

Lubra and the *Mdos rgyab* ritual

The recorded history of Lubra goes back to the 11th C; archaeological data recovered by a series of projects in the Muktinath valley, which is found a short distance to the north in the Kali Gandaki drainage, suggest that southern Mustang was occupied at least as early as 1200 BCE.[3] According to these historical records, the original inhabitants of Lubra were descended from a clan from the Tibetan Plateau. The documents that describe their origins indicate that they were likely to be Bonpos upon their arrival, and further, had lived well to the north of Lubra in a village called Bonkhor.[4] As we shall see below, the likelihood of a historical presence of Bon practitioners in Upper Mustang is significant for and relevant to the claims made in this manuscript.

As described by Ramble, the *Mdos rgyab* ritual has both sacred and secular components. The sacred aspect of the ritual is a year-end exorcism of the demons and other baleful entities that plagued the community over the past year. In effect, it is meant to cleanse the community so that it will prosper in the coming year. The ceremony lasts up to 19 days, and over that time, rites and rituals are conducted in the temple of the monastery in the community. Dances and other activities are also performed. The culmination of the sacred event is the creation, then destruction, of the *mdos*, which is a complex construction of string, dough effigies that have been placed upon on a series of platforms, parchments, and other objects. The *mdos* is carried from the temple, hacked apart, then burned.[5]

The secular aspects of the ritual are primarily concerned with the rules and arrangements for feeding the participants as they perform its various activities. These are quite formulaic and specific quantities of different foods, their manner or preparation, and the details of

---

2 See Ramble 2000.

3 See Aldenderfer in press.

4 Ramble 2000: 291.

5 Ramble 2000: 302.

their presentation are important aspects of the ritual process. Two "stewards" (*spyi pa*) act as overseers for the duration of the ceremony. These stewards also held the role of village headman (*rgan pa*) and served for the preceding year as supervisors of communal activity, which generally includes dispute resolution, tax collection, and similar duties. These steward/headmen are replaced at the end of the *Mdos rgyab* ritual and new ones appointed.[6]

Among the many secular activities that surround the ritual, the one of greatest interest to this manuscript is the annual transfer of stewardship.[7] Conducted at the end of the ceremony, the transfer acknowledges the outgoing stewards and consecrates those incoming. It takes place within the temple and includes strict protocols in seating, the offering and consumption of beer, and the singing of songs by both men and women.

Two kinds of traditionally prepared beer are consumed: *chang* (which is called *yang gyab* in this context) which is usually made from either barley or buckwheat, and is a yellowish color, and *tsemo*, a rice beer with a whitish color. Both kinds of beer are placed in large pans and the container for the *tsemo* sits upon an iron tripod that is wrapped with white wool or a white khata. A ceremonial wooden flask holds some of the *yang gyab*; beer is poured from this flask into a ladle, which is then used to pour the beer into four wooden bowls, one for each of the incoming and outgoing stewards. The *yang gyab* is consumed first, and the *tsemo*, also called *A-bse* (the name of a prominent Bon protector), is consumed as the final act of the ceremony. The transfer of authority to the new stewards is now complete.

Wooden or metal objects used in this setting are 1) pans or vessels to hold the *yang gyab*; 2) an iron tripod that supports the pan holding the *tsemo*; 3) a wooden flask; 4) a ladle; and 5) bowls used for drinking beer. Other, more perishable items used include 1) butter; and 2) white wool or a white fabric.

Samdzong and Samdzong 5

Samdzong is a mortuary site that consists of ten shaft tombs found in the façade of a cliff face on the east side of the Samdzong Khola at an elevation of ca. 4000 m (Fig. 1 and 2). The tombs were exposed by a seismic event that shook off the cliff face, thus exposing the chambers. This event collapsed the ceilings of the tombs and mixed their contents. Although we have been able to infer the basics of the treatment of the dead, the remains are jumbled and certainly moved from their original placements. Some artifacts were broken during the event as well. Despite these obstacles, we recovered the remains of at least 105 individuals and numerous artifacts

6 Ramble 2000: 303.

7 Ramble 2000: 311-314.

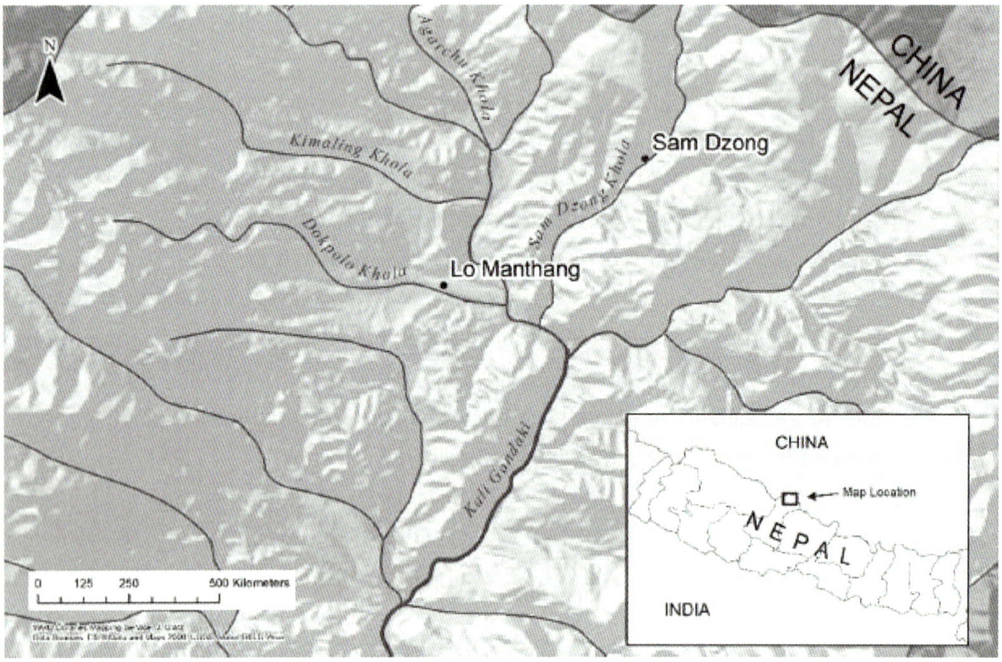

Fig. 1 General location of Samdzong in Upper Mustang (J. Glatz, Western Michigan University).

Fig. 2 The site of Samdzong. Numbers indicate the tomb complex (photo: M. Aldenderfer).

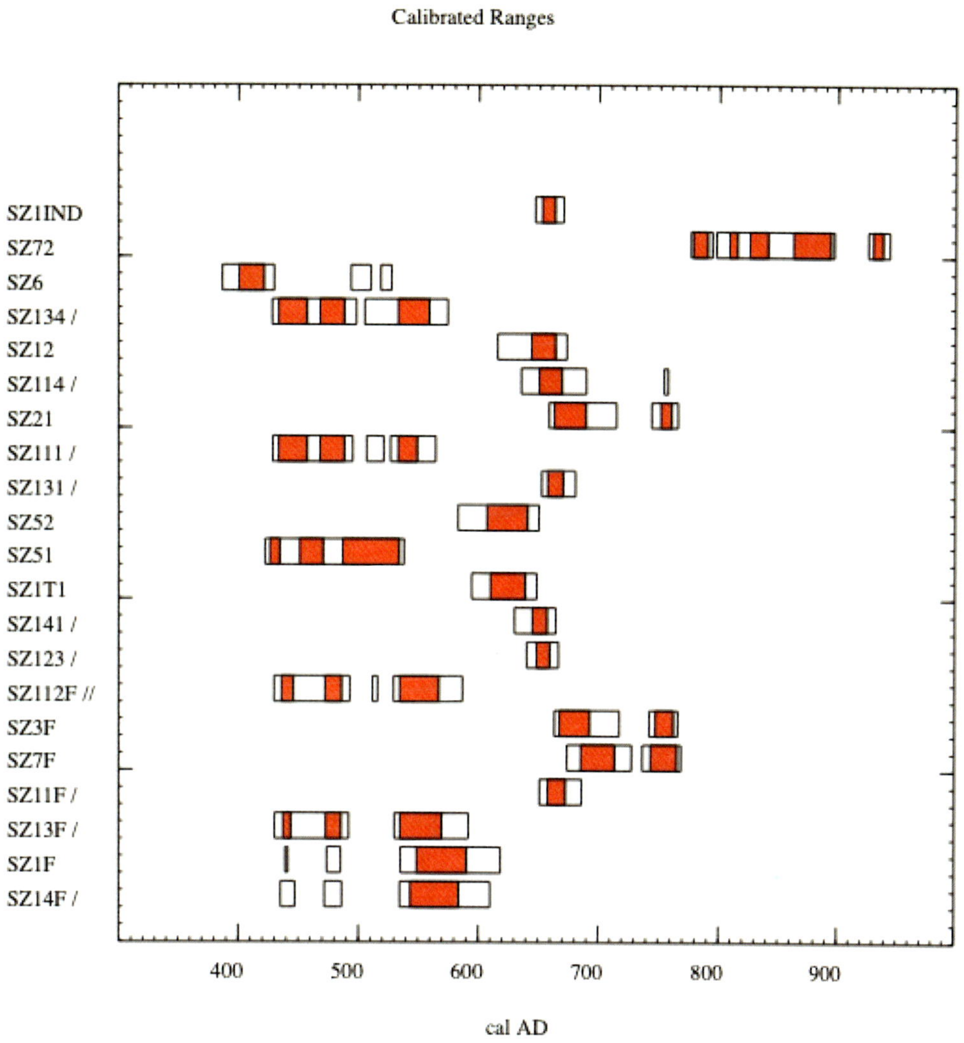

Fig. 3 Calibrated radiocarbon dates from Samdzong (http://calib.org/calib/calib.html accessed June 5, 2019).

including glass beads, fabrics, metals, wooden objects, and ceramics.[8] A comprehensive program of radiocarbon dating, exclusively from the human and animal remains found within the tombs indicates that the site was occupied from 450-750 CE (Fig. 3); one of the tombs, Samdzong 7, dates after 800 CE, but reflects a very different mortuary treatment when compared to the other tombs.

8 Eng and Aldenderfer 2011, 2017.

Fig. 4 The archaeological context of Samdzong 5. Note the iron tripod (Photo: P. Athans).

Samdzong 5 is the tomb of greatest interest to this manuscript. This context was the most complex at the site; artifacts recovered from it include an almost-square wooden coffin that contained a single individual, a gold/silver mask, copper vessels, an iron tripod, wooden and bamboo cups, wooden trays, Chinese silks, a bronze mirror, and thousands of glass beads.[9] The remains of horses, sheep/goat, and a large bovid (possibly a yak) were also discovered. The coffin contained the remains of a single adult individual of indeterminate sex. Radiocarbon dating of the remains returned an age of 1580±20 RCYBP or cal CE 422-538 and a median probability of CE 483 (calibrated with Calib 7.11 http://calib.org/calib/calib.html). The contents of the tomb were disturbed by the collapse of the ceiling following the seismic event (Fig. 4). These findings

9 Gleba, M., Vanden Berghe and Aldenderfer 2016; Massa, Aldenderfer, and Martin-Torres 2019.

Fig. 5 Copper vessels recovered from Samdzong 5
a) ladle b) handle of ladle with remnants of iron c) small copper bowl d) large copper cauldron (Photos: G. Massa).

suggest that the inhabitant of the coffin in Samdzong 5 was a local elite; the kin of this person were able to mobilize artifacts from many places in South, Central, and Western Asia.[10]

The metal, bamboo, and wooden artifacts from Samdzong 5

The copper vessels include a large cauldron, a smaller bowl, and a ladle (Fig. 5). The chemical composition of the large cauldron, including lead isotope analysis, as well as stylistic features of the artifact, suggest that it was produced in South Asia.[11] The other two objects are similar in composition, and likely have a South Asian origin as well. The ladle once had an iron handle,

10 Massa, Aldenderfer, and Martin-Torres 2019: 13.

11 Massa, Aldenderfer, and Martin-Torres 2019: 3, 13.

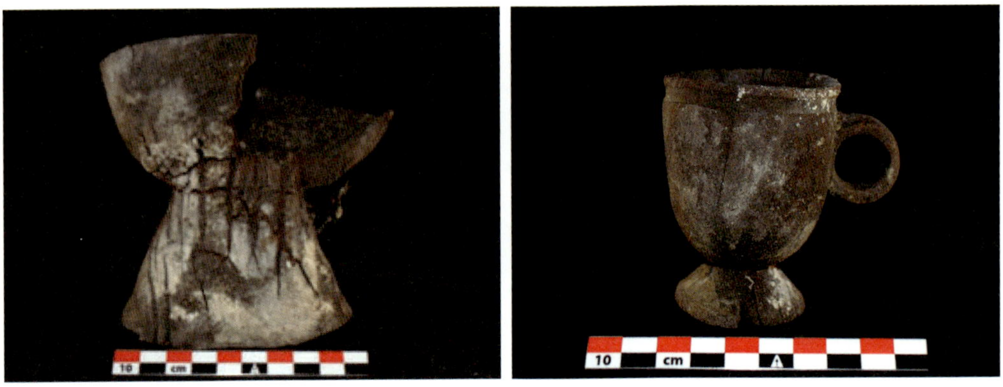

Fig. 6 Left: large wooden cup Right: small wooden cup (Photo: M. Aldenderfer).

remnants of which can still be observed. Finally, the iron tripod was highly corroded and missing part of one of its legs. Each of these artifacts were found near the wooden coffin.

Three cups were found in the tomb, one of bamboo and two of wood. The bamboo cup is cylindrical in form, has a single node of the bamboo plant as its base and a hollow internode. There is no handle or other attachment to the cup, which has been broken. The wooden cups appear to have been carved out of a single piece of a soft wood (Fig. 6). The largest of the two wooden cups has a large, ovoid bowl that is supported by an expanding, but hollow, stem. The bowl of the cup has been broken, and it has been warped by the pressure of the deposit. The base, however, is mostly intact but cracked longitudinally. The second cup is smaller, has a tapering cylinder that is supported by a small base. It has a circular ring-shaped handle. It is intact and in remarkably good condition.

Residue analysis of vessel contents

Although the collapse of the ceiling of the tomb introduced debris into some of the vessels, most were not affected. Some, such as the wooden cups, were trapped under the debris but were not filled with it. Some roof fall did enter the cauldron, but some of the slats of the wooden coffin prevented it from being filled with it. In any case, the debris was easily removed after excavation. Following routine cleaning, the interior surfaces of each vessel were inspected for deposits, encrustations, and signs of use. Any identified residues were carefully sampled and exported for analysis.

Macroscopic, microscopic, and chemical analyses were performed on these residues. Although these studies are only preliminary, their results are significant and critical for obtaining data on their use. These analyses, under the supervision of Christina Warinner of the

Max Planck Institute for the Science of Human History[12] resulted in the following (Table 1).

Table 1. Preliminary findings from Samdzong funerary vessels

ID	Vessel	Macrobotanical	Metagenomics	Proteomics
SAM1	Large wooden cup	Amorphous residue, rice husks	-	Rice, wool
SAM3	Bamboo cup	Amorphous residue	-	Rice, wool
SAM4	Small copper bowl	Amorphous residue, bone	Wheat, barley, rice, millet (*Setaria italica*)	-
SAM5	Copper cauldron	Amorphous residue, plant fibers, bone	Wheat, barley, fermentation fungi	-
SAM6	Copper ladle	Amorphous residue	-	-

Residues were recovered from each of the vessels. The large wooden cup had rice husks and grain fragments present, and proteomics analysis (the study of proteins as expressed by an organism) identified both rice and wool proteins. The bamboo cup had both rice and wool proteins. Metagenomic analysis (the study of genetic material from environmental samples) identified the presence of other plants in the small copper bowl and the presence of fermentation fungi, including barley, in the copper cauldron. Given the archaeological context of these tombs and the fact they were sealed from environmental contamination until very recently, these results are likely to reflect the uses of these objects before they were placed within in the tomb context.

Although wheat and barley are known subsistence crops cultivated in the region,[13] rice is a low-elevation domesticate and cannot be grown in the highlands of Upper Mustang. While the source of the rice cannot be identified with certainty, rice is not grown today in elevations above 3000m,[14] so it is clear that it had to have been imported. The presence of rice husks supports this assertion.

Discussion

Although there are real differences between the assemblage of artifacts used in the transfer of authority ceremony in the *Mdos rgyab* ceremony in Lubra and the assemblage of artifacts found in Samdzong 5, there are enough points of contact to suggest that the artifacts at Samdzong

12 Christina Warinner, personal communication, 2018.

13 Knorzer 2000.

14 Paudel 2013.

reflect aspects of it. Granted, the context is quite different: artifacts found in a mortuary facility versus a set of artifacts used, then stored, over the course of a year in a temple. But as was argued above, it is not necessary for these assemblages to be identical in content and setting to be suggestive that some form of transfer of authority of the *Mdos rgyab* ceremony may be reflected at Samdzong 5.

The most direct similarities are the iron tripod, the ladle, and the wool proteins. Rice grains and proteins are found in the wooden and bamboo cups. This suggests that the rice was consumed as a beverage, and not as a meal. Although the color of the beverage cannot be inferred from the proteins, it is quite likely that the beverage was similar to *tsemo*. In the copper cauldron, metagenomics reveals the presence of wheat and barley as well as fermentation fungi. The presence of these proteins suggests that it was used to serve or store the yellow beer, or *yang gyab*. Likewise, the presence of wool proteins in the cups suggests that wool was present and perhaps wrapped on or was near the iron tripod. The ladle was likely used to serve both beers, which were consumed in the bamboo and wooden cups.

Aside from the different contexts, there are other points of dissimilarity. In the modern ceremony, bowls are used, not cups, to drink the beer. At Samdzong, there is nothing that resembles the ceremonial flask used to offer the beer into the serving bowls. Although the small copper bowl has more genetic material present than just rice, the remains of these other plants may reflect earlier uses not related to the ceremony itself. The assemblage at Samdzong 5, then, is an imperfect reflection of the modern ceremony.

If these points of similarity are valid, they suggest that the ceremony has changed over time. At Samdzong 5, the entire collection of artifacts in the tomb indicates that a politically or socially prominent person was interred. This person may have been a local leader but of an unknown position. Upon death, not only were wealth objects placed in the tomb, such as the golden mask, but also the artifacts that symbolized authority, such as the ladle, iron tripod, and copper vessels. It is not possible to know if any type of ceremony, such as the consumption of the beers, was conducted in the tomb although given its small size, this is unlikely. It is also unknown (and unknowable) if the placement of these artifacts in the tomb represents a transfer of authority as it does in the modern performance or is instead a reflection of a status position. Despite all of these caveats, however, the assemblage in Samdzong 5 has a strong resemblance to the modern Mdos rgyab ceremony.

A deeper question remains to be answered: does the material recovered from Samdzong 5 reflect the practice of a Bon ceremony and thus the presence of Bon in Upper Mustang in the late 5th C? To answer this requires looking at other possible manifestations of Bon in the wider region. Gold masks similar to that found at Samdzong 5 (indeed, two other gold/silver masks were found in Samdzong tombs 1/4) are found in the western Himalayas at a series of mortuary sites in western Tibet and northwestern India.[15] The western Tibetan masks have a median age probability of 281 and 194 cal BCE; the northwestern Indian mask is said to date around 100 BCE, and similar masks are found throughout Central Asia and date from CE 100-500.

Not all of these masks are necessarily indicative of a Bon religious tradition, but Tong and Li[16] in passing suggest that at least the western Tibetan masks may be of Bon origin. I have extended this suggestion and have argued on the basis of textual evidence developed by Samten Karmay[17] that these masks are an important part of Bon mortuary practice.[18] If this argument is valid, the presence of artifacts in Samdzong 5 similar to the modern Mdos rgyab ceremony supports this assertion. At a general level, then, we can say that a religious tradition with elements of Bon was in place in Upper Mustang at least by the 5th C.

Conclusions

The artifacts found in Samdzong 5, combined with careful archaeometric analysis, support an assertion that they reflect at least in part aspects of the modern Mdos rgyab ceremony, especially those activities related to the transfer of village authority and stewardship, as it is practiced in Lubra. These findings provide additional support to the hypothesis that elements of Bon religion were present in Upper Mustang at least by the 5th C.

Bibliography

Aldenderfer, M. 2010. "Gimme that Old Time Religion: Rethinking the Role of Religion in the Emergence of Social Inequality." In *Pathways to Power*, ed. T.D. Price and G. Feinman. New York: Springer, 77-95.

—— 2013. "Variation in Mortuary Practice on the Early Tibetan Plateau and the High Himalayas." In *Journal of the International Society for Bon Studies* 1: 273-298.

—— 2016. "The Golden Masks from the Western Himalayas: Evidence for Bon Mortuary Ritual?" Paper presented at the International Conference on Bon: Ancient and Modern. Shenten Dargye Bon Congregation, Blou, France. June.

15 Aldenderfer 2013; Tong and Li 2015, 2016.

16 Tong and Li 2016: 90.

17 Samten Karmay 2019.

18 Aldenderfer 2016.

—— In press. "Defining a Shangshung Presence in Ancient Mustang (Lo and Se-rib), Nepal." In *Proceedings of First Lhasa Shangshung Culture International Academic Seminar.*
Eng, Jacqueline and M. Aldenderfer. 2011. "Bioarchaeological Analysis of Human Remains from Mustang, Nepal, 2010." In *Ancient Nepal* 178: 9-32.
—— 2017. "Bioarchaeological Profile of Stress and Dental Disease among Ancient High Altitude Himalayan Communities of Nepal." In *American Journal of Human Biology* 00: e22998. https://doi.org/10.1002/ajhb.22998
Gleba, M.; Vanden Berghe and M. Aldenderfer. 2016. "Textile Technology in Nepal in the 5th-7th Centuries CE: the Case of Samdzong." In *Science and Technology of Archaeological Research* 2(1): 1-11.
Karmay, S. 2019. "The Gold Masks Found in Shang shung and the 'Five Supports of the Soul (*rten lnga*)' of the Bon Funerary Tradition." In *Ancient Civilization of Tibetan Plateau. Proceedings of the First Beijing International Conference on Shang Shung Cultural Studies, Vol.* 2, ed. T. Tsar and T. Sharshorn, 330-344.
Knorzer, K-H. 2000. "3000 Years of Agriculture in a Valley of the High Himalaya." In *Vegetation History and Archaeobotany* 9(4): 219-222.
Massa, G. 2013. *The Funerary Metals of Samdzong: Material Characterisation of Artefacts from Pre-Buddhist Nepal.* Msc dissertation, Institute of Archaeology, University College, London.
Massa, G.; M. Aldenderfer and M. Martin-Torres. 2019. "Of Gold Masks, Bronze Mirrors and Brass Bracelets: Analyses of Metallic Artefacts from Samdzong, Upper Mustang, Nepal 450-650 CE." *Archaeological Research in Asia.* 18: 68-81.
Paudel, M. 2013. "Rice (Oryza sativa L) Cultivation in the Highest Elevation of the World." In *Agronomy Journal of Nepal.* 2: 31-41. https://doi.org/10.3126/ajn.v2i0.7519.
Ramble, C. 2000. "The Secular Surroundings of a Bonpo Ceremony: Games, Popular Rituals and Economic Structures in the *mDos-rgyab* of Klu-brag Monastery (Nepal)." In *New Horizons in Bon Studies: Bon Studies 2,* eds. Samten G. Karmay and Yasuhiko Nagano, Osaka: National Museum of Ethnology, 289-316.
Tong Tao and Li Linhu. 2015. 仝涛、李林辉 . "Ouya shiye nei de Ximalaya huangjin mianju." 欧亚视野内的喜马拉雅黄金面具 [The Himalayan Gold Masks from the Eurasian Perspective]. *Kaogu* 考古 */Archaeology* 2: 92-102.
—— 2016. "The Himalayan Gold Masks from the Eurasian Perspective." *Chinese Archaeology* 16: 85-90.

◆ Author: Mark Aldenderfer, John D. and Catherine T. MacArthur Distinguished Professor, Department of Anthropology and Heritage Studies, University of California

Knucklebones
An Archaeological and Ethnohistorical Inquiry into one of Tibet's Oldest Gaming and Divination Objects

John Vincent Bellezza

Abstract: Through archeological and ethnographic sources this article furnishes a comprehensive perspective on the Tibetan cultural purposes of the ovicaprid ankle bone called astragalus or knucklebone. It sets forth criteria for the identification of culturally significant astragali in Tibetan tombs and assesses the functional implications of examples in burials in other parts of Eurasia for comparison. A copper alloy astragalus of ostensible Tibetan origin is examined, also supplying some insight into the ancient cultural status of this bone on the plateau. The article also investigates the role of astragali in Tibetan gaming, divination, tallying, ritual traditions, and concepts of the sacred. Finally, attention is turned towards cross-cultural aspects of the utility and symbolism of ovicaprid astragali and what they might tell us about the nature and extent of transcultural exchange in Eurasia in the Late Prehistoric era (ca. 1200 BCE to 600 CE) and in historic times.

Introduction[1]

This article reviews the archaeology and ethnohistory of the ovicaprid knucklebone on the Tibetan plateau, one of the most enduring and widespread of cultural symbols.[2] The knucklebone is located in the tarsus of the rear legs of domestic sheep (*Ovis aries*), goats (*Capra hircus*) and other artiodactyls. It is a squarish bone that has been used for a variety of purposes by humans, its cultural associations having spread widely in Europe, the Middle East, Central Asia, and China by the Iron Age. That there are only two per sheep or goat lends the astragalus intrinsic value and its blocky form and high density make for a durable, tactile and visually appealing object. The work considers archaeological and ethnographic evidence regarding this storied implement and symbol, examining its ancient and contemporary functions in gaming, divination and protection in Tibet and other regions of Eurasia. By probing the material and abstract significance of the astragalus a new channel of inquiry into Tibet's place in the cultural map of the continent is opened. It is the author's hope that this preliminary study will stimulate further interest in the subject among historians, anthropologists and archaeologists working on the Tibetan plateau.

The astragali of sheep and goats and their facsimiles are one of the most widely distributed objects in archaeological and anthropological contexts in Eurasia, Tibet being no exception. They have been discovered in ancient settlements and tombs and served as popular gaming pieces in many places on the continent until well into the 20th century. It is generally believed that astragali are the precursors of jacks and dice, the etched markings on the latter sometimes matching those on knucklebones. The bone may also have contributed to the creation of other games such as boules. Recreational activities featuring astragali in the archaeological and ethnographic settings are mostly associated with children but adults participated as well and this is reflected in the premodern cultural scene of Tibet too. There are a number of gambling games using ovicaprid knucklebones that were traditionally played by adults in Tibet until the end of the last century. However, they have now disappeared or are in steep decline. Copper alloy imitations of astragali were cast in ancient Greece, Rome, central China, and probably Tibet. The wide distribution of knucklebones and knucklebone imitations in Eurasia is mirrored in cowries, a marine mollusk collected from the Indian and Pacific oceans, which also had

1 The writing of this article was supported by a grant awarded me by the Lumbini International Research Institute (LIRI), Lumbini, Nepal. I especially want to thank the acting director of LIRI, Christoph Cüppers, for his support of my work. I also heartily thank Prof. Huo Wei and Zhang Changhong for arranging my attendance at the Seventh International Conference of Tibetan Archaeology & Art, in Chengdu, October 19-21, 2018, and for the excellent hospitality I received whilst in Chengdu.

2 In English it is also known as astragalus/astragal (pl. astragali/astragals), talus (pl. tali), and huckle-bone. The term "knucklebones" also denotes games played with this bone.

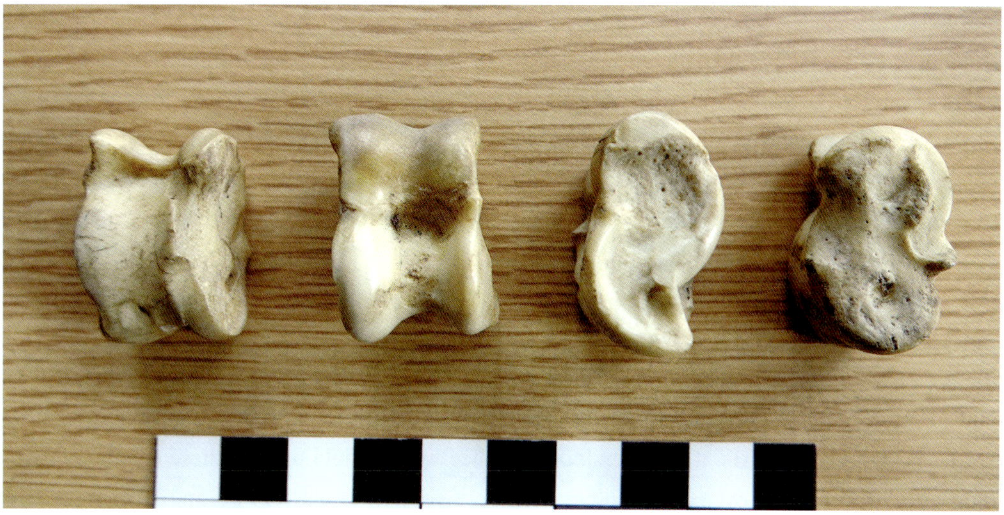

Fig. 1 The four sides of ovicaprid astragali
Left: plantar; Middle left: dorsal; Middle right: lateral; Right: medial.

a broad array of functions, serving as ornaments, talismans and a medium of exchange for various Eurasian peoples, including Tibetans. Cowries were reproduced in Tibet and other locations on the continent using copper alloys and other substances.[3]

The astragali of sheep and goats are known by a variety of names on the Tibetan plateau (Fig. 1). In Khams and A mdo (eastern Tibetan plateau)[4] and in the Hor and A pha Hor regions of Nag chu, it is generally called *the ge*. In parts of A mdo such as Rnga ba the knucklebone is rendered *be ke*, a regional variant of *the ge*. In Lhasa and southern areas of the Tibet Autonomous Region, the astragalus is referred to as *A cug*. In Gtsang and Stod (including Ting ri, Skyi grong, Spu rangs and the western Byang thang) the astragalus is styled *long mo*, a constituent of the ankle joint (*long tshig/long rdog*). More generally, the knucklebone and ankle in Tibetan are called *long bu* and *Ong bu*. In Spiti (Spyi ti) a sheep or goat astragalus is known as *mug lo*. There are also more localized names for sheep and goat astragali in Tibet. For example, in the Gling tshang dialect of Sde dge, the bone is designated *sa ga*, while in Dkar mdzes and Brag 'go, located further east in Khams, it is the *A 'gram* (spelling?). There are likely to be other synonyms for ovicaprid astragali in sundry Bodic languages and dialects but more research is required to confirm this.

The Tibetan *the ge* and *long mo* appear to be older indigenous terms. *Long* as an initial syllable of Tibetan words is well attested and those having to do with the abdomen, intestines

3 For a preliminary study of both knucklebones and cowries in Tibet, see Bellezza 2014.

4 Incorporated into the Chinese provinces of Yunnan, Sichuan, Gansu, and Qinghai.

and bulging shapes probably share a root with *long mo/long bu*. This semantic cluster appears to be derived from the Old Tibetan language. *The ge*, by virtue of its orthography, also seems to be of ancient origins. It can be traced to either Old Tibetan or the Zhang zhung language (both *the* and *ge* occur in Zhang zhung lexicons). The term *the ge* and other common Tibetan names for the knucklebone do not seem to occur in the Dunhuang manuscripts. The reasons for this absence in extant Old Tibetan texts is a matter for deliberation. The restricted and highly fragmentary state of the corpus might indicate that it is simply left out by chance. Nevertheless, this common gaming object and symbol does not appear to play a part in the Old Tibetan funerary, healing and curative texts that have come down to us. In the Dunhuang text ITJ 739, the term *cho lo* (refers to dice or dominoes) is cited four times in the explication of the positive and negative outcomes of a divination ritual (*mo*).[5] While not explicitly mentioned in other Dunhuang divination texts, it is understood that dice were widely used in these rituals. Perhaps then by the time these divination documents were written down (ca. 8th to 10th century CE) manufactured dice had replaced natural astragali in divination, at least in more formal ritual settings. The Spitian word *mug lo* appears to be of Zhang Zhung linguistic origins and thus derived from an ancient linguistic source.[6] In various Turkic languages words for astragalus include *asyk*, *ashyk*, *chükö*, and the related Tajik word is *oshuq*. It is from one of these terms or an etymon that the Central Tibetan *A cug* is derived. The closest word phonologically to the Lhasa term is the Tajik *oshuq*, which may suggest that the Sogdians or Sassanians were responsible for the introduction of the term into the Central Tibetan vernacular during the Imperial period (ca. 650-850 CE).[7] The word *sa ga* is almost certainly borrowed from the Mongolian *shagai* (*šagai*; knucklebones). We might conjecture that the formation of the Mongol chiliarchy of Bi ri in the wider region in the 13th century CE may have influenced the adoption of this term in Sde dge. Etymological interconnections with north Inner Asian languages are reflected in parallel knucklebone games and the beliefs of Tibetans and speakers of Turco-Mongolian and Iranian languages.[8]

5 On dice divination in Old Tibetan manuscripts, see Dotson 2015; Nishida 2018. On ancient forms of Tibetan dominoes (*sbag*) divination, see Norbu 2009: 204-10; on the Tibetan dice game of *sho*, see Murakami 2014.

6 On this term and its apparent Zhang zhung etymology, see Bellezza 2013a.

7 Modern Persian: *ashiq*; Modern Turkish: *aşık*. On the complex Indo-European etymological links for "knucklebone", "astragalus" and "dice", consult the relevant dictionaries. The Persian *band angusht* and Sanskrit *asthi aṅguṣṭha* (literally, knuckle bone) are linked through Indo-Iranian antecedents, the Persian more closely interrelated to the Turkic and Tajik words for astragalus. Neither the Persian nor Sanskrit term are directly related to the Tibetan *A cug*.

8 "North Inner Asia" as defined in this work is a geographic denomination encompassing eastern Kazakhstan, eastern Uzbekistan, Tajikistan, Kyrgyzstan, northeastern Afghanistan, Mongolia, southern Siberia, and northwestern PRC. The Tibetan Plateau and far northern Pakistan constitute south Inner Asia.

An archaeological review of knucklebones in Tibet and other parts of Eurasia

Knucklebones were employed in games, divination and cult practices over a wide swathe of Eurasia by the Late Bronze Age and Iron Age. There is still much lore attached to this most intriguing of animal bones in living cultures of Central Asia, Mongolia and Tibet. Some of the earliest examples of intentionally modified ovicaprid astragali as cultural objects comes from the northern Balkans and are thought to date to the middle and late Neolithic. At the Chalcolithic settlement of Gumelniţa, Iepureşti, southern Romania, a group of twenty-five ovicaprid astragali purposefully abraded and perforated were discovered in a burned house.[9] Other early mostly non-funerary sites in Romania have also yielded humanly modified astragali, some pigmented with red ochre or placed in ceramic pots alone or with other objects.[10] In the eastern Mediterranean and Anatolia ovicaprid astragali as gaming pieces and objects with religious and symbolic functions are traced to the Bronze Age. The oldest known occurrence of astragali as grave goods in Italy occurs in Tires, an alpine site in Bolzano dated to the end of the Bronze Age or the beginning of the Iron Age.[11] Astragali with worked edges and sacrificial sheep remains were found in the fortified settlement of Kamenny Ambar (Olgino) in the western Steppe belonging to the chariot-using and sheep-rearing Sintashta culture (ca. 2100-1800 BCE).[12] Astragali, including polished and pierced examples, were also widespread in the ancient Persian world,[13] particularly from the second half of the second millennium BCE and in children's graves.[14] Moreover, disarticulated astragali are regularly recovered from Late Bronze Age and Iron Age graves in the Altai, in tombs of the Slab Grave culture of Mongolia (ca. 11th to 5th centuries BCE), and in other regions of Inner Asia.

Ovicaprid knucklebones were widely used as gaming pieces in Eurasia.[15] It is commonly held that they are the historical antecedents to dice and jacks. The functions of knucklebones in the classical world are determined through archaeological, artistic and literary sources of

9 Kogălniceanu *et al.* (2014: 292-94) consider several possible functions for the twenty-five abraded and perforated ovicaprid astragali found in the Copper Age settlement of Gumelniţa in Romania: tools for making pottery decorations or leather working, gaming, markers of social status, amulets, and primitive currency.

10 Kogălniceanu *et al.* 2014: 294-98. Sidéra and Vornicu 2016: 381-82.

11 de Grossi Mazzorin and Minniti 2013: 372-74.

12 Koryakova *et al.* 2011: 68.

13 Muscarella 1974: 80 [n. 21].

14 Schädler and Dunn-Vaturi 2009.

15 A forthcoming volume of collected papers has been announced by the De Gruyter publishing conglomerate for publication in early 2020 under the title, *Astragalomania: New Perspectives in the Study of Knucklebones in the Ancient World.* According to the publisher's website, this volume will offer various perspectives on the archaeological contexts and actual and symbolic traditions of astragali.

evidence. Ovicaprid knucklebones are found in a variety of settings in the Mediterranean and Asia Minor, including houses, public buildings, temples, sanctuaries, tombs, and boundary markers. In addition to natural examples made of bone, replicas were fabricated from copper alloys, silver, lead, stone, glass, ivory, and terracotta. In an Egyptian tomb-painting a nobleman is shown playing his favorite game in the afterlife in which he gestures with an astragalus above a board arrayed with figures.[16] In ancient Italy astragali had ritual applications in divination, profane uses in gaming and metrology,[17] and functioned as protective devices for the dead during their journey to the netherworld.[18] Perego observes[19] that the magic connected to amuletic objects like ovicaprid astragali had important social functions as materializations of religious practices, class structures and gender differences, as well as relaying emotional experiences.[20] Ovicaprid astragali were central to a number of commonplace games in the Roman empire involving throwing and pickup, striking targets, playing boards, and gambling contests, which are attested in texts, paintings and sculptures.[21] The many astragali cached in elite tombs of ancient Italy may have been markers of wealth too, since they imply possession of considerable livestock, while the many astragali discovered in children's tombs frequently represent toys, a common plaything in the ancient Mediterranean. Astragali buried in the tombs of children, however, may also have functioned as amulets to protect the living from the untoward circumstances and bad luck associated with such deaths.[22] In the Iron Age Levant ovicaprid astragali also appear in modified forms and seem to have been used in wide-ranging ways as gaming pieces, instruments of augury, amulets, funerary and cult offerings, pious records of sacrifices, and

16 David 1962: 5, 18.

17 Roman authors state that astragalus games were played primarily by children and young women. The Greek poet Homer writes that when Patroclus was a child, he became so angry over a game of knucklebones that he nearly killed his opponent (David 1962: 4). Dobbs (2018: 33, 41) notes that this account in the *Iliad* depicts the severe consequences arising from destructive emotions unleashed in knucklebone games as well cosmic analogies concerning humans being the pawns of the gods.

18 de Grossi Mazzorin and Minniti 2013.

19 Perego 2010: 67-68.

20 Pindar (5th century BCE) records that divination took place at Greek temples by casting astragali (Lebo 2016: 423). In his *Guide to Greece*, Pausanias (2nd century CE) mentions the practice of astragalomancy in a sanctuary dedicated to Heracles (Affanni 2008: 84, after Pauli and Wissowa 1924). Cicero (106-43 BCE) in his *De Divinatione* famously refers to games of chance such as those played with astragali as characterized by luck and recklessness. In the *Lives of the Twelve Caesars* by Suetonius (died 126 CE), Emperor Tiberius is recorded as flinging several golden knucklebones into a spring to learn of his future (Sidéra and Vornicu 2016: 380). David (1962: 15, 16) describes oracular functions employing four or five astragali in Greek and Roman temples. They were also common votive objects at Greek and Roman temples and shrines (Lebo 2016: 423). For a review of temple excavations in Turkey where astragali are thought to have been used in divination, see Tahberer 2012: 9-10.

21 On coins of the classical Mediterranean world embossed with images of astragali, dating to the 5th to 3rd centuries BCE, see Tahberer 2012.

22 Perego 2010: 78, 69, 80. de Grossi Mazzorin and Minniti 2013: 377.

primitive money.[23] The multifarious functions and structural modifications of astragali attested in the archaeological record in Eurasia quite closely matches traditional practices in the Tibetan ethnographic record.

It is as grave goods that the earliest ritualistic uses of ovicaprid astragali in Inner Asia are attested. While the deposition of knucklebones in Inner Asian tombs may have been envisioned as objects for amusement in the afterlife, they also appear to have had specific functions in funerary rites as auspicious offerings, apotropaic instruments and eschatological signs. Ovicaprid skeletal remains including astragali occur in burials in most regions of the Tibetan plateau. They have been found in tombs of all ancient cemeteries professionally excavated in western Tibet and Mustang except for Chokhopani.[24] These tombs are broadly dated from ca. 600 BCE to 800 CE.[25] As Aldenderfer notes, the earliest known ovicaprid depositions in western Tibet are represented in burials at Rgyal gling thang and Chu 'thag.[26] Sheep bones were also found in shaft tombs excavated outside Lhasa by Aufschnaiter in 1950.[27] A perusal of Chinese archaeological literature would uncover many other instances of this burial practice on the plateau (many hundreds of tombs have been excavated since the 1980s). Nonetheless, there

23 Affanni 2008: 83-87. On the archaeological context of the gaming and ritual functions of worked (smoothed, perforated and weighted) and unworked ovicaprid astragali in the Levant and eastern Mediterranean, also see Gilmour 1997. For ovicaprid astragali (including perforated specimens and glass and lead models) found with Aramaic divination ostraca dating to the second half of first millennium BCE, compelling evidence of the former being used in cleromancy (divination by lots) in Maresha, Shephelah, Israel, see Eshel and Stern 2017. On criteria for determining primitive forms of money and their economic and relgious functions, see Holmgren 2004: 215-18.

24 Aldenderfer 2018: 133. Thirteen mummified sheep and goat heads were found in burial contexts at Me brag (ca. 450 BCE to 100 CE), and ovicaprid skulls and other parts of the skeleton at Bsam rdzong (ca. 400-650 CE). See Aldenderfer 2013: 304, 305.

25 On ovicaprid bones deposited in substantial numbers in the tombs of Chu 'thag, Gu-ge, see Institute of Archaeology, CASS and Cultural Relics Conservation Institute of Tibet Autonomous Region 2014, 2015. Ovicaprid bones have also been identified in a burial in Malari (3300 m), Uttarakhand, India (Bhatt *et al.* 2008-2009: 5). The presence of a gold burial mask in this shaft tomb links funerary traditions of Malari with Transhimalayan sites in Mustang and Gu ge where such masks have also been discovered.

26 On the basis of the extant evidence, Aldenderfer (2013: 310, 311) holds that the mortuary tradition of including ovicaprid remains in Tibetan tombs probably does not predate 500 BCE. Nonetheless, controlled excavations in western Tibet predating that period have not been carried out, or if they have, they are not adequately dated. Given the growing body of evidence for the wholesale adoption on the Tibetan plateau of cultural and technological traditions via north Inner Asia beginning in the Late Bronze Age, it may yet be shown that the internment of ovicaprid skulls and bones in upper Tibet predates 500 BCE. On Late Bronze Age and Iron Age customs and traditions introduced on the Tibetan plateau originating in or transmitted through north Inner Asia and the interactive processes underlying them, see Bellezza forthcoming-a, forthcoming-b, 2017, 2016, 2008. Lu 2015. On a tomb in the western Byang thang dated to ca. 10th to 9th century BCE, see Bellezza 2017, 2008: 91-92, forthcoming-a.

27 Aufschnaiter 1956: 81. On the possible dating of these tombs to the second half of the first millennium BCE, see Bellezza forthcoming-a.

is still very little information available regarding differentiation of ordinary ovicaprid bones from their role as artifacts.

Despite ovicaprid skeletal remains being a common element in burials on the Tibetan plateau in the Iron Age (ca. 600-100 BCE) and Protohistoric period (ca. 100 BCE to 600 CE), little is known yet about their osteological, molecular and stable isotope characteristics. This deficit in archaeological study obscures a picture of sheep populations, diet, health, and rearing practices in ancient Tibet. Detailed inventories of bones and their spatial relationship (planar and stratigraphic) with each other and other tomb materials are also mostly absent from archaeological studies carried out to date. To obtain spatial data the location of each bone or bone fragment and other grave goods are pinpointed on a three-dimensional grid, permitting an assessment of the configuration of interments and how these may have changed since the time of burial due to geomorphological, waterborne, and anthropogenic disruptions. The general lack of findings concerning the nature and location of ovicaprid entombment in Tibet impedes a determination of whether they were deposited as whole animals, heads only and/or as specific parts of the post-cranial frame. While ovicaprid astragali are often part of larger skeletal assemblies, their numerical proportions as compared to other types of bones must be ascertained on a tomb by tomb basis. Also, it is crucial to determine whether bones were intentionally altered by scoring, bisection, abrading, polishing, perforation, painting, or heating. Without a solid understanding of the physical state, placement and quantity of buried ovicaprid bones little can be said about their potential mortuary functions.

The collection and analysis of spatial and qualitative data takes on added significance as archaeologists in China open more and more graves. Generally speaking, isolated deposition of ovicaprid astragali, especially when cached in large numbers, is evidence for cultic and ritual functions. The deliberate placement of astragali with manmade objects may also be an indication of specialized religious functions, the lineaments of which might be inferred by the kinds of burial goods in the assemblage. From the plans of Tibetan tombs in Chinese publications it appears that animal remains (ovicaprid, equid and bovid, etc.) are often arrayed in different groups across the floor of shaft tombs, at various levels of a tomb structure, and in subsidiary spaces such as shelves and niches in the walls of burial chambers. The complex arrangement of ovicaprid bones in tombs may indicate variable functions as part of funerary traditions with elaborate ideological and procedural components.

Tibetan archaic funerary texts furnish a complex picture of death rituals pertaining to the use and sacrifice of sheep.[28] However, these texts do not specifically mention exploitation of ovicaprid astragali in funerary rites. The three major functions of sheep in Tibetan archaic

28 For detailed information on the funerary function of the sheep in Tibetan funerary ritual literature, see Bellezza 2008, 2013b. Also see Stein 1970, 1971. Macdonald 1971: 373-75. Lalou 1953: 357 [n.3]. Haarh 1969: 370, 373, 376-78.

funerary literature can be summed up as follows: 1) as provisions (food and livestock) for use in the afterlife, 2) offerings to appease demons interfering with the passage of deceased to the afterlife, 3) psychopomps aiding the deceased in the journey across the land of infernal spirits to the afterlife.[29] Although none of these texts can be dated before the 8th century CE, they appear to have considerable bearing on Late Prehistoric (ca. 1200-600 BCE) as well Early Historic (ca. 600-1000) burials on the Tibetan plateau and have some relevance to mortuary practices in other regions of Inner Asia. One of the most pronounced examples of carryover from the prehistoric archaeological record to the Tibetan literary record is the use of horned headdresses on psychopomp horses. They first manifest in so-called Scytho-Siberian burials (Pazyryk, Tuketa, Berel, etc.) of the mid-first millennium BCE and feature much later in Old Tibetan funerary ritual manuscripts. The inclusion of ovicaprid remains in tombs has been documented for many agri-pastoralist cultures in north Inner Asia commencing in the Late Bronze Age. One of the most widespread occurrences is in tombs of the complex of Central Asian cultures known as Andronovo (ca. 1800-900 BCE), whose economy was based on sheep and cattle rearing, members of which practiced tin-bronze metallurgy and may have spoken Indo-Iranian languages.[30] In addition to the sequestering of astragali (sometimes in ceramic vessels), positioning on or near corpses, integration with other objects in tombs, and evidence for their modification through filing and drilling indicate specific functions in burial rites and in the host culture more generally.[31] Moreover, the recurring of astragali with specific types of inhumations (e.g., juvenile, female, etc.) may also offer some insight into their cultural purposes. Some progress in identifying the possible functions of ovicaprid astragali has been

29 Goats are also specifically noted in four Old Tibetan funerary manuscripts: *Rnel drĭ 'dul ba'i thabs sogs, Sha ru shul ston rabs,* PT 1134, and ITJ 731r. See Bellezza 2013b: 149, 99, 205, 06, 23, 37.

30 For a review of the spread of domesticated sheep from their putative source in eastern Anatolia in the 8th millennium BCE across the entire steppes by the Late Bronze Age, one accompanied by the theoretical spread of Indo-European languages, see Anthony 2007.

31 The drilling of holes in and the filing down of astragali are widely attested in Eurasia. Ancient bone astragali in the Middle East frequently have holes drilled in them for suspending from a cord, which appear to have chiefly functioned as children's toys but may have also been worn as pendants and amulets (British Museum n.d: 36). Astragali with holes found in the Veneto region of Italy dating to the Iron Age are hypothesized to have possibly functioned as amulets, ornaments or gifts to the dead (Perego 2010: 78). Numerous studies note that Greek and Roman ovicaprid astragali were modified by being filed, filled or cut for gaming and amuletic purposes. For tallies and an analysis of astragali that were perforated and smoothed in various ways from Iron Age sites in northern and central Italy, see de Grossi Mazzorin and Minniti 2013. It is noted that the smoothing of the lateral and medial or plantar and dorsal sides may be related to different functions, gaming among them (de Grossi Mazzorin and Minniti 2013: 378). It has been demonstrated that some astragali with smooth faces were employed in ancient Italy in leather working and ceramic making (Perego 2010: 78, after Riedel and Tecchiati 2001). Closer to our area of study, ovicaprid knucklebones with drilled holes have been found in a tomb of the Bohai culture, eastern Mongolia, dated to the 11th century CE (Kradin and Ivliev 2008: 441, 42 [fig. 4.3]).

Fig. 2 Left: Copper alloy ovicaprid astragalus (dorsal side) obtained in Tibet (3.2 cm in length). Right: Plantar side of the same object (Late Shang Nyima Collection).

made in Xinjiang.[32] A good example of ovicaprid astragali in a ritualized context in Inner Asia is afforded by a non-burial mound excavated at Beiram, Uvs aymag, in the Mongolian Altai.[33]

Linguistic, ethnographic and archaeological evidence allude to the deeply ingrained status of ovicaprid astragali in gaming and divination on the Tibetan plateau. Archaeological findings from other parts of north Inner Asia suggest that this bone was already accorded particularized cultural functions in Tibet in the Late Prehistoric era. Another piece of evidence suggestive of ancient knucklebone ritualism and/or talismanic functions in Tibet is a copper alloy facsimile in the collection of the late Shang Nyima, Kathmandu (Fig. 2). All major anatomical features of the bone are discernable in this copper alloy replica. Other than it being purchased in Tibet in the 1980s or early 1990s, no other information on its provenance could be obtained from its owner. Versed in the old material culture of Tibet, Shang Nyima highly prized this object

32 The discovery of sheep knucklebones in tombs of the early phase of the Shamirshak culture (attributed to the Bronze Age), northern Xinjiang, suggests ritual and other functions (Jia and Betts 2010: 298). For ovicaprid astragali in specialized contexts in burials of Xinjiang in the late second and first millennia BCE, see Chen and Hiebert 1995: 262, 63, 71, 81.

33 Large numbers of sheep, bovid and wild ungulate astragali were discovered at this site, which is estimated to date to the mid-first millennium BCE based on structural and artifactual parallels with Saka burials. The Beiram mound is thought to have been constructed for ritual or other religious purposes. In the center of the mound there was a wooden box containing five sheep astragali and other votive objects but no human remains. In total, 3192 sheep astragali were recovered from Level 1 of the Beiram mound. The astragali cached in large numbers at the site are believed to have been used in divination. Also, a sheep astragalus with a swastika carved on it and one pierced by a hole were found at the site. The hole was probably for suspending, possibly indicating it was worn as an amulet. On this site, see Davis-Kimball 2000: 91, 92, 97.

and believed it was of ancient manufacture. However, its age and place of production have not been verified, obscuring its significance to the cultural disposition of ovicaprid astragali. The lack of corrosion, a well-developed patina and heavy wear are indicative of an heirloom passed down over the generations (rather than it being buried in the ground for a long time). The object differs in stylistic details from European and Chinese bronze astragali, reinforcing attribution to Tibet. Metallurgical analysis might help pinpoint its place of manufacture or at least differentiate it from those made in other parts of Eurasia.

Antique small copper alloy objects in Tibet are known as *thog lcags* and *thog rde'u* and were well distributed among the population. They are believed to fall from the sky with lightning strikes and to offer their owners protection and good luck. In reality, *thog lcags* are a heterogenous class of manmade objects originally functioning as amulets, horse tack, implements, insignia, etc. They appear to be of considerable age and mostly cast between the Late Bronze Age and 1500 CE.[34] As a *thog lcags* the Shang Nyima astragalus can probably be viewed as "ancient". However, it is one of only three examples of an astragalus in this body of artifacts to have come to my attention. In addition to these specimens, those fabricated from rock crystal, nephrite and ivory are known in Tibet. Furthermore, pieces of turquoise and coral were carved into the shape of an astragalus and used as settings in rings. These rings are still worn by Khams pa today.

Bronze ovicaprid astragali are rare as compared to natural bone specimens. They were produced in classical Greece and Rome but these are found buried and lack the fine patina of the Shang Nyima specimen.[35] A copper alloy pendant from the Caucasus mountains in the form of a life-size astragalus with a hole for suspension, dated to 11th-7th centuries BCE, is in the British Museum. It is comparable to another copper alloy specimen with a holed drilled in it from the Koban necropolis.[36] Bronze ovicaprid astragali were also produced in mainland

34 On *thog lcags*, see, for example, Bellezza 1998. John 2006. Lin 2003. Weihreter 1998, 2002. Tucci 1973.

35 There are numerous archaeological works illustrating bronze astragali from Greece and Rome. For example, see Davidson 1952: 222 (no. 1755), pl. 100. Doyen 2018. For online images of Greek and Roman imitation bronze astragali, see the *Metropolitan Museum of Art* website: bronze astragalus, circa 3rd century BCE to 2nd century CE, Greek or Roman, 2.6 cm in length (http://www.metmuseum.org/collections/search-the-collections/256765); *Harvard Art Museums* website: bronze astragalus, Greek, 400-300 BCE, 3.2 cm in length (http://www.harvardartmuseums.org/art/304304), copper alloy knucklebone, Greco-Roman, 5th to 1st century BCE (https://www.harvardartmuseums.org/art/178245); *British Museum* website: Greek or Roman copper alloy astragalus: (https://www.britishmuseum.org/research/collection_online/collection_object_details.aspx?objectId=464118&partId=1&searchText=Gaming+piece&sortBy=imageName&page=1), also see http://archaeologicalmuseum.jhu.edu/the-collection/object-stories/archaeology-of-daily-life/childhood/knucklebones/. Note: I have selected links to online images of copper alloy astragali that have been stable for more than five years. For the famous giant bronze astragalus (37 × 21 cm × 23 cm) with a Greek inscription indicating that it was from the sanctuary of Apollo at Didyma before being looted by the Persians and taken to Susa, see, for example, Luce 2011.

36 British Museum n.d: 36, after Chantre 1885-87.

China.[37]

The ritual, divinatory and talismanic uses of ovicaprid astragali as well as the production of imitations in Tibet are bracketed by Eurasian cultures to the west and the Han culture of the Central Plains to the east. If the copper alloy astragalus obtained in Tibet postdates the 11th century CE, its manufacture may possibly be related to those made in China dated ca. 1000-1600 CE. However, should the Tibetan astragalus prove older, as appears likely, other cultural sources for its creation must be sought. A Protohistoric attribution (100 BCE to 600 CE) could possibly permit it to be related to those of the ancient Greek and Romans; its creation perhaps inspired by trade or other exchanges. As an Early Historic period (600-1000 CE) artifact, the Shang Nyima astragalus could either represent a relict cultural trait or be an example of Tibetan cosmopolitanism ushered in by international contacts and conquests during the Imperial period.

Knucklebones in Tibetan cultures

This section of the article explores the recreational, practical and sacral functions of ovicaprid astragali on the Tibetan plateau. Findings are based on fieldwork carried out by the author in Tibetan communities since 2014. The study reviews salient features of this bone in gaming, divination and other traditions. Nevertheless, this is a vast topic of which it is only possible to give an introduction in an article-length work.[38]

The astragali of sheep and goats are known all over the Tibetan plateau as children's toys. They remained very popular until the proliferation of manufactured goods in the last two or three decades. Nowadays, with mandatory schooling, modernization and extraneous cultural pressures, knucklebones are rapidly disappearing in Tibet. Still, it is not uncommon for children in pastoralist ('brog pa) communities to use ovicaprid astragali as imaginary livestock in miniature play camps.[39] There is much nostalgia surrounding this recreational tradition among middle-aged and elderly Tibetans interviewed for this article. The small, compact astragalus of sheep and goats makes an ideal gaming piece and appears to be one of the oldest and most ubiquitous diversions in Tibet. That these naturally occurring objects have ancient cultural

37 For Chinese bronze and iron astragali dated 1000-1600 CE, see: http://www.anythinganywhere.com/commerce/relic/chin-misc.htm; for more heavily stylized Chinese bronze astragali possibly dating to the Han dynasty, see http://www.anythinganywhere.com/commerce/relic/chin-chuanweights.htm. Note: I have selected online images of copper ally astragali from a commercial site with URLs that have proven stable for more than five years.

38 Tibetan language publications that examine astragali cultural functions would constitute an important additional avenue of study. However, no such publications were available to me at the time of writing this study.

39 Use of astragali as toys in Tibet is noted in Rinjing Dorje 1987. Tibetans often equate them to horses. In his *Historia Animalium*, Aristotle describes the astragalus as resembling a small sculpture of a sheep (Affanni 2008: 85).

underpinnings is supported by a widely shared belief in Tibet assigning them to antiquity.

As in other parts of the world, knucklebones are probably the precursor of still popular dice games in Tibet (*cho lo, sho*). In both Tibetan knucklebones and dice, the outcome of each throw is determined by the assigned value of the face that lands upright after a throw. In modern Tibet *sho* has almost completely replaced knucklebones as the gambling game of choice for men. Nevertheless, as is often the case with ancient traditions, knucklebone games are much broader in scope and have ceremonial and symbolic dimensions that dice do not possess. While both dice and knucklebones are exhilarating and emotive pastimes, the latter has acquired a deep cultural significance that the former lacks. Elders report encouraging the playing of knucklebones among youth, claiming that it was superior to *sho* or *mahjong* (of Chinese origins), games that Tibetans consider morally questionable.

There are many different knucklebone games in Tibet, each with its own rules and customs. They are variously played by adults and children, male and female. The games deviate from region to region and are particularly popular among pastoral sections of the population. The basis of all games is the competitive tossing or shooting of astragali. This is referred to as "to throw" (*rgyab/rgyag*), "to strike" (*'khrab*) and "to race" (*rgyug*). In places like Snyan-rong in Hor and Skye rgu mdo in Khams, entire villages come out in their best clothes to enjoy knucklebones during the New Year (Lo gsar) celebrations.[40] Traditionally, residents of Yul shul prefecture would gather in public places and play knucklebone games during the fourth and fifth day of the holiday (Figs. 3-5). Reportedly, this tradition is still observed but to a much smaller extent than before. [41]

In all Tibetan regions and knucklebone games each of the six sides of the astragalus is assigned a special name and value. In some instances, the four flatter faces are equated with the cardinal directions. Most commonly in Tibet, the six sides of the bone are identified with animals and other metaphorical representations as follows:

- Dorsal side-goat: second-most inferior face. This side with the hollow is also called *stong pa* and *ltogs*, as in an empty stomach.
- Plantar side-sheep: second-most superior of the four main faces. This arched side is also known as *gang, brgyags* and *'grang*, as in a full stomach after eating.

40 According to Tucci (1966: 153), beginning on the third day of the New Year celebrations and continuing for some days afterwards, residents of all ages in Skye rgu mdo played a knucklebone game called "goat astragalus sheep astragalus" (*ra the lug the*) with colored bones.

41 A single man in Yul shul has acquired more than 1000 old astragali used for gaming and divination, the largest collection in the prefecture according to him. He believes that some in his possession are more than 100 years old. The owner, an avid player in his youth, reports that the average person possessed twenty to forty astragali. Through winnings, the best players could attain more than one hundred pieces. Knucklebones is now much reduced in Yul shul, as the accumulation of so many by a single person indicates. Also, the keeping of sheep is much less prevalent in Yul shul today, making replenishment of gaming pieces more difficult.

Fig. 3 Bronze sculptures of Tibetans playing knucklebones, central Skye rgu mdo.

Fig. 4 A close-up of the same installation of sculptures showing a player poised to flick an ovicaprid astragal at others on the playing board.

Fig. 5 A Tibetan man teaching the rudiments of a popular knucklebone game to the author in Skye rgu mdo.

- Lateral side-horse: most superior face. This side has a pronounced rim and is also called the "front" (*kha*).
- Medial site-donkey or mule: most inferior face. This flatter side is also called the "base" (*gsham*). [42]
- The proximal surface with two keeled extensions (tibial trochlea): horned eagle (*khyung*). In Hor regions these protuberances are styled "fingernails" (*sen mo*). In certain games this is the best of the six sides of an astragalus.
- The distal surface with two rounded ends (trochleated head) has various names in Tibetan. In parts of Khams it is referred to as the dog's hind-end (*khyi rkub*). In Hor regions it is called the "rear end" (*Ong*). In pastoral regions of western Tibet, it is the "tiger" (*stag*). In some knucklebone games this is the worst of the six sides of the bone.

For gaming the lateral and medial sides of astragali were sometimes filed and polished, giving them smoother and more regular surfaces and a more cubic form. The proximal surface was occasionally filed down as well. By working an astragalus in this manner it becomes faster and will flip, spin and slide in a less erratic manner. I have seen sleek astragali gaming pieces with rich patinas that have hardened with age, as moisture is slowly lost and perhaps through chemical treatment as well. The decorated cloth or leather sack in which gaming and divinatory astragali are stored is called *the khug*.

Traditionally, astragali only became available with the slaughter of goats and sheep, limiting the available supply. Their value was further accentuated by specially preparing the bone in a variety of ways. These included chemical treatments and ornamental alterations. Occurring naturally as light-colored bones, astragali were processed and colored by Tibetans using a variety of techniques, a noteworthy demonstration of household ingenuity. Many colored astragali are given names from Tibetan horse terminology because this bone when resting on its lateral side is said to have the shape of a horse. Some names of the different colored horses used to describe astragali can be traced to Old Tibetan literature.[43] An epithet for the astragalus found in some western Tibet pastoral regions is the "horse rider astragalus" (*rta pa long mo*). According to the cultural luminary Tshe ring chos 'phel, pointed microliths (*rdo mdung rtse*; stone spearpoint), which are quite common in upper Tibet, served as the horseman placed on top of an astragalus in children's games. Another epithet for this bone in western Tibet is "full-hungry" (*'grangs ltogs*), as in the stomach before and after eating. This

42 The relative values given to the four main sides of an astragalus in Tibet have substantial correspondence with those in ancient Greece and Rome. From a study of classical writings, scholars of the Italian Renaissance computed that in knucklebones the planar side is counted as four, the dorsal side as three; the lateral side as six and the medial side as one (David 1962: 7).

43 On horse fur coloration and patterns in the Old Tibetan mytho-ritual funerary text PT 1060, a particularly fecund source, see Bellezza 2005: 468 (n. 154), 2013b: 44 (n. 65).

nickname reflects the variable outcomes, positive and negative, in gaming and divination. During games there are different verses spoken for each type of astragalus. This more or less formalized speech is known as the "calling of the astragalus" (*the 'bod*). The lines spoken, some of which are of ancient origins, vary from place to place and region to region. This constitutes an important Tibetan oral tradition that deserves far more scrutiny than it has received so far.

According to elders from various parts of Tibet, among the many types of astragalus gaming pieces are the following:

- *Bsag-pa* (literally, ochre one): an astragalus thickly coated in red ochre and named after a reddish horse.
- *Rta ngang pa* (goose-horse): an astragalus upon which ochre is lightly applied. It is then covered in mud and gently heated in a fire until assuming an orange tint. It is named for a horse with orange highlights.
- *Rta rgya bo*: this gaming piece is made by covering an astragalus in yak manure and gently heating it in fire. It is named for a horse with brownish coloring and yellowish face markings.
- *'Ol ba rting dkar*: an astragalus darkened by the application of manure but in such a manner that the rounded distal surface is left white. It is named after a black horse with white fetlocks.
- *Rrgya bo gdong dkar*: a dark-colored astragalus but with the horn-like proximal tips left white. This nomenclature denotes a brownish horse with yellowish face markings and a white spot on the forehead.
- *Rta gro dkar*: an astragalus with dark lines painted along the edges. It is named for a gray horse with white markings.
- *Bsag khra* and *dmar khra*: astragali and horses with red and light-colored markings.
- *Sngo ril* and *ser ril*: a blue astragalus and a yellow astragalus respectively. These names reflect the manner in which the bones are rolled in dye to give them color and the way in which they spin during gaming.
- *Ja bzos mdog* (literally, tea-cooked color): a purplish astragalus created by boiling the bone in a very strong solution of tea.
- *Sog dkar* (literally, white shoulder blade): an astragalus with the arched part of the plantar side left white on an otherwise darkened bone. This white spot is said to resemble a shoulder blade (*sog pa*).
- *Ong do* (literally, buttocks): a white astragalus darkened on its rounded distal surface.
- *Sbus the* (literally, "swollen astragalus" in the Hor dialect of Nag chu; equivalent of the Tibetan *'bur*): astragali from immature sheep and goats. The less defined features of the juvenile bone are thought to make them look like they are swollen.

Astragali are also classified as to whether they come from castrated sheep (*shab zan* [spelling?]) or stud rams (*lug rub bzang/lug thug*). These astragali are called *shab the* and *rub the* respectively. Astragali are also classified as mother (*mo*) and father (*pho*) bones, reflecting their bilateral arrangement in ovicaprid anatomy. In the "father astragalus" (*pho the*) the proximal or horn-like extension faces outward when the goat face is rested against the right palm. In the "mother astragalus" (*mo the*) the horns or fingernails (tibial trochlea) point outwards in the left palm.

Fancier types of knucklebones were created by adults for gaming. One of these is the *mtho ril*, an astragalus in which lead studs are placed in small holes bored in one or more of the four main sides.[44] The proximal horn-like extensions and rounded arch on the sheep side of the bone may also be filed down in this kind of knucklebone. These actions create much faster playing pieces and ones more likely to land with the superior sheep and horse faces upright. Sometimes a turquoise was inserted into the hollow on the goat side of the astragalus. The relatively balanced squarish configuration of an astragalus is ideal for the randomization of sequences in throwing events. However, as the four faces vary in size and form, the probability of landing on any one of them in each throw is unequal. The most frequent outcomes from throwing an astragal on a flat surface is for it to land upright on one of the four main faces (goat, sheep, donkey, or horse) sides. The righting of a piece on its proximal (*khyung* horns) or distal (butt) surfaces facing upwards is far less common but the incidence increases when there are many pieces on a playing board and astragali become propped up by others.

In Yul shul the most popular knucklebone game of men and boys is largely one of chance in which pieces are wagered with each throw. I provide a rough outline here of this fast-moving activity. At least two players are needed but larger groups (up to ten players) add much intensity and excitement to the proceedings. Each player begins with a pile of thirteen astragali and takes turns tossing three pieces on the playing surface (any flat expanse will do). If a matching pair is thrown (e.g., two sheep), the next player engages in a shootout, trying to hit one of the pieces in the pair with the other to make it jump, while not touching any other astragalus on the board. If the strike is successful the active player takes possession of the piece hit, adding it to his or her pile. This procedure lends an element of skill to the game. As pieces are lost and acquired, each player's stock rises or dwindles until there are no more bones left on the board. Larger throws of four to six astragali commonly take place and if several pairs appear on the board at one time, multiple pieces can be won in a single hand. Throws of up to nine pieces are possible. The stakes are raised further when a player betters the result of the last player, potentially allowing him to add all the pieces on the board to his pile.

I will now describe briefly several other knucklebone games as has been communicated to me by Tibetan players. I have not observed any of these games firsthand, thus my

44 The practice of filling a hole in an astragalus with a piece of bronze, copper, iron, or lead was widespread in the ancient Mediterranean world (Lebo 2016: 425).

characterization of them is bound to be imperfect. There are probably dozens of different knucklebone games on the Tibetan plateau, the survey given here an introduction to their flavor and diversity. It is reported that there is a game in Yul shul where players (male and female) attempt to toss astragali into a bowl. According to my informants, one of the most universal games of children in Tibet is called "knucklebone strike" (*the ge rgyab*) or "knucklebone race" (*the ge rgyug*). This game is likened to a horserace. The players begin by each tossing an astragalus on the ground. Those that come up on the horse side are the last ones in the race. The remaining astragali are tossed, excluding those landing on the horse side, until only two pieces remain. Their players begin striking each other's pieces to prevent one from remaining on the horse side. The winner of the horserace is the last astragalus to stay on the horse side after a round of striking.

Another common Tibetan knucklebone pastime is called *the spu rgyab*. This fast-moving enterprise entails the striking of opponent's astragali, in order that one's own piece stays in the most advantageous position (horse and sheep sides). In a series of rounds, players try to capture all the astragali of their rivals. The game of *the sho*, is played just like the Tibetan game of dice.

An elaborate Tibetan knucklebone game is *dmag the* (army knucklebones), where a large playing field is set up with groups of astragali piled up in different ways by players to represent a king, two ministers and eight generals. The king is set in the most protected position in the rear of the playing field, in front of which are placed the ministers and then the generals. In addition to these arrays of astragali, there are many individual pieces representing soldiers (*dmag mi*). The players flick army men with their fingers in order to upset the king, ministers and generals. The player possessing the last king standing is the winner. This energetic game is very challenging because soldiers tend to increasingly obstruct the playing field, forcing shooters to adopt special offensive and defensive strategies. Tibetans report that in addition to other knucklebone games, there are variations on the few I have covered.

Besides recreation, ovicaprid astragali have a number of other functions. These alternative applications also appear to be of ancient origins. In Tibetan astragalomancy (*the mo*) the six sides of the knucklebone possess the same names as they do in gaming (Fig. 6). According to the way in which a tossed astragalus falls, it is thought to auger a certain outcome or destiny.[45] In some forms of astragalomancy four or five bones of different colors were used, representing the elements, cardinal directions, families of spirits, etc. Unlike gaming, astragali in divination must be thrown on a table or other clean surface and not on the ground. Well-formed astragali that have not been used for other purposes are employed. The application of astragali in Tibetan divination appears to have preceded forms of prognostication with dice and dominoes.

45 The cubic shape of an astragalus lends itself to dualistic equations such as life and death, yes and no, and good and evil, etc., useful in an instrument of divination (Holmgren 2004: 217).

Fig. 6 Five different colored antique Tibetan ovicaprid astragali, such as those used for divination. Collected by a Khams pa and used in Khams.

Another function for the ovicaprid astragalus was as a calculating tool for keeping accounts. In the system explained to me an astragalus is equivalent to one hundred units of something in weight or number. Small tally sticks called *bcu shing* were used to represent ten units of something. These accounting devices were stored in a sack and consulted over the long-term to determine one's financial position.

The sacred and ritualistic qualities of sheep are epitomized by the astragalus, one of the most distinctive and portable symbols of the animal. Astragali are strung together to form long garlands (*the star*) in Tibet. These are hung in kitchens and on the "father pillar" (west pole) of the black yak hair tent as harm repulsing and good-fortune bestowing instruments. In pastoral areas it is thought that this garland of bones prevents a tent from being struck by lightning and livestock from being eaten by wild animals. The theme of the retention of the good fortune potential (*g.yang*) of livestock emphasizes the talismanic value of knucklebones and invests them with a sacral quality. Ordinary sheep in Tibet have divine analogues, specially colored animals that function as offerings to elemental spirits and as their mounts and emanations. [46] The identity of these animals is marked by their color (e.g., white for the *lha*, reddish for the *btsan*, bluish for the *klu*). There is an entire pantheon of spirits in the form of sheep preserved by spirit-mediums (*lha pa, dpa 'bo*) in upper Tibet, which participate in curative and prosperity rituals.[47]

A special talisman consists of a particularly large sheep astragalus with a prominent horn-like proximal surface joined at the tips, called the "great fingernail" (*se chen*). Typically, a

46 On these divine species of sheep, see Bellezza 2008: 454 (n. 314); 2005: 456-72.

47 For the *lug lha* in the spirit-mediumship of upper Tibet, see Bellezza 2015: 18, 28, 29; 2011: 15, 19; 2012: 12, 13.

string was tied through the natural loop in the bone and it was placed in a good fortune sack (*g.yang khug*) or good fortune box (*g.yang sgam*) for safekeeping. Alternatively, it was added to the head of a garland of other astragali. Sometimes Tibetan children would wear this most precious of astragali for prestige and as a good luck charm when playing knucklebones. In the Hor region of Snyan rong (and possibly in other areas as well), there is a special astragalus called *mu the* (hunger astragalus). This astragalus comes from a big, healthy sheep with much fat. Typically, a few of these were carried on pilgrimage and other long journeys in case food became unavailable. It is believed that by placing one of these bones in the mouth hunger could be forestalled for long periods of time. It is reported in Mnga' ris that astragali may have been used in the marriage ceremonies of western Tibetan herders but this custom seems to have completely died out. Earlier practices and their ideological substructure may deviate from contemporary patterns, but the sacral status of ovicaprid astragali almost certainly predates the introduction of Buddhism to Tibet, a salient example of the persistence of archaic religious customs and beliefs. Although archaeological evidence is still pending, attributing the cultural functions of astragali on the Tibetan plateau to the Late Prehistoric era finds much resonance in traditions attested throughout much of Eurasia.

The cross-cultural dimensions of knucklebones

Even a cursory survey of knucklebone games in Eurasia, past and present, reveals many parallels with those on the Tibetan plateau. Striking knucklebones with others, aiming at targets from afar and games of chance are well represented on the continent.[48] The profane and sacred uses of astragali in ancient times constitute two overlapping categories of function and meaning. Aspects of recreation, myth, cosmology and cult were interrelated in Eurasian astragalus traditions. This is no less true of Tibet, where astragalus gaming, divination, protection, and symbolism were tied together in cultural expression.

The ancient Greco-Roman game of *pentalitha* (played with ovicaprid astragals from other animals thrown in the air, their value gauged by the side that lands upright) is still played in Turkey today and is known as *beş taş*.[49] Another game played in Turkey is *kuru*, where

48 A (blog) with colorful illustrations on the ancient and contemporary uses of astragali in gaming as well as a historical perspective on their recreational functions is entitled "Five Stones". It is found on the literary website *Poemas del río Wang*. "Five Stones" cites the commonly held hypothesis that astragalus gaming spread along the Silk Road, reaching China from Central Asian nomadic tribes and coming to the ancient Mediterranean from the east. See: http://riowang.blogspot.in/2011/05/five-stones.html. This website page has been stable for more than five years. The origins of knucklebone gaming in ancient Greece were often attributed to the Lydians of Asia Minor (Davis 1962: 6).

49 See Tahberer 2012.

players attempt to flip over astragali from the upright position by striking it with another.[50] *Bojul* is played with ovicaprid astragali in Khorasan, northeastern Iran, and links two sides of the bone with the donkey and horse, a game that appears to be of ancient origins based on archaeological discoveries of astragali in the region.[51] *Qāb-bāzī* ("knucklebones") is a game of chance with complicated rules played with sheep astragali by Iranian nomads that also probably dates to antiquity.[52] Schädler and Dunn-Vaturi[53] caution however that apart from chess and backgammon, little is known about games in ancient Persia and the archaeological evidence is often inconclusive.[54] Similarly, the impression of researchers and players in other parts of Eurasia is that many of these games have very old lineages. Nevertheless, the absence of continuous streams of documentary evidence from deep in the past to the present means that conjecture and conviction regarding the perdurability of astragalus gaming is not likely to yield to scientific certainty anytime soon (but this does not render it any less plausible).

Looking eastward from Iran, the next big northern territory that comes in line is Mongolia. Given their geographic proximity, it is not surprising that astragali traditions in Mongolia closely resemble those on the Tibetan plateau. Knucklebones are used in Mongolia in gaming, life-cycle rituals, amulets, sacrificial objects, tools of divination, and in in trials of martial strength.[55] Mongolian knucklebones have been elevated to a national pastime and are recognized by UNESCO as a cultural heritage of international importance.[56] While often a form of recreation in Mongolia there is a game played at New Year with a sacral character, the winner of the competition destined to be the most fortunate in the coming year.[57] Holmgren discusses[58] a study by Kabzinska-Stawarz (1991), linking the fertility of livestock to the astragalus (each of its four sides representing a different domestic animal), a bone believed to have magical properties that strengthens the life-force of animals and increases the size of flocks. In the *Secret History of the Mongols* (13th century CE), astragali are not only playthings

50 Holmgren 2004: 214.

51 See Sabori *et al.* 2016.

52 See Vahman 1989.

53 See Schädler and Dunn-Vaturi 2009.

54 Muscarella (1974: 80 [n. 21]) notes that workers often asked for astragali recovered from archaeological sites excavated in Iran so that they could give them to their children as toys.

55 Birtalan 2003.

56 Inscribed by the Intergovernmental Committee for the Safeguarding of the Intangible Cultural Heritage of Humanity on November 27, 2014. The enduring strength of shamanistic practices and ideologies in Mongolian cultural world probably helps explain the high profile of knucklebones in the steppes. Generally speaking, the sheer dominance of Buddhism on the Tibetan plateau eliminated or dampened many archaic traditions and probably had an effect on astragalus gaming and lore as well.

57 Birtalan 2003: 48.

58 Holmgren 2004: 213.

of children and adults but a solemn object for divination and sacrifice.[59] According to historical sources, while still children, the future Mongol chieftains Temujin and Jamukha entered into a sworn alliance sealed with the exchange of astragali.[60]

A wide range of knucklebones games were played on the Tibetan plateau and in Mongolia where pieces were either tossed or flicked.[61] Some of these games are similar, others are unique to each territory. One of the most common in Tibet and Mongolia is the horserace, which is played in a similar manner. In Tibet and Mongolia, the four main sides of an ovicaprid astragalus represents a group of animals with three members in common. In Mongolia these are the horse, camel, goat, and sheep; in Tibet the horse, donkey, goat, and sheep. As in Tibet, the luckiest sides are the horse and sheep in Mongolia. Mongolians also color astragali for gaming and divination. Their avid use of horse astragali however is not matched in Tibet. In addition to astragalomancy, scapulimancy (shoulder blade divination) was practiced in both Tibet and Mongolia. The belief that ovicaprid astragali have talismanic and prosperity-and life-enhancing qualities appears to be deeply anchored in both the Mongolian and Tibetan pastoralist context.

Certain similarities between Tibetan and Mongolian knucklebone gaming, divination, and symbolism are probably attributable to processes of cross-fertilization. Agents of transmission from ca. 11th-18th century CE could possibly have included the Tanguts, Jurchens, Kitans, and/or various groups of Mongols. The cultural and political impact of the Mongols in Tibet was especially powerful and far reaching, and the linguistic, gaming and religious evidence presented in this work suggests that their influence extended into the realm of astragali as well.[62] Interactions between Mongolia and the Tibetan plateau in the Late Prehistoric era must also be considered. The rise of nomadic pastoralism in Mongolia and other regions of north Inner Asia in the Late Bronze Age may have acted as a springboard for the broadcast of astragalus-related traditions south onto the Tibetan plateau, as part of a suite of herding customs and their ritual and symbolic props. My research demonstrates that Mongolia and southern Siberia and Tibet exhibit cognate chariot, mascoid, big game hunting with the recurve bow, combat, and Eurasian Animal Style rock art,[63] the raising of standing stones and slab wall constructions at funerary

59 Birtalan 2007-2008: 49.

60 Birtalan 2007-2008: 47. Yamakoshi 2016: 89.

61 There are many online sources for Mongolian knucklebone gaming, which may involve multiple teams and hundreds of players. For a summary of a study endorsing the value of knucklebones in the cognitive development of young children in Mongolia, see Sarantuya and Erdenetsetseg 2014.

62 An examination of the vectors of transmission potentially responsible for the adoption and enrichment of knucklebones games played by the Chinese (*zhuā guǎi*) is beyond the scope of this article. Mainland China is an eastern terminus in the tradition, where games of tossing and catching ovicaprid and pig astragali played by children have analogues across Eurasia.

63 Parallels in the themes, subjects and motifs of rock art are particularly strong in Mongolia and Ladakh. See Bellezza forthcoming-a.

sites,[64] similar kinds of copper alloy objects,[65] common archaic funerary rites,[66] and interrelated pastoral practices, etc. It would be in keeping with the prevailing patterns of transmission if these vibrant and extensive cultural and technological links between Mongolia and Tibet beginning in the Late Bronze Age extended to astragalus traditions as well.

Any such bilateral relationship between Tibet and Mongolia is liable to be but one facet in a complex sphere of interactions in Eurasia beginning much earlier with the diffusion of ovicaprid stockbreeding eastward. However, unravelling the complex web of transference accounting for the dissemination of ovicaprid astragalus traditions in Eurasia and the trade, diplomatic, military, cultural, and religious processes involved is a formidable task. To properly assess the spread of astragalus games, lore and ritual over the breadth of the continent would require substantial collective effort and comprehensive study of the archaeological, ethnographic and linguistic records of many peoples, past and present.

To illustrate interactions across the breadth of Eurasia that may have a bearing on Tibetan astragalus traditions, I take just one example regarding the assigned values of the four sides of the bone. The Mongolian game of *dörwön berx* (four difficulties) is "very similar" to the Greco-Roman divination tradition known as the venus-throw.[67] The numerical values accorded the faces of an astragalus by the Greeks and Romans finds correspondence in the Iron Age site of Geoy Tepe, western Azerbaijan.[68] Analogous numerical associations are found in Mongolia and the Tibetan plateau. These appear to have been engendered along a corridor extending from the Mediterranean to Inner Asia via western Asia. Be that as it may, the archaeological data required to translate the circumstantial evidence for spatio-temporal ties into verifiable findings is not yet available to us.

The diffusion of astragalus traditions in Eurasia over the last three millennia is almost certainly not merely the result of a down-the-line transfer from one people to another. It is much more likely that multilateral transmissions in which activities and ideas were combined and recombined over the long haul are implicated. To explain the deep-seated and pervasive nature of astragalus traditions in Eurasia and their possible effects on the Tibetan plateau, I tender a model predicated on different chrono-cultural stages of development. Despite the historical linkages propounded being hypothetical, this model helps situate astragalus cultural complexity in a framework amenable to further scrutiny and amendment. I propose that the following four chrono-cultural stages are represented in the dissemination of astragalus traditions on the Tibetan plateau:

64 See Bellezza 2008: 92-99, 106-108; 2017; forthcoming-a; forthcoming-b.

65 See Bellezza 2008: 99-106; 2016; forthcoming-b.

66 See Bellezza 2008: 544-59.

67 Birtalan 2007-2008: 48; a different number appearing on each upright side of four tali thrown simultaneously.

68 Schädler and Dunn-Vaturi 2009.

1) Late Bronze Age and Early Iron Age (ca. 1500-600 BCE) transfer from Inner Asian pastoralist groups in the wake of the expansion of Andronovo cultural traits in Xinjiang and eastern Kazakhstan.
2) Iron Age and Protohistoric (ca. 600 BCE to 300 CE) transfer potentially encompassing the classical world and involving the Saka and possibly Achaemenid and Parthian intermediaries.
3) Imperial period (ca. 600-850 CE) transfer effected through cultural borrowing and consolidation spurred on by Tibetan imperial expansion.
4) Later historical period (1000-1700 CE) transfer through north Inner Asian cultures that had extensive contacts with Tibetans.

While cultures of north Inner Asia were well suited to serve as a cultural purveyor of ovicaprid astragalus traditions to the plateau, independent innovation appears to have played a role in molding unique aspects of the Tibetan declension, reflecting the distinctive cultural, religious and social environment of the plateau. Functional similarities in ovicaprid pastoralism and responses to similar conditions arising from it may also account for affinities in astragalus traditions among different peoples. Yet, independent innovation and functional convergence do not appear to have deterred successive waves of interactions in Eurasia, the force of seminal ideas, things and activities often transcending geographic, cultural and linguistic barriers. Finally, as so little is known about the historical dispersal of astragali as cultural objects and symbols, Tibet as a generator of tradition to other parts of the continent must also be considered in the mix of factors contributing to large-scale assimilation on the continent.

Conclusion

This article furnishes a bird's eye view of the cultural significance of ovicaprid astragali on the Tibetan plateau. It presents both archaeological and ethnohistoric data in a comprehensive review of the subject. Nonetheless, this study is but an initial step in the examination of astragalus phenomena in Tibet. The role of knucklebones in gaming, divination, tallying, and religious beliefs and customs demands far more attention from archaeologists, historians and anthropologists working on the Tibetan plateau than it has received to date. An exhaustive look at Tibetan historical references to knucklebones in gaming and divination is bound to provide valuable insights into their functions and symbolism, supplementing what may have been already written on the subject by contemporary native authors. The typological and regional classification of astragalus gaming and the analysis of its linguistic and ideological components has a very large purview, ensuring that much work remains to be done.

I trust this study has demonstrated that knucklebones are not just a matter of curiosity but a vital tool in understanding the course of Tibetan civilization and its interactions with a host of other peoples over the last 3000 years. Perhaps no other single object offers such a large window onto transcultural relationships that helped shape the sportive, religious and intellectual complexion of Tibet and the entire Eurasian continent.

Bibliography

Affanni, Giorgio. 2008. "Astragalus bone in Ancient Near East: Ritual depositions in Iron Age I in Tell Afis." In *Proceedings of the 5th International Congress on the Archaeology of the Ancient Near East, Madrid, April 3-8 2006. Actas del V Congreso Internacional de Arqueología del Oriente Próximo Antiguo*. J. Mª Córdoba, *et al.* eds., Madrid: Centro Superior de Estudios sobre el Oriente Próximo y Egipto, 1: 77-92.

Aldenderfer, Mark. 2013. "Variation in Mortuary Practice on the Early Tibetan Plateau and the High Himalayas." In *The Journal of the International Association for Bon Research*. Montreal: The International Association for Bon Research, 1: 293-318.

——2018. "Archaeological Evidence and the definition of Zhangzhung." In *Ancient Civilization on Tibetan Plateau: Proceedings of the First Beijing International Conference on Shang Shung Cultural Studies*. Tsering Thar Tongkor and Tsering Dawa Sharshon eds., Xining: Mtsho-sngon mi-rigs dpe-skrun khang, 123-45.

Anthony, David, W. 2007. *The Horse, the Wheel and Language: How Bronze Age Riders from the Eurasian Steppes Shaped the Modern World.* Princeton: Princeton University Press.

Aufschnaiter, Peter. 1956. "Prehistoric sites discovered in inhabited regions of Tibet." In *East and West* 7.1: 74-88.

Bellezza, John V. 1998. "Thogchags: Talismans of Tibet." In *Arts of Asia* 28.3: 44-64.

—— 2005. *Calling Down the Gods: Spirit-Mediums, Sacred Mountains and Related Bon Textual Traditions in Upper Tibet.* Tibetan Studies Library 8. Leiden: Brill.

—— 2008. *Zhang Zhung: Foundations of Civilization in Tibet. A Historical and Ethnoarchaeological Study of the Monuments, Rock Art, Texts and Oral Tradition of the Ancient Tibetan Upland.* Philosophisch-Historische Klasse Denkschriften 368. Wien: Verlag der Österreichischen Akademie der Wissenschaften.

—— 2011. "The Liturgies and Oracular Utterances of the Spirit-mediums of Upper Tibet: An Introduction to their *bSang* Rituals." In *Revue d'Etudes tibétaines* 20: 5-31. Paris: CNRS. http://www.himalaya.socanth.cam.ac.uk/collections/journals/ret/pdf/ret_20_01.pdf

—— 2012. "Spirit-mediumship in Upper Tibet: The Vocation of one expert practitioner." In *Bulletin of Tibetology*, 48.2: 7-32. P. Roy ed., *Exploring Tibet's History and Culture. Proceedings of the International Conference held in New Delhi, 2009.* Samyak Vak Series 17. Varanasi: Central University of Tibetan Studies, 2011: 379-410.

—— 2013a. "A Review of the Early Cultural History of Spiti — Part Two", "Non-Tibetan vocabulary in the dialect of Spiti." In *Tibetan Archaeology,* June 2015. http://www.tibetarchaeology.com/june-2015/

—— 2013b. *Death and Beyond in Ancient Tibet: Archaic Concepts and Practices in a Thousand-Year-Old Illuminated Funerary Manuscript and Old Tibetan Funerary Documents of Gathang Bumpa and Dunhuang.* Philosophisch-Historische Klasse Denkschriften 454. Wien: Verlag der Österreichischen Akademie der Wissenschaften.

—— 2014. "Bronze cowries and a bronze knucklebone: Markers of cosmopolitanism in the ancient artifacts of Tibet." In *Tibet Archaeology*, May 2014. http://www.tibetarchaeology.com/may-2014/

—— 2015. "The Voice of the Gods in Upper Tibet: The trance-induced invocations and songs of praise of the spirit-medium Phowo Sridgyal." In *The Illuminating Mirror*. O. Czaja and G. Hazod eds., Contributions to Tibetan Studies 12. Wiesbaden: Dr. Ludwig Reichert Verlag, 15-40.

—— 2016. "A Preliminary Study of the Origins and Early Development of Bronze Metallurgy on the Western Tibetan Plateau." In *Tibet Archaeology*, February and March 2016. http://www.tibetarchaeology.com/february-2016/ http://www.tibetarchaeology.com/March-2016/

—— 2017. "Talus-blanketed Red House Necropolis of Upper Tibet: Cross-cultural exchanges with the north at the end of the Bronze Age — section 2: The wider Inner Asian archaeological context." In *Tibet Archaeology*, January 2017. http://www.tibetarchaeology.com/January-2017/

—— Forthcoming-a. *Besting the Best: Warriors and War in the Religious and Cultural Traditions of Tibet. A historical, ethnographic and archaeological survey on the nature of martial activities over the last three millennia.* Lumbini: Lumbini International Research Institute.

—— forthcoming-b. *Tibetan Silver, Gold and Bronze Objects and the Aesthetics of Animals in the Era before Empire: Cross-cultural Reverberations on the Tibetan Plateau and Soundings from other Parts of Eurasia.* British Archaeological Reports International Series. Oxford: BAR Publishing.

Bhatt, R. C.; Kvamme, K. L.; Nautiyal, V.; Nautiyal, K. P.; Juyal, S. and Nautiyal, S. C. 2008-2009. "Archaeological and Geophysical Investigations of the High Mountain Cave Burials in the Uttarakhand Himalaya." In *Indo-Kōko-Kenkyū-Studies in South Asian Art and Archaeology* 30: 1-16.

Birtalan, Ágnes. 2003. "Ritualistic Use of Livestock Bones in the Mongolian Belief System and Customs." In *Proceedings of the 45th Permanent International Altaistic Conference (PIAC), Budapest, Hungary, June 23-28, 2002.* A. Sárközi and A. Rákos eds., Budapest: Research Group for Altaic Studies, Hungarian Academy of Sciences, Department of Inner Asian Studies, Eötvös Loránd University.

—— 2007-2008. "Rituals of Sworn Brotherhood (Mong. anda bol-, Oir. and, ax̨ düü bol -)

in Mongol Historic and Epic Tradition." In *Chronica. Annual of the Institute of History, University Szeged. 7-8*, I. Zimonyi ed., Szeged: Institute of History, University of Szeged, 44-56.

British Museum. N.d. "Objects from the Central Caucasus (The Koban Culture)." https://www.britishmuseum.org/pdf/2%20koban%20integ-opt-sec.pdf

Chen, Kwang-tzuu and Hiebert, Fredrik T. 1995. "The Late Prehistory of Xinjiang in Relation to its Neighbors." In *Journal of World Prehistory* 9.2: 243-300.

David, F. N. 1962. *Games, Gods and Gambling*. New York: Hafner Publishing.

Davidson, Gladys R. 1952. "The Minor Objects". In *Corinth*. Athens: American School of Classical Studies at Athens, 12: iii-366.

Davis-Kimball, Jeannine. 2000. "The Beiram Mound: A Nomadic Cultic Site in the Altai Mountains (Western Mongolia)." In *Kurgans, Ritual Sites, and Settlements: Eurasian Bronze and Iron Age*. J. Davis-Kimball *et al*. eds., BAR International Series 890. Oxford: Archeopress, 89-105.

De Grossi Mazzorin, Jacopo. and Minniti, Claudia. 2013. "Ancient use of the knuckle-bone for rituals and gaming piece." In *Anthropozoologica* 48.2: 371-80. Paris: Muséum national d'Histoire naturelle. http://sciencepress.mnhn.fr/sites/default/files/articles/pdf/az2013n2a13.pdf

Dobbs, Christopher S. 2018. "Not Just Fun and Games: Exploring Ludic Elements in Greek and Latin Literature." Doctoral dissertation, University of Missouri.

Dotson, Brandon. 2015. "The Call of the Cuckoo to the Thin Sheep of Spring: Healing and Fortune in Old Tibetan Dice Divination Texts." In *Tibetan and Himalayan Healing: An Anthology for Anthony Aris*. C. Ramble and U. Roesler eds., Kathmandu: Vajra Publications, 147-60.

Doyen, Charles. 2018. "Knucklebones or Weights? Metal Astragali in the Classical World." in *DIAR.pr Research Publications*. https://dial.uclouvain.be/pr/boreal/object/boreal:203134

Eshel, Esther and Stern, Ian. 2017. "Divination Texts of Maresha-Archeology and Texts." In *Archaeology and Text: A Journal for the Integration of Material Culture with Written Documents in the Ancient Mediterranean and Near East*. Ariel University and Lehigh University, 1: 7-25.

Gilmour, Garth H. 1997. "The Nature and Function of Astragalus Bones from Archaeological Contexts from the Levant and Eastern Mediterranean." In *Oxford Journal of Archaeology* 16.2: 167-75.

Haarh, E. 1969. *The Yar-luṅ Dynasty: a study with particular regard to the contribution of myths and legends to the history of Ancient Tibet and the origin and nature of its kings*. Copenhagen: G.E.C. Gad's Forlag.

Holmgren, Richard. 2004. "'Money on the hoof' The astragalus bone-religion, gaming and primitive money." In PECUS. *Man and animal in antiquity. Proceedings of the conference at the Swedish Institute in Rome, September 9-12, 2002*. B. Santillo Frizell ed., Rome: The Swedish Institute in Rome, 212-19.

Institute of Archaeology, CASS and Cultural Relics Conservation Insitute of Tibet Autonomous Region. 中国社会科学院考古研究所、西藏自治区文物保护研究所 2014. "The Excavation of the Gurugyam Cemetery in Gar County, Ngari Prefecture, Tibet Autonomous Region in 2012." 西藏阿里地区噶尔县故如甲墓地 2012 年发掘报告 . In *Kaogu Xuebao* 考古学报 / *Acta Archaeologica Sinica* 4: 563-93.

—— 2015. "New Discoveries at Gurugyam Cemetery and Chu vthag Cemetery in Ngari, Tibet" (trans. T. Tong). On *The Institute of Archaeology CASS* website. http://www.kaogu.cn/en/Special_Events/Top_10_Archaeological_Discoveries_in_China_2014/2015/0410/49819.html

Jia, Peter Wei Ming and Betts, Alison, V. G. 2010. "A reanalysis of the Qiemu'erqieke (Shamirshak)." In *The Journal of Indo-Europen Studies*, vol. 38.3/4: 275-317.

John, Gudrun. 2006. *Tibetische Amulette aus Himmels-Eisen*. Rahden: Verlag Marie Leidorf.

Kogălniceanu, Raluca; Ilie, Ana; Mărgărit, Monica; Simalcsik, Angela; Dumitraşcu, Valentin. 2014. "A hoard of astragals discovered in the Copper Age settlement at Iepureşti, Giurgiu County, Romania." In *Documenta Praehistorica* 41: 283-304.

Koryakova, L. N.; Krause, R.; Epimakhov, A. V.; Sharapova, S.V.; Panteleyeva, S. E.; Berseneva, N. A.; Fornasier, J.; Kaiser, E.; Molchanov, I. V.; Chechushkov, I. V. 2011. "Archaeological Studies of the Kamenny Ambar (Olgino) Fortified Settlement." In *Archaeology Ethnology & Anthropology of Eurasia* 39.4: 61-74.

Kradin, Nikolay N. and Ivliev, Alexander L. 2008. "Deported nation: The fate of the Bohai people of Mongolia." In *Antiquity* 82.316: 438-45.

Lalou, Marcelle. 1953. "Rituel Bon-po des funérailles royales (fonds Pelliot tibétain 1042)." In *Journal Asiatique* 240.1: 339-63.

Lebo, Patrick. 2016. "Astragalomancy in Etruria: An Analysis of the Astragali at Cetamura del Chianti." In *Proceedings of The National Conference on Undergraduate Research (NCUR)*. Ashville: University of North Carolina, 420-30.

Lin, Tung-Kuang. 2003. *Antique Tibetan Thogchags and Seals* (trans. B. Li). Taiwan: Liao, Yue-Tao.

Luce, Jean-Marc. 2011. "From miniature objects to giant ones: The process of defunctionalisation in sanctuaries and graves in Iron Age Greece." In *Pallas. Revue d'Études Antiques* 86: 53-73.

Lu Hongliang 吕红亮 . 2015. *Trans-Himalayan Interaction: An Archaeological Study of the Prehistory of Western Tibet* 跨喜马拉雅的文化互动 ：西藏西部史前考古研究 . Beijing: Science Press 北京 ：科学出版社 .

Macdonald, A. 1971. "Une lecture des Pelliot tibétain 1286, 1287, 1038, 1047, et 1290. Essai sur la formation et l'emploi des mythes politiques dans la religion royale de Sroṅ-bcan sgam-po." In *Études Tibétaines dédiées à la mémoire de Marcelle Lalou.* A. Macdonald ed., Paris: Adrien Maisonneuve, 190-391.

Murakami, D, 2014. "Aspects of the Traditional Gambling Game known as Sho in Modern Lhasa-religious and gendered worldviews infusing the Tibetan dice game." In *Revue d'Etudes Tibétaines* 29: 245-70. http://himalaya.socanth.cam.ac.uk/collections/journals/ret/pdf/ret_29_08.pdf

Muscarella, Oscar White. 1974. "The Iron Age at Dinkha Tepe, Iran." In *Metropolitan Museum Journal* 9: 35-90.

Namkhai Norbu, 2009. *The Light of Kailash: A History of Zhang Zhung and Tibet,* vol. 1. Merigar: Shang Shung Publications.

Nishida, Ai. 2018. "'Two Dice Divination Texts' from Dunhuang: Pelliot tibétain 1046B and IOL Tib J 740." In *Central Asiatic Journal.* Special Issue: Old Tibet and its Neighbours (eds. L. Doney et al.) 61.1: 133-50.

Perego, Elisa. 2010. "Magic and Ritual in Iron Age Veneto, Italy." In *Papers from the Institute of Archaeology University College London,* 20: 67-96. London. http://www.pia-journal.co.uk/article/view/pia.342/54

Rinjing Dorje, 1987. *Food in Tibetan Life,* London: Prospect Books.

Sabori, Hadi; Basafa, Hasan; Hejininezhad, Esmaeil; Bolandi, Reza; Norouzi Khorasani, Mina. 2016. "Game Pieces of Knucklebones: Evidence about the Continuation of Local Games in Khorasan, Iran." In *The Silk Road* 14: 209-212. The Silk Road Foundation.

Sarantuya, S. And Erdenetsetseg, E. 2014. "Impact of Mongolian National Game «Shagai» on the Development of Cognitive Processes in Preschool Children." In *A Game and Toys in the History and Culture, Development and Education,* 85-88. Materials of the III International Scientific Conference on April 1-2, 2014. Prague: Vědecko Vydavatelské Centrum Decko Vydavatelské Centrum. Http://www.sociosphera.com/Files/Conference/2014/K-04_01_14.Pdf#Page=85

Schädler, Ulrich and Dunn-Vaturi, Anne-Elizabeth. 2009. "Board Games in pre-Islamic Persia." In *Encyclopædia Iranica,* online edition. http://www.iranicaonline.org/articles/board-games-in-pre-islamic-persia .

Sidéra, Isabelle and Vornicu, Andreea. 2016. "The Archaeology of Games: Playing with Knucklebones in the Early Chalcolithic of the Balkans." In *Southeast Europe and Anatolia in Prehistory. Essays in Honor of Vassil Nikolov on his 65th Anniversary.* Universitätsforschungen zur Prähistorischen Archäologie, 293. Bonn: D. R. Rudolfhabelt GMBH, 379-88

Stein, R. A. 1970. "Un document ancien relatif aux rites funéraires des Bon-po tibétains." In *Journal Asiatique* 258: 155-85.

—— 1971. "Du récit au rituel dans les manuscrits Tibétains de Touen-houang." In *Études Tibétaines dédiées à la mémoire de Marcelle Lalou.* A. Macdonald ed., Paris: Adrien

Maisonneuve, 479-547.
Tahberer, Bekircan. 2012. "Astragaloi on Ancient Coins: Game Pieces or Agents of Ancient Prophesy?" In *The Celator* 26.4: 6-20, 56.
Tucci, Giuseppe. 1966. *Tibetan Folk Songs from Gyantse and Western Tibet.* With two appendices by N. Norbu. Ascona: Artibus Asiae.
—— 1973. *Transhimalaya* (trans. J. Hogarth). Reprint, Delhi: Vikas Edition.
Vahman, Fereydūn. 1989. "Bāzī." In *Encyclopædia Iranica*, online edition. http://www.iranicaonline.org/articles/bazi-games
Weihreter, Hans. 1988. *Schmuck aus dem Himalaja.* Graz: Akademische Druck-u., Verlagsanstalt.
—— 2002. *Thog-lcags: Geheimnisvolle Amulette Tibets.* PDF document on CD-ROM. Augsburg.
Yamakoshi, Yasuhiro. 2016. "Predicative non-past participles in the Secret History of the Mongols." In *Altai Hakpo* 26: 85-101.

◆ Author: John Vincent Bellezza, Senior Research Fellow, University of Virginia.

唐初的中尼交通：资料的再审视

王邦维

内容摘要：蕃尼古道的存在有很长的历史，考古发现证明其最早可以追溯到旧石器时代。对于蕃尼古道的历史，可以分为唐代以前、唐代、唐以后至明清时期这三个大的时段来理解和研究。具体到唐初的蕃尼古道，应该考虑东亚与南亚甚至中亚当时各个方面的形势、文献记载的时间层次、考古新发现等方面的问题，同时有关蕃尼古道研究的文献，虽然大多早已经被人注意到和引用过，但仍然存在不少问题，研究其实还可以深入。此外，我们还要注意求法僧与外交使节以及商人的关系，当时求法僧行进经常跟使节和商人搭伴，所以他们当时求法的路线实际上也就是商路。

2019 年 1 月 5-6 日，四川大学中国藏学研究所举办“蕃尼古道工作坊——碑铭、图像、写本”，我有幸受邀参加。我对蕃尼古道历史的研究很早就开始了，从 20 世纪 70 年代末至今已经近四十年。蕃尼古道的存在有着很长的历史，十分古老，在有文献记载之前古道早已经存在。近年来的考古发现证明，人类在青藏高原上的活动，可以追溯到旧石器时代。有人类的活动就有人的迁徙和人群的交往，也就有道路，蕃尼古道也是如此。在有文献记载的历史之前，通过神话传说等，也可以来追溯早期人类迁徙留下的痕迹，包括古道。

对于蕃尼古道的历史，我认为可以大分为几个时段来理解和研究。

第一个时段：唐代以前，可以称为神话和传说的时代。对于这个时段的历史，我们需要思考如何将传说的线索与考古实证串接起来，其意义不仅限于对蕃尼古道的历史考察，还涉及神话学、宗教学、文献学、文本的形成与流传、族群的迁徙等方面的问题。

第二个时段：唐代，这一时期开始出现文献记载，同时也有碑铭等考古发现，需要把文献与考古发现结合起来进行研究。当然碑铭也可以看做是某个时间点在特定条件下固化的一种文献，典型的例子是中尼边境吉隆发现的《大唐天竺使出铭》，价值非常重要[1]。

第三个时段：唐以后直至明清时期，这一期间史料越来越丰富，考古实物也越来越多，而且材料不仅有汉文、藏文，还有尼泊尔文和更晚一些的英文，如何处理和理解这些材料是我们需要面对的问题。

总起来说，自有人类以来，族群之间生产技术、物资交换、宗教文化的交流，从来就是多向度、多方位、多层次，包括交流的物质背景——交通道路。

具体到唐初的蕃尼古道，我以为应该考虑以下三个方面的问题。

一是东亚与南亚，甚至包括中亚当时各个方面的形势，不仅是吐蕃和尼婆罗，同时要考虑到唐代中原地区与印度的文化、外交、政治及其他的交往。尤其是这一时期新的变化，包括吐蕃的兴起、唐政权的政治及外交活动、汉地求法僧西行求法运动路线的变化等，我们要注意几个地区间的互动，因为上述变化都发生在这样的大背景下。

二是文献方面的记载，从史源学和史料学的角度来看，这些文献是有时间层次的。其中最早的是与汉地求法僧有关，如《大唐西域求法高僧传》《大唐西域记》，两者都有明确的写作年代。稍晚一点的是使臣的记载，如王玄策的《中天竺行记》，这部书虽然亡佚了，但在《释迦方志》《法苑珠林》，甚至包括《一切经音义》中都有部分保留。同时还有唐末到宋代撰写的史书，如《旧唐书》《新唐书》《通典》《唐会要》《册府元龟》等。此外还有印度、尼泊尔、克什米尔的相关碑铭与文献资料，这些材料该如何收集

1　参见西藏自治区文管会文物普查队：《西藏吉隆县发现唐显庆三年〈大唐天竺使出铭〉》，《考古》1994（7）：619-623；霍巍：《大唐天竺使出铭及其相关问题的研究》，[日]《东方学报》（京都）第66册，1994：253-270；陆庆夫：《关于王玄策史迹研究的几点商榷》，《敦煌研究》1995（4）：171-178；孙修身：《王玄策事迹钩沉》，乌鲁木齐：新疆人民出版社，1998；林梅村：《〈大唐天竺使出铭〉校释》，收入氏著《汉唐西域与中国文明》，北京：文物出版社，1998：420-442；霍巍：《〈大唐天竺使出铭〉相关问题再探》，《中国藏学》2001（1）：37-50；Wang Bangwei, *New Evidence on Wang Xuance's Missions to India, India and East Asia: Culture and Society*, ed. N. N. Vohra, Delhi: Shipra Publications, 2002: 41-46. 佟柱臣：《大唐王玄策天竺使出铭考》，《藏学学刊》第一辑，成都：四川人民出版社，2004：101-110；郭声波：《〈大唐天竺使之铭〉之文献学研识》，《中国藏学》2004（3）：108-118。

和处理？以与王玄策、玄奘有关的印度戒日王（Harṣavardhana）为例，有关戒日王的印度文献有梵文的*Harṣacarita*，还有被认为是他自己写的*Nāgānanda*，有*Priyadarśikā*和*Ratnāvalī*三种文学作品或者说梵剧，此外还有一组与戒日王有关的碑铭。但印度方面的文献有一个普遍性的问题，那就是很多都与神话和传说纠缠在一起，和汉文文献相比，可信度要差很多，因此需要谨慎使用，而碑铭材料又相对简单，对史实介绍不多。最近张远的《戒日王研究》一书收集了很多材料[2]，可以提供参考。阿闍黎·启昼教授关于离车族（Licchivi）碑铭的研究，排了一个很好的序列，碑铭材料很重要，不过也有局限，就是所提供的信息量往往有限，而尼泊尔的编年史14世纪才开始出现，克什米尔的编年史Kalhana's *Rajatarangini*也是12世纪才出现的文献。

三是新的考古发现，是近代或者近几十年来才有的事。如高宗显庆三年（658年）的《大唐天竺使出铭》，极为重要。此外还包括遗址的发掘、古道的勘定，其中也涉及一些专题性的人物和事件研究，如王玄策出使印度的过程，考古材料的重要性不言而喻。

此外，与蕃尼古道研究有关的文献，虽然大多早已经被人注意到和引用过，但仍然存在不少问题，需要继续深入研究。举例来说，《大唐西域求法高僧传》一书中明确讲到，经蕃尼古道到印度的求法僧共十一位，包括玄照、道希、师鞭、玄太、玄恪、道方、道生、末底僧诃等，他们中很多还有梵名。其中玄照两次经过吐蕃，行程涉及文成公主，而第一次赴印度时则有新罗僧人玄恪同行。道希“行至吐蕃，中途危厄，恐戒检难护，遂便暂舍。行至西方，更复重受”[3]，这可以让我们对松赞干布时代西藏佛教流行的程度做具体的思考，显然当时佛教在西藏的某些区域并没有得到接受。同时道希“在大觉寺造唐碑一首。所将唐国新旧经论四百余卷，并在那烂陀矣”[4]，而王玄策在印度也有造碑，根据吉隆发现的王玄策碑，可以发现使团中有专门的书写、刻工和记录者。似乎都对在印度造碑一事很重视。另外，汉地求法僧到印度，除学习梵文经典外，他们也将中国的汉译经论[5]带到印度。道生“以贞观末年从吐蕃路往游中国……在那烂陀，学为童子王深所礼遇”[6]，此处“中国”指中印度[7]，这段记载对研究印度历史也有帮助。还有两位求法僧，“是吐蕃公主奶母之息也”[8]，这里的“吐蕃公主”，法国汉学家沙畹在翻译该书时认为

2　张远：《戒日王研究》，北京：社会科学文献出版社，2018：1-495。
3　（唐）义净原著，王邦维校注：《大唐西域求法高僧传校注》，北京：中华书局，1988：36。
4　（唐）义净原著，王邦维校注：《大唐西域求法高僧传校注》，1988：36。
5　（唐）义净原著，王邦维校注：《大唐西域求法高僧传校注》，1988：36。
6　（唐）义净原著，王邦维校注：《大唐西域求法高僧传校注》，1988：49。
7　（唐）义净原著，王邦维校注：《大唐西域求法高僧传校注》，1988：49。
8　（唐）义净原著，王邦维校注：《大唐西域求法高僧传校注》，1988：65。

是吐蕃的公主，但根据汉文史书里一贯的称谓，例如汉代的“乌孙公主”，这里应该是指文成公主，而不是其他人。其中的“奶母之息”，王玄策碑碑文里恰好就有这个“息”字，是指儿子，《大唐西域求法高僧传》中也不止一处提到王玄策。

同时，我们还要注意求法僧与外交使节以及商人的关系，当时求法僧行进经常跟使节和商人搭伴，所以他们当时求法的路线实际上也就是商路。唐初道宣撰写的《释迦方志》，卷上《遗迹篇》讲唐初通印度有三条道路，“自汉至唐往印度者，其道众多，未可言尽。如后所纪，且依大唐往年使者，则有三道。依道所经，具覩遗迹，即而序之”[9]。道宣把它们分别称为“北道”“南道”和“东道”，其中“北道”“南道”相当于《汉书·西域传》讲的“南道”“北道”，也就是玄奘来回行经的两条道，即塔克拉玛干沙漠南缘和北缘的两条道，而“东道”则有如下记载：

> 其东道者，从河州西北度大河，上曼天岭，减四百里至鄯州。又西减百里至鄯城镇，古州地也。又西南减百里至故承风戍，是隋互市地也。又西减二百里至清海，海中有小山，海周七百余里。海西南至吐谷浑衙帐。
>
> 又西南至国界，名白兰羌，北界至积鱼城，西北至多弥国。又西南至苏毗国，又西南至敢国。又南少东至吐蕃国，又西南至小羊同国。
>
> 又西南度呾仓法关，吐蕃南界也。又东少南度末上加三鼻关，东南入谷，经十三飞梯、十九栈道。又东南或西南，缘葛攀藤，野行四十余日，至北印度尼波罗国（此国去吐蕃约为九千里）。[10]

“东道”此前未见记载，这是道宣记载的的一条新的路线，很多研究者结合王玄策碑对此已有很好的解释。但是为什么叫“东道”呢？实在不好理解，这条道路从长安出发，明明是向西，从吐蕃通过是往西走，为什么不叫“西道”却叫“东道”？道宣难道连东西的方向都分不清楚？但他这样说，应该有他的依据。笔者推测道宣知道这条路线，大概是从吐蕃人那里听来的，如果把吐蕃通向唐的道路称作“东道”，就没什么问题了。道宣参加过玄奘的译经，后来住在长安的西明寺，他与王玄策是有个人接触的。可以相信，道宣这段话，其说法来源的大部分，尤其是关键部分，来自王玄策，因此道宣讲的“东道”，最后一段很可能指的就是吉隆道。这条道路，不是王玄策首先开通，而是吐蕃

9 （唐）道宣撰，范祥雍点校：《释迦方志》，上海古籍出版社，2011：10。
10 （唐）道宣撰，范祥雍点校：《释迦方志》，2011：10-11。

人先已开通，王玄策只是利用而已，因此道宣说“东道”，而不说“西道”。《法苑珠林》也存在类似情况，其编撰者道世与道宣同门，当时也住在西明寺，他编书时也应该与王玄策有个人的接触。目前我们所见到的有关王玄策的碑刻，确定的有两处，除吉隆的《大唐天竺使出铭》外，在龙门石窟也有发现。

最后谈一下宋代求法僧继业的行程问题[11]。北宋初乾德四年（966年），僧行勤等一行一百五十多人，赴印求法，继业在其中，回程时“又至磨逾里。过雪岭，至三耶寺。由故道，自此入阶州”[12]。此处“三耶寺”应该就是桑耶寺。至于“磨逾里”，应该是指芒域，这当然就与蕃尼古道有关系了，反映了蕃尼古道宋代的情况。

此外，关于尼泊尔方面的情况，《大唐西域记》讲到了泥婆罗国，大致就是今天的加德满都地区。但玄奘到过迦毗罗卫，没到过今天的加德满都。与《大唐西域记》同时或稍晚的文献中更有一些关于泥婆罗的记载。所有这些记载，哪些可信？哪些不可信？哪些是准确的？哪些不准确？信息材料来自哪里？都需要做具体的研究。当然，我们今天做研究的目的，就是要解决这些问题。

编者按：2019年1月5-6日，四川大学中国藏学研究所成功举办“蕃尼古道工作坊——碑铭、图像、写本”学术活动，本文为王邦维教授在此次工作坊结束时的发言，由王文波整理。

◆ 王邦维　北京大学东方文学研究中心教授

11　参见王邦维：《峨眉山继业三藏西域行程略笺释》，《南亚研究》1993（2）：36-40；修订稿载永寿主编：《峨眉山与巴蜀佛教——峨眉山与巴蜀佛教文化学术讨论会论文集》，北京：宗教文化出版社，2004：179-186。

12　范成大撰：《吴船录》，北京：中华书局，1985：14-15。

Uncovering Amoghavajra's legacy in the Hexi Corridor and Tibet [1]

Yury Khokhlov

Abstract: This research analyses the images from Mogao and Yulin caves, which have been traditionally ascribed to Tibetan influence and believed to represent the early Tibetan style. Contrary to this common opinion, the author shows that these images are in fact influenced by Southern Indian art and in particular by the art of the Pallava kingdom in Tamil Nadu and closely affiliated with teachings introduced to China by Vajrabodhi (金刚智 , 671-741), a renowned Buddhist master from the Pallava Kingdom, in the first half of the 8th century and specifically propagated in Hexi by Amoghavajra (不空 Bukong, 705-774) in the mid 8th century. He argues that these images belong to a distinctive artistic tradition, which was established by Vajrabodhi who was also known in China as a great painter. The presence of these images in artwork from the Tibetan period merely signifies the continuation of the

1 The paper expands on a talk given at the Seventh International Conference on Tibetan Archaeology & Arts in Chengdu (October, 2018). Many people helped me in various stages of preparing it. I would like to thank in particular Tristan Bruck, Analicia Busha, Geoffrey Goble, Shawo Khacham, Rory Lindsay and Darik Thokmay for their assistance with my studies on various topics discussed in this paper; and Emmanuel Francis, Yuko Fukuroi, Amy Heller, Deepanjana Klein and Arno Klein for sharing with me their photographic archives. I am immensely grateful to Andrea Acri, Claudine Bautze-Picron, Rolf Giebel, Yannick Laurent, Robert Mayer, Neil Schmid, Per Sørensen, Jeffrey Sundberg, Joie Szu-Chiao Chen, Sam van Schaik, Peter Sharrock and Zhang Changhong who read my manuscript, corrected my errors and offered me their extremely valuable feedback. All remaining errors are of course my own.

artistic and religious trends that existed in Hexi before the Tibetan conquest. Furthermore, the article argues that the Tibetan conquest of the Hexi corridor enabled the Tibetan appropriation of Chinese religious and artistic trends, which were popular in the region. This conclusion well supports Christopher Beckwith's theory according to which the Tibetan adoption of Buddhism as a state religion was inspired by the Chinese model of state-protective Buddhism established by Amoghavajra.

Introduction

As a starting point, this research analyses the imagery in a distinctive Indian artistic mode[2] found in various paintings from Mogao and Yulin caves.[3] The material under review belongs to the 8th to 11th century and often features Esoteric Buddhist imagery.[4] Since some of the early examples within this group belong to the period of the Tibetan occupation of the Hexi Corridor,[5] their artistic mode has often been ascribed — erroneously, in my view — to the cultural influence of Tibet. Several recent publications on this topic provoked me to address the issues that I see in such attributions.[6] Contrary to this common opinion, I will argue that this artistic mode is in fact influenced by Southern Indian[7] art and, in particular, certain stylistic and iconographic features can

2 The term "artistic mode" is used as a broader category than artistic style and refers to a general way of representation. Additionally, "imagery in an Indian artistic mode" refers to Indianized images that were made to look as if they were Indian as opposed to images in a traditional local artistic mode, which for the area discussed in this essay is Chinese.

3 A list of these paintings can be found in Appendix 1.

4 The term "Esoteric Buddhism" is notoriously complex and problematic; in this article it is used mostly as a reference to teachings, which were introduced to China during the Tang and possessed instructions in the use of mantra, dhāraṇī, and maṇḍala. "Esoteric Buddhist imagery" refers here to representations of deities associated with these teachings. An extensive discussion on the term "Esoteric Buddhism" can be found in Orzech, Sørensen, and Payne 2011: 3-18.

5 In this article, I adopted the dates of the Tibetan conquest of the Hexi corridor from van Schaik and Galambos 2012: 62-63. Guazhou (瓜州), the prefecture where the Yulin caves are located, was captured by the Tibetans in 776, while Shazhou (沙州), Dunhuang, fell in 786. After the collapse of the Tibetan empire, the whole Hexi Corridor was once again under Chinese rule by 851.

6 Recent publications that argue for the Tibetan origin of the discussed imagery include Kapstein 2004, 2009, 2014; Sha 2013; McCoy 2016; M. Wang 2018; Debreczeny 2019. See footnotes 53, 134 and 144 for details.

7 Geographically, the Indian subcontinent has been divided into the Northern and Southern parts. While the Northern part includes the northern mountains and the Indo-Gangetic plains, the Southern part is comprised of the Indian Peninsula. An imaginary division line between the two parts goes along the Vindhya Mountains and the Satpura Range which separate the Gangetic plains and the Deccan plateau (see Map 1, where it is shown as a black dashed line). The two parts of the subcontinent, being interconnected on many levels, are, nevertheless, characterized by different histories, economies and cultures, and often by distinctive artistic styles. See Thapar 2003: 37-68. There is yet another distinction which is particularly important for this research. While the cultural influence of Northern India mostly spread along land-bound trade routes, Southern Indian influence is mostly noticeable in territories with which Southern Indian polities engaged in sea trade. From this perspective, landlocked Tibet belongs to the Northern Indian sphere of influence, while China was naturally predisposed to receive influence from both Northern and Southern parts of India.

be traced exclusively to the art of the Pallava kingdom in Tamil Nadu and the Pallava influenced art of the Western Deccan, thereby ruling out alleged artistic influences from Tibet. Moreover, the discussed images are closely affiliated with teachings introduced to China by Vajrabodhi (金刚智 , 671-741) in the first half of the 8th century and specifically propagated in Hexi by Amoghavajra (不空 , 705-774) in the mid 8th century. Thus, the presence of such depictions in artwork from the Tibetan period merely signifies the continuation and Tibetan appropriation of the artistic and religious trends that existed in Hexi *before* the Tibetan conquest. Furthermore, it will be shown that this artistic mode was transmitted to Central Tibet during the Tibetan occupation of the Hexi Corridor and can be recognized in sculptures from a number of early Central Tibetan temples. I argue that this artistic transmission was a result of significant religious transmission, which included, but was not limited to, the cult of Vairocana and the eight great bodhisattvas, as well as the teachings of the Yoga tradition (i.e. Yoga Tantras according to the Tibetan classification).

This article is divided into four major parts. **Part 1** presents a brief historical overview of Buddhism and artistic trends in Hexi before the Tibetan conquest. **Part 2** discusses the most representative depictions within this group of materials and their connection to Southern Indian art and Amoghavajra's textual heritage. In **Part 3**, I will provide an overview of Southern Indian influence on Buddhist art in China in general and situate this Hexi group of images within a larger picture. In **Part 4**, I will demonstrate that the artistic mode under review and its corresponding teachings were transmitted from Hexi to Tibet during the period of Tibetan occupation. Sites mentioned in the article are shown in **Map 1**, which also illustrates major land and maritime routes between South and East Asia in the first millennium CE.[8]

Part 1. Historical Setting

By the Han dynasty (206 BC-220 CE), the Hexi Corridor was already a strategic part of the Silk Road and a gateway to China for those travelling from India and Central Asia. This area was an early recipient of Buddhist teachings and artistic styles arriving to China from the West. Frequent contacts with the West led to a highly cosmopolitan Buddhist culture that encouraged a close imitation of foreign artistic models. Imperial Buddhist patronage and expansion of the Tang dynasty to the West in the Tarim Basin created a steady traffic of monks travelling between China and Northern India through Hexi. Indian monks travelling to China and Chinese monks returning to China from India carried with them Buddhist texts and imagery as tribute to the court. This process resulted in a rapid transmission of the newest — and increasingly Esoteric — teachings and in the popularity of Indian icons and Indianized styles in China in general and in Hexi in

8 Routes on the Tibetan plateau are not shown in the map.

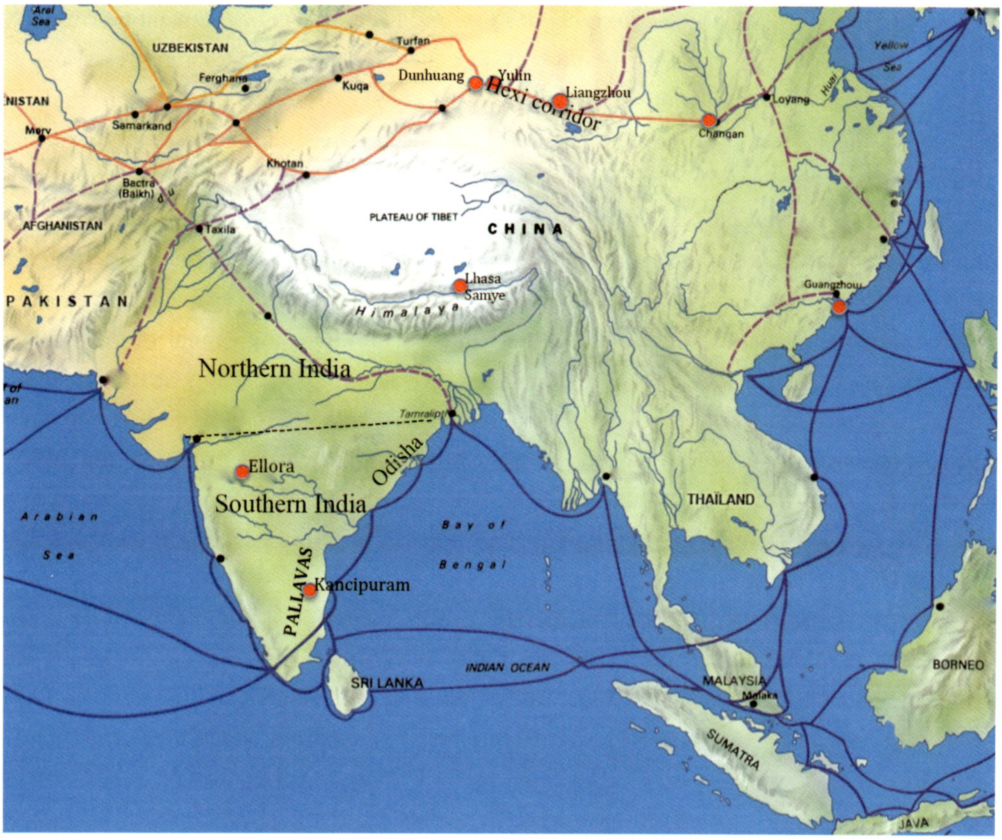

Map. 1 Major land and maritime routes between South and East Asia in the first Millennium CE and sites mentioned in the article. Routes on the Tibetan plateau are not shown (Based on a map from https://en.unesco.org/silkroad/about-silk-road).

particular.[9]

Whereas the cultural influence of Northern India mostly spread along land-bound trade routes, including those known as the Silk Road, the impact of Southern Indian culture is mostly noticeable in territories with which Southern Indian polities engaged in sea trade. Recent scholarship has recognized that maritime relations played an equally important role in the spread of Buddhist ideas and artistic styles.[10]

Perhaps one of the most important maritime Buddhist imports to Tang China was the

9 The most recent and comprehensive research on travelling monks as agents of religious and artistic transmission from India to China is in Wong 2018. On Esoteric Buddhism in Dunhuang and depictions of Esoteric deities in Dunhuang art during the Tang, see Schmid 2011.

10 On the spread of Buddhism through maritime networks, see Acri 2016, 2018.

Vajroṣṇīṣa Yoga (金 刚 顶 瑜 伽 *Jin gang ding yu qie*; lit. the Yoga of Adamantine Crown)[11] teachings from Southern India. This tantric system includes eighteen structural texts, out of which only the *Sarvatathāgatatattvasaṅgraha Tantra* (*STTS*),[12] also known as the *Vajraśekhara Sūtra*, was transmitted to China during the Tang dynasty. The tradition based on the *STTS* (hereafter the Yoga tradition) became the foundation for a Buddhism of national protection in China in the second half of the 8th century.[13] The propagation of the Yoga tradition in China is attributed to the activities of the Indian monk Vajrabodhi (or Vajrabuddhi)[14] and his pupil Amoghavajra.[15] Vajrabodhi studied the Vajroṣṇīṣa Yoga under Nāgajñāna (Nāgabodhi or Nāgabuddhi) in Southern India, most likely at Kāñcīpuram,[16] the capital of the Pallava Kingdom and a great center of religious and Sanskrit learning equal almost to Nālandā.[17] Nāgajñāna in turn was a disciple of Nāgārjuna, who is also believed to be from Kāñcīpuram,[18] and who according to legend obtained the Vajroṣṇīṣa Yoga teachings from an "iron stūpa" which was probably located in Tamil Nadu or Andra Pradesh.[19] Vajrabodhi was famed as a great Esoteric master and performer of miraculous deeds, and before traveling to China he was active at the Pallava court in Kāñcīpuram. [20]

The core territory of the Pallava Kingdom roughly corresponds to the modern-day state of Tamil Nadu. The Pallavas were a major military and cultural power in the Peninsula and Tamil merchants historically played a key role in maritime commerce with Southeast Asia and China.[21] In the late 7th and early 8th centuries, the Pallavas' relations with China in particular

11 As was shown by Rolf Giebel, *Vajroṣṇīṣa* is a correct Sanskrit reconstruction of the Chinese title 金刚顶瑜伽 , which is traditionally known as *Vajraśekhara*, see Giebel 1995: 109. The Vajroṣṇīṣa Yoga is understood as "the Esoteric tradition that encompasses the doctrines and practices contained in the eighteen texts of the Vajroṣṇīṣa Yoga cycle and the lineage concerning the legitimate transmission of them." See Yang 2018: 10.

12 On the *STTS* and its English translation, see Giebel 2001.

13 Yang 2018: 120-158. On the notion of National Protection Buddhism in Tang China, see Orzech 1998: 1-9; 135-209.

14 On Vajrabodhi, see Sundberg and Giebel 2011.

15 On Amoghavajra and his teachings, see Chou 1945: 284-307; Goble 2012; Orzech, Sørensen and Payne 2011: 263-285; Yang 2018.

16 Sundberg and Giebel 2011: 151

17 On Kāñcīpuram, see Thapar 2003: 344. Lokesh Chandra even suggested Kāñcīpuram as the location of Uḍḍiyāna. Although this issue was recently solved by Sanderson, who has sufficiently proved that Uḍḍiyāna is located near Kashmir, Chandra's article provides a useful discussion on Kāñcīpuram as a centre of Esoteric Buddhism, see Chandra 1980. On the location of Uḍḍiyāna, see Sanderson 2007: 265.

18 Sundberg and Giebel 2011: 195, n.110.

19 The story of the "iron stūpa" is found in Amoghavajra's "Instructions on the Gate to the Teaching of the Secret Heart of the Great Yoga of the Scripture of the Diamond Summit." (金刚顶经大瑜伽秘密心地法门义诀 Jin gang ding jing da yu qie mi mi xin di fa men yi jue, T.1798.39:808a19-b28). See Orzech, Sørensen, and Payne 2011: 152. Amoghavajra's account is translated integrally in Orzech 1995. See also Tanaka 2018: 309-311.

20 Sundberg and Giebel 2011: 7-9.

21 On the history of maritime relations between these regions, see Guy 2014: 3-13.

strengthened and it is recorded that the two states exchanged several diplomatic missions.[22] The Pallava king Narasiṁhavarman II (r. 700-728) is credited with building a Buddhist temple in the Chinese style at the port city of Nāgapaṭṭinam for Chinese Buddhists arriving by sea.[23] On the Southern Chinese shore, three temples (Hindu or Buddhist) for Tamil merchants were erected in the port city of Guangzhou (广 州) in the 8th century or even earlier.[24] Xuanzang (玄奘 , c. 602-664) visited Kāñcīpuram by land routes in the mid 7th century and reported the presence of about 100 Buddhist temples and 10,000 Buddhist monks.[25]

Intent on propagating Buddhism in China, Vajrabodhi joined a Pallava diplomatic mission and travelled to the Tang court as an envoy of the Pallava king. Navigating along established sea routes through Sri Lanka and Sumatra, the mission arrived at Guangzhou, from whence they reached Luoyang (洛阳) in the year 720. Vajrabodhi brought to China various Buddhists texts, including a short version of the Vajroṣṇīṣa Yoga scripture (a complete one hundred thousand verse text of the scripture was purportedly lost on the way during a storm) and a copy of the *Mahāprajñāpāramitā Sūtra* offered to the Chinese emperor by the Pallava king Narasiṁhavarman II.[26] The master spent the remaining 21 years of his life in China propagating the Yoga tradition and working on translation projects.[27] It is especially relevant for this study that Vajrabodhi was known in China as a great painter, who was particularly good at painting Indian Buddhist images. He was included in *the Record of Famous Painters of Successive Dynasties* (历代名画记 *Li dai ming hua ji*; 9.16b-17a), compiled by Zhang Yanyuan (张彦远) in 847.[28] The master himself painted numerous maṇḍalas as well as designed wooden sculptures for the Luoyang Guangfu Temple and a stūpa of Vairocana, which was considered as an excellent piece of work. None of Vajrabodhi's works are known to have survived, but it could be surmised that they were most likely executed in the Pallava style.

Vajrabodhi's disciple Amoghavajra, whom he met during his journey to China, is regarded as a towering figure in the history of Chinese Buddhism. Amoghavajra studied under Vajrabodhi for more than 20 years and became a prolific translator, second only to Xuanzang, and an imperial preceptor for three successive Tang emperors: Xuanzong (玄宗 , r. 712-756), Suzong (肃 宗 , r. 756-762), and Daizong (代 宗 , r. 762-779).[29] In 742-746, Amoghavajra travelled to Sri Lanka and Southern India, where he received Esoteric initiations and acquired more than five hundred Buddhist texts, including a complete scripture of the eighteen texts of

22 Sen 2016: 26; Sundberg and Giebel 2011: 144-145.

23 Sundberg and Giebel 2011: 145.

24 Guy 1993: 295.

25 Sundberg and Giebel 2011: 154.

26 Sundberg and Giebel 2011: 138, 147.

27 Yang 2018: 27-28.

28 Chou 1945: 276 n. 30, 280; Sundberg and Giebel 2011: 4 n.10.

29 Goble 2012: 62.

the Vajroṣṇīṣa Yoga.[30]

Amoghavajra made his first significant translations of the texts obtained during his journey, including the first part of the *STTS*, in the Hexi Corridor, in the regional capital city of Liangzhou (凉州 , modern Wuwei) between 754 and 756. He was sent to Hexi upon request of the military governor Geshu Han (哥舒翰 , 700-757) to assist the troops with ritual support in the battlefield against the Tibetans who constantly harassed the northwestern frontier.[31] In Hexi, Amoghavajra initiated thousands of people into the secret practices of the Yoga and gained many followers amongst the local nobility, government, and military. The Yoga teachings were propagated in Hexi on an unprecedented scale. This can be illustrated by an excerpt from Amoghavajra's official biography, composed upon his death in 774, which describes the events in 754:

> In the thirteenth year [of Tianbao], [Bukong] arrived in Wuwei, where he resided at the Kaiyuan Monastery. From the military commissioner to officials of the lowest rank, [Bukong] conducted the service of abhiṣeka for all; as many as several thousand people, both the gentry and commoners, ascended the altar [to receive the service of abhiṣeka]. [Bukong] imparted the teachings of the Five Divisions to his clerical disciple, Hanguang. Next, [he] administered the abhiṣeka ritual of the Five Divisions for Li Yuancong, now the Commissioner of Merit, [with the prestigious rank of] Opening Bureau, and instructed him in the teachings of the Great Maṇḍala of the Diamond Realm.[32]

It is important to note that Amoghavajra gained his renown as an Esoteric master in Hexi, and from there it spread to the capitals via Hexi officials and military commanders who were his disciples.[33] In addition, Hexi came to be regarded as the master's ancestral place; towards the end of his life, he was awarded the title of Duke of Su and given a nominal fief of 3000 households in Suzhou (肃州), a district in the northwestern part of the Hexi Corridor.[34]

During the turbulent events of the An Lushan rebellion and the war with the Tibetans, Amoghavajra significantly strengthened his religious and political influence at court. He performed countless Esoteric initiations and protective rituals for the imperial troops, the

30 Yang 2018: 33-35, 256-257. It is not known what regions Amoghavajra visited while in India; the sources are extremely vague about the Indian part of his trip and give detailed information only on his stay in Sri Lanka. Bearing in mind the shortness of the trip and that Amoghavajra spent most of his time in Sri Lanka, it is unlikely that he travelled beyond Southern India.

31 Yang 2018: 41-42, 264-265.

32 Yang 2018: 265. "The teachings of the five divisions" refers here to the Yoga tradition, while "the Great Maṇḍala of the Diamond Realm" stands for the Vajradhātu maṇḍala. See Yang 2018: 30.

33 Yang 2018: 41-45.

34 Yang 2018: 170-171, 362.

state, and the emperor. The institutionalization of a close group of his disciples as a form of governmental organization for the purpose of serving the state by performing apotropaic rituals can be regarded as one of Amoghavajra's major achievements.[35] At the same time and as Robert Sharf has argued, the Esoteric practices propagated by Vajrabodhi, Amoghavajra and alike should not be regarded as an independent tradition/sect/school. What these masters promoted was essentially a new ritual technology intended for members of the ruling elite who could afford spending considerable resources on elaborate rituals conducted for the simultaneous achievement of mundane and supermundane goals. Sharf has emphasized that in China in the 8th century these new teachings were transmitted to monastics from a variety of backgrounds and beyond sectarian lines imposed by later traditions. [36]

Amoghavajra and his Buddhist institution reached the peak of their power during the reign of Daizong (762-779). The master had a vast network of supporters and disciples, including the most powerful people of the empire; all the court officials and commanders of the imperial guards were required to be initiated into the Vajradhātu maṇḍala and to participate in rituals orchestrated by Amoghavajra.[37] Among the master's other deeds are the translation of a great number of Buddhist texts and the promotion of the cult of Mañjuśrī and Mount Wutai.[38]

Liangzhou, where Amoghavajra translated the *STTS* and initiated thousands of people into secret practices of the Yoga tradition in 754-756, fell to the Tibetans in 758 and became a major centre of the Tibetan administration over the eastern areas.[39] It is worth remembering that Tibetan Buddhism and the Tibetan Buddhist order were at this time in their early formative stage. Only in the 760s Buddhism started to be promoted by the Tibetan emperor Trisong Detsen (Tib. Khri srong lde btsan, r. ca. 742-797); the first Tibetan monastery of Samye (Bsam yas) was consecrated in 779.[40] In general, the Tibetan ruling elite was highly suspicious towards Esoteric teachings, however the *STTS* and closely related texts (in general correspond to Yoga Tantras according to the Tibetan classification) were not only permitted, but, in parallel with the contemporaneous developments in Chinese state Buddhism, became a foundations for official Buddhist ceremonies in the late 8th century (this will be discussed in detail in Part 4).[41] It is also clear that Tibetan interest in the Yoga tradition emerged in close temporal proximity to Amoghavajra's propagation of this tantric system in the Hexi region which soon after became a part of the Tibetan Empire.

35 Yang 2018: 194-195.

36 Sharf 2017: 85-86, 114.

37 Yang 2018:188-200.

38 Yang 2018: 147-160.

39 van Schaik and Galambos 2012: 46.

40 Kapstein 2000: 60.

41 Weinberger 2010: 140-150.

Amoghavajra died in 774, two years before the Tibetan conquest of Guazhou (瓜州 , the prefecture containing the Yulin caves). With the conquest of Shazhou (沙州 , the prefecture containing Dunhuang) in 786, the whole Hexi Corridor came under Tibetan rule. Tibetans continued the patronage of existing Buddhist institutions in Hexi, which were numerous and many were large, and sponsored building of several new monasteries and temples.[42] However, Tibetan impact on Buddhist thought and Buddhist art in Hexi during this period of occupation remains largely unclear, since major developments with regard to the Tibetan appropriation of Buddhism took place during or after the conquest of the Hexi corridor. One undisputable sign of the Tibetan input on Dunhuang art, however, is depictions of Tibetans and a Tibetan emperor in several caves at Mogao and Yulin.[43] The Chinese emperor continued to be depicted as well and his superior status was not diminished. For instance, in a painting in Mogao Cave 231 dated to circa 839, which shows the debate between Mañjuśrī and Vimalakīrti, a Chinese emperor retains his exalted position as the Buddhist authority and is shown in the entourage of Mañjuśrī, while a Tibetan emperor leads a procession of foreign kings on the side of Vimalakīrti.[44] The Dunhuang manuscripts mention some mixed Sino-Tibetan Buddhist communities and show no signs of opposition between Chinese and Tibetan Buddhists.[45] Given the richness of Buddhist culture in Hexi and written records describing Tibetans eagerly seeking to learn the Dharma from the Chinese, the impact of Hexi Buddhist culture on what was to become known as Tibetan Buddhism and Tibetan Buddhist art must have been significant.[46] The Tibetan period in Hexi lasted until the mid 9th century, when, following the collapse of the Tibetan Empire, most of the region was again under Tang control. Despite this political upheaval, many Tibetans remained in the region and the Tibetan language continued to be widely used.[47]

To summarize, when Tibetans arrived in Hexi, they found themselves in a highly sophisticated Buddhist environment, where Esoteric teachings, especially those of the Yoga tradition, enjoyed great prestige. The Buddhist art in Hexi was characterized by an increasing popularity of Indianized styles and Esoteric imagery.

---

42 Sha 2013: 152-156; van Schaik and Galambos 2012: 62. On Buddhist institutions in Hexi during the Tibetan period, see Horlemann 2012.

43 Just a few examples: Yulin Cave 25 and Mogao Caves 158, 231, 359. See Sha 2013: 53-81.

44 For a discussion on the symbolism of representations of the Mañjuśrī-Vimalakīrti debate in Dunhuang, see Schmid 2006: 183-185. For a reproduction of the scene from Cave 231, see Debreczeny 2019: 50, fig.1.2.

45 H. Sørensen 2000: 41.

46 For example, according to the *Testament of Ba*, two Tibetan delegations were sent to the Chinese capital to learn Buddhist teachings in the second half of the 8th century. It is also stated that one thousand Buddhist texts were granted by the Chinese emperor and brought to Tibet by one of these delegations. See Wangdu and Diemberger 2000: 16-17, 21, 42 n.91, 49 n. 121-122, 52 n. 136, 138, and 70 n. 245. Moreover, this source shows that Buddhism in 8th century Tibet was strongly associated with China and sometimes even referred to as the doctrine of China. See Wangdu and Diemberger 2000: 37 n.71.

47 van Schaik and Galambos 2012: 62-69.

Part 2. Definitions and Origins

A list of paintings executed in the artistic mode discussed in this article is presented in Appendix 1. It is by no means exhaustive and includes only the most significant published examples. The majority of the paintings depict maṇḍala-like compositions. Common central figures include Vairocanābhisaṁbodhi (see section 2.2),[48] Vajrasattva, a Buddha, four-armed Amoghapāśa (see section 2.3), and two-armed Avalokiteśvara. As will be shown these images mostly draw from repertoire of the Yoga tradition. Other subjects include Vairocanābhisaṁbodhi with the eight great bodhisattvas (see section 2.1) as well as Kubera with attendants (see section 2.4). In addition, the list includes portable paintings with single figures of bodhisattvas (see section 2.5) and paintings with stylistically mixed imagery (see section 2.6).

Before proceeding to a detailed discussion on the paintings under review, it is necessary to mention that for almost all of them potential textual sources can be found in both the Chinese and Tibetan traditions. Since it has been historically maintained that Tibetan Esoteric Buddhism stems directly from the Indian tradition, possible relationships between the parallel Chinese and Tibetan texts have been rarely seriously considered. Moreover, it is commonly believed that developed Esoteric Buddhism did not exist in Dunhuang/Hexi before the Tibetan conquest. Thus, a decisive factor for the attribution of the discussed images to the Tibetan tradition has often been a combination of their Indianized style (as opposed to the Chinese style), which was understood as Tibetan, with Esoteric subject matter. In the following, I will challenge the validity of this approach.

2.1 Representations of Vairocanābhisaṁbodhi with the Eight Great Bodhisattvas in Hexi and their spread to Eastern Tibet

2.1.1 Yulin Cave 25

2.1.1.1 Description of the Cave and the State of Scholarship

The scholarship on Yulin Cave 25 perfectly illustrates issues surrounding the attribution of the imagery under review to Tibetan influence and therefore I discuss it first and at greatest length. The cave was excavated during the period of Tibetan rule in Guazhou and is currently dated by

48 Vairocanābhisaṁbodhi refers here to bejewelled Vairocana displaying *dhyāna mudrā*, as this form was initially described in the *Vairocanābhisaṁbodhi Tantra (VAT)*. See Wayman and Tajima 1998: 8. However, images of Vairocana in this form do not necessarily signify the context of the *VAT*.

Fig. 1 Vairocana and the eight great bodhisattvas, the east wall of the main chamber, late 8th C., Tibetan period in the Hexi corridor, Yulin Cave 25, China (Extant section (in color): Dunhuang Academy 2014: pic. 10; The lost section (in b/w): Kapstein 2009: fig. 9).

the Dunhuang Academy to the early years of the Tibetan period (i.e. 776-781).[49] The centre of the cave is occupied by a sculptural representation of Vairocana perhaps dating to the Qing dynasty, which could be a replica of the original sculpture. The wall paintings are regarded as originals. The central wall of the main chamber consists of Indianized images of Vairocanābhisaṁbodhi and the eight great bodhisattvas (Fig. 1).[50] The bodhisattvas are identified by Chinese inscriptions as Ākāśagarbha, Kṣitigarbha, Maitreya, Mañjuśrī, Vajrapāṇi, Avalokiteśvara, Sarvanivāraṇaviṣkambhin, and Samantabhadra, who together are known as the eight great bodhisattvas.[51] This group of nine — Vairocanābhisaṁbodhi and the eight great bodhisattvas — will henceforth be abbreviated as VAEGB. The rest of the paintings in the cave are executed in the Chinese mode. They include the Pure Lands of Maitreya and Amitābha on the northern and southern walls respectively; the bodhisattvas Mañjuśrī and Samantabhadra with attendants and Sudhana on the western wall (Fig. 2); and six standing bodhisattvas, whose identities are not

49 A review of scholarship on the attribution of the cave to the Tibetan period can be found in Kapstein 2009: 56-57. The date period 776-781 is provided by the Dunhuang Academy in https://www.edunhuang.com/cave/10.0001/0001.0002.0025 (accessed 22.04.2019).

50 Only four bodhisattvas on the left side have survived to the present day. The group on the right side is shown in the old photographs taken in 1940s that are currently preserved in the Lo Archive, Princeton.

51 Wang 2018: 108-109. The most comprehensive study on the eight great bodhisattvas as a group is in Bautze-Picron 1997.

Fig. 2 Bodhisattvas Samantabhadra (left) and Mañjuśrī (right) with Sudhana and retinue, late 8th C., Tibetan period in the Hexi corridor, the west wall of the main chamber, Yulin Cave 25, China (Dunhuang Academy 2014: pics.32, 33).

Fig. 3 Left: Face of Vairocana, detail of fig. 1
Right: Face of attending bodhisattva from Samantabhadra retinue, detail of fig. 2
(https://www.e-dunhuang.com/cave/10.0001/0001.0002.0025).

entirely clear, and who are depicted on the corners of the cave. These Indianized and Chinese images show identical line structures and shading, and the faces of some figures between the two groups bear a striking resemblance (Fig. 3). From this it is clear that, differences in style notwithstanding, all the paintings in the cave were likely executed by the same group of artists.

A publication produced in 2000 by the Dunhuang Academy for a centennial commemoration of the discovery of the library in Mogao cave 17 briefly mentions that the central composition (VAEGB) of Yulin cave 25 "indicates close ties to Master Amoghavajra's spread of Tantrism in the Hexi region."[52] This idea has been ignored in later scholarship. Instead, the coexistence of the two artistic modes, as well as the coexistence of Esoteric and traditional Pure Land subjects within the cave have been ascribed to the cultural influence of Tibet. The style of the composition of VAEGB has been understood either as the Tibetan style or as the Pāla style of northeastern India being transmitted through Tibet.[53] In the following, I

52 Unfortunately no arguments supporting this attribution were given. See Zhang 2000: 31.

53 The publications include Kapstein 2004, 2009, 2014; Sha 2013; Wang 2018; Debreczeny 2019.

In a series of articles, Matthew Kapstein has developed a theory that Yulin Cave 25 should be identified as a temple built by Tibetans to commemorate a peace treaty between the Tibetan and Tang empires made in 821-822. Although the iconographic program of Yulin Cave 25 only partially matches a description of the temple found in the Dunhuang manuscripts, the author develops his idea by pointing to the popularity of Vairocana cult in the Tibetan Empire and to existence of roughly contemporaneous rock carvings of VAEGB in Eastern Tibet (Kapstein 2009: 53, 58). As stylistic evidence, the figure of Vairocana from Cave 25 was compared with an undated sculptural representation of the same deity that was ascribed to the Imperial period. The sculpture, however, is executed in a considerably different style, which makes it difficult to accept the author's point. Summarizing his argument, Kapstein emphasizes the coexistence of the two styles in the cave and concludes: "In both iconography and style, Anxi Yulin 25 thus expresses the coexistence of the Tibetan and Chinese Buddhist worlds. On the surface at least, it seems an especially fitting memorial to a peace accord between the two powers." (Kapstein 2009: 54). Recently, the author revised his initial notion and suggested instead that Yulin Cave 25 could be either an earlier Tibetan model for the treaty temple or its copy (Kapstein 2014). I will discuss issues concerning the Tibetan rock carvings in section 2.1.2. As for the coexistence of Indianized and Chinese depictions, as well as Esoteric and Pure Land subjects, such mixed imagery can be already found in Tang dynasty caves predating the Tibetan period. I will discuss some examples in the next chapter.

Sha Wutian's research on Cave 25 was published in his monograph devoted to Dunhuang art of the Tibetan period. The author postulates that the figures of VAEGB in Cave 25 represent the Tibetan style and more specifically the northeastern Indian Pāla style as transmitted through Tibet. These statements seem to ignore the fact that no comparable depictions that can be dated to the period before the Tibetan occupation of Hexi are known from Tibet. Moreover, the discussed material certainly does not belong to the Pāla artistic tradition. See Sha 2013: 360-382, 470-492. Sha 2016: 119-122.

Michelle Wang in her recent publication *Maṇḍalas in the Making* came to the conclusion that the depiction of VAEGB in Cave 25 belongs to the Tibetan Buddhist tradition and is executed in the Tibetan style, which she defines as a "Nepalese-derived Tibetan style." The author compared the images from the cave to Tibetan and Nepalese sculpture and noted various similarities. Significant differences were, however, overlooked. The Eastern Tibetan rock carvings and the coexistence of the two artistic modes in Cave 25, named as "stylistic bilingualism," were regarded as evidence for the Tibetan origin of the cult of VAEGB in Hexi. See Wang 2018: 91-121.

In the latest contribution to this subject, Karl Debreczeny sees the group of VAEGB in Yulin Cave 25 as a manifestation of the new aesthetic and religious interests introduced under Tibetan rule. The author's argument is essentially based on the works by Kapstein, Sha and M. Wang and therefore has the same shortcomings. See Debreczeny 2019: 24-25.

Fig. 4 Two bodhisattvas (detail of the wall painting), Early Tang dynasty (618-712), the east wall of the main chamber, Mogao Cave 329, China (https://www.e-dunhuang.com/cave/10.0001/0001.0001.0329).

will argue against the current scholarly consensus and demonstrate that neither such thematic and stylistic diversity nor the style of the group of VAEGB can be ascribed to the Tibetan or Pāla-Indian influence.

2.1.1.2 Stylistic Considerations

Indian and Chinese Modes in Hexi Art before the Tibetan Conquest

Indianized imagery started to appear early on in Tang dynasty caves.[54] For example, Fig. 4 shows two bodhisattvas from Mogao Cave 329 (datable to the early Tang period, 618-712).[55] A bodhisattva on the right is depicted in the Chinese mode, characterised by a round halo, long scarves wrapped around the body, and a voluptuous lower garment. The bodhisattva on the left, on the other hand, is shown in the Indian mode. It is similar to what is found in Yulin Cave

54 For example, Mogao Caves 202, 321, 329, and 335. See Sha 2013: 133-134.

55 For a description of this cave and additional images, see https://www.e-dunhuang.com/cave/10.0001/0001.0001.0329 (accessed 22.04.2019).

Fig. 5 Bodhisattva Bhaiṣajyarāja with eight bodhisattvas and two lokapalas, 766-776, Tang dynasty, slopped ceiling inside the niche on the north wall of the main chamber, Mogao Cave 148, China (Dunhuang Academy 2013: fig.29).

25 (Fig.1), where the bodhisattvas also have inverted U-shaped halos and wear similar lower garments resembling trousers.

Another example of such coexistence of the two modes can be found in Mogao Cave 148, which contains depictions of the Buddha's Parinirvāṇa and various Pure lands painted in the Chinese mode and Esoteric imagery (e.g. various multi-armed forms of Avalokiteśvara) painted in the Indian mode. According to the inscription engraved on the stele at the entrance, the cave was completed sometime between 766 and 776 — that is within the decade leading up to the Tibetan conquest of Guazhou in 776.[56] Particularly interesting are six rectangular panels painted inside the niches. They contain compositions akin to that of VAEGB in Yulin Cave 25 (Fig. 1).

Fig. 5 is one of the panels, and it depicts the bodhisattva Bhaiṣajyarāja surrounded by eight bodhisattvas and two Lokapālas. It has a similar layout to the image in Yulin Cave 25 (Fig.1), with a large central figure placed under a canopy and flanked by two groups of smaller figures shown symmetrically on either side. The lotus seats of the central figure and the two chief bodhisattvas are almost identical to the lotus seats in the Yulin composition. In both paintings, the stems of the lotus seats of the bodhisattvas grow from the seat of the central divinity. The small lotus flowers and leaves in the intermediate space are similar in both compositions as well.

It is thus evident that the coexistence of the Indian and Chinese artistic modes as well as of Pure Land and Esoteric imagery within Yulin Cave 25 is a continuation of the trend that started in early Tang dynasty caves. Similarly, the depiction of the group of VAEGB itself is based on a template that was popular in Hexi before the Tibetan conquest.

56 Mogao Cave 148 is discussed in Lee 2010: 181-201. Esoteric imagery in the cave is discussed in Liu 2008.

Southern Indian Artistic Mode

Esoteric teachings were transmitted not only through texts, but also through their accompanying images.[57] Although none of the original Indian illustrations survive in China, the fact that they existed is evident from Chinese translations made by Indians. For example, Śubhākarasiṁha (善无畏 , 637-735), an Indian translator-monk living in Tang China, frequently made references to iconographic illustrations in his texts.[58] In addition, the importance of imagery in the transmission of Esoteric teachings was stressed by Kūkai (空海 , 774-835), who studied in China under Amoghavajra's successor Huiguo (惠果 , 746-806). In his inventory (dated 806), Kūkai states: "The secret wisdom of the true words is hidden and implicit in scriptural texts; only through imagery can it be properly transmitted."[59] In China, original Indian illustrations were copied by local artists, and, as in the case of Vajrabodhi, many Indian monks themselves were able to produce such images. In any case, works with Indian background were considered extremely valuable; they were carefully recorded and praised in monastic inventories. Furthermore, accuracy in the copying of these images was regarded crucial for the authenticity and efficacy of replicas in Esoteric rituals.[60] Another important feature of Chinese practice was the standardization of religious imagery. Standardized models and templates for replication were known as *yang* (样). In her recent book, Hsueh-man Shen (沈雪曼) describes many Tang dynasty scrolls with *yang* of iconic images of various deities, including a group of the eight great bodhisattvas.[61]

It is through these processes of copying, standardization, and replication that elements of Indian costumes and decorations were adopted in Chinese art. In this regard, tracing the origins of distinctive decorative elements in early Chinese Esoteric depictions yields an important trace for determining the provenance of the artistic tradition, to which Indian prototypes belonged, and, by extension, the provenance of the corresponding teachings.

The group of VAEGB in Cave 25 was likely based on standardized models. The figures of the bodhisattvas are essentially of the same type. They are shown either frontally or in a three-quarter profile and have almost identical decorations. Diversity is achieved through different hand gestures, leg positions, and attributes.

Although the figures are overall similar to the imagery in Mogao Cave 148 (Fig. 5), they show certain stylistic peculiarities (see an enlarged image of Vairocana in Fig. 6) such as:

57 This was recently discussed by Kimiaki Tanaka, see Tanaka 2018: 125-126.

58 Tanaka 2018: 125-126.

59 Shen 2019: 154.

60 Hsueh-man Shen shows that the inventories of objects taken from China to Japan during the Tang specifically comment on images produced by Indian masters or originated from India, see Shen 2019: 154. The earliest extant example of iconographical drawings is an early 9th century Chinese scroll, known as the *Gobu shinkan* (五部心观), see Tanaka 2018: 293-294.

61 Shen 2019: 149-155.

Fig. 6 Vairocana and close-ups of the crown and armband, details of fig. 1 (https://www.e-dunhuang.com/cave/10.0001/0001.0002.0025).

- elongated Y-shaped torsos;
- crowns and armbands with spikes of pearls or little spears (henceforth spiked crowns and armbands), see close-ups in Fig. 6;
- broad necklaces with swags of pendants (henceforth swagged necklaces);
- and earrings with large pendants.

These elements are the defining characteristics of the artistic mode that this article is concerned with, though it is not always the case that all of them are present in a given image. Of the four characteristics, the spiked decorations are the most distinctive and persistent feature (see close-ups in Fig. 6). It is a matter of fact that such decorations are almost exclusively associated with Southern Indian art (see examples in Figs. 7, 8, 9, 10, 19, 23, 24). In this regard, they are neither found in Tibetan art prior to the occupation of Hexi, nor in the art of Northern India, Nepal, or Central Asia, artistic traditions which, along with that of China, contributed to the formation of Buddhist art in Tibet. As such, this indeed eliminates the currently assumed possibility of the alleged Tibetan background of the discussed imagery.

In contrast, this Southern Indian stylistic trace corresponds well to the Southern Indian current in Chinese Esoteric Buddhism represented by Vajrabodhi and Amoghavajra.

In the 7th and 8th centuries, there were two regions in Southern India where Esoteric Buddhism was prominent and these exact kinds of spiked jewelry were common in artistic representations. They are Tamil Nadu in the southeastern part of the Indian Peninsula and the Western Deccan. With regard to Sri Lanka, which was an important destination for both Vajrabodhi and Amoghavajra, it is unlikely that the discussed artistic mode in Hexi art has a Sri Lankan origin. Although Sri Lankan Mahāyāna and Vajrayāna Buddhism and associated art were greatly influenced from the Pallava Kingdom of Southern India,[62] the spiked decorations are not particularly common in Sri Lankan Buddhist depictions. [63]

Connections with the art of Tamil Nadu are not surprising as this region was the home of Esoteric teachings propagated by Vajrabodhi and Amoghavajra.[64] Moreover, Vajrabodhi as a painter most likely belonged to the Pallava artistic tradition that flourished in Tamil Nadu. Having in mind the records about imagery produced by Vajrabodhi in China and the Chinese practices of copying, standardization, and replication, we can assume that a Chinese artistic tradition based on Pallava art and closely associated with Vajrabodhi emerged in the Tang capitals by the mid-8th century and spread from there to Hexi/Dunhuang. The existence of religious and artistic interexchange between Dunhuang and the Tang capitals is well recorded[65] and thus Vajrabodhi's teachings and related imagery likely reached Hexi already during the master's lifetime. Nevertheless, the tradition undoubtedly owes its greater popularity in the region to Amoghavajra. As discussed, the master not only taught in Hexi, but also made his first major translations there.

Regarding the Western Deccan, the existence of Esoteric Buddhism in the 8th century there is evident from Ellora cave sculpture. It has been also suggested that the region could have

62 On the Pallava Buddhist and artistic influence in Sri Lanka, see Indrapala 2005: 189-192; Dohanian 1983.

63 On Sri Lankan Mahāyāna imagery, see Dohanian 1977. The most comprehensive research on Sri Lankan Buddhist sculptures can be found in von Schroeder 1990. It has to be noted, however, that remaining Esoteric Buddhist material is only lately being studied and the chronology of Sri Lankan Buddhist art of that period is debatable because of a lack of firmly datable material.

64 On Esoteric Buddhism in Tamil Nadu, see Yang 2018: 179-180, n. 370. In particular, on Kāñcīpuram as a centre of Esoteric Buddhism, see footnote 17. Esoteric Buddhism in Tamil Nadu was probably part of the larger tradition encompassing the neighboring Andhra region, the motherland of the Pallavas. On the development of Esoteric Buddhism in Andhra, see Barber 2008.

65 Fraser 2004: 52-53.

been the origin place of such fundamental scripture as the *VAT*.[66] At the same time, numerous cross-regional military raids of the Pallavas (ruling in Tamil Nadu), and the Cālukyas (ruling in the Deccan) in the 7th and 8th centuries intensified cultural exchange across the peninsula and it is not unlikely that the respective Buddhist communities were in conversation, influencing each other and sharing major scriptures.[67] For example, the earliest surviving images displaying iconography that could be related to the *STTS* can be found in the Western Deccan, at Ellora Cave 12 (early 8th century).[68] In general, Ellora sculptures from the 8th century onwards reflect increasing influence from the South of the Peninsula, and in particular the Pallava influence.[69]

Regrettably, we do not know the specific regions Amoghavajra visited while in India; the sources are extremely vague about the Indian part of his trip and give detailed information only on his stay in Sri Lanka.[70] It is fair to assume, however, that Tamil Nadu, a place where Vajrabodhi studied the Yoga tradition before going to China, would have been Amoghavalra's prime destination, though a small possibility that he visited other regions, including the Western Deccan, cannot be entirely excluded. In addition, it is possible that materials collected by Amoghavajra in Sri Lanka were of an Indian origin, as the introduction of Esoteric Buddhism to Sri Lanka is associated with Tamil Buddhists who migrated to the island in the 7th and 8th centuries fleeing from the antagonistic movements in Śaivism and Vaiṣṇavism that were specifically directed against Buddhists and Jains.[71]

As a result of the anti-Buddhist campaigns, only a handful of Pallava Buddhist images survived. Most of them have been vandalised and were found in the vicinity of Hindu temples which suggests a violent expropriation and conversion of Buddhist establishments.[72] For our purposes, the Pallava stylistic features can be reconstructed from abundant examples of Brahmanic imagery. For instance, Pallava sculptures in Figs. 7 and 8 possess all major characteristic of the discussed artistic mode in Hexi art and show remarkable similarities to the aesthetics of the Yulin images (Figs. 1, 6): Y-shaped torsos, tall headdresses, spiked crowns and armbands, swagged necklaces, and large earrings.

In the Western Deccan, Buddhist material heritage largely survived. Ellora Caves 11 and 12, which are traditionally dated to the early 8th century, represent the last large-scale Buddhist

66 On the development of Esoteric imagery in the Western Deccan, see Huntington 1981, Malandra 1993, Bautze-Picron 2000. On possible geographical origins of the *VAT*, see Wayman and Tajima 1998: 11-12.

67 On artistic and architectural connections between these regions see D. Dayalan.

68 Tanaka 2018: 265, fig. 4.9.

69 Malandra 1993: 116-117. The most striking example of the Pallava influence is a famous Kailāsanātha monument, which was built in the mid-8th century and partially patterned on Kailāsanātha temple in Kāñcīpuram.

70 Yang 2018: 256-257.

71 Indrapala 2005: 181, 192-193; Yang 2018: 180-181; Davidson 2002: 192.

72 Rao 1915; Verardi 2018: 296ff, fig. 4.

Fig. 7 Śiva as Gaṅgādhara (detail), stone relief, 7th C., Pallava period, Lalitankura cave, Tiruchirapalli, Tamil Nadu, India (Photograph courtesy of Emmanuel Francis).

Fig. 8 Viṣṇu, copper alloy, 8th-9th C., Pallava period, 47 cm, Thyagaraja temple, Thiruvarur, Tamil Nadu, India (Asha Rani 1988: 147, fig. 7).

undertaking in the region.[73] The eight great bodhisattvas as a group assume prominent positions in both caves. While Cave 11 contains two groups of the standing bodhisattvas, Cave 12 has one group of the seated and two groups of the standing bodhisattvas. Fig. 9, from the first floor of Cave 12, shows two groups of the four bodhisattvas flanking a statue of the Buddha with *dharmacakra mudrā*. Their identities were reconstructed by Malandra and Bautze-Picron according to their attributes and they appear to be the same bodhisattvas as the bodhisattvas in Yulin Cave 25.[74] The Ellora and Yulin bodhisattvas are visually similar as well and convey

73 For a detailed analysis of Buddhist art at Ellora in general and these caves in particular, see Malandra 1993.

74 Malandra 1996: 197; Bautze-Picron 1997:10-11.

Fig.9 Eight Bodhisattvas, first floor, early 8th C., Ellora Cave 12, Maharastra, India (www.elloracaves.org, Photographs courtesy of Deepanjana and Arno Klein).

Fig. 10 Left: Detail of fig. 9; Right: Detail of fig. 1 (https://www.e-dunhuang.com/cave/10.0001/0001.0002.0025).

late Pallava aesthetics (see comparison in Fig. 10). They have elongated and Y-shaped torsos, crowns with spikes, and swagged necklaces. The armbands display similar leaf-like elements decorated with spikes. Spikes in the armbands of the sculptures are not clearly visible in the pictures as the decorations were finished with plaster which is largely lost now.

It is evident that stylistically the images in Yulin Cave 25 depended on Southern Indian prototypes and that the defining characteristics of the discussed artistic mode have a Southern Indian origin. Therefore, from here onwards this mode in Hexi art will be labelled as Southern Indian.

2.1.1.3 Iconographical Considerations

Ellora Caves 11 and 12 and their Iconographic Innovations

According to Geri Malandra, Ellora caves 11 and 12 reflect Esoteric teachings, which were new for the Deccan, and this new iconography was executed in a new style that shows a noticeable influence from the South of the Peninsula.[75] She suggested that the teachings reflected in the caves were imported to the Deccan and that they might have had the same origin as the sculptures' new style. In support for her theory, Malandra noted that contemporaneous or slightly later representations of the eight great bodhisattvas are found in Odisha and Java that points to the Southern (as opposed to Northern) source of the innovations.[76] Indeed, Northern Indian depictions of the eight great bodhisattvas mostly date from the 9th century and later.[77] In addition, the popularity of the cult of the eight great bodhisattvas in the 8th century is evident in the Malay Peninsula,[78] as well as in China (discussed in this Part and in Part 4.). This distribution implies that the cult of the eight great bodhisattvas was popular in the eastern coastal areas of the Indian Peninsula that historically played a key role in maritime relations of Southern Indian polities with Southeast Asia, and China. Moreover, the Pallava influenced style of the Dunhuang depictions points specifically to Tamil Nadu as a source of the cult in China. Similarly, the Pallava influenced style of the Ellora sculptures should be regarded as evidence for a Tamil Nadu origin of the respective teachings in the Western Deccan as well. As was already discussed, travelling monks and pilgrims were instrumental in the transmission of new teachings and their art forms. Ellora was an important holy site (*tīrtha*), a place of pilgrimage that attracted people from distant lands and different religious communities; its sacred status encouraged commissioning religious imagery at the site. Lisa Owen has recently shown, for instance, that Ellora Jain caves reflect activities of the Jain communities associated with Tamil Nadu and Karnataka (see discussion in section 2.4).[79] Although donors of the discussed

75 Malandra 1993: 116-117; Malandra 1996: 206.

76 Malandra 1996: 205-206.

77 Bautze-Picron 1997: 14-27.

78 Skilling 2011: 375-377; Sharrock and Bunker: 2016: 244; Acri 2018.

79 Owen 2012: 16, 20, 160-163.

Buddhist caves remain unknown, there is a possibility that they hailed from the South as well.[80] It is also possible that some Buddhist communities migrated from Tamil Nadu to the Western Deccan during the period of interreligious antagonism in their homeland.

The Aṣṭamaṇḍalakasūtra

In addition to the sculptural groups of the eight bodhisattvas, Ellora Cave 12 contains five wall reliefs of maṇḍalas of the eight great bodhisattvas centred around a *dhyāna-mudrā* Buddha, identified by scholars as Vairocana (Fig. 11). The bodhisattvas in the maṇḍalas were identified according to their attributes and they also happen to be the same bodhisattvas as those depicted in Yulin Cave 25.[81] According to Kimiaki Tanaka, the group of Vairocana and the eight great bodhisattvas ultimately originates from the *Aṣṭamaṇḍalakasūtra* (*The Sūtra of the Mandala of the Eight Great Bodhisattvas*) which was also the most probable source of the Ellora maṇḍalas.[82] The central figure of the Tathāgata is only briefly described in the text[83] and this perhaps explains an iconographic variety of his representations. He can be depicted unadorned, like in the Ellora maṇḍalas (Fig.11), or bejewelled, like in the Yulin composition (Fig.1), and with the *bhūmisparśa-*, *dharmacakra-* or *dhyāna-mudrā*. Examples of the group with the central figure displaying the *dhyāna-mudrā* are relatively rare in India and found only in the Southern part, namely in the Western Deccan (Ellora) and Odisha (Ratnagiri).[84] Thus, it is evident that the iconography of the group depicted in Yulin Cave 25 was particularly common in Southern India. The *Aṣṭamaṇḍalakasūtra* was translated by Amoghavajra (T1167)[85] and the central deity of the maṇḍala in his text is described as "Tathāgata in His True Golden Form Body" (如来真金色身).[86] This epithet perhaps refers to Vairocanābhisaṃbodhi, a form of

80 Buddhist monks from Tamil Nadu and Andhra were active even in Northern India. Bautze-Picron has recently discussed a number of stone and bronze images from Kurkihar dating from the 8th to 11th century which bear inscriptions mentioning donors who hailed from Kāñcīpuram and Andhra. Notable among these are two circa 9th century stone slabs which show a set of the eight great bodhisattvas around the Buddha. See Bautze-Picron 2015: fig. 91, 92. In a private communication on 09.08.2019, Bautze-Picron remarked that these slabs would seem to suggest that the cult of the eight great bodhisattvas might have been introduced to Bihar from Tamil Nadu and Andhra.

81 On the identification of the figures in these maṇḍalas, see Malandra 1996: 197, 201; Tanaka 2018: 141-144.

82 Tanaka 2018: 92-93. This sutra is also known as the *Aṣṭamahābodhisattvamaṇḍalakasūtra.*

83 For the description of the eight great bodhisattvas and the central figure in the text, see de Viser 1915: 15-17.

84 Northern Indian examples show Buddha/Vairocana either in the *bhūmisparśa-* or *dharmacakra-mudrā.* See Bautze-Picron 1997; Tanaka 2018: 81-82.

85 The *sūtra* was initially translated into Chinese by Puṇyodaya in the 7th century (T486), but it became particularly popular in the translation by Amoghavajra, who assigned to this maṇḍala a much greater importance, see Li-Kuang Lin 1935. There are two Tibetan versions of the *sūtra*, both are believed to be translated around 800, see Skilling 2011: 376, n. 9, 10, 11.

86 I am grateful to Geoffrey Goble for sharing this information. Personal communication 25.07.2018.

Fig. 11 Maṇḍala of the eight great bodhisattvas, Ellora Cave 12, early 8th C., Maharastra, India (www.elloracaves.org, Photograph courtesy of Deepanjana and Arno Klein).

Vairocana, which is initially appeared in the *VAT* and described there as having a golden body (in contrast, for example, with Vajradhātu-Vairocana whose colour is white) bejewelled and displaying the *dhyāna-mudrā*.[87] This is precisely how Vairocana is depicted in Yulin Cave 25.

To summarise, in both style and iconography the Yulin group of VAEGB is closely related to Southern Indian examples.

87 For a description of Vairocana in the *VAT*, see Wayman and Tajima 1998: 101. The relation between the maṇḍala of the eight great bodhisattvas and the *VAT* was earlier suggested by Malandra and Tanaka. See Malandra 1996: 76; Tanaka 2018: 77-78.

The Bhadracarī

The popularity of the eight great bodhisattvas in Southern Indian Buddhism is well reflected in Amoghavajra's textual heritage. In addition to the translation of the *Aṣṭamaṇḍalakasūtra*, Amoghavajra integrated the eight great bodhisattvas into practices of such popular prayers as the *Bhadracarī* and the *Uṣṇīṣavijayā dhāraṇī*.[88] These combinations were proabably meant to employ the power of the boddhisattvas to magnify the efficiency of these prayers. According to the *Aṣṭamaṇḍalakasūtra*, the mantras and maṇḍala of the eight great bodhisattvas are effective in fulfillment of one's wishes, eradicating one's sins, setting one on the path to swift enlightenment and protection from harm.[89]

I believe that although the *Aṣṭamaṇḍalakasūtra* is the ultimate source for the VAEGB group, the depiction of VAEGB in Yulin Cave 25 is not a maṇḍala, as the bodhisattvas do not encircle the central figure, and is actually based on another Amoghavajra's work entitled *Puxian pusa xing yuan zan* (普贤菩萨行愿赞) (T297).[90] The text was composed between 756 and 774 and consists of four parts, where the first part is a translation of the *Samantabhadrācāryap ranidhānarāja* (普贤行愿品), also known as the *Bhadracarī*;[91] the second part is a eulogy to the eight great bodhisattvas, which is a part of the *Aṣṭamaṇḍalakasūtra* (T1167); and the third and final parts are a *dhāraṇī* and a praise of this *dhāraṇī*.

In short, the work includes the cult of the eight great bodhisattvas of the *Aṣṭamaṇḍalakasūtra* into the practice of the *Bhadracarī*, an immensely popular aspirational prayer in which one vows to worship the buddhas and become enlightened for the sake of all beings.

The Bhadracarī is known as an independent work and as the final part of the *Gaṇḍavyūha Sūtra* (入法界品),[92] which itself is a part of the *Avataṁsaka Sūtra* (华严经), a core scripture of the Avataṁsaka (华 严 Huayan) Buddhist tradition.[93] According to modern scholarship, the Vairocana of Esoteric Buddhism developed from the Vairocana of the *Avataṁsaka Sūtra*,

88 See Amoghavajra's works T297 and T972. On Amoghavajra's ritual manual for the *Uṣṇīṣavijayādhāraṇī sutra* (T972), see Wang 2018: 47-50, Lin 2014: 139-43. Amoghavajra produced the manual in 764 and it became the most influential redaction in Tang China (several earlier redaction are known, including the one by Śubhākarasiṃha). The manual introduces a maṇḍala which is known in Japanese Buddhism as Sonshō Maṇḍala in the Amoghavajra tradition. The maṇḍala is similar to the maṇḍala of the eight great bodhisattvas of the *Aṣṭamaṇḍalakasūtra*, but, in addition, it includes two wrathful deities, Acala and Trailokyavijaya. See Tanaka 2018: 88, 95.

89 Granoff 1968/1969: 2; Geoffrey Goble, private communication 25.07.2018.

90 On this text, see Dessein 2003.

91 The *Bhadracarī* is discussed in Osto 2010.

92 The *Bhadracarī* is included in the translation of the *Gaṇḍavyūha Sūtra* made by Prajña 般若 , which was finished in 798 and was based on the Sanskrit copy that had been presented to the Chinese emperor by the King of Odisha. The extant Tibetan translation of the *Gaṇḍavyūha* was made during the imperial period and also concludes with the *Bhadracarī*. See Osto 2010: 2-3.

93 See Cleary 1993 for a translation of the sūtra.

who is featured in the sūtra under the special name of Rocana (卢舍那 Locana). The Huayan tradition integrated various Esoteric teachings, and the Huayan Vairocana and Vairocana of Esoteric Buddhism were sometimes "fused iconographically."[94]

The image of Vairocana in Yulin Cave 25 is an example of such fusion. A cartouche next to it contains the Chinese inscription 清净法身卢那舍佛 (the Pure Dharmakāya Locana Buddha) which refers to Vairocana of the *Avataṁsaka Sūtra.*[95] Thus, we have Locana Buddha accompanied by the eight great bodhisattvas of the *Aṣṭamaṇḍalakasūtra*. This combination corresponds to the *Puxian pusa xing yuan zan* (普贤菩萨行愿赞) (T297), where the eight great bodhisattvas of the *Aṣṭamaṇḍalakasūtra* are understood as guardians of Locana of the *Avataṁsaka Sūtra.*[96] Therefore, the Yulin painting (Fig. 1) represents the deities of the *Aṣṭamaṇḍalakasūtra* in the Huayan context. However, in contrast with the *Aṣṭamaṇḍalakasūtra*, which prescribes a strictly circular layout for the bodhisattvas, the *Puxian pusa xing yuan zan* (T297) does not provide any guidance in this regard. I believe, this explains a variety of spatial arrangements found in the representations of the group (discussed below).

Furthermore, not only the central composition, but also the whole iconographic program of Yulin Cave 25 can be understood in the Huayan context. First of all, the characteristic Huayan depictions of Mañjuśrī, Samantabhadra, and Sudhana occupy the western wall (Fig. 2).[97] The depictions of Amitābha's and Maitreya's Pure Lands as a pair are common in Dunhuang art and their compositions are based on respective sūtras.[98] However, their presence in Cave 25 might reflect an additional level of symbolism. For example, aspiration for rebirth in Amitābha's Pure land is emphasized in the *Bhadracarī*,[99] while Maitreya is one of the most important spiritual friends of Sudhana who visits Maitreya's abode in the narrative of the *Gaṇḍavyūha Sūtra*. Therefore, Yulin Cave 25 can be understood as a manifestation of the donor's practice of the *Bhadracarī* and of their aspiration for enlightenment.

As a matter of fact, references to the *Bhadracarī* and/or the *Gaṇḍavyūha Sūtra* can be found in almost all representations of VAEGB in Hexi and Tibet.[100]

94 Orzech, Sørensen, and Payne 2011: 91-92.

95 The characters na 那 and she 舍 have been transposed. See Wang 2018: 109-110.

96 Dessein 2003: 332. As was noted by Wang, Dessein mistakenly replaces bodhisattva Sarvanivāraṇaviṣkambhin with Acalanātha, see M. Wang 2018: 258, n. 59.

97 Paired images of Mañjuśrī and Samantabhadra, the major bodhisattvas of the Huayan tradition, were often depicted in Dunhuang caves starting from the early Tang dynasty. According to M. Wang, this pair reflects the interest in the *Gaṇḍavyūha Sūtra* narrative and the *Bhadracarī*. See Wang 2018: 247.

98 For example, Mogao Caves 329 and 321. See Wang 2005: 382-386.

99 Osto 2010: 5-6.

100 This also finds parallels at Borobudur, Java. Panel IV-3 from the *Gaṇḍavyūha* reliefs contains images of Sudhana and the eight great bodhisattvas. See Bautze-Picron 1997: 28, 54 schema 11; Fontein 2012, p. 173; Long 2009: 165-168. I am very grateful to Claudine Bautze-Picron for drawing my attention to the Borobudur depiction and providing these references.

2.1.2 Other Representations of VAEGB in Hexi and Eastern Tibet

2.1.2.1 A Wooden Shrine

One striking example is a wooden shrine from the Nelson-Atkins Museum of Arts (Fig. 12). The shrine has attracted considerable scholarly attention and was variously ascribed to Central Asia, Kashmir, or Tibet.[101] On stylistic grounds, I argue that it most likely originates from Hexi, as is evident from the Chinese facial features of the figures, the combination of the Indian and Chinese artistic modes, and the spiked armbands worn by Vairocana, which is a characteristic of the Southern Indian mode in Hexi art (see a close-up of the armbands in Fig. 12). The central section of the shrine shows Vairocana flanked by two vertical rows of four bodhisattvas who alltogether most likely represent the eight great bodhisattvas.[102] Such a layout can be found in Southern Indian art from the 6th century onwards and this particular group is depicted in the same manner in a 9th or 10th century stone stele from Odisha.[103] In the shrine, three more figures are placed below Vairocana. While Granoff and M. Wang identify this group as a representation of an *abhiṣeka* ceremony, Linrothe argues that it depicts a donor of the shrine being blessed by the bodhisattvas.[104] I would argue that this group likely symbolises Sudhana's spiritual path towards enlightenment. The two bodhisattvas thus represent Mañjuśrī (on the left) and Samantabhadra (on the right), who together with a central figure of Vairocana (here Locana of the *Avataṁsaka Sūtra*) form the typical trinity of Huayan Buddhism. Therefore, a figure seated on a rug represents Sudhana who is customarily depicted in Chinese art as a little boy with a shaven head.[105] Accordingly, the depiction of Sudhana together with Mañjuśrī and Samantabhadra symbolises his spiritual journey as described in the *Gaṇḍavyūha Sūtra*; in his search for enlightenment, Sudhana meets fifty-three spiritual fiends (*kalyānamitra*) starting from Mañjuśrī and ending with Samantabhadra.[106] At the same time, these three are part of the final stage of Sudhana's pilgrimage which culminates in the pronouncement of the *Bhadracarī*. Before his final meeting with Samantabhadra, the boy sees Mañjuśrī again and

101 The most notable publications include Granoff 1968/69; Linrothe 2014; M. Wang 2018. While Granoff ascribes the shrine to Central Asia, Linrothe suggests a Kashmiri provenance, and M. Wang argues for a Tibetan origin. See Granoff 1968/69: 81; Linrothe 2014: 31; Wang 2018: 83.

102 They were identified as such by Granoff. See Granoff 1968/69: 90-91.

103 For a 6th century example in Cave 23 at Nasik, see Bautze-Picron 2000: fig.9-10. For the Odisha stele, see Tanaka 2018: fig. 1.15.

104 Granoff 1968/69: 90; Linrothe 2014: 31; Wang 2018: 72.

105 On representations of Sudhana in Chinese art, see Fontein 1968: 23-110.

106 The representations of Mañjuśrī, Samantabhadra and Sūdhana in Yulin Cave 25 likely have the same meaning. Fig. 2 shows Sudhana depicted in the right corner of the Mañjuśrī painting and in the left corner of the Samantabhadra painting.

receives from him various kinds of teachings.[107] In our composition, Mañjuśrī is shown offering Sudhana a round object. A depiction of this meeting can be also found in a wall painting in Mogao Cave 85 (late 9th century), where it is identified by an accompanying cartouche.[108] There Mañjuśrī is also depicted offering Sudhana a round object. This object probably represents the jewel of the teaching, references to which can be found in the sūtra. For example, during their first meeting, Sudhana

Fig. 12 Shrine, wood with traces of polychrome and gold, 9th-10th C., probably from the Hexi corridor, 31.1 × 35.6 cm., the Nelson-Atkins Museum of Arts, Kansas City, USA. Object number 44-18 (Linrothe 2014: fig. 1. 1).

107 Cleary 1993: 1502.

108 Wang 2018: 250, fig. 119.

supplicates to Mañjuśrī: "Instruct me, O King, with the jewel of the wheel of teaching."[109] Properly prepared by Mañjuśrī, Sudhana sees Samantabhadra (depicted in the shrine as a bodhisattva with his right hand placed upon Sudhana's head).[110] The crucial moment of their meeting, which takes place at the feet of Vairocana/Locana (exactly as shown in the shrine), culminates in the pronouncement of the *Bhadracarī* and is described in the *Gaṇḍavyūha Sūtra* as follows:

> "Just as in this world, in the presence of Vairocana Buddha, the enlightening being Universally Good (bodhisattva Samantabhadra) extended his right hand and laid it on Sudhana's head ... And just as facets of truth entered Sudhana as he was touched by the hand of Universally Good at the feet of Vairocana Buddha, likewise facets of truth entered Sudhana in various ways as he was touched by the multitudes of hands extended from the bodies of all the Universally Goods."[111]

I believe that an image of an elephant, the vehicle of Samantabhadra, placed in the centre of the Vairocana's throne is a reference to the *Bhadracarī*. Douglas Osto remarked that Samantabhadra and the *Bhadracarī* were "associated with each other in the sense that Samantabhadra is thought to embody the aspirations contained in the verses."[112] In addition and as was pointed out to me by Claudine Bautze-Picron, lion(s) and elephant(s) form a pair, which is often encountered in the ornamentation of the pedestal of throne in India from an early period. The meaning imparted to the two animals is rich, but, in short, an elephant refers to enlightenment and a lion to the teaching.[113]

The Nelson-Atkins shrine carries an unobtrusive and mostly illegible Tibetan inscription on the back. It opens with an initial Tibetan mark (*yig mgo*) followed by the syllables *byang chub*. As was suggested by Robert Linrothe, these syllables may have originally stood for the words "awakening" (*byang chub*), "bodhicitta" (*byang chub sems*), "bodhisattva" (*byang chub sems dpa'*), which would correspond well to the proposed symbolism of the central scene. According to Yannick Laurent, the syllables may have alternatively stood for a personal Tibetan

---

109 Cleary 1993: 1175.

110 A similar representation of the scene where Samantabhadra lays his hand on Sudhana's head can be found in the *Gaṇḍavyūha* narrative panels located on the east wall on the fourth level at Borobudur, panel IVB-82. See https://www.photodharma.net/Indonesia/11-Gandavyuha-Level-4/11-Gandavyuha-Level-4.htm, picture 82; Fontein 2012: 147 fig. 33.

111 Cleary 1993: 1508.

112 Osto 2010: 5.

113 Bautze-Picron, private communication 09.08.19. This symbolism is also evident in Huayan art, where the lion is the vehicle of Mañjuśrī, an embodiment of the teaching, while the elephant is the vehicle of Samantabhadra, an embodiment of the enlightenment. On the symbolism of these two animals in Indian art, see Bautze-Picron 2008.

name (i.e. Jangchub).[114] It has to be also noted that there is no way to know when and where the inscription was added and its presence per se does not signify a Tibetan provenance of the shrine. It merely suggests that the shrine was at some point used by Tibetan-speaking people.[115]

2.1.2.2 A Portable Painting from Mogao Cave 17

Another version of the group of VAEGB can be found in a portable painting from Mogao Cave 17, which could be dated to the late 9th century on stylistic grounds (Fig. 13).[116] The bodhisattvas are partially identified by Tibetan inscriptions and partially by iconographic attributes. As with the Yulin painting (Fig. 1), the figures display all defining characteristics of the Southern Indian mode. The layout of the composition is similar to that in the Nelson-Atkins shrine (Fig. 12) and the same as in the already mentioned stele from Odisha.[117] The bottom foreground of the painting contains representations of sand hills and birds which are normally associated with depictions of Amitābha's Pure Land. As mentioned earlier, the *Bhadracarī* contains a reference to Amitābha's Pure Land that perhaps explains why its features are depicted in the painting. [118]

2.1.2.3 Eastern Tibetan Rock Carvings

There are three rock carvings in Eastern Tibet which depict a group of VAEGB (Fig. 52-54).[119] They have often been offered as evidence for the Tibetan provenance of the composition

114 Linrothe 2014: 31-34; Yannick Laurent, personal communication, August 2019. Laurent further remarked that the foreign provenance of this Buddhist shrine and its now effaced epigraph make it difficult to determine the nature of this Tibetan inscription. In comparison with other non-Tibetan portable images bearing Tibetan inscriptions, the epigraph of the shrine may have acted as a laudatory inscription, a descriptive caption, or even as an expression of ownership, as shown by Laurent during his presentation at the 15th Seminar of the International Association for Tibetan Studies in Paris, July 2019.

115 On a wide use of Tibetan language in Hexi and even in correspondence between non-Tibetan parties, see van Schaik and Galambos 2012: 67-68; Takata 2019.

116 For an overview of the scholarship and the latest discussion on the painting, see Wang 2018: 111-113.

117 Bautze-Picron; 1997: 27, 53 schema 10; Tanaka 2018: fig. 1.15.

118 This was noted by Michelle Wang as well. See Wang 2018: 258 n. 59.

119 For an overview of the carvings, see Huo 2018.

a) Renda high relief rock carving, dated 804/816, Brag gyab County, Chamdo Prefecture of TAR. On this carving see Heller 1994; Shanxi Province Academy of Archaeology and TAR Relics Preservation Institute 2014.

b) Sgar thog high relief rock carving, near the town of Sgar thog in Smar khams county, Chamdo Prefecture of TAR. On this carving, see Yang Qingfan, Lu Suwen and Zhang Yanqing 2017.

c) 'Bis khog high relief rock carving (also known as Bimda), dated 806, Yushu Tibetan Autonomous Prefecture, Qinghai province. On the most recent research on this carving and for an overview of the previous scholarship, see Huo 2017.

Fig. 13 Vairocana and the eight great bodhisattvas, ink and color on silk, 10th C., from Mogao Cave 17, 63.5 × 17.95 cm, the British Museum, London. Museum number 1919,0101,0. 50 (Ch. 0074) (Wang 2018: fig. 2).

in Yulin Cave 25.[120] The carvings are concentrated in the areas bordering Tang empire and date to the early 9th century. At least two, if not all, of them were commissioned by the same person — Ye shes dbyangs, who was identified as a high-profile Tibetan monk who was listed in a Chan lineage in the later Dunhuang texts, and who, according to an inscription at Renda, commissioned many other carvings in the area.[121] Altogether this strongly suggests that the carvings were created under the cultural influence of the Hexi Corridor.[122]

I argue that these rock carvings are associated with the *Bhadracarī* and, like the examples from Hexi, reflect the practice established by Amoghavajra in the *Puxian pusa xing yuan zan* (T297). A complete text of the *Bhadracarī* is carved about 100 meters away from the group of VAEGB at 'Bis khog.[123] The inscription is considered part of the monument and covers a large portion of the rock that gives it an exceptional prominence at the site. In addition, a prayer to Vairocana and the eight great bodhisattvas is carved in 23 lines to the right of VAEGB.[124] This prayer corresponds to the eulogy to the eight great bodhisattvas in the Amoghavajra's text. A single religious text accompanies the rock carving at Renda. It was initially identified as an excerpt from the *Bhadracarī*, but this was questioned by Amy Heller.[125] At present, the text is understood to be a short prayer, probably a local creation, which focuses on the bodhisattva Samantabhadra and is inspired by the *Bhadracarī*.[126]

In addition, the historical inscriptions at Renda and 'Bis khog have clear references to the main qualities of the *Bhadracarī*. They praise the path to enlightenment and dedicate the monuments to the wellbeing of the Tibetan Emperor, *tsenpo* (btsan po).[127] Sam van Schaik and Lewis Doney have shown that the *Bhadracarī* was one of the most popular Buddhist prayers in Imperial Tibet and that it was understood as having the power to give the *tsenpo* longevity. Since many Tibetan copies of the prayer were found among the Dunhuang manuscripts, they have remarked that its popularity among Tibetans might have been due to Chinese influence.[128] Indeed, even the link between the *Bhadracarī* and the *tsenpo* finds parallels in Chinese practice, as Amoghavajra's translation of the *Bhadracarī* was intended as a eulogy to the Chinese emperor as well.[129] Furthermore, out of three extant Chinese translations, the one by

120 See footnote 53.

121 Heller 1994; On Ye shes dbyangs see also, van Schaik 2015: 163-174.

122 Huo Wei also argues that these carvings should be understood in the context of the Sino-Tibetan relations, see Huo 2018.

123 Huo 2017: 6-7.

124 Huo 2017: 5.

125 Heller 1994: n 6.

126 Shanxi Province Academy of Archaeology and TAR Relics Preservation Institute 2014: 14.

127 Heller 1994; Huo 2017: 6.

128 van Schaik and Doney 2007: 185 n. 19.

129 Dessein 2003: 331-332.

Amoghavajra most closely corresponds to the Tibetan version.[130]

Regarding artistic features, the groups of VAEGB in the carvings were depicted either in the Tibetan mode, with the figures clad in Tibetan-style robes (Figs. 53 & 54), or in the Indian mode (Fig. 52).[131] The iconography of the group of VAEGB in the carvings corresponds to the Southern Indian and Hexi examples (Vairocana is shown with the *dhyāna-mudrā*). Compositionally, the Renda group is organized in the same way as the group in a portable painting from Mogao Cave 17 (Fig. 13) and in the stele from Odisha.[132] It displays typical elements of Chinese design such as a canopy above Vairocana, which is almost identical to that in the Hexi examples (Fig. 1 & 5), and two *apsarasas* flying on Chinese-style clouds. The two other carvings follow the layout of the composition in Yulin Cave 25, though the bodhisattvas are depicted standing, as at the Ellora caves. Discussion on the transmission of the cult of VAEGB from Hexi to Tibet will continue in Part 4.

2.1.3 Summary of section 2.1

The depictions of VAEGB in Hexi and Eastern Tibet reflect the popularity of the *Bhadracarī*. The central figure in these depictions represents Vairocana of the *Avataṁsaka Sūtra*, whose iconography was fused with that of Vairocana of the *Aṣṭamaṇḍalakasūtra*. The connection between the *Bhadracarī* and the *Aṣṭamaṇḍalakasūtra* was established in Amoghavajra's work the *Puxian pusa xing yuan zan* (T297), which integrated the eight great bodhisattvas of the *Aṣṭamaṇḍalakasūtra* into the practice of the *Bhadracarī*. The Southern Indian stylistic elements detected in the Hexi depictions confirm the context of the Amoghavajra teachings and, by extension, the Southern Indian origin of the cult of VAEGB in Hexi. The Tibetan occupation of the Hexi Corridor in the mid-8th century enabled religious and artistic transmission from this region to Tibet. In this regard, the discussed eastern Tibetan rock carvings bear material witness of that process.

2.2 Maṇḍala-like compositions featuring Vairocanābhisaṃbodhi

At both Mogao and Yulin, Vairocanābhisaṁbodhi and the retinue figures are consistently depicted in the Southern Indian mode. Figures 14, 16, and 17 show maṇḍala-like

130 Osto 2010: 2.

131 It is difficult to go beyond this general observation, as in their current state 'Bis khog and Renda figures are freshly plastered and painted, while the Sgar thog carving is significantly damaged. Initially, the reliefs were likely covered with plaster, in which smaller details were made. Such details could have been lost over time and/or altered during subsequent renovations.

132 See footnote 117.

Fig. 14 Maṇḍala-like composition centered around Vairocana, wall painting, second half of the 9th C., Guiyijun period (848-1036), Mogao Cave 14, Gansu, China (Wang 2018: fig. 73). Circles indicate offering goddesses.

compositions[133] from Mogao Cave 14, Yulin Cave 20, and Yulin Cave 38 dating from the 9th to 11th centuries.[134] The compositions feature Vairocanābhisaṁbodhi surrounded by bodhisattvas, Offering Goddesses, gatekeepers and/or guardians of the directions. Each of these maṇḍalas is accompanied by a second maṇḍala in the same style depicted on the same or opposite wall and centred around Vajrasattva in Mogao Cave 14 (Fig. 15), and a Buddha in the two other caves.

133 Although these compositions look like maṇḍalas, it is not clear if they were created and used in a ritual context that established their function as maṇḍalas. For a definition of "maṇḍala," see Orzech, Sørensen, and Payne 2011: 81-82.

134 For a review of the scholarship and a discussion on these compositions as well as for additional images, see Wang 2018: 156-168, fig. 28, 29, 72, 73, 74, 80, 81. On the ground of their style, M. Wang ascribes the maṇḍalas to the Tibetan tradition. She designates them as "Maṇḍala of eight great bodhisattvas" and groups them together with the previously discussed depictions of VAEGB. In my view, this can be misleading, as the maṇḍala of the eight great bodhisattvas contains only nine deities and is based on the *Aṣṭamaṇḍalakasūtra*. Compositions with more deities are based on different texts and can feature different eight bodhisattvas. Moreover, the eight great bodhisattvas in the maṇḍala of the *Aṣṭamaṇḍalakasūtra* are not the same eight bodhisattvas as those found in maṇḍalas of the Yoga cycle, to which the discussed examples most likely belong. See, for example, Tanaka 2018: 194-195.

Fig. 15 Maṇḍala-like composition centered around Vajrasattva, wall painting, second half of the 9th C., Guiyijun period (848-1036), Mogao Cave 14, Gansu, China (Wang 2018: fig. 75).

Textual sources behind these twin-maṇḍalas have not been identified.[135] What is clear, however, is that they display iconography similar to that of basic maṇḍalas of the Yoga tradition, which, for instance, can be recognized by the presence of such distinctive deities as four or eight Offering Goddesses who also sometimes are depicted in male forms as offering bodhisattvas (marked by circles in the images).[136] For example, Cave 14 has the maṇḍala-like compositions centred around Vairocanābhisaṁbodhi (Fig. 14) and Vajrasattva (Fig. 15). Somewhat similar maṇḍalas with the same central deities are described in the Amoghavajra's translation of the *Prajñāpāramitānaya Sūtra* (般若理趣经) (T243). According to Kimiaki Tanaka, this sūtra is the oldest in the Yoga cycle and it greatly influenced the development of the other texts,

135 The central deities in the maṇḍalas in Yulin Cave 20 are identified by accompanying inscriptions, which give the same name "the pure dharmakāya Vairocana Buddha" (*qingjing fashen Piluzhena fo* 清净法身毘卢遮那佛), see Wang 2018: 165. The name Piluzhena fo corresponds to the name of Vairocana in the eight fascicle translation of the *Avatamsaka sūtra* (T279: 39a 17-18), see Wang 2018: 109. Similarly with the case of Yulin cave 25, this likely reflects adaptation of Esoteric teachings for the Huayan context.

136 On the Offering Goddesses as features of the basic maṇḍalas of the Yoga cycle, see Tanaka 2018: 279-288. In fig.15, it is difficult to distinguish Offering Goddesses/bodhisattvas from other bodhisattvas.

Fig. 16 Maṇḍala-like composition centered around Vairocana, wall painting, second half of the 9th C., Guiyijun period (848-1036), Yulin Cave 20, Gansu, China (Wang 2018: fig. 28). Circles indicate offering goddesses.

including the *STTS*.[137]

Thus, it is clear that there is a strong affiliation between the Southern Indian artistic mode and the Yoga tradition.

2.3 Seated Amoghapāśa with four arms

There are three portable paintings from Mogao cave 17, which depict maṇḍalas centred on

137 On the maṇḍalas of the *Prajñāpāramitānaya Sūtra*, see Tanaka 2018: 248-280. The first and second maṇḍalas described in the text are centred around Vairocanābhisaṁbodhi (21 deities) and Vajrasattva (17 deities), respectively. There are versions, where the second maṇḍala is centred on the Buddha instead of Vajrasattva (see Tanaka 2018: 204) that corresponds to examples in Yulin caves 20 and 38. In Cave 14, the central deities of the maṇḍalas are swapped, with the Vairocanābhisaṁbodhi maṇḍala containing 17 deities and the Vajrasattva maṇḍala containing 21 deities.

Fig. 17 Maṇḍala-like composition centered around Vairocana, 10th/11th C., Guiyijun period (848-1036), Yulin Cave 38, Gansu, China (Wang 2018: fig. 80). Circles indicate offering goddesses/bodhisattvas.

seated Amoghapāśa with four arms (Figs. 18, 20, 21).[138]

The painting in Fig. 18 is traditionally dated to the 8th or 9th century.[139] While four-armed Amoghapāśa in the centre is identified by a noose held in the upper left hand, the presence of four Offering Goddesses (marked by circles in Fig. 18) points the context of the Yoga teachings.[140]

Amoghapāśa is an Esoteric variant of Avalokiteśvara; he can manifest in different forms, including peaceful and wrathful, standing and seated, with four, six, eight or more arms, and so on. There are nine Chinese translations of several versions of the *Amoghapāśadhāraṇīsūtra* dating from the 7th to 10th centuries, including one by Amoghavajra.[141] Iconographic

138 The paintings were discussed by Kimiaki Tanaka, who relates two of them (Figs. 18 and 20) to the Yoga tradition, see Tanaka 2000: 39-71.

139 It was discussed by Karl Debreczeny in Brauen 1997: 80-81, where its Indianized style was ascribed to Tibetan influence.

140 See footnote 136.

141 Wong 2007a: 152.

Fig. 18 Amoghapāśa Maṇḍala (shown without mount), 8th-9th C., from Mogao Cave 17, 204.5 × 107.5 cm with mount, the Musée Guimet, Paris. Museum number ART 371790 (Brauen 2009: plate 1). Circles indicate offering goddesses.

Fig. 19 Left: Viṣāpaharaṇa Śiva, 9th C., Pallava period, copper alloy, H 62 cm, Government Museum, Chennai, Tamil Nadu, India (American Institute of Indian Studies photo archive, https://vmis.in/ArchiveCategories/gallery?search=visapaharana). Right: Amoghapāśa, detail of fig. 18.

descriptions are rarely given in the texts and it is often simply mentioned that Amoghapāśa looks like Śiva.[142] This probably explains the great varieties of his iconographic forms, since Śiva has many iconographic forms as well. At the same time, at least three translations mention Amoghapāśa with one head and four arms.[143]

Amoghapāśa and his retinue in our painting (see close-up in Fig. 19 on the right) are depicted in the Southern Indian mode. Although no comparable Southern Indian images of Amoghapāśa are known, there are many contemporaneous images of four-armed Śiva seated with one leg pendant. These images can represent different forms of Śiva depending on the presence or absence of accompanying figures, hand gestures, and attributes. The late Pallava sculpture of Viṣāpaharaṇa Śiva in Fig. 19 (on the left) is very close to Amoghapāśa in the

142 Reis-Habito 1999: 48.

143 These are the translations by Maṇicintana (宝思惟 ; 693), Li Wuchan (李无谄 ; 670), and Bodhiruci (菩提流支 ; 707-9). See Reis-Habito 1999: 52.

Fig. 20 Amoghapāśa Maṇḍala, ink and color on silk, from Mogao Cave 17, 10th C., 115 × 65 cm, the Musée Guimet, Paris, France. Museum number EO. 3579 (Giès 1994-96: plate 99). Circles indicate offering goddesses.

painting. Both figures have three eyes and are adorned with large armbands decorated with spikes. The similarities in their proportions and in the position of the second pair of the arms are striking.

The two other maṇḍalas are shown in Figs. 20 and 21.[144] They date to around the 10th century and display some iconographic and stylistic variations in comparison to the earlier example. Nevertheless, the deities in the paintings show distinctive elements of the Southern Indian mode (spiked decorations, swagged necklaces) as well. The eight Offering Goddesses (marked by circles) are clearly recognisable, see Fig. 20. The composition in Fig. 21 is organized similarly to that in Fig. 18, though only eight deities are depicted and the identities of some of them remain debatable. The colours of the four figures marked by circles match

144 Recent discussions and a review of the scholarship on the painting in Fig. 20 can be found in McCoy 2016 and Wang 2018: 184-187. The authors argue for a Tibetan background of the painting.

Fig. 21 Amoghapāśa Maṇḍala, ink and color on silk, from Mogao Cave 17, 10th C., 89.6 × 60 cm, the Musée Guimet, Paris, France. Museum number EO. 1131 (Giès 1994-96: plate 80).

the colours of the Offering Goddesses in Fig. 19 and at least two of them are clearly female.[145] Overall, the painting gives an impression that it was either unfinished or reworked.[146]

To summarise, all three paintings (Figs. 18, 20, 21) depict the deities in the Southern Indian mode and, at least two of them are clearly related to the Yoga tradition.

2.4 Yulin Cave 15

Yulin Cave 15 also contains a composition executed in the Southern Indian mode (Fig. 22).[147] It features a god known under various names, including Kubera and Vaiśravaṇa. While the

145 Tanaka identifies them as deities of the Lotus family of the *VAT*. He dates the painting to the second half of the 8th century. Such an early date cannot be accepted from a stylistic point of view. Tanaka 2000: 39-44.

146 It looks like one figure is missing in the top of the painting; also the figure in the upper left corner curiously has three arms.

147 Sha Wutian argues that the painting is executed in the Tibetan style. See Sha 2013: 117-118.

etymology of the former is debatable, the latter derives from the name of his father Viśravis.[148] In India, Kubera is the guardian of the North in a group of the eight *dikpālas* and the king of yakṣas and other demigods.[149] In China, the god is mostly known as Vaiśravaṇa (多闻天王), the guardian of the North in a group of the four heavenly kings.[150] Vaiśravaṇa is traditionally depicted in an armoured form, which probably has a Central Asian origin.[151] In Cave 15, the god is represented as a *yakṣa* holding a club and a mongoose, which corresponds to the iconography of Kubera.

Close parallels can be found amongst sculptures of *yakṣas* at Ellora, two of which are shown in figures 23 and 24. These and many other similar examples belong to Ellora's Jain caves.[152] Lisa Owen has recently discovered that these caves reflect the patronage of Jains from the regions of Tamil Nadu and Karnataka.[153] This observation corresponds well to the Pallava influenced style of the sculptures. Owen has remarked that few comparable depictions survived in Tamil Nadu and Karnataka,[154] and thus the Ellora sculptures are especially valuable with regard to reconstructing artistic traditions of these regions. This observation provides evidence for a probable Tamil Nadu background of the Yulin painting. In terms of iconography, images of Brahmanic, Buddhist and Jain *yakṣas* represent a shared concept of wealth and protection and display only minor differences.[155]

Like the Yulin Kubera, the Ellora *yakṣas* are placed under an arched canopy formed by a tree with luxuriant foliage and flowers. Such design with a tree as part of a throne back and luxuriant foliage depicted above a divinity is unusual for the art of the Deccan, but is common in the examples from Tamil Nadu.[156] The figures are seated with one leg pendant and flanked by two attendants, one of which (on the right) carries a purse made of mongoose skin. In contrast to the Ellora *yakṣas*, who are mounted atop elephants (a typical vehicle of the Jain *yakṣas*), the

148 On *yakṣa* cult and iconography, see Misra 1981; Bautze-Picron 2002. In particular, on Kubera/Vaiśravaṇa, see Misra 1981: 59-71.

149 On the iconography and symbolism of the guardians of the directions, *dikpālas*, in India, see Wessels-Mevissen: 2001.

150 On the development of iconography and symbolism of the four heavenly kings in Central and East Asia, see Shim 2013.

151 Shim 2013: 82-112.

152 On Ellora's Jain caves, see Owen 2012. In particular, on depictions of *yakṣas* at Ellora, see Owen 2012: 81-127.

153 Owen 2012: 16, 20, 160-163.

154 Owen 2012: 127-129.

155 Owen 2012: 127-129; Bautze-Picron: 2002.

156 I am grateful to Claudine Bautze-Picron who has drawn my attention to this. Comparable examples can be found in the Jain rock carvings at Kalugumalai, the 9th or early 10th century, Tamil Nadu, see Owen 2010: figs 3, 11. Also, see a 9th century Buddha from Tamil Nadu, now in the Museum of Fine Arts, Boston (accession numbers 1970.3 and 67.4a-b); and a 10th century Buddha with two bodhisattvas, from Nāgapaṭṭinam, Tamil Nadu, now in the Government Museum Chennai (accession number 81212).

Fig. 22 Kubera with attendants, wall painting, Tibetan period in the Hexi corridor, Yulin cave 15, China (Dunhuang Academy 2014: pic. 40).

Yulin Kubera is seated on a throne.[157] Nevertheless, both figures are similarly decorated with swagged necklaces and spiked crowns and armbands. Additionally, the images in Figs. 22 and 24 have almost identical square backrests and halos of an inverted U-shape.

The appearance of such Kubera images in Hexi could be related to protective rituals centred on Vaiśravaṇa, rituals which Amoghavajra regularly performed to provide imperial

157 Kubera seated on a throne is depicted in the early 8th-century Ellora Cave 25, but the image is significantly damaged. See Owen 2012: fig. 57.

Fig. 23 Fig. 24 Yaksa with attendants, early 9th C., Ellora Cave 32, Maharastra, India (American Institute of Indian Studies photo archive, https://vmis.in/ArchiveCategories/collection_gallery_zoom?id=923&search=1&index=57339&searchstring=ellora,%20cave,32).

troops with supernatural assistance. The earliest recorded instance of Amoghavajra performing the Vaiśravaṇa rituals is specifically linked to the Tibetan siege of Liangzhou.[158] There are five texts in the Taishō Canon attributed to him that specifically invoke Vaiśravaṇa for military magic.[159] In these texts, the god is consistently referred to as a king of *yakṣas*. Frustratingly, his physical appearance is not always described and where it is given, the description is of his armoured form.[160] However, Yulin Kubera is shown with the same two attendants as those

158 Yang 2018: 86-87.

159 These rituals and texts have been discussed in Goble 2013.

160 Geoffrey Goble, private communication 23.07.2018.

Fig. 25 Bodhisattva Samantabhadra, ink and color on silk, from Mogao Cave 17, 9th-10th C., 59.8 × 17.8 cm, the Musée Guimet, Paris, France. Museum number MG. 1770 (Giès 1994-96: plate 4).

Fig. 26 Bodhisattva, ink and color on silk, from Mogao Cave 17, 17.4 × 18.5 cm, 9th C., the British Museum, London, UK. Museum number Ch. lv. 007 (Whitfield 1982-85: plate 53).

that are normally depicted with Vaiśravaṇa in Dunhuang art.[161] This suggests that, despite the differences in iconography, he was understood to be the same god as Vaiśravaṇa.[162] It can be surmised that the aforementioned protective rituals were of an Indian origin and therefore they must have been initially centred on Kubera, whose images likely accompanied the original Indian texts, but who was replaced with his well known local equivalent, Vaiśravaṇa, in the Chinese translations.

2.5 Portable Paintings with Single Figures of Bodhisattvas

Figs. 25 and 26 show images of solitary standing bodhisattvas in the Southern Indian mode. Their vertical format implies that the paintings were displayed on banners and possibly produced in sets representing a group of eight bodhisattvas. Parallels can be found at Ellora as well, where Caves 11 and 12 contain several groups of the eight great bodhisattvas depicted standing.[163]

An outstanding painting in Fig. 27 was likely conceived of as an individual icon. The bodhisattva sports a tubular and extremely tall hairstyle (*jaṭāmukuṭa*), a typical feature of Pallava imagery and Sri Lankan imagery in the Pallava style. A figure attributed as Tārā from the British Museum in Fig. 28 is one striking example of this. The sculpture was discovered in Sri Lanka, but it possibly has a Pallava provenance.[164] The bodhisattva and Tārā are clad in lower garments of a similar design and their headdresses are secured by nearly-identical leaf-like crown elements. Unlike the other discussed images, the crown and armbands of the bodhisattva do not have spiked elements. This, however, does not rule out a possible Pallava background as decorations without spikes were also common in Pallava art. Alternatively, the painting could have been based on a Sri Lankan original, as spiked decorations were not prominent in Sri Lankan art.[165] Although the painting is currently attributed to the 9th century,

161 See, for example, a woodblock print dated to 947 in the British Museum collection (1919.0101.0.245). The attendants are a female attendant with a tray of jewels (identified by the museum as Goddess Śrī) and a *gandharva* (a class of demigods) wearing a tiger-head helmet that covers his head and shoulders. On depictions of *gandharva* in Chinese art, see Wong 2019: 73 fig 2.14, 120 fig. 3.8. Another example of Vaishravana attended by *gandharva* is a 9th century painting 1919,0101,0.38, in the British Museum collection.

162 The conflation between the *dikpālas* and the heavenly kings is also evident in the compositions in Figs. 14 and 15, which were discussed in the previous section. While the North, South, and West directions are guarded by the *dikpālas* (Kubera is depicted in the right top corner in Fig.14 and in the left top corner in Fig.15; Yama and Varuṇa are in the bottom corners), the East is guarded by the heavenly king of the East, Dhṛtarāṣṭra, who is clearly recognized by his attribute, a lute.

163 Malandra 1993: figs. 222, 223, 251, 252.

164 Srinivasan 1999: 110.

165 See footnote 64.

Fig. 27 Bodhisattva, ink and color on silk, 8th C., from Mogao Cave 17, 57.5 x 38.1 cm, the British Museum, London, UK. Museum number Ch. 18003 (Whitfield 1982-85: plate 53).

Fig. 28 Tara, copper alloy, 8th C., Sri Lanka, H 143 cm, the British Museum, London, UK. Museum number 1830,0612. 4 (https://www.britishmuseum.org/research/collection_online/collection_object_details.aspx?objectId=251954&partId=1).

its almost pure Pallava/Sri Lankan aesthetics suggest the 8th-century date.

2.6 Examples of Mixed Imagery

As discussed in section 2.1, the bodhisattvas in Yulin Cave 25 (Fig. 1) were likely painted in accordance with standardized models known in Chinese art as *yang*. Several portable paintings discovered in Mogao Cave 17 suggest that *yang* models of bodhisattvas in the Southern Indian mode were perhaps also used for depicting attending bodhisattvas in heavenly assemblies where the rest of the figures are in the Chinese mode.

Perhaps the earliest example of such imagery is a portable painting shown in Fig. 29,

Fig. 29 Pure Land of Bhaiṣajyaguru, ink and color on silk., from Mogao Cave 17, dated 836, Tibetan period, 152.3 × 177.8 cm, the British Museum, London, UK, Museum number Ch.xxxvii.004 (Whitfield 1982-85: plate 16).

which belongs to the Tibetan period and is dated to 836. The painting contains Chinese and Tibetan inscriptions and displays a mixture of the Chinese and Indian artistic modes. It has been suggested that the Indianized images in the painting represent the Tibetan style and their appearance along with Chinese images is a sign of Tibetan influence, which materialized in Dunhuang art during the period of the Tibetan occupation.[166] I would argue that neither in terms of iconography nor in terms of style can this painting be ascribed to Tibetan influence. The painting was likely centred on Cintāmaṇicakra, Thousand-armed Avalokiteśvara, and Amoghapāśa, which was a popular grouping in Dunhuang. Their images are largely lost, but the deities are mentioned in the accompanying Chinese inscription. Cults of these Esoteric forms of Avalokiteśvara gained popularity during the reign of Empress Wu (武 则 天 , r. 684-705) and were promoted by the court along with the Huayan doctrine.[167] As a result, images of these deities are often found along with those belonging to the Huayan context.[168] In this painting too, characteristic figures of two main bodhisattvas of the Huayan tradition, Samantabhadra riding an elephant and Mañjuśrī riding a lion, are depicted right above the Esoteric versions of Avalokiteśvara. Finally, an assembly of Buddha Bhaiṣajyaguru occupies the top of the painting.

166 Karmay 1975: 8-14; Wang 2018: 98-107.

167 On cults of Esoteric deities during the Tang, see Wong 2018: 184-200.

168 On Esoteric imagery in Huayan context, see Wong 2012: 223-260.

Fig .30 Ten stages of the bodhisattvahood according to the *Avataṁsaka Sūtra*, ink and color on silk, from Mogao Cave 17, 10th C., 286 × 189 cm, the Musée Guimet, Paris, France. Museum number MG 26465 (Giès 1994-96: plate II-1).

All these subjects were popular in Dunhuang before the Tibetan period and altogether they can be found at already discussed Mogao Cave 148, which was excavated between 766-776 (i.e. in the decade before the Tibetan conquest).[169] As with Mogao Cave 148 and Yulin Cave 25, the painting shows the coexistence of the two artistic modes. The bodhisattvas flanking the figure of Bhaiṣajyaguru are shown in the Indian mode, while the rest of the figures are depicted in the Chinese mode. These bodhisattvas represent the same type as that in the VAEGB composition of Yulin Cave 25 (Fig. 1) and display the characteristics of Southern Indian art such as spiked decorations and swagged necklaces (see a close-up of the bodhisattva in Fig. 29). A large rectangular cartouche in the centre of the painting contains Chinese and Tibetan inscriptions. The Chinese inscription is almost completely faded and illegible to the naked eye, while the

169 The iconographic program of Mogao cave 148 includes sculptural representations of Cintāmaṇicakra and Amoghapāśa (no longer extant) and a painted image of Thousand-armed Avalokiteśvara along with distinctively Huayan images of Samantabhadra riding an elephant and Mañjuśrī riding a lion as well as several heavenly assemblies including that of Buddha Bhaiṣajyaguru. See Lee 2010: 91.

Tibetan inscription is relatively clear.[170] The Chinese inscription includes the date and was read with the help of infrared photography. Although the inscriptions are similar in their content, it is clear that they are not translations of each other. The Tibetan one mentions an image of Pariṇatacakra instead of Amoghapāśa in the Chinese inscription, and furthermore dedicates the painting to all living beings, whereas the Chinese inscription dedicates it to the donor's deceased parents. Bearing in mind that the Chinese inscription is faded and the majority of the painting is lost, it could be that the painting was restored at some point and then rededicated with the Tibetan inscription. It is also worth remembering that during the Tibetan period the Tibetan language was the language of the ruler and was used in Hexi in parallel with the Chinese and not only by Tibetan people.[171] In this regard, a Tibetan inscription per se cannot be regarded as evidence for the Tibetan religious and/or artistic influence.

Another example of a similar synthesis is a 10th century painting from the Musée Guimet (Fig. 30) that depicts the ten stages of bodhisattvahood according to the *Daśabhūmika Sūtra*, which itself is a part of the *Avataṁsaka Sūtra*. The bodhisattvas in the Southern Indian mode are included in one of the assemblies whereas the other figures are depicted in the Chinese mode.[172]

The examples discussed in this chapter likely reflect the general popularity of Indian icons in Tang China as well as the creativity of Dunhuang artists.[173]

2.7 Conclusion for Part 2

The images from Mogao and Yulin discussed above share a great deal of iconographic and stylistic similarities with Pallava and Pallava-influenced examples from Southern India. Most of them can be related to the Yoga and other teachings propagated by Vajrabodhi and Amoghavajra. Their stylistic consistency, which is already evident in the earliest examples (late 8th century), confirms that this artistic tradition emerged earlier and thus it should be associated with Vajrabodhi as a painter, who was active in the Tang capitals from 720 to 741. The popuiarity of such imagery in Dunhuang art in the second half of the 8th century is in all

170 For the photograph of the inscriptions, see Wang 2018: 102, fig. 44.

171 On the use of Tibetan language in Hexi during and after the Tibetan period, see van Schaik and Galambos 2012: 67-68; Takata 2019.

172 The iconography of the painting is discussed in Wong 2007b: 343. According to Wong, the painting is only known illustration of this subject.

173 In addition, in a British Museum painting from Mogao cave 17 (Ch.XXVI. a. 007), which represents Huayan Mañjuśrī riding a lion, the bodhisattva is depicted in the Southern Indian mode as well. Another example from the British Museum collection where attending bodhisattvas are shown in the Southern Indian mode is a painting Ch.ivi.0034.

likelihood related to Amoghavajra's activities in the region. Since the dates of the discussed imagery span from the 8th to the 11th century, it can be surmised that Amoghavajra's teachings were adopted by the Tibetans in Hexi and remained popular in the region even after the collapse of both the Tibetan and Tang empires. They were, nevertheless, suppressed by new tantric teachings which started arriving to Hexi from northeastern India in the late 10th century.[174] This new wave of Esoteric transmission brought along new aesthetics characterised by the Pāla artistic style.

Part 3. A Brief Overview of the Southern Indian Influence on Buddhist Art in China

This part aims to demonstrate that the existence of a Southern Indian mode in Hexi art should not be perceived as disturbing or exceptional. There are other examples in Tang Buddhist art that complement the Hexi material and reflect the centuries-long interactions between the polities of Southern India, Sri Lanka, Southeast Asia, and China.

Historical records from the 3rd century CE onwards tell us about a great number of Buddhist monks travelling between India and China by sea.[175] Sri Lanka, whose Buddhist culture was intimately linked to that of Southern India, was an important transit stop for many of them. Early examples of these travelling monks include Faxian (法显 , 337/342-422), who spent two years in Sri Lanka on his way from Northern India to China; and Bodhidharma (菩提达摩), the founder of Chinese Chan Buddhism, who travelled from the Pallava Kingdom to China in the late 5th or early 6th century.

Indianized polities of Southeast Asia played an important intermediate role in Buddhist and artistic transmission from Southern India to China. The Indianization of the region started in the early historical period and was facilitated by Tamil seafaring merchants. The process included the adoption of Southern Indian religious cults, models of statehood, languages, scripts, and artistic styles. Early Buddhist and Brahmanic icons found in Southeast Asia display a dominating Southern Indian influence.[176] According to Chinese sources, the Southeast Asian

174 In the late 10th century, a large number of Chinese monks were sent to northeastern India through the Hexi corridor in search of new Esoteric teachings. At the same time, many Indian monks arrived in China attracted by the lavish Buddhist patronage of the early Song emperors. It can be assumed that travelling through the Hexi Corridor, these monks shared teachings and imagery with local Buddhist communities. On these movements, see van Schaik and Galambos 2012: 35-61; Sen 2016: 102, 110-125. The earliest examples of Pāla style imagery in Hexi are found in the early 11th-century Mogao Cave 76, see Toyka-Fuong 1998. On Pāla-style imagery in Hexi art, see Khokhlov, forthcoming.

175 On Buddhist monks travelling between China and India by sea, see Acri 2018.

176 Guy 2014: 3-21.

Fig. 31 Buddha, painted stone, Northern Qi dynasty (550-577), H 156 cm, excavated in Longxing monastery, Qingzhou, Shandong province, China (Okada 2004: fig. 21-4).

Fig. 32 Buddha, stone, Ikshvaku period (3rd-4th C.), H 293 cm, from Nagarjunakonda valley, Archeological survey of India, Nagarjunakonda, Guntur district, Andra Pradesh, India (http://www.museumsofindia.gov.in/repository/record/nkm_hyd-mar-scu-0008-7).

polities of Funan (Mekong delta, territory of Cambodia), Lynyi (territory of Central Vietnam) and Panpan (Malay peninsula, territory of Thailand) often sent Buddhist monks, texts, and images to the dynasties of Southern China.[177]

Although Buddhist art of the Southern Chinese dynasties before the Tang is almost completely lost, in his pioneering research on textual sources Alexander Soper argued that in the late 5th and 6th centuries it was greatly influenced by the Southern Indian artistic tradition transmitted by maritime routes as well as through the Indianized polities of Southeast Asia.[178] Soper states that artists from Southern China were famed as great specialists in rendering "Indian Buddhist icons" and their legacy can be traced in Buddhist art from the Northern Qi (550-557) to the Northern Song dynasties (960-1127).[179] Soper supported his argument by pointing to Southern Indian features found in some Northern Qi examples.[180] His theory can be further confirmed thanks to sculptures recently excavated in the eastern coastal area of

177 Wade 2014: 25-31.

178 Soper 1960.

179 Soper 1960: 88-89.

180 Soper 1960: 95-96, fig.20.

Shandong province.[181] A Northern Qi Buddha sculpture in Fig. 31 shows typical features of the late Amaravati tradition of Southern India and it is comparable to a Buddha sculpture from Nāgārjunakoṇḍa in Fig. 32. Both figures have a low *uṣṇīṣa*, elongated and columnar bodies clothed in the distinctive Amaravati way with a garment cloth pulled diagonally across the body that leaves the left shoulder bare.

As was discussed in Part 1, interactions between Southern India and China increased dramatically during the Tang dynasty. However, the resulting artistic current in Tang art has rarely been highlighted in art historical literature. The problem partially lies in the lack of surviving material from Chang'an and Luoyang where foreign influences on art were especially strong. The capitals were prime destinations and places of residence for the majority of foreign monks and this was also true for Vajrabodhi and Amoghavajra. These metropolises suffered badly from the calamities of Chinese history and none of their hundreds of Buddhist temples have survived.[182] Nevertheless, in addition to the discussed Dunhuang images, the Southern Indian facet of Tang Buddhist art can be further illustrated by a few more examples.

3.1 Longmen Buddha Sculptures

About a hundred of sculptures depicting the Buddha seated in *bhadrāsana* are distributed in several caves at Longmen (龙门) and Gongxian (巩县) (Fig. 33). Each one of them is about one meter high and is dated by inscriptions to the period between 655 and 680. These inscriptions name the sculptures as "Buddha of the King of Udayana."[183] Amy McNair argues for a Northern Indian stylistic origin of these images and compares them with a Buddha figure from Sarnath. This attribution ignores clear features of Southern Indian art present in the sculptures, such as low *uṣṇīṣa*, bare right shoulder, and ankle-sweeping robes, a vestige of the Amaravati tradition. The closest comparable examples are metal sculptures excavated in Andhra Pradesh and Tamil Nadu and datable to around the 6th century (Fig. 34).[184] Several sculptures with similar stylistic characteristics are also known from Southeast Asian polities that suggests a possibility of the transmission through Southeast Asia as well.[185]

181 For a discussion on this group of sculptures, see Okada 2004.

182 Wong and Field 2008: 132-135.

183 On these sculptures, see McNair 2007: 102-103.

184 In addition to the image in Fig. 34, see Buddha figures from the Buddhapad hoard, now in the British Museum collection (1905.1218.2; 1905.1218.3): https://www.britishmuseum.org/research/collection_online/collection_object_details.aspx?objectId=225203&partId=1&searchText=buddhapad&page=1
https://www.britishmuseum.org/research/collection_online/collection_object_details.aspx?objectId=225204&partId=1&searchText=buddhapad&page=1

185 See Guy 2014: cat. 20-23, 50, 51.

Fig. 33 The "King Udayana Buddha" images, stone, ca. 655-680, Tang dynasty, H ca. 100 cm, Longmen, Henan province, China (Revire 2012: fig. 11. 8).

Fig. 34 Buddha, copper alloy, 5th-6th C., from Nagapattinam, Tamil Nadu, India, H 40.6 cm, the Metropolitan Museum, New York, USA. Accession number 1998.414 (https://www.metmuseum.org/art/collection/search/45449).

3.2 Two Metal Sculptures

The Metropolitan Museum of Art has a metal figure of a bodhisattva (Fig. 36) that was reportedly found in Vietnam and dated by the museum to the 7th century. Another similar figure attributed to the Sui Dynasty (581-618) of China has been recently published (Fig. 35).[186]

These figures show a synthesis of Chinese and Southern Indian aesthetics, similar to what is found in the Mogao painting in Fig. 25. Both display distinctive swagged necklaces, while the crown of the bodhisattva in Fig. 35 is decorated with spikes. The date of their production is unlikely to be earlier than the 8th century, as the figures show closer connections with late Pallava material, such as the sculpture in Fig. 37. The fact that the territory of Northern Vietnam (Da Viet, Red river delta) belonged to Tang China suggests a probable southern Chinese origin for these sculptures. The occurrence of such imagery in southern China is logical, as Guangzhou was a major entry point to China for seafaring merchants and monks arriving from

186 Schulenburg, Hessel, Schmidt, and Wagner 2015: 150-151.

Fig. 35 Bodhisattva, copper alloy, 8th C., Tang dynasty, China, 43 cm, private collection (Schulenburg, Hessel, Schmidt, Wagner K., Brauen 2015: fig. 24).

Fig. 36 Bodhisattva Avalokitesvara, copper alloy, 8th C., Tang dynasty, China, 36.5 cm, the Metropolitan Museum, New York, USA. Accession number 1993.387. 14 (https://www.metmuseum.org/art/collection/search/51170).

Fig. 37 Bodhisattva Maitreya, copper alloy, 8th-9th C., Pallava period, 39.5 cm, from Tanjor, Tamil Nadu, formerly in the Government Museum, Chennai, India, stolen, present whereabouts unknown (Snellgrove 1978: fig .90).

South Asia. As was previously mentioned, three Tamil temples existed in Guangzhou in the 8th century that clearly demonstrates significant religious transmission. Moreover, Amoghavajra's teachings were popular in the area as well. The master preached in Guangzhou right before his trip to South Asia. He attracted a great number of local followers, converted thousands of people to Buddhism, and conferred Esoteric initiations on members of the ruling elite.[187] In

187 Yang 2018: 33. Chou 1945: 288-289.

Fig. 38 Buddha Shakyamuni preaching, silk embroidery, probably Chinese work, 8th C., Tang Dynasty, 207×157 cm, Nara National Museum, Japan (https://www.narahaku.go.jp/english/collection/647-0.html).

addition, upon his return to China, Amoghavajra was temporarily banished from the court and spent four years (749-753) in the Guangzhou area.[188]

It is worth noting that the sculptures under discussion are visually close to a famous icon of the Nanzhao and Dali kingdoms, the Acuoye Guanyin, which can also ultimately be aligned with a Pallava model.[189] Taken together, these examples reflect the considerable Southern Indian influence in the region.

188 Yang 2018: 41.

189 On South-East Asian stylistic connections of this icon, see Guy 1995: 86.

Fig. 39 Left: Buddha, stone, 7th C., Pallava period, 240 cm, excavated on the territory of Kamakshidevi Temple, Kancipuram, Tamil Nadu, Government Museum, Chennai, Tamil Nadu, India (Photograph courtesy Yuko Fukuroi). Right: Buddha, Detail of Fig.38.

3.3 Nara Embroidery and Hōryūji murals

An embroidery in Fig. 38 belongs to the Nara National Museum in Japan. It has traditionally been dated to the early 8th century and is believed to have been produced in China, likely in one of the Tang capitals.[190] The work depicts a heavenly assembly with the Buddha attended by a retinue of bodhisattvas, monks, and lay people. I regard images of the Buddha with two leading bodhisattvas as heavily influenced by Southern Indian and Sri Lankan prototypes.

190 Wong 2018: 153-154.

Fig. 40 Left: Bodhisattva, copper alloy, 8th-9th C., H 17.9 cm, Sri Lanka, Los Angeles County Museum of Art, USA (https://collections.lacma.org/node/247426).

Fig. 41 Middle: Bodhisattva, detail of fig. 38.

Fig. 42 Right: Bodhisattva, copper alloy, 8th C., Sri Lanka, National museum, Colombo, Sri Lanka (Boisselier 1979: fig. 52).

The Buddha exhibits the same iconography as that of the Longmen sculptures (Fig. 33). At the same time, his bulky proportions and a robe drape in the Amaravati style are strikingly similar to his counterpart in a circa 7th-century Pallava sculpture in Fig. 39.[191] The folds of the robes in both figures are arranged in a similar and distinctive fashion. They are concentrated along the upper edge and below the waist, creating a flat area on the stomach.

The two chief bodhisattvas with their wide shoulders and almost naked torsos stand out visually from the group (see a close-up in Fig. 41). They represent a particular type of

191 On this sculpture, see Rao 1915; Aiyappan and Srinivasan 2000: 70-72.

Fig. 43 Buddha Amida Pure Land, wall painting, panel 6, West wall, Kondo, Hōryūji, 8th C., Ikaruga, Nara Prefecture, Japan. Not extant anymore (Wong 2008: plate 12).

bodhisattva which was popular in Pallava and Sri Lankan art (Fig. 40 & 42).[192] Bodhisattvas of this type are characterized by an upright posture, and by the *abhaya* or *vitarka mudrā* (right hand) and *kaṭaka mudrā* (left hand), which are performed distinctively at elbow-level. These figures can be bejeweled or unadorned, but always wear a distinctive flat and wide sash, which

192 A number of metal sculptures representing bodhisattvas of this type were recovered in Indonesia and Thailand and it is assumed that they were imported from the Pallava Kingdom or Sri Lanka. See, Guy 2014: cat. 6, a Pallava example is cat. 7.

probably represents the skin of a black deer (*kṛṣṇājina*) worn in the manner of the sacred thread (*yajñopavīta*).[193] It is loosely wrapped across the torso forming a loop on the left shoulder and drapes down to the right hip. The bodhisattvas in the embroidery follow this model closely. As has been recently shown by Osmund Bopearachchi, this model likely represents bodhisattva Avalokiteśvara as a protector of mariners.[194] Such images were often found along river and sea trade routes that points to maritime transmission of this iconographic form to China.

It has long been noted that the two bodhisattvas in this piece of embroidery are visually close to the bodhisattvas in the murals that used to adorn the main hall of Hōryūji Temple in Japan (Fig. 43).[195] These murals depicted heavenly assemblies of four buddhas and eight unidentified bodhisattvas. It is commonly thought that the murals date to the early 8th century and represent the metropolitan Tang style that has largely been lost in China. Moreover, it is thought that the figures in the murals were most likely executed with the help of full-sized stencils, which are believed to have been brought to Japan from one of the Tang capitals.[196]

Fig. 44 compares the bodhisattva images from Yulin Cave 25, the embroidery, and the Hōryūji murals. Other than certain variations in decorations, the figures look strikingly similar in their linear structures, proportions, postures, gestures, and facial features. What unite them the most are their elongated and almost naked torsos, remarkably broad shoulders, and contrasting narrow waists. Though located thousands of miles apart, the Hōryūji and Yulin bodhisattvas, with their almost identical swagged necklaces of the Southern Indian type, and similarly drawn sash and *kṛṣṇājina*, look as if they are from the same painting. Such similitude suggests that the images were based on standardized models. As was already mentioned, many of these *yang* — standardized models and templates for the replication of images — recorded in official inventories of objects transferred from Tang China to Japan have been described by Hsueh-man Shen.[197] The Hōryūji example also shows that artistic models were transmitted from China to Japan even with the help of full-sized stencils. Sarah Fraser demonstrated that significant artistic interexchange existed between Dunhuang and the Tang capitals as well.[198]

In my view, taken as a group the imagery from Yulin Cave 25, the Nara embroidery, and the Hōryūji murals confirm the existence of the distinctive tradition in Tang Buddhist art,

---

193 It was attributed as such by Dohanian. See Dohanian 1977: 41.

194 Bopearachchi 2014: 161-187.

195 On the Hōryūji and its murals, see Wong and Field 2008.

196 Wong and Field 2008: 147-152.

197 Shen 2019: 149-155.

198 Fraser 2004: 52-53.

Fig. 44 Left: Bodhisattva, detail of fig. 43.
Middle: Bodhisattva, detail of fig.1(https://www.e-dunhuang.com/cave/10.0001/0001.0002.0025).
Right: Bodhisattva, detail of fig. 38.

which was most likely established by Vajrabodhi as a painter.[199] It should be mentioned that the Southern Indian influence on the Hōryūji murals has previously been suggested by at least two other scholars. Jeannine Auboyer noted similarities in clothing between the Hōryūji figures and Ellora statues, while Marilyn Rhie argued that the facial features of the bodhisattvas reflect the influence of Southern Indian art, an influence she saw as resulting from the maritime exchange of Tang China with Southern Indian polities.[200]

Part 4. From the Hexi Corridor to Central Tibet

Tibetan rule in the Hexi Corridor lasted roughly from the mid-8th till the mid-9th century and coincided with a period of the most intense promotion of Buddhism in the Tibetan Empire. As was discussed in Parts 1 and 2, the region was one of the major centres for the teaching and practice associated with the Southern Indian tradition of the Yoga literature, which became dominant in the official Buddhist ceremony and doctrine of both Tang China and Tibetan Empire in the latter half of the 8th century.

The Tibetan religious tradition ascribes the introduction of the Yoga teachings in Tibet to Northern Indian master Buddhaguhya, who was supposedly active in the 8th century. However, his identity and life story cannot be historically verified and modern scholarship cast doubt on his influence in Tibet.[201] On the other hand, the *Testament of Ba* (*Dba' bzhed / Sba bzhed*), a historical account on the origin of Buddhism in Tibet that was probably compiled in the 11th or 12th century, attests to significant activities of Chinese monks from Hexi in Central Tibet in the second half of the 8th century. It says, for example, that the Buddhist master Moheyan from Dunhuang was patronized by the Tibetan court and had a majority of followers in Tibet.[202] According to the *Testament of Ba*, tensions developed between the Chinese and newly arrived Indian teachers, who allegedly taught a different path towards enlightenment. The *Testament of Ba* further states that these tensions were resolved in a formal debate, where the Chinese side was defeated and expelled from Tibet. As was discussed by Sam van Schaik, this episode has no documentary value and was likely designed to validate new Indian lineages, which

199 Remarkable similarities between the images of bodhisattvas from Yulin Cave 25, the Nara embroidery, and the Hōryūji murals would also seem to suggest that they were created in a relatively close temporal proximity. Out of the three, only the Yulin image is securely datable. It was created between 776 and 851, but most likely in the late 8th century. In contrast, the Hōryūji murals and the Nara embroidery are traditionally dated to the beginning of the same century that, in the light of the presented analysis, should perhaps be reconsidered.

200 Auboyer 1941: 71; Rhie 1988: 27-28.

201 Weinberger 2003: 30, 83-90; Nagasawa: 2017.

202 Wangdu and Diemberger 2000: 76 n 287; van Schaik 2015: 14-17.

started arriving in Tibet in the 11th century, as the only genuine source of Buddhism.[203] It has been traditionally understood that the Chinese party represented the Chan tradition in its modern understanding, which emphasized a concept free meditation and the immediate presence of enlightenment in the mind as opposed to the scholastic Indian tradition advocating the graduated path and the multitude of methods including Esoteric teachings. In the light of recent scholarship, however, this picture looks not only simplified, but also anachronistic. As was argued by Robert Sharf, the very notion that, Chan and Esoteric teachings constituted independent traditions in China in the 8th century can be misleading. Moreover, these teachings had a few areas of congruence, and were likely practiced in the same Buddhist circles.[204] With regard to Hexi, Sam van Schaik has demonstrated that monks in Dunhuang in the 8th and 9th centuries, who were identified as members of Chan lineages in the later texts, practiced various Esoteric rituals, including those associated with the Yoga tradition in general and the Vajradhātu maṇḍala in particular.[205] Furthermore, several Chinese and Tibetan sources suggest that Moheyan himself was proficient in Esoteric rituals as well.[206] These traits find striking parallels in the teachings of the Nyigmapa (Rnying ma pa), the oldest school of Tibetan Buddhism, which traces its origin back to the Imperial period. According to David Snellgrove, there was a considerable vogue of Yoga Tantras in Imperial Tibet and many Mahāyoga Tantras of the Nyigmapa, which were largely rejected by the later Tibetan schools "as unorthodox and probably Chinese," conform to the content and style of "orthodox Yoga Tantras" such as the *STTS*.[207] In addition, the Nyigmapa tradition of Dzogchen (Rdzogs chen, the Great Perfection), which includes elements of both the Mahāyoga and Chan teachings, was viewed by some 13th and 14th century authoritative Tibetan scholars as the Chinese doctrine of Moheyan.[208]

Altogether this would seem to suggest that Buddhist masters from Hexi, who have been perhaps misleadingly labelled as Chan monks in modern scholarship,[209] were instrumental in the transmission of the Yoga tradition and possibly many other "not Chan" teachings to the Tibetans in the 8th and 9th centuries. This can be also well supported by the example of Ye shes dbyangs, a Tibetan monk, who has been identified as a member of the Chan lineage in the later Dunhuang texts and, who propagated the cult of VAEGB as part of Amoghavajra's practice of the Bhadracarī (discussed in section 2.1.2.3).

According to Weinberger and Dalton, it is nearly certain that the *STTS*, the root Tantra of

203 van Schaik 2015: 15.

204 Sharf 2017: 53.

205 van Schaik 2015: 168.

206 van Schaik 2015: 132-133.

207 Snellgrove 1987: 457-460.

208 S. Karmay 2007: 11, 140-142.

209 For example, see Kapstein 2000: 43.

the Yoga tradition, was transmitted to Tibet and probably even translated into Tibetan during the Imperial period, though no details of the translation are known and the text is missing from the Imperial catalogues.[210] In contrast, the Chinese translations are much better documented and historically attested, and it is not impossible that the early Tibetan translation could have been based on the Chinese texts. The earliest work in Chinese summarizing the principles of the *STTS* dates to 723 and is authored by Vajrabodhi. It was followed by Amoghavajra's translation of the first part of the *STTS* produced in Liangzhou in 753.[211]

As a matter of fact, the Chinese legacy in Tibetan Buddhism was deliberately minimized by later Tibetan historiographies and by a practice of editing the colophons and texts of Tibetan translations from non-Sanskrit sources in order to connect them directly to the Indian tradition. This practice started in as early as the 9th century.[212] As James Gentry put it, "the general unreliability of translation colophons and centuries of scribal and editorial activity, which often included efforts during the Imperial period and thereafter to standardize Tibetan scriptural translations according to an imperially-decreed common lexicon, have obscured the process by which these collections and their translations came into being and were transmitted. As a result, the role of Chinese and other language translations of Indic texts in Tibetan translation activity and the formation of Tibetan scriptural language remains little understood."[213] Regarding the Tibetan lineages of transmission, it is clear that for such important religious traditions like that of the Yoga, they were of great political consequence, and, therefore, there is no a priori reason to assume that they are much more reliable than the colophons.

4.1 The Main Temple of Samye

As was noted by Steven Weinberger, one of the strongest pieces of evidence for the importance of the Yoga tradition in early Tibetan Buddhism is the first Tibetan monastery of Samye.[214] The iconographic program of its main temple, which was seriously damaged during the Cultural Revolution, can be reconstructed from various historical sources including the *Testament of Ba* and a Tibetan Chronicle *The Mirror Illuminating the Royal Genealogies* (*Rgyal rabs gsal ba'i me long*).[215] In the following, I will try to make sense of it with the help of Kimiaki Tanaka's

210 Weinberger 2010: 146-150; Dalton 2017: 329-330.

211 Weinberger 2003: 9.

212 Issues concerning the Chinese legacy in Tibetan Buddhism were discussed in Li 2016: 95. Specifically on doubtful colophons in tantric material, see van der Kuijp 1992, Almogi 2008.

213 Gentry 2019.

214 Weinberger 2010: 140.

215 English translations of these sources can be found in Wangdu and Diemberger 2000 and Sørensen1994.

recent interpretation.[216]

The main temple had three floors and a Chinese-type roof.[217] On the first floor, the central icon was Buddha Śākyamuni, which was surrounded by sculptures of the eight great bodhisattvas, two additional bodhisattvas, Acala and Trailokyavijaya. As Tanaka remarked, the combination of the Buddha/Vairocana with the eight great bodhisattvas, Acala, and Trailokyavijaya corresponds to a mandala introduced by Amoghavajra in a ritual manual for recitation of the *Uṣṇīṣavijayā dhāraṇī* (T972).[218] Amoghavajra was the most enthusiastic propagator of this *dhāraṇī*; he elevated its status from being a scripture with salvific and protective properties for individuals, to a scripture of the national defence and protection.[219] Bearing in mind the nationwide significance of Samye, the emphasis on apotropaic qualities of Buddhist teachings in its iconographic program would have made perfect sense. It is not unlikely that the enormous power ascribed to the *Uṣṇīṣavijayā dhāraṇī* in Tang China led to the appropriation of the related rituals in Tibet. A textual fragment in the Tibetan language found in Dunhuang, which describes a ritual involving Vairocana, the eight great bodhisattvas, Acala, and Trailokyavijaya, could be regarded as possible evidence for such appropriation.[220]

The second floor was centred on Vairocana of an unknown affiliation flanked by the eight great bodhisattvas and two additional bodhisattvas, the same as those on the first floor. Buddhas of the past, present and future; Medicine Buddha; and Buddha Amitābha were installed in front of the Vairocana and bodhisattvas. A pair of Chinese gatekeepers holding a *vajra*, known as King and Kang, was also included in the composition. It is tempting to suggest that the sculptures of Vairocana and the eight great bodhisattvas on this floor might have represented the practice of the *Bhadracarī*, which, as we discussed, was an extremely popular aspirational prayer in Imperial Tibet and was believed to prolong the *tsenpo*'s life (see section 2.1.2.3). In this regard, it is worth mentioning that other depictions related to the *Avataṁsaka Sūtra* subjects were present at Samye as well. While Sudhana's spiritual journey from the *Gaṇḍavyūha Sūtra* was illustrated in a wall frieze in the great courtyard, the *Daśabhūmika Sūtra*, which describes the ten stages of bodhisattvahood, was illustrated in murals of the main temple's third floor.[221]

The only known illustration for the *Daśabhūmika Sūtra* comes from Dunhuang (Fig. 30) and a similar composition could have been depicted at Samye (for a discussion on the

216 Tanaka 2018: 83-85.

217 Sørensen1994: 376-381.

218 See footnote 88.

219 Lin 214: 139-140. For example, Emperor Daizong, under the thread from advancing Uighurs and Tibetans in 765, ordered Amoghavajra to install a group of monks at court to chant the *dhāraṇī* for the sake of the nation. In 776, Daizong ordered all nuns and monks of the country to chant the *dhāraṇī*, see Yang 2018: 159.

220 The text title is *Rnam par snang mdzad 'khor dang bcas pa la bstod pa*. It is found in P.T. 7a and in IOL TIB J 366/3. See Tanaka 2018: 81; Tanaka 2000; Heller 1997; Dalton and van Schaik 2006: 97-98.

221 van Schaik and Doney 2007: 187-188; Sørensen1994: 379.

Dunhuang painting (fig.30), see section 2.6; for a discussion on depictions of Vairocana and the eight great bodhisattvas in the *Avataṁsaka* context, see section 2.1).

A principal image of the third floor represented Vairocana with four heads (facing four directions), surrounded by eight unidentified bodhisattvas, two for each head, and many other deities. This group has traditionally been understood as representing the Sarvavid-Vairocana maṇḍala of the *Sarvadurgatipariśodhana Tantra* (hereafter the *SDP*).[222] However, as Kimiaki Tanaka has pointed out, Vairocana with four heads could just as well stand for the Vajradhātu-Vairocana, the central deity of the *STTS*.[223] Tanaka further notes that images of the four Buddhas of the Vajradhātu maṇḍala depicted back-to-back were installed at Samye during the modern reconstruction.[224] Moreover, a Tibetan historical source *Lde'u Chos 'byung* explicitly states that all images at the third floor were erected as a depiction of the god-assembly of the Vajradhātu.[225] The *SDP* was specifically associated with mortuary rites and thus the alleged installation of the Sarvavid-Vairocana maṇḍala as the central composition of the principal temple requires further explanation. In contrast, a version of the Vajradhātu maṇḍala fits perfectly with the official status of Samye. As discussed, this maṇḍala was the cornerstone of the Yoga tradition and a central element of state protection rituals in contemporaneous China.[226]

In addition, the main temple at Samye can be compared to the Golden Pavilion of Jin'ge monastery (金阁寺) constructed in 767 on Mount Wutai.[227] The construction of the monastery was initiated by Amoghavajra, who started promoting the cult of Mount Wutai towards the end of his life. Built with lavish imperial sponsorship, Jin'ge became one of the principal monasteries responsible to carry out apotropaic rituals for the sake of the state. Similarly to Samye, the Golden Pavilion, a main temple of the monastery, had a three-storey design with a vertically oriented iconographic program centred around Vairocana, which, as was suggested

222 Weinberger 2010: 140. The *SDP* is regarded as an explanatory Tantra on part two of the *STTS*, see Tanaka 2018: 321. It is centred on Buddha's Uṣṇīṣa deities and mirrors the narrative found in various versions of the *Sūtra of the Revered and Victorious Dhāraṇī of the Buddha's Uṣṇīṣa (Uṣṇīṣavijayā dhāraṇī)*. Both the *SDP* and the *Uṣṇīṣavijayā dhāraṇī* were specifically employed for mortuary rituals, see Wang 2018: 25, 42-50. Weinberger 2010: 146. The history of the early translation of the *SDP* into Tibetan is far from clear. The text is listed in the Imperial catalogue and the colophon, which dates to the 8th century, gives the names of Indian and Tibetan translators, see Weinberger 2010: 148-149. However, the colophon is proven to be unreliable and the identity of the translators has been questioned, see van der Kuijp 1992.

223 Vajradhātu-Vairocana can be depicted with four heads as well, but in contrast with like Sarvavid-Vairocana, who performs the *dhyāna mudrā*, Vajradhātu-Vairocana performs the *bodhyaṅgī mudrā*. See Tanaka 2018: 83; On four-faced Vairocana in the *STTS*, see Weinberger 2003: 187.

224 Tanaka 2018: 84.

225 Sørensen 1994: 379 n 1260.

226 There is strong evidence showing that the Vajradhātu maṇḍala was known in Tibet in the 8th century. See Weinberger 2010: 144.

227 On the Golden Pavilion and Jin'ge monastery, see Lin 2014: 131-154.

by Wei-Cheng Lin, was likely conceived to represent a three-dimensional version of the Vajradhātu maṇḍala whose five-fold system correlated with the five monasteries and five peaks of Mount Wutai.[228] The Tibetans must have been aware of these developments in China as the popularity of Wutai Shan in Tibetan Empire is well attested in historical sources and according to the *Old Dynastic History of the Tang*, the Tibetan *tsenpo* once even requested a picture of Mount Wutai from the Tang court.[229] Remarkably, the first representations of Mount Wutai appeared in Dunhuag art during the Tibetan period.[230]

The discussed parallels are striking and suggest that the decision to built Samye might have been motivated by apotropaic qualities of certain Buddhist teachings. I have later come across a 1983 article by Christopher Beckwith, where he put forward a theory suggesting that the Tibetan adoption of Buddhism as a state religion in general and the building of Samye in particular were inspired by the Chinese model of National Protection Buddhism maintained by Amoghavajra, and were, at least partially, dictated by a need to resolve the crisis of legitimacy faced by the Tibetan emperor Trisong Detsen.[231] I was delighted to learn that I came to the same conclusion independently, but from a different angle. Regrettably, no original images survived from Samye, as they could provide art historical evidence for sources of their corresponding teachings. Nevertheless, I argue that Samye's aesthetics can be reconstructed from artwork created at the earliest stage of the Buddhist revival in Tibet in the late 10th and 11th centuries.

11th century Clay Sculptures from Central Tibetan Temples

After the collapse of the empire in the mid-9th century, Tibet lost its colonies and went to a so-called period of fragmentation. The monastic tradition perished to be reintroduced only in the late 10th century with a religious movement known in Tibetan history as the "later spread" of the Dharma (*phyi dar*). Although most of Hexi was recaptured by the Tang forces, its capital and a former Amoghavajra's seat, Liangzhou, remained under local Tibetan rule up to the 11th century, when it was absorbed into the Xi Xia Empire.[232] The region undoubtedly continued to hold a position of Buddhist authority in Central Tibet, as in the late 10th century a group of men from there were sent to the areas of Liangzhou and its neighbor, the Tibetan kingdom of Tsongkha, in order to bring the monastic tradition back to Central Tibet.[233] Being ordained in these areas, the new monks, sometimes labeled as the Eastern Vinaya monks, returned to

228 Lin 2014: 149.

229 Debreczeny 2011: 8-9; Wong 1993: 39.

230 Wong 1993: 41.

231 Beckwith 1983. On the notion of National Protection Buddhism in Tang China, see Orzech 1998. In particular, on the term "National Protection Buddhism", see Orzech 1998: 3 n. 9.

232 van Schaik and Galambos 2012: 64-65.

233 van Schaik and Galambos 2012: 68-74.

Central Tibet and initiated the formation of Buddhist communities, the reconstruction of old temples, and the building of new ones. Although Samye and other royal temples were not in use and in a poor state, they still contained sculptures and paintings.[234] In addition, a network of small temples continued to function under the patronage of local rulers. According to Tibetan historical sources, hundreds of Buddhist establishments were renovated and built in Central Tibet during the 11th century. Renovation of old temples, symbols of Tibet's ancient glorious past and the Imperial past, was a top priority during this period[235] and it can, therefore, be surmised that survived specimens of Imperial art were renovated and replicated in the new temples. For example, Samye monastery was not only renovated, but also taken as a model for Grwa thang monastery (founded in 1081).[236] Thus, it is the artistic styles of the late Imperial period that would have been prevalent in Buddhist art of central Tibet in the late 10th and 11th century.

In this regard, I would like to draw attention to a group of clay sculptures from the Central Tibetan temples/monasteries of G.ye dmar, Rtis gnas gsar, Zhwa lu Gser khang, Rkyang bu, Grwa thang, Zho nang, and Snye thang.[237] Although most of them were lost during the Cultural Revolution, their images can still be seen in pre-1950 photographs taken by Li Gotami Govinda and Giuseppe Tucci's expedition.[238] Luckily, the sculptures of Snye thang monastery have survived.[239]

These temples were founded or renovated at the earliest stage of the Buddhist revival in the 11th century. Despite the fact that some of these temples are located at a considerable distance from one another, their sculptures demonstrate remarkable stylistic consistency. This, I believe, confirms that the sculptures reflect Buddhist aesthetics of the Imperial period, which must have been a common source of inspiration for artists throughout Central Tibet in the 10th and 11th centuries.[240] With regard to the iconographic programs, much of the subject matter depicted in these temples had already been popular during the Imperial period as well. For example, four-faced Vairocana with retinue and Vairocana grouped with eight bodhisattvas

234 Davidson 2005: 94-95.

235 On the activities of the eastern Vinaya monks and the general situation in Central Tibet at the time, see Davidson 2005: 84-115.

236 Vitali 1990: 49; Heller 2002: 40-41; Stoddard 2018: 96-97.

237 The temples were discussed in Vitali 1990: 37-69; Lo Bue: 2000; von Schroeder 2001: 836-851.

238 Many photographs are reproduced in publications listed in the previous footnote. Also, see Govinda 1979: 40-50.

239 For description and images of the sculptures, see von Schroeder 2001: 860-869. Although von Schroeder dates the sculptures to circa 1200, I believe they belong to the 11th century.

240 Along the same lines, Heather Stoddard suggested that surviving murals at Grwa thang reflect the aesthetics employed at Samye in the late 8th century. Stoddard 2018: 96-97. In addition to the imagery in the early style, the murals also include some depictions in the Pala style of northeastern India, which was introduced to Tibet in the 11th century. On the history and paintings of Grwa thang, see Heller 2002.

Fig. 45 Vairocana

Fig. 46 Amoghasiddhi

Part of the sculptural Vajradhātu mandala, clay sculptures, 11th C., Rkyang bu temple, Central Tibet. Not extant anymore (von Schroeder 2001: fig. XIII-17, 19).

can be found in the iconographic programs of Samye and the temples under discussion. Most remarkably, the sculptures, which depict these groupings, show the same distinctive elements of the Southern Indian artistic mode as they are found in the imagery from Mogao and Yulin.

For example, Rkyang bu temple was established shortly before 1037[241] and contained a sculptural representation of the Vajradhātu maṇḍala with four-faced Vairocana at its centre (Fig. 45).[242] Vairocana in this form had likely been installed, as suggested above, on the third floor of the main temple at Samye. Another four-faced Vairocana is recorded in a temple with a Chinese roof (*rgya phibs*) at Rtis gnas gsar, which was founded during the Imperial period and renovated in the 11th century.[243] The Vajradhātu sculptures in Rkyang bu temple are decorated with spiked armbands and swagged necklaces that are characteristic of the Southern Indian mode found in Hexi art (Figs. 45, 46, 47). The sculptures' style and splendor show striking

241 Vitali 1990: 56-59.

242 This figure was misidentified as Sarvavid-Vairocana in earlier scholarship.

243 Vitali 1990: 51; von Schroeder 2001: 840-841.

Fig. 47 Ratnasambhava and attending deities as a section of the sculptural Vajradhātu maṇḍala, 11th C., Rkyang bu temple, Central Tibet. Not extant anymore (von Schroeder 2001: fig. XIII-21).

Fig. 48 One of sixteen bodhisattvas surrounding a figure of Vairocanābhisaṁbodhi (worshipped as Amitāyus), 11th C., G.ye dmar temple, Central Tibet (Photo: Lionel Fournier, courtesy of Amy Heller).

parallels with the 8th and 9th century Hexi imagery (see examples in Figs. 14, 15, 16). Their square and tiered thrones are similar to those in the Hexi depictions as well. It is important to stress that these sculptures are more closely related to the earlier Hexi examples than to contemporaneous 10th and 11th century ones (see Figs. 17, 20, 21). The contemporaneous imagery from the Hexi corridor shows a considerable decline in artistic quality that does not match the refinement and monumentality of these Tibetan sculptures. This would seem to confirm that the sculptures represent the revival of the Imperial aesthetics, which in turn were influenced by the 8th and 9th century art from the Hexi Corridor.

Groups of the eight bodhisattvas are recorded in all the temples. In addition, at G.ye dmar there was a group of sixteen bodhisattvas, which probably represented the sixteen bodhisattvas

Fig. 49 One of eight bodhisattvas surrounding a figure of Vairocanābhisaṁbodhi.
Fig. 50 Vairocanābhisaṁbodhi and one of eight attending bodhisattvas.
Both worshipped as Amitāyus, 11th C., G.ye dmar temple, Central Tibet (Govinda 1979: 45).

of the Bhadrakalpa, a prominent group in the Yoga tradition and members of the Vajradhātu maṇḍala.[244] In all these groups, the bodhisattvas accompany crowned figures displaying the *dhyāna mudrā*, who have been identified either as Vairocanābhisaṁbodhi or as Amitābha/Amitāyus.[245] These deities are differentiated only by the presence/absence of a bowl/vase in their hands. It is possible that initially all of them represented Vairocanābhisaṃbodhi. The

244 On the sixteen bodhisattvas of the Bhadrakalpa, see Tanaka 2018: 169-170.
245 von Schroeder 2001: fig. xiii-8, 9, 11, 13, 34B.

Fig. 51 Vairocanābhisaṁbodhi (worshiped as Amitāyus) and one of eight attending bodhisattvas, clay sculptures, 11th C., H 310 cm and 330 cm, Snye Thang monastery, Central Tibet (photo: Alain Bordier, 1998; von Schroeder 2001: pics. 199A, 200F).

bowls/vases could have been added later when the cult of Vairocana declined in popularity.[246] As discussed, examples of bodhisattvas surrounding Vairocana displaying the *dhyāna mudrā* are relatively rare and, apart from Tibet, can be found in Southern India and in the Hexi Corridor. The Tibetan sculptures under review depict Vairocana and bodhisattvas either in the Tibetan mode (clad in Tibetan-style robes) (Figs. 48, 49, 50), or the Indian mode (Fig. 51). These two modes of representation can already be found in the early 9th century rock carvings in Eastern Tibet (Figs. 52, 53, 54) discussed in section 2.1.2. Significantly, the sculptures in both Tibetan and Indian modes are adorned with spiked armbands that is a clear indication of the influence from the Hexi corridor. In Figs. 48, 49, and 50, I have highlighted the armbands

246 The same conversion is evident in the early 9th-century rock carving at 'Bis khog in Eastern Tibet, where Vairocana (identified by inscription) holds a bowl in his hands (see Fig. 53) . Another example of such a conversion can be seen in the main temple of Tabo. See Klimburg-Salter and Luczanits 1998: 101, 143-146, fig.146.

Fig. 52 Sketch of Renda high relief rock carving, dated 804/816, Bragyab county, Chamdo prefecture of TAR, China (Shanxi Province Academy of Archaeology and TAR Relics Preservation Institute: 2014: 9).

Fig. 53 Sketch of 'Bis khog high relief rock carving (also known as Bimda), dated 806, Yulshul, Qinghai, China (Huo 2017: 8).

Fig. 54 Sketch of Sgar thog high relief rock carving, early 9th C. near the town of Sgar thog in Smar khams county, Chamdo prefecture of TAR, China (Yang, Lu and Zhang 2017: 236).

with blue arrows; in Fig. 51, some remaining spikes are clearly visible in the armbands of the bodhisattva. Despite substantial renovation, the figures of Vairocana and the bodhisattva in Fig. 51 still convey the same splendid aesthetics that we see in the late 8th century images from Yulin Cave 25 (in particular compare Vairocana in Fig. 51 with Vairocana in Fig. 6).

As it was already stated, since no direct contacts between Tibetan Empire and Southern Indian polities are known, the source of the Southern Indian features in Tibetan art can only be Hexi/China. Also, it is very important to note that not all of the discussed sculptures display these elements. They are mostly found in sculptures which represent subjects of the Yoga tradition and groups of Vairocanābhisaṁbodhi with bodhisattvas.[247] The same correlation is evident in Hexi art. Imagery played a pivotal role in the transmission of Esoteric teachings, hence it can be deduced that these parallels between the Tibetan and Hexi depictions reflect not only an artistic transmission, but also the transmission of the Yoga teachings as well as of the cult of VAEGB from the Hexi corridor to Tibet. Although the Chinese textual antecedents and visual evidence from Hexi provide solid grounds for this conclusion, much research needs to be done in the area of Tibetan textual scholarship. Such research could potentially uncover additional textual evidence as well as possible traces of Chinese lexical influence in the relevant Tibetan texts. From a larger perspective, these stylistic and iconographic traits from Hexi detected in the early Tibetan imagery provide a strong support to the theory of the apotropaic function of Samye and, by extension, to the theory of the Chinese background of the Tibetan adoption of Buddhism.

Finally, in parallel with the Southern Indian mode in Hexi art, the artistic mode represented by these Tibetan sculptures gradually vanished in Tibet after the 11th century. Its disappearance likely reflects a decline of interest for the older teachings and their imagery caused by the arrival of new Tantric teachings and imagery in the Pāla style from northeastern India.[248]

Conclusion

In tracing the artistic background and doctrinal affiliations of a group of images from Mogao and Yulin this research elucidates the intricate web of politics, religion and art that connected the Pallava Kingdom of Southern India, Tang China and Imperial Tibet. Addressing a period of particularly intense Buddhist interexchange between South and East Asia, this article

247 For depictions, which do not display the element of the Southern Indian mode, see sculptures at G.ye dmar in von Schroeder 2001: fig.xiii-10; and murals at Grwa thang in Vitali 1990: Plates 29-34.

248 In the forthcoming article, I argue that in this process the Hexi corridor played a crucial role as well, and these northeastern Indian teachings and Pala aesthetics were initially introduced to Tibet from the Hexi corridor. See footnote 174 and Khokhlov: forthcoming.

contributes to reshaping our understanding of several key issues.

Firstly, it highlights considerable Southern Indian traits in Buddhist art of Tang China and identifies a distinctive artistic tradition, which was most likely established in China by Vajrabodhi, a renowned Buddhist master as well as a painter from the Pallava Kingdom of Southern India. Specific stylistic and iconographic features found in the Dunhuang imagery can be confidently traced to the art of the Pallava kingdom in Tamil Nadu and the Pallava influenced art in the Western Deccan. The subjects of these Dunhuang images belong to the Yoga tradition and the cult of the eight great bodhisattvas, which were propagated in China by Vajrabodhi and Amoghavajra.

On the other hand, this article helps in reconstructing artistic features of Buddhist art of Tamil Nadu, which was largely lost in India. In addition, the Pallava influenced styles of the discussed Chinese and Tibetan images constitute material evidence for the popularity of the Yoga tradition and the cult of the eight great bodhisattvas in Tamil Nadu in the 8th century.

Lastly, but not least, this research defies the idea of "early Tibetan Buddhist art" as represented by the artwork created in the Hexi Corridor during and after the period of Tibetan rule. In fact, it shows quite the opposite and suggests that the conquest of the Hexi Corridor enabled the Tibetan appropriation of Chinese religious and artistic trends, which were popular in the region in the 8th century. Furthermore, the artistic and iconographical considerations presented in this research support the theory that the Tibetan adoption of Buddhism as a state religion was most likely based on the Chinese model of National Protection Buddhism established by Amoghavajra.

Appendix 1

A list of paintings from Mogao and Yulin that display the Southern Indian artistic mode discussed in this article.

This list is not exhaustive and contains only the most important published examples.

1) A wall painting of Kubera with two attendants in Yulin Cave 15. The cave is traditionally dated to the Tibetan period, but it could have been executed earlier, at some point between 750 and 776. Discussed in section 2.4, Fig. 22.
2) A wall painting of Vairocanābhisaṁbodhi and the eight great bodhisattvas in Yulin Cave 25. The deities are identified by accompanying Chinese inscriptions. Tibetan period, late 8th century. Discussed in section 2.1, Fig. 1.
3) A portable painting of the Amoghapāśa maṇḍala from Mogao Cave 17. $8^{th}/9^{th}$ century. Musée Guimet, Paris. MG 26466. Discussed in section 2.3, Fig.18.
4) A portable painting identified as the Pure Land of Bhaiṣajyaguru from Mogao cave 17.

Dated to 836. British Museum. Ch.xxxvii.004. Discussed in section 2.6, Fig.29.

5) Two wall paintings depicting maṇḍala-like compositions centred around Vairocanābhisambodhi and Vajrasattva, Mogao Cave 14. Second half of the 9th century. See section 2.2, Fig. 14 & 15.
6) A portable painting depicting a heavenly assembly from Mogao Cave 17. 9th century. British Museum. Ch.ivi.0034.
7) A portable painting depicting Mañjuśrī riding a lion from Mogao Cave 17. 9th century. British Museum. Ch.XXVI. a. 007.
8) Four large images of seated Avalokiteśvara with four Offering Goddesses, painted on four slopes of the ceiling in Mogao Cave 161. 9th/10th century. Discussed in Wang 2018: 145-150, Fig. 63-66.
9) Two wall paintings depicting maṇḍala-like compositions centred around Vairocanābhisambodhi and a buddha, Yulin Cave 20. 9th century. Discussed in section 2.2, Fig.16.
10) A portable painting depicting a standing figure of Samantabhadra, Mogao Cave 17. 9th/10th century. Musée Guimet. MG. 17770. Discussed in section 2.5, Fig. 25.
11) A portable painting depicting a standing bodhisattva, Mogao Cave 17. 9th/10th century. British Museum. Ch. Iv. 007. See section 2.5, Fig. 26.
12) A portable painting depicting a standing bodhisattva, Mogao Cave 17. 9th/10th century. British Museum. Ch.Iv.0031.
13) A portable painting depicting a standing bodhisattva, Mogao Cave 17. 9th/10th century. British Museum. Ch.Iv.004.
14) A portable painting depicting a seated figure of Avalokiteśvara, Mogao Cave 17. Dated by the museum to the 9th century, but likely belongs to the 10th century. British Museum. Ch.00401.
15) A portable painting depicting seated bodhisattva, Mogao Cave 17. Dated by the museum to the 9th century, but likely belongs to the 10th century. British Museum. Ch.00377.
16) A portable depicting a maṇḍala of Avalokiteśvara, Mogao Cave 17. Dated by the museum to the 8th century, but likely belongs to the 10th century. British Museum. Ch.xxii.0017.
17) A portable depicting a maṇḍala of Avalokiteśvara, Mogao Cave 17. Dated by the museum to the 8th-9th century, but likely belongs to the 10th century. British Museum. Ch.Iv.0024.
18) A portable painting of Vairocanābhisaṁbodhi and the eight great bodhisattvas (the deities are partially identified by Tibetan inscriptions), Mogao Cave 17. Late 9th or early 10th century. British Museum. Ch.0074. Discussed in section 2.1, Fig. 13.
19) A portable painting of the Amoghapāśa maṇḍala, Mogao Cave 17. 10th century. Musée Guimet. EO.3579. Discussed in section 2.3, Fig. 20.
20) A portable painting of Amoghapāśa maṇḍala, Mogao Cave 17. Dated by the museum to the 8th century, but likely belongs to the 10th century. Musée Guimet. EO.1131. Discussed

in section 2.3, Fig. 21.

21) A portable painting of the ten stages of bodhisattvahood, Mogao Cave 17. 10th century. Musée Guimet. MG. 26465. Discussed in section 2.6, Fig.30.

22) Two wall paintings depicting maṇḍala-like compositions centred around Vairocanābhisaṃbodhi and a buddha, Yulin Cave 38. 10th/11th century. Discussed in section 2.2, Fig. 17.

23) Wall paintings inside a Heavenly King stūpa (天王堂) at Mogao. 10th century. The content was only partially published. Six multi-armed deities, each surrounded by four Offering Goddesses, are painted on the ceiling; eight or more standing bodhisattvas and other deities are painted on the walls. Published in the Dunhuang Research Academy's 2003 The *Complete Collection of Dunhuang Grottoes,* Volume 10, pp. 197-212.

Bibliography

Acri, Andrea. 2016. *Esoteric Buddhism in Mediaeval Maritime Asia: Networks of Masters, Texts, Icons*. Singapore: I. SEAS-Yusof Ishak Institute.

—— 2018. "Maritime Buddhism." In *Oxford Research Encyclopedia of Religion*. Oxford University Press. http://oxfordre.com/religion/view/10.1093/acrefore/9780199340378.001.0001/acrefore-9780199340378-e-638, accessed 14.11.19.

Aiyappan, Ayinapalli and Srinivasan, P.R. 2000. *Story of Buddhism with Special Reference to South India*. Chennai: Commissioner of Museums, Govt. Museum.

Almogi, Orna. 2008. "How Authentic Are Titles and Colophons of Tantric Works in the Tibetan Canon? The Case of Three Works and Thier Authors and Translators." In *Beitrage Zur Zentralasienforschung* 14: 87-124.

Asha Rani, Mathur. 1988. *The Great Traditions: Indian Bronze Masterpieces*. New Delhi: Festival of India.

Auboyer, Jeannine. 1941. *Les Influences et les Réminiscences Étangères au Kondō Du Hōryūji, Dessins de l'Auteur*. Paris: P. Geuthner.

Barber, A. W. 2008. "Two Mahāyāna Developments Along the Krishna River." In *Buddhism in the Krishna River Valley of Andhra*, eds. Sree Padma (Holt) and A.W Barber. Albany: State University of New York Press, 151-167.

Bautze-Picron, Claudine. 1997. "Le groupe des huits grandes bodhisatva en Inde: genèse et développement." In *Living a Life in Accord with the Dhamma: Papers in Honor of Professor Jean Boisselier on his Eightieth Birthday*, ed. Natasha Eilenberg. Bangkok: Silpakorn University, 1-55.

—— 2000. "Nasik: The Late Mahāyāna Caves 2, 15, 20 & 23-24." In *South Asian Archaeology 1997, Proceedings of the Fourteenth International Conference of the European*

Association of South Asian Archaeologists. Rome: Istituto Italiano per l'Africa e l'Oriente, 1201-27.

—— 2008. "Antagonistes et complémentaires, le lion et l'éléphantdans la personnalité du Buddha." In *Penser, dire et représenter l'animal dans le monde indien*, eds. Nalini Balbir and Georges-Jean Pinault, Paris: Librairie Honoré Champion, Éditeur (Bibliothèque de l'École des Hautes Études, Sciences historiques et philologiques, Tome 345), 523-72.

—— 2015. *The Forgotten Place: Stone Images from Kurkihar, Bihar*. New Delhi: Archaeological Survey of India.

Beckwith, Christopher. 1983. "The Revolt of 755 in Tibet." In *Contributions on Tibetan Language, History, and Culture. Proceedings of the Csoma de Karas Symposium held at Velm-Vienna, Austria*, eds. Ernst Steinkener and Helmut Tauscher, Vol. I. Vienna: Arbeitskreis fur Tibetische und Buddhistische Studien Universitat Wien, 1-16.

Boisselier, Jean. 1979. *Ceylon Sri Lanka*. Geneva: Nagel Publishers.

Bopearachchi, Osmund. 2014. "Sri Lanka and the Maritime Trade. Bodhisattva Avalokiteśvara as the Protector of Mariners." In *Asian Encounters exploring connected histories*, eds. Parul Pandya Dhar and Upinder Singh. New Delhi: Oxford University Press, 161-87.

Brauen, Martin. 1997. *The Mandala: Sacred Circle in Tibetan Buddhism*. 1st ed. Boston: Shambhala.

Chandra, Lokesh. 1980. "Oḍḍiyāna: A New Interpretation." In *Tibetan Studies in Honour of Hugh Richardson*. eds. Aris, M. and Aung San Suu Kyi. Warminster and Oxford: Aris and Phillips, 73-78.

Chou, Yi-liang. 1945. "Tantrism in China." *Harvard Journal of Asiatic Studies* 8.3-4: 241-332.

Cleary, Thomas. F. 1993. *The Flower Ornament Scripture*. Boston: Shambhala.

Dalton, Jacob. P. 2011. *The Taming of the Demons: Violence and Liberation in Tibetan Buddhism*. New Haven and London: Yale University Press.

—— 2017. "On the Significance of the Arya-Tattvasamgraha-Sadhanopayika and Its Commentary." In *Chinese and Tibetan Esoteric Buddhism*. eds. Yael Bentor and Meir Shahar, Leiden: Brill, 321-337.

Dalton, Jacob.P. and van Schaik, Sam. 2006. *Tibetan Tantric Manuscripts from Dunhuang: A Descriptive Catalogue of the Stein Collection at the British Library*. Leiden and Boston: Brill.

Dayalan, Duraiswamy. *Art, Architecture and Cultural Link Between Maharastra and South India (Andhra Pradesh & Tamil Nadu)*. https://www.academia.edu/25250507/ART_ARCHITECTURE_AND_CULTURAL_LINK_BETWEEN_MAHARASHTRA_AND_SOUTH_INDIA_ANDHRA_PRADESH_and_TAMIL_NADU.

Davidson, Ronald M. 2002. *Indian Esoteric Buddhism: A Social History of the Tantric Movement*. New York: Columbia University Press.

—— 2005. *Tibetan Renaissance: Tantric Buddhism in the Rebirth of Tibetan Culture*. New

York: Columbia University Press.

de Visser, Marinus Willem. 1915. *The Bodhisttva Ti-tsang (Jizō) in China and Japan*, Berlin: Oesterheld & Co. Verlag (Erste Sonderveröffentlichung der Ostasiatischen Zeitschrift).

Debreczeny, Karl. 2011. "Wutai Shan: Pilgrimage to Five-Peak Mountain." In *Journal of the International Association of Tibetan Studies*, no. 6: 1-133.

—— 2019. "Faith and Empire: An Overview." In *Faith and Empire: Art and Politics in Tibetan Buddhism*, ed. Karl Debreczeny. New York: Rubin Museum of Art, 17-53.

Dessein, Bart. 2003. "The Glow of the of the Vow of the Teacher Samantabhadra 'Puxian Pusa Xingyuan Zan' (T.297) Samantabhadracaryapranidhanaraja." *Acta Orientalia Academiae Scientiarum Hungaricae* 56 (2/4): 317-38.

Dohanian, Diran K. 1977. *The Mahāyāna Buddhist Sculpture of Ceylon*. New York: Garland House.

—— 1983. "Sinhalese Sculptures in the Pallava Style." *Archives of Asian art* 36: 6-21.

Dunhuang Academy ed. 敦煌研究院编 2003. *Dunhuang shiku quanji* 敦煌石窟全集 / *The Complete Collection of Dunhuang Grottoes*, vol. 10. Hong Kong: The Commercial Press 香港：商务印书馆.

—— 2013. *Zhongguo shiku: Dunhuang Mogaoku 4* 中国石窟·敦煌莫高窟 4/ *Chinese Grottoes: Dunhuang Mogao Grottoes*. Beijing: Cultural Relics Publisher 北京：文物出版社.

—— 2014. *Yulin Ku* 榆林窟 / *The Yulin Grottoes*. Nanjing: Jiangsu Arts Publisher 南京：江苏美术出版社.

Fontein, Jan. 1968. *The Pilgrimage of Sudhana. A Study of Gaṇḍavyūha Illustrations in China. Japan and Java.* The Hague: Mouton.

—— 2012. *Entering the Dharmadhātu, A Study of the Gandavyūha Reliefs of Borobudur*, Leiden/Boston: Brill (Studies in Asian art and archaeology, vol. 26).

Fraser, Sarah E. 2004. *Performing the Visual: The Practice of Buddhist Wall Painting in China and Central Asia, 618-960.* Stanford, CA: Stanford University Press.

Gentry, James. 2019. "An Inquiry into Source-Text Multilingualism in Tibetan Scriptural Translations." abstract of a talk delivered at the 15th Seminar of the International Association for Tibetan Studies in Paris, July 2019. [https://www.academia.edu/39792552/An_Inquiry_into_Source- Text_Multilingualism_in_Tibetan_Scriptural_Translations.]

Giebel, Rolf W. 1995. "The Chin-kang-ting ching yü-ch'ieh shih-pa-hui chih-kuei: An Annotated Translation." In *Journal of Naritasan Institute for Buddhist Studies* 18: 107-201.

—— 2001. *Two Esoteric Sutras: The Adamantine Pinnacle Sutra, the Susiddhikara Sutra.* Berkeley, Calif: Numata Center for Buddhist Translation and Research.

Giès, Jacques. ed. 1994-96. *Les Arts de l'Asie Centrale*. 2 vols. London: Serindia.

Goble, Geoffrey. 2012. "Chinese Esoteric Buddhism: Amoghavajra and the Ruling Elite." PhD

thesis. Indiana University.
—— 2013. "The Legendary Siege of Anxi: Myth, History, and Truth in Chinese Buddhism." *Pacific World: Journal of the Institute of Buddhist Studies* 3 (15): 1-32.
Govinda, Li Gotami. 1979. *Tibet in Pictures: Text and Photos*. Berkeley, CA: Dharma Pub.
Granoff, Phyllis. 1968/69. "A Portable Buddhist Shrine from Central Asia." In *Archives of Asian Art* 22: 80-95.
Guy, John. 1994. "The Lost Temples of Nagapattinam and Quanzhou: A Study in Sino-Indian Relations." In *Silk Road Art and Archeology* 3: 291-310.
—— 1995. "The Avalokitesvara of Yunnan and Some South East Asian Connections." In *South East Asia and China: Art, Commerce and Interaction, Percival David Foundation Colloquies on Art and Archeology of Asia*, eds. Rosemary Scott and John Guy. London: University of London, 64-83.
—— 2014. "Introducing Early Southeast Asia." In *Lost Kingdoms: Hindu-Buddhist Sculpture of Early Southeast Asia.* ed. John Guy. New York: Metropolitan Museum of Art.
Heller, Amy. 1994. "Ninth Century Buddhist Images Carved at Ldan Ma Brag to Commemorate Tibeto-Chinese Negotiations." *Tibetan Studies: Proceedings of the 6th Seminar of the International Association for Tibetan Studies, Fagernes, 1992.* Oslo: Institute for Comparative Research in Human Culture, 335-49.
—— 1997. "P.T. 7A , P.T. 108 , P.T. 240 and Beijing Bstan 'gyur 3489: Ancient Tibetan Rituals Dedicated to Vairocana." In *The Pandita and the Siddha: Tibetan Studies in Honor of E. Gene Smith,* ed. Gene Smith. Dharamsala: Amnye Machen Institute, 85-91.
—— 2002. "The Paintings of Gra thang: History and Iconography of an 11th century Tibetan Temple." In *Tibet Journal* 27(1/2): 39-72.
Horlemann, Bianca. 2012. "Buddhist Sites in Amdo and former Longyou from the 8th to the 13th Century." In *Old Tibetan Studies Dedicated to the Memory of Ronald E. Emmerick,* PIATS Oxford 2003. ed. Cristina Scherrer-Schaub. Leiden: Brill, 119-157.
Huntington, John C. 1981. "Cave Six at Aurangabad: A Tantrayana Monument?" In *Kalādarśana: American Studies in the Art of India*, ed. J.G. Williams. Leiden: E.J. Brill, 47-55.
Huo Wei 霍巍 . 2017. "Qinghai Yushu Darirulai fotang de kaogu diaocha yu xinfaxian" 青海玉树大日如来佛堂的考古调查与新发现 [Archaeological Investigation on Parinirvana in Yushu of Qinghai and New Findings]. *Qinghai Minzu Yanjiu* 青海民族研究 */Qinghai Ethnic Research* 28 (1): 4-9.
—— 2018. "Zangdong Tubo moya zaoxiang yu Tangbo jiaoliu shiye xia de Jiannan Yizhou" 藏东吐蕃摩崖造像与唐蕃交流视野下的剑南益州 [Rock Reliefs in East Tibet and Yizhou in the Context of Cultural Exchanges between Tang and Tubo]. *Zangxue xuekan* 藏学学刊 */Journal of Tibetology* 16: 301-313.
Indrapala, Karthigesu. 2005. *The Evolution of an Ethnic Identity The Tamils in Sri Lanka c.300*

BCE to c.1200 CE. Sydney: MV Publications for the South Asian Study Centre.

Kapstein, Matthew T. 2000. *The Tibetan Assimilation of Buddhism: Conversion, Contestation, and Memory.* Oxford University Press.

—— 2004. "The Treaty Temple of De-Ga G.Yu-Tshal: Identification and Iconography." In *Xizang Kaogu Yu Yishu* 西藏考古与艺术 / *Tibetan Arachaeology and Art*. ed. Huo Wei and Y. Li. 霍巍，李永宪编 Chengdu: Sichuan renmin chubanshe 成都：四川人民出版社，98-127.

—— 2009. "The Treaty Temple of the Turquoise Grove." In *Buddhism Between Tibet and China*, ed. Matthew T. Kapstein. Boston: Wisdom Publications, 21-72.

—— 2014. "The Treaty Temple of De ga g.yu tshal: Reconsiderations." *Zangxue xuekan* 藏学学刊 /*Journal of Tibetology* 10: 32-34.

Karmay, Heather. 1975. *Early Sino-Tibetan Art*. Warminster: Aris and Philips lts.

Karmay, Samten Gyaltsen. 2007. *The Great Perfection (rDzogs chen) A Philosophical and Meditative Teaching of Tibetan Buddhism*. Leiden and Boston: Brill.

Khokhlov, Yury. (forthcoming). The abstract: https://www.academia.edu/36748689/From_India_to_the_Doorstep_of_China_Indian_Pala_Style_in_the_Hexi_Corridor, accessed 14.11.19.

Klimburg-Salter, Deborah E. and Christian Luczanits. 1998. *Tabo: A Lamp for the Kingdom: Early Indo-Tibetan Buddhist Art in the Western Himalaya*. New York: Thames and Hudson.

Lee, Sonya S. 2010. *Surviving Nirvana: Death of the Buddha in Chinese Visual Culture*. Hong Kong University Press.

Li, Channa. 2016. "Translationship Lost in Transmission: Elusive Attributions of Two Tibetan Sūtra Translations." *Revue d'Etudes Tibétaines* 37: 207-30.

Lin Li-Kuang. 1935. "Puṇyodaya (Na-t'i), un propagateur du tantrisme en Chine et au Cambodge à l'époque de Hiuan-tsang." *Journal Asiatique* 227: 83-100.

Lin Wei-Cheng. 2014. *Building a Sacred Mountain: The Buddhist Architecture of China's Mount Wutai*. Seattle: University of Washington Press.

Linrothe, Robert N. 2014. "What They Saw: Kaśmīrā in the Eyes of Western Himalayas." In *Collecting Paradise: Buddhist Art of Kashmir and its Legacies*, exh. cat. New York: Rubin Museum of Art, 29-107.

Liu Yongzeng 刘永增. 2008. "Mogaoku di148ku nanbeikan tianjing tuxiang jieshuo" 莫高窟第148窟南北龛天井图像解说 [Explanation of the Ceiling Images in the Southern and Northern Alcoves of Mogao Cave 148]. In *Dunhuang bihua yishu jicheng yu chuangxin guoji xueshu yantaohui lunwenji* 敦煌壁画艺术继承与创新国际学术研讨会论文集 / *The Inheritance and Innovation of Dunhuang Wall Art: Proceedings of the International Conference*. ed. Duhuang Academy 敦煌研究院编. Shanghai cishu chubanshe 上海辞书出版社. 518-536.

Lo Bue, Erberto. 2000. *Tibet. Templi scomparsi fotografati da Fosco Maraini*, Torino: Ananke.

Long, Mark. 2009. *Caṇḍi Mendut, Womb of the Tathāgata, written, compüiled, translated and illustrated*, New Delhi: Aditya Prakashan..

Malandra, Gery Hockfield. 1993. *Unfolding a Mandala: The Buddhist Cave Temples at Ellora.* Suny Series in Buddhist Studies. Albany, N.Y.: State University of New York Press.

—— 1996. "The Mandala at Ellora/Ellora in the Mandala." *Journal of the International Association of Buddhist Studies* 19: 181-207.

McCoy, Michelle. 2016. "Maṇḍala of Avalokiteśvara of the Unfailing Lasso (Amoghapāśa)." In *Cave Temples of Dunhuang: Buddhist Art of China's Silk Road.* eds. Neville Agnew, Marcia Reed and Tevvy Ball. Los Angeles: J. Paul Getty Trust, 236-39.

McNair, Amy. 2007. *Donors of Longmen: Faith, Politics, and Patronage in Medieval Chinese Buddhist Sculpture.* Honolulu: University of Hawai'i Press.

Misra, R.N. 1981. *Yaksha Cult and Iconography.* New Delhi: Munshiram Manoharlal.

Nagasava, Jake. 2017. https://treasuryoflives.org/biographies/view/Buddhaguhya/10546, accessed on 01.10.2019.

Okada, Ken. 2004. "Observations on Buddhist Stone Sculptures from the Longxing Monastery." In *New Perspectives on China's Past: Chinese Archaeology in the Twentieth Century.* ed. Xiaoneng Yang. New Haven, CT: Yale University Press, 381-91.

Orzech, Charles D. 1995. "The Legend of the Iron Stūpa." In *Buddhism in Practice*, ed. Donald S. Lopez, Jr. NJ: Princeton University Press, 314-17.

—— 1996. "Maṇḍalas on the Move: Reflections from Chinese Esoteric Buddhism Circa 800." *Journal of the International Association of Buddhist Studies* 19: 209-45.

—— 1998. *Politics and Transcendent Wisdom The scripture for Humane Kings in the Creation of Chinese Buddhism.* University Park: The Pensilvania State University Press.

Orzech, Charles D., Sørensen, Henrik H. and Payne, Richard K. eds. 2011. *Esoteric Buddhism and the Tantras in East Asia.* Leiden and Boston: Brill.

Osto, Douglas. 2004. *The Gaṇḍavyūha-sūtra: a study of wealth, gender and power in an Indian Buddhist narrative.* Ph.D. dissertation, School of Oriental and African Studies, University of London.

—— 2010. "A New Translation of the Sanskrit Bhadracari with Introduction and Notes." *New Zealand Journal of Asian Studies* 12 (2): 1-21.

Owen, Lisa N. 2010. "Demarcating Sacred Space: The Jina Images at Kalugumalai." In *International Journal of Jaina Studies* 6 (4): 1-28.

—— 2012. *Carving Devotion in the Jain Caves at Ellora.* Leiden: Brill.

Padma, Sree and A.W Barber. 2008. *Buddhism in the Krishna River Valley of Andhra.* Albany: State University of New York Press.

Rao, Gopinatha T.A. 1915. "Bauddha Vestiges in Kanchipura." *Indian Antiquary* 44: 127-29.

Reis Habito, Maria. 1999. "The Amoghapasa Kalparaja Sutra: A Historical and Analytical

Study." *Studies in Central and East Asian Religions* 11: 39-67.

Revire, Nicolas. 2012. "New Perspectives on the Origin and Spread of Bhadrāsana Buddhas throughout Southeast Asia (7th-8th centuries)." In *Connecting Empires and States. Selected Papers from the 13th Conference of the European Association of Southeast Asian Archaeologists*, Vol. 2, eds. Mai Lin Tjoa-Bonatz, Andreas Reinecke and Dominik Bonatz. Singapore: NUS Press, 127-143.

Rhie, Marilyn M. 1988. *Interrelationships between the Buddhist Art of China and the Art of India and Central Asia from 618-755 A.D.* Napoli: Istituto universitario orientale.

Sanderson, Alexis. 2007. "The Śaiva Exegesis of Kashmir." In *Mélanges tantriques à la* mémoire d'Hélène *Brunner, Tantric Studies in Memory of Hélène Brunner*, eds. Dominic Goodall and Andre Padoux. Collection Indologie 106, EFEO, Institut français de Pondichéry (IFP), 231-442.

Schmid, Neil. 2006. "The Material Culture of Exegesis and Liturgy and a Change in the Artistic Representations in Dunhuang Caves, Ca.700-1000." *Asia Major*, 3d series, Vol.19, No 1/2, China at the Crossroads: a Festschrift in Honor of Victor H. Mair, 171-210.

—— 2011. "Dunhuang and Central Asia." In *Esoteric Buddhism and the Tantras in East Asia*, ed. Charles Orzech, Henrik Sørensen and Richard Payne, Leiden and Boston: Brill, 365-374.

Sen, Tansen. 2016. *Buddhism, Diplomacy, and Trade: The Realignment of India-China Relations, 600-1400*. Lanham: Rowman & Littlefield.

Skilling, Peter. 2011. "Buddhism and the Circulation of Ritual in Early Peninsular Southeast Asia." In *Early Interactions between South and Southeast Asia: Reflections on Cross-cultural Exchange*, eds. Pierre-Yves Manguin, A. Mani, Geoff Wade. Singapore: Institute of Southeast Asian Studies. New Delhi: Manohar, 371-384.

Sha Wutian 沙武田 2013. *Tubo tongzhi shiqi Dunhuang shiku yanjiu* 吐蕃统治时期敦煌石窟研究 / *Studies on Dunhuang Grottoes during the Tubo Period*. Beijing: Zhongguo shehui kexue chubanshe 北京：中国社会科学出版社.

——2016. *Yulinku di 25ku* 榆林窟第25窟 / *The Yulin Cave 25*. Beijing: The Commercial Press 北京：商务印书馆.

Shanxi Province Academy of Archaeology and TAR Relics Preservation Institute 陕西省考古研究院，西藏自治区文物保护研究所 2014. "Xizang Chayaxian Danmazha moya zaoxiang kaogu diaocha jianbao" 西藏察雅县丹玛札摩崖造像考古调查简报 [Archaeological Report on Brag gYab County lDan Ma Brag Cliff Carvings]. *Kaogu yu wenwu* 考古与文物 /*Archaeology and Relics* 6: 7-14, 52-3.

Sharf, Robert. 2017. "Buddhist Veda and the Rise of Chan." In *Chinese and Tibetan Esoteric Buddhism*. eds. Yael Bentor and Meir Shahar. Leiden and Boston: Brill, 85-120.

Sharrock, Peter D. and Emma C. Bunker. 2016. "Seeds of Vajrabodhi: Buddhist Ritual Bronzes from Java and Khorat." In *Esoteric Buddhism in Mediaeval Maritime Asia: Networks of*

Masters, Texts, Icons. Singapore: I. SEAS-Yusof Ishak Institute, 237-252.

Shen, Hsueh-man. 2019. *Authentic Replicas: Buddhist Art in Medieval China*. Honolulu: University of Hawai'i Press.

Shim, Yeoung Shin. 2013. "Four Heavenly Kings: Iconography and Symbolism seen Through Literary Evidence and Imagery." Unpublished PhD thesis. The University of Pennsilvania.

Snellgrove, David L. 1978. *The Image of the Buddha*. London: Serindia Publications: UNESCO.

—— 1987. *Indo-Tibetan Buddhism Indian Buddhists and their Tibetan Successors*. London: Serindia Publications.

Soper, Alexander C. 1960. "South Chinese Influence on the Buddhist Art of the Six Dynasties Period." *Bulletin of the Museum of Far Eastern Antiquities* 32: 47-112.

Sørensen, Henrik H. 2000. "Perspectives on Buddhism in Dunhuang during the Tang and Five Dynasties Period." In *The Silk Roads: Highways of Culture and Commerce*, ed. Vadime Elisseeff. New York and Oxford: Berghahn Books, 27-48.

—— 2011. "Central Divinities in Esoteric Buddhist Pantheon in China." In *Esoteric Buddhism and the Tantras in East Asia*, ed. Charles Orzech, Henrik Sørensen and Richard Payne. Leiden and Boston: Brill, 90-132.

Sørensen, Per. 1994. *The Mirror Illuminating the Royal Genealogies: Tibetan Buddhist Historiography: an Annotated Translation of the XIVth century Tibetan Chronicle: rGyal-rabs gsal-ba'i me-long*. Weisbaden: Harrassowitz.

Srinivasan, Sharada. 1999. "Lead Isotope and Trace Element Analysis in the Study of over One Hundred South Indian Metal Icons." *Archaeometry* 41: 91-116.

Stoddard, Heather. 2018. "Drathang Monastery." In *Murals of Tibet*, eds. Thomas Liard, Robert Thurman, Heather Stoddard, Cameron Bailey, Jakob Winkler. Milan, New York, Berlin, London: Taschen, 96-105.

Sundberg, Jeffrey R. and Rolf Giebel. 2011. "The Life of the Tang Court Monk Vajrabodhi as Chronicled by Lü Xiang (吕向) : South Indian and Śrī Laṅkān Antecedents to the Arrival of the Buddhist Vajrayāna in Eighth-Century Java and China." *Pacific World: Journal of the Institute of Buddhist Studies* 13 (3): 129-222.

Takata, Tokio. 2019. "Tibetan Dominion over Dunhuang and the Formation of a Tibeto-Chinese Community." In *Buddhist Road Paper 6.1. Special Issue: Central Asian Networks. Rethinking the Interplay of Religions, Art and Politics Across the Tarim Basin (5th-10th c.)*, ed. E. Forte, 85-106.

Tanaka, Kimiaki. 2000. *Tonkō: Mikkyō to bijutsu* 敦煌：密教と美术 . Kyoto: Hōzōkan.

—— 2018. *An Illustrated History of the Maṇḍala : From Its Genesis to the Kālacakratantra*. Boston: Wisdom Publications. Google books. https://play.google.com/store/books/details/An_Illustrated_History_of_the_Mandala_From_Its_Gen?id=l8VWDwAAQBAJ&hl=en_US

Thapar, Romila. 2003. *Early India: From the Origins to AD 1300*. Berkeley, CA: University of California Press.

Toyka-Fuong, Ursula. 1998. "The Influence of Pala Art on 11th-Century Wall-Painting of Grotto 76 in Dunhuang." In *The Inner Asian International Style 12th-14th Centuries*, eds. Deborah Klimburg-Salter and Eva Allinger. Vienna: Verlag der Osterreichischen Akademie der Wissenschaften, 67-96.

van der Kuijp, Leonard W.J. 1992. "Notes Apropos of the transmission of the Sarvadurgatipariśodhanatantra in Tibet." *Studien zur Indologie und Iraninistik (StII)* 16: 109-125.

van Schaik, Sam. 2015. *Tibetan Zen: Discovering a Lost Tradition*. Boston and London: Snow Lion.

van Schaik, Sam. and Lewis Doney. 2007. "The Prayer, the Priest, and the Tsenpo: An Early Buddhist Narrative from Dunhuang." *Journal of International Association of Buddhist Studies* 30 (1-2): 175-217.

van Schaik, S. and Imre Galambos. 2012. *Manuscripts and Travellers: The Sino-Tibetan Documents of a Tenth-Century Buddhist Pilgrim*. Berlin: De Gruyter.

Verardi, Giovanni. 2018. *The Gods and the Heretics, Crisis and Ruin of Indian Buddhism*, New Delhi/Buenos Aires: Aditya Prakashan & Fundación Bodhiyāna.

Vitali, Roberto. 1990. *Early Temples of Central Tibet*. London: Serindia Publications.

von der Schulenburg, Stephan., Elke Hessel, Karsten Schmidt, Matthias Wagner eds. 2015. *Buddha: 108 Begegnungen/Encounters*. Koln: Wienand Verlag.

von Schroeder, Ulrich. 1990. *Buddhist Sculptures of Sri Lanka*. Hong Kong: Visual Dharma Publications

—— 2001. *Buddhist Sculptures in Tibet*. Hong Kong: Visual Dharma Publications.

Wade, Geoff. 2014. "Beyond the Southern Borders: Southeast Asia in Chinese Texts to the Ninth Century." In *Lost Kingdoms: Hindu-Buddhist Sculpture of Early Southeast Asia*, ed. John Guy. New York: Metropolitan Museum of Art.

Wang, Eugene Y. 2005. *Shaping the Lotus Sutra Buddhist Visual Culture in Medieval China*. Seattle and London: University of Washington Press.

Wang, Michelle C. 2018. *Maṇḍalas in the Making: The Visual Culture of Esoteric Buddhism at Dunhuang*. Leiden: Brill.

Wangdu, Pasang and Hildegard Diemberger. 2000. *dBa' bzhed: The Royal Narrative Concerning the Bringing of the Buddha's Doctrine to Tibet*. Wien: Verlag der Österreichischen Akademie der Wissenschaften.

Wayman, Alex and Ryujun Tajima 1998. *The Enlightenment of Vairocana*. Delhi: Motilal Banarsidass Publishers.

Weinberger, Steven N. 2003. *The Significance of Yoga Tantra and the Compendium of Principles (Tattvasaṃgraha Tantra) within Tantric Buddhism in India and Tibet*. Ph.D.

dissertation, University of Virginia.
—— 2010. "The Yoga Tantras and the Social Context of Their Transmission to Tibet." *Chung-Hwa Buddhist Journal* 23: 131-66.
Wessels-Mevissen, Corinna. 2001. *The Gods of the Directions in Ancient India: Origin and Early Development in Art and Literature (Until c. 1000 A.D.)*. Monographien zur indischen Archäologie, Kunst und Philologie, Band 14. Berlin: Dietrich Reimer Verlag.
Whitfield, Roderik. 1982-86. *Art of Central Asia: The Stein Collection in the British Museum.* 3 vols. Tokyo: Kodansha International, in cooperation with the Trustees of the British Museum.
Wong, Dorothy C. 1993. "A Reassessment of the Representation of Mt Wutai from Dunhuang Cave 61." *Archives of Asian Art*, 27-52.
—— 2007a. "The Case of Amoghapasa." *Journal of Inner Asian Art and Archeology* 2: 151-58.
—— 2007b. "The Huayan/Kegon/Hwaŏm Paintings in East Asia." In *Reflecting Mirrors: Perspectives on Huayan Buddhism*, ed. by Imre Hamar. Wiesbaden: Harrassowitz.
—— 2012. "The Art of AvataṁsakaBuddhism at the Courts of Empress Wu and Emperor Shomu/Empress Komyo." in *Avataṁsaka Buddhism in East Asia: Huayan, Kegon, Flower Ornament Buddhism: Origins and Adaptation of a Visual Culture*, eds. Imre Hamar and Robert M. Gimello. Wiesbaden: Harrassowitz Verlag, 223-260.
—— 2018. *Buddhist Pilgrim-Monks as Agents of Cultural and Artistic Transmission: The International Buddhist Art Style in East Asia, ca. 645-770*. Singapore: NUS Press.
Wong, Dorothy C. and Eric M. Field. 2008. *Hōryūji Reconsidered.* Newcastle: Cambridge Scholars.
Yang Qingfan, Lu Suwen and Zhang Yanqing 杨清凡，卢素文，张延清. 2017. "Xizang Mangkang Gatuozhen xinfaxian Tubo moya shike diaocha jianbao" 西藏芒康嘎托镇新发现吐蕃摩崖石刻调查简报 [Archaeological Report on the Newly Discovered Tubo Dynasty Rock Sculptures in the Town of Sgar thog in Smar khams County, Tibet]. *Zangxue xuekan* 藏学学刊 */Journal of Tibetology* 16: 233-251.
Yang Zeng. 2018. *"A Biographical Study on Bukong 不空 (aka. Amoghavajra, 705-774): Networks, Institutions, and Identities."* Unpublished Ph.D thesis. The University of British Columbia.
Zhang Wenbin ed. 张文彬编 2000. *Dunhuang: Jinian Dunhuang cangjingdong faxian yibai zhounian* 敦煌：纪念敦煌藏经洞发现一百周年 / *Dunhuang: A Centennial Commemoration of the Discovery of the Cave Library*. Beijing: Chaohua Chubanshe 北京：朝华出版社.

◆ Author: Yury Khokhlov, Independent researcher, the United Kingdom.

关于藏文蓝黑纸（མཐིང་ཤོག）写经的初步考察：以文献为中心 *

朱丽双

内容摘要：蓝黑纸（མཐིང་ཤོག）是藏族文化中一种特制的纸张。蓝黑纸的制作主要分三个步骤，首先将数层纸粘合在一起，然后在纸张表面涂一层特制的墨汁、颜料或染液，最后研磨打光。蓝黑纸主要用于书写佛经，其中最珍贵且常用的是用金汁或金银汁隔行书写。蓝黑纸包括汉地所谓的瓷（磁）青纸，但二者不能等同。

མཐིང་ཤོག 是一种特制的纸张。《藏汉大辞典》藏语释作 ཤོག་བུ་སྔོན་པོ，汉语释作"黑色书写纸。可用金银末浆写经书的蓝黑色厚纸"。[1] 耶什克《藏英字典》于 ཤོག་བུ 词条下列出 མཐིང་ཤོག 和 ནག་ཤོག，释意作书写金字和银字的深蓝色或黑色纸张[2]。མཐིང་ཤོག 这个词中

* 本文为国家社科基金项目"吐蕃统治时期的于阗研究"（18BZS123）的阶段性成果。在研究资料收集方面，笔者得到好友杨鸿蛟博士、沈琛博士、罗帅博士和周文欣博士的诸多帮助，谨此深致谢意！

1 张怡荪主编：《藏汉大辞典》，北京：民族出版社，1993：1209。

2 Heinrich A. Jäschke, *A Tibetan English Dictionary with Special Reference to the Prevailing Dialects*, first published in 1881 by Routledge & Kegan Paul Ltd; repr. London: Routledge, 1990: 563.

的 ཤོག 意为纸，མཐིང 似指一种蓝色或深色染料。或认为此处 མཐིང 意为深黑色[3]，但据藏文文法，形容词当置于名词之后，若按此理解，则应作 ཤོག་མཐིང。对于 མཐིང་ཤོག，英译常作 blue paper、black paper、dark blue paper、blue-black paper[4]；汉译一般作“蓝纸”“碧纸”；也有学者译作瓷青纸，不过实际瓷青纸或磁青纸（瓷、磁相通）恐怕只是 མཐིང་ཤོག 的一种。本文将采用《藏汉大辞典》的解释，暂译作“蓝黑纸”。不过这个译法仍是权宜之计，因为 མཐིང་ཤོག 这种纸张的颜色并不固定，或深蓝，或纯蓝，或黑色，或同时具黑色和蓝色。

一、蓝黑纸（མཐིང་ཤོག）的制作

从文献记载看，蓝黑纸的制作材料和方法非常多样，有些方法会用到动物脑浆（གླད་པ）、牦牛皮胶（སྤྱིན）、煤烟（སྲི་ནག）或者由熬开的油（སྣུམ）或油松（སྒྲོན་མེ་ཤིང）制作的油烟，当然还有纸（ཤོག་བུ）。纸必须强劲坚韧，能经受湿润的颜料多次上色及随后对其表面进行研磨打光[5]。另外的方法会用到藏青果（ཨ་རུ་ར）、泽漆（ཟར་ནུ）、黑矾（ནག་མཚུར）、硼砂（ཚ་ལ）。还有的用靛蓝（རམས）。另有称蓝黑纸写经的前面数页往往由许多层纸粘贴在一起，并由一根小小的皮钉（ཀྲུན་བུ）合在一起，使之变厚，便于凸显文字和描绘图像，从而达到装饰性美学效果[6]。

汉堡大学纸张专家 Helman-Ważny 博士概述了制作蓝黑纸的四种方法。她所说的第一种方法是把面粉浆糊煮开，洒在纸上，等纸晾干，用布把它擦干净，然后在干纸上加一层湿纸。如此数次，直到纸张达到合适厚度。接着在墨槽上用手混合油松制成的黑墨，加入煮开的牦牛脑和羊脑，混合并再次煮开。在这个混合液中加入融化的豆粉纤维，等它变得温凉，即可涂到已经粘合好的纸张表面。然后把涂好墨汁的纸张放在光滑的桦树

3 James Canary, “*Thingshog (mthing shog)*: Luxury Illuminated Manuscripts on Blue-black Paper,” in Hildegard Diemberger, Mark Elliot, Michela Clemente eds, *Buddha's Word: The Life of Books in Tibet and Beyond*, Cambridge: Museum of Archaeology and Anthropology, University of Cambridge, 2014: 109.

4 参见如 Agnieszka Helman-Ważny, *The Archaeology of Tibetan Books*, Leiden: Brill, 2014: 42; James Canary 2014: 109-110; Dorji Wangchuk, “Sacred Words, Precious Materials: On Tibetan Deluxe Editions of Buddhist Scriptures and Treatises,” in Orna Almogi ed., *Tibetan Manuscript and Xylograph Traditions: The Written Word and Its Media within the Tibetan Culture Sphere*, Hamburg: Department of Indian and Tibetan Studies, Universität Hamburg, 2016: 402.

5 James Canary 2014: 109-110.

6 James Canary 2014: 109-110.

木板表面，用猫睛石（གཟི）研磨打光。一次研磨后，再次涂上墨汁，并再研磨打光[7]。看来，这种方法所用的原料主要是油松制成的黑墨和牦牛脑与羊脑脑浆，以这种方法制作出来的纸张应是黑色的，似即下文所谓墨纸（སྣག་ཤོག）。这种纸可能与明代的羊脑笺比较接近。

第二种方法制造出来的蓝黑纸是蓝色的，主要原料为黑矾、泽漆、硼砂和藏青果，其蓝色染液的制作方法如下：先让黑矾溶液沉淀，等到上清液完全与沉淀物分开。然后泡好泽漆，加入硼砂，用布过滤；加入发酵的麦酒（ཐྲོ་ཆང）；煮开。再加入少许黑矾、较多的麦酒和泽漆。注意保持这三种物质的比例。然后在白纸上试验这个混合液是否合适：如果白纸变暗，说明这个混合液成功了。接着让它冷却到温凉，即可涂到传统的质量上乘的藏纸上面，让它晾干。下一步是煮开藏青果浆，用布过滤，然后涂到纸张上面，直到出现想要的蓝色[8]。

第三种方法被认为是汉地的作法。其蓝色溶液是用西藏的麦酒、豆蔻粉（ཛ་ཏི）和焚烧出来的白色海贝（འགྲོན་བུ）粉制作而成。用这种方法准备的纸张先令其晾干，然后折起来，撒上藏青果汁。

第四种方法是用靛蓝染色[9]。用这种方法制作出来的纸张，笔者推测应即汉地所谓的瓷青纸了。

剑桥大学的Canary博士亦描述了制作蓝黑纸的一种方法：首先调制墨汁，即用手掌将牦牛、绵羊或山羊的脑浆和经过仔细研磨的黑色煤烟粉末及一小部分熬过的皮胶捏合在一起。注意动物脑浆不可过多，否则会使纸张太油而难以书写，而且以后可能在纸张表面产生皂化问题。其次是将制好的墨汁涂到纸张表面，让其晾干。最后用一块光滑的海贝或多数情况下用猫睛石研磨，直到表面变得光滑漂亮，便于书写[10]。这种方法基本接近于上述Helman-Ważny博士所述的第一种方法，但在加工细节上有所区别。

汉堡大学的多杰旺秋（Dorji Wangchuk）教授提到了有关蓝黑纸制作的五种藏文文

7 Agnieszka Helman-Ważny 2014: 42.

8 Agnieszka Helman-Ważny 2014: 42.

9 Agnieszka Helman-Ważny 2014: 42-43,

10 James Canary 2014: 109.

献，其中包括现代藏族学者撰写的有关文章[11]。笔者阅读这些文献后，发现蓝黑纸的制作还有其他工艺，比如一份 13 世纪的医学文献是这样描述的：

> 敲碎藏青果，放入水中煮，直至汁液变成黄色，令纸浸泡其中，晾干；再泡入土矾和酒的混合液中，让其晾干，即为 མཐིང་ཤོག。[12]

再如 17 世纪一位竹巴噶举派（འབྲུག་པ་བཀའ་བརྒྱུད）上师德乌玛 · 丹增彭措（དེའུ་དམར་བསྟན་འཛིན་ཕུན་ཚོགས། 1672-?）所述黑纸（ཤོག་ནག）和墨纸（སྣག་ཤོག）的制作工艺与前述虽不完全相同，但又有些相似。其述墨纸的制作方法如下：

> 若制墨纸，将少量 (?) 墨胶（སྣག་སྦྱིན）和适宜牲畜的脑浆一起煮，丢弃血水；若使腐烂，需要无垢之金银；脑浆需要柔滑，具有光泽；将脑胶（ཀླད་སྦྱིན）涂抹到研磨良好的、དམ་སྦྱར་བ（?）的墨汁中，使厚薄均匀，研磨时用猫睛石（གཞི）和青白亚玛瑙（མཆོང）；只在用墨汁抄写时才涂抹。[13]

此方法与 Helman-Ważny 博士所述的第一种方法及 Canary 博士描述的方法相当接近，但细节仍有差别。甚至这里对用这种方法制作出来的纸张亦不叫蓝黑纸（མཐིང་ཤོག），而作墨纸（སྣག་ཤོག）。看来，蓝黑纸的制作工艺十分多样，且用不同工艺制作出来的纸张可能还有专称。综合起来看，蓝黑纸的制作似可分三个步骤，首先用面粉浆糊将数层纸粘合在一起；然后在纸张表面涂一层特制的墨汁、颜料或染液；最后研磨打光。

Canary 博士称，有些 མཐིང་ཤོག 的表面全部为黑色，并研磨得如同漆过；另外一些只

---

11 Dorji Wangchuk 2016: 403. 分别是 1) བྲང་ཏི་དཔལ་ལྡན་རྒྱལ་མཚན། མན་ངག་གསེར་བྲེ་མ་དང་དངུལ་བྲེ་མ། པེ་ཅིན་། མི་རིགས་དཔེ་སྐྲུན་ཁང་། BDRC: W17713, 2004: 143. 2) བཀྲ་ཤིས་དོན་གྲུབ། ཤིང་ཤོག་བཟོ་བའི་གོ་རིམ་རགས་བསྡུས། 载 སྤྱང་རྒྱན་མེ་ཏོག་རྩོམ་སྒྲིག་ཁང་། བོད་ཀྱི་དམངས་སྲོལ་གཅེས་བཏུས། པེ་ཅིན། མི་རིགས་དཔེ་སྐྲུན་ཁང་། BDRC: W21679, 1999: 119-120. 3) དཀོན་མཆོག་བསྟན་འཛིན། འཕྲིན་ལས་རྒྱལ་མཚན་དང་པདྨ་གཡུ་སྒྲོན། བོད་ཀྱི་ལག་ཤེས་ཀུན་འདུས་ཆེན་མོ། པེ་ཅིན་། ཀྲུང་གོའི་བོད་རིག་པ་དཔེ་སྐྲུན་ཁང་། 2010: 245-246. 4) སློབ་དཔོན་པདྨ་དང་བློ་སྦྱང་སོགས། བཟོ་རིག་གི་ལག་ལེན་རབ་པ་ཏུ། 载 དཀོན་མཆོག་བསྟན་འཛིན། བཟོ་རིག་ཕྱོགས་བསྒྲིགས་རིན་ཆེན་སྒྲོམ་བུ། པེ་ཅིན་། ཀྲུང་གོའི་བོད་རིག་པ་དཔེ་སྐྲུན་ཁང་། 2011: 549-550. 5) རྒྱལ་མོ་འབྲུག་པ། བཀའ་བསྟན་འབྲི་བཤུ་པར་འདེབས་ཤོག་བཟོའི་ལག་རྩལ་སྐོར་ལ་དཔྱད་པ། 载 རྒྱལ་མོ་འབྲུག་པའི་ཆེད་རྩོམ་ཕྱོགས་བསྒྲིགས། པེ་ཅིན། ཀྲུང་གོའི་བོད་རིག་པ་དཔེ་སྐྲུན་ཁང་། 2016: 163-184. 其中第 5 种文献主要据下列著作介绍西藏各种有色纸的制作方法：དེའུ་དམར་བསྟན་འཛིན་ཕུན་ཚོགས། "རིག་པ་བཟོ་ཡི་གནས་ཀྱི་ལས་ཚོགས་ཕྲན་ཚོགས་འདོད་རྒྱུ་སྒྲུབ་པ་ཕྲ་ཕབ་འོད་ཀྱི་སྣང་བརྙན་ཞེས་བྱ་བ་བཞུགས་སོ།" in མཁན་པོ་དམ་ཆོས་ཟླ་བས་བསྒྲིགས། ཟློས་གར་དང་བཟོ་རིག། ཁྲི་ཞིང་། མཚོ་སྔོན་མི་རིགས་དཔེ་སྐྲུན་ཁང་། BDRC: W30012, 2004: 879-974.

12 བྲང་ཏི་དཔལ་ལྡན་རྒྱལ་མཚན། མན་ངག་གསེར་བྲེ་མ་དང་དངུལ་བྲེ་མ། 2004: 143.

13 དེའུ་དམར་བསྟན་འཛིན་ཕུན་ཚོགས། རིག་པ་བཟོ་ཡི་གནས་ཀྱི་ལས་ཚོགས་ཕྲན་ཚོགས་འདོད་རྒྱུ་སྒྲུབ་པ་ཕྲ་ཕབ་འོད་ཀྱི་སྣང་བརྙན། 2004: 879-974.

有准备书写文字的部分制成黑色，其四周用靛蓝染色[14]。但只有用他所述的方法制作出来的蓝黑纸才是那样。实际并非所有 མཐིང་ཤོག 皆呈黑色，比如用靛蓝染色的 མཐིང་ཤོག 一般呈纯蓝色或深蓝色。

很多材料都可用来写在蓝黑纸之上，但最珍贵且常用的是金汁，其字称为金字（གསེར་ཡིག）。不过并非所有金汁都是纯金，有时亦掺用黄铜合金[15]。另外用金银汁隔行书写的佛经也比较常见。蓝黑纸上常可见到经微描画出来的栏线，可能用金粉描，也可能用朱砂（མཚལ）描。一般情况下，蓝黑纸上的字多用藏文楷体（དབུ་ཅན）书写[16]。

据研究，藏文金汁写本的纸张往往特制。实际上任何纸张皆可使用，但不同类型的纸制要求不同的加工程序。一般情况下，汉地的纸用桑树、竹、麦秆或青草制成，较软，用靛蓝染色；反过来，西藏纸用瑞香或结香属（Daphne/Edgeworthia）植物的纤维制成，其表面往往用刷子涂一层颜料[17]。不过实际情况可能较此复杂。

二、从蓝纸（ཤོག་བུ་མཐིང་ག）到蓝黑纸（མཐིང་ཤོག）

西藏用纸始于吐蕃时期，《旧唐书·吐蕃传》："高宗嗣位（650年），……[弄赞]献金银珠宝十五种，请置太宗灵座之前。高宗嘉之，进封为賨王，赐杂彩三千段。因请蚕种及造酒、碾、硙、纸、墨之匠，并许焉。"[18] 看来7世纪中叶时，造纸之术已传入吐蕃。但吐蕃记事最初多用木牍，藏文作 ཁྲམ，《吐蕃大事纪年》744/745年条有"红册换成黄纸"的记载，但木牍仍大量使用，今新疆麻札塔格、米兰等地出土的大量吐蕃时期的藏

14 James Canary 2014: 109-110.

15 དེའུ་དམར་བསྟན་འཛིན་ཕུན་ཚོགས། རིག་པ་བཟོ་ཡི་གནས་ཀྱི་ལས་ཚོགས་ཕྲན་ཚོགས་འདོད་རྒུ་སྒྱུར་བ་ཕྲ་ཕབ་འོད་ཀྱི་སྣང་བརྙན། 2004: 871: མཐིང་ཤོག་དང་ཤོག་ནག་ལ་ཡི་གེ་བྲི་ན། གསེར་དམ་སྙིན་སྣག་དམ་གྱི་ཕྱེད་ཙམ་དང་། ཟར་ཁུ་གར་མོ་དགོས། འདི་བཞིན་གཤའ་ཟངས་རག་གསུམ་དུལ་མས་བྲིས་བྲུག་བྱེད་ཀྱང་དམ་སྦྱར་གསེར་དང་འདྲ་བ་ལས་ཁྱད་མེད་དོ།། "在蓝黑纸和黑纸上写字时，金或墨胶约一半，加上浓稠的胡麻汁，还有纯熟黄铜，以之抄写，与纯金一般无别。"

16 James Canary 2014: 109-110.

17 Agnieszka Helman-Ważny 2014: 103-104. 巴桑旺堆指出，制作藏纸的原料之一是瑞香狼毒，藏语 རེག་ཅག，这种植物有一定毒性，制作出来的纸质地坚韧，不遭虫蛀，经久耐用。见其文《关于古藏文写本的研究方法的再探索》，《中国藏学》2009（3）：63。

18 《旧唐书》卷一九六上《吐蕃传》上，北京：中华书局，1975：5222。

文木牍即是明证[19]。

据文献记载，吐蕃时期已开始使用“蓝纸”，用来书写盟书誓文。比如《贤者喜宴》在叙述赤松德赞（ཁྲི་སྲོང་ལྡེ་བཙན། 742-c.800）颁布兴佛证盟诏书时：

> [赤松德赞] 忆昔玛尚仲巴结（མ་ཞང་ཁྲོམ་པ་སྐྱེས）等灭佛之事，为此后不再发生类似事情，遂制定吐蕃任何人亦不得灭佛之诏书，郑重盟誓，如此两次行之，其第一道诏书云：
>
> 赞普赤松德赞之时，将诏书以金粉书于蓝纸（མོག་དུ་མཐིང་ག）之上，置于金匣之内，存于桑耶寺之府库中。……其第二道诏书：赞普赤松德赞之时，置兴佛历史（?ཡོ་དྭང）之文书副本，以颇罗弥（ཕྲ་སྦྱིན）书写，置于金匣之内，存于吉祥桑耶寺之府库中。[20]

其中第一道诏书的 མོག་དུ་མཐིང་ག 这个词，意为“蓝纸”[21]，有学者认为即后世的 མཐིང་ཤོག[22]。虽然此判断尚待进一步证实，但必定是一种非常贵重的纸张。第二道诏书所用的书写材料 ཕྲ་སྦྱིན，敦煌文献一般作 ཕྲ་མེན[23]，为一种金涂银之物，音译作颇罗弥，不过第二道诏书究竟书于何种书写材质上，史载不明。总之，不论是金粉和颇罗弥，还是蓝纸，都是非常贵重的书写材料，赤松德赞将其兴佛诏书用金粉书于蓝纸上，又置于金匣之内，当然是为郑重其事，表明他对佛法的虔诚之心和兴佛的决心。

赤松德赞之子赤德松赞（ཁྲི་ལྡེ་སྲོང་བཙན། ?-815）时，建噶迥寺（དཀར་ཆུང་རྡོ་རྗེ་དབྱིངས་ཀྱི་ལྷ་ཁང），同时与臣工属民盟誓不毁佛法，《贤者喜宴》记其事云：

> 子赤德松赞之时，以金粉书写 [诏书] 于蓝纸（མོག་དུ་མཐིང་ག）之上，置于

19 Brandon Dotson, *The Old Tibetan Annals: An Annotated Translation of Tibet's First History. With an Annotated Cartographical Documentation by Guntram Hazod*, Vienna: Verlag der Österreichischen Akademie der Wissenschaften, 2009: 52-53, 124. 参见 H. Uebach, “From Red Tally to Yellow Paper: The Official Introduction of Paper in the Tibetan Administration in 744/745”, *Revue d'Études Tibétaines* 14, 2008: 57-69; Agnieszka Helman-Ważny and Sam van Schaik, “Witnesses for Tibetan Craftsmanship: Bringing together Paper Analysis, Palaeography and Codicology in the Examniation of the Earlies Tibetan Manuscripts,” *Archaeometry* 55.4, 2013: 707.

20 དཔའ་བོ་གཙུག་ལག་ཕྲེང་བ། མཁས་པའི་དགའ་སྟོན། པེ་ཅིན། མི་རིགས་དཔེ་སྐྲུན་ཁང་། 2006: 195-196.

21 黄颢、周润年译注：《贤者喜宴——吐蕃史译注》，北京：中央民族大学出版社，2010：183。

22 པད་མ་བཀྲ་ཤིས། བོད་ཡིག་གནའ་དཔེའི་རྣམ་བཤད། ལྷ་ས། བོད་ལྗོངས་མི་དམངས་དཔེ་སྐྲུན་ཁང་། 2013: 31.

23 参见如 P.t.1089. 关于 ཕྲ་མེན 的可能词源，参见 Dorji Wangchuk 2016: 374-375, note 12.

颇罗弥匣内，存于桑耶寺其父王兴佛证盟诏书之旁。[24]

从上可见，赤松德赞和赤德松赞父子为示弘扬佛教的决心，是用最贵重的材料来书写兴佛证盟诏书，看来“蓝纸”在吐蕃时期是极其珍贵的书写材质。据潘吉星，中土在魏晋南北朝时已生产包括蓝色在内的各种色纸，其中染蓝用靛蓝，取自蓼科的蓼蓝（*Polygonum tinctoria*）、十字花科的菘蓝（*Isatis tinctoria*）、豆科的木蓝（*Indigofera tinctoria*）、爵床科的马蓝（*Strobilanthes flaccidifolius*）及十字花科的青蓝（*Isatis indigotica*）之茎叶，经发酵、水解及氧化而制成[25]。到了唐朝又有所谓“云蓝纸”，潘吉星推测其蓝色即来自靛蓝染料[26]。对于赤松德赞父子所用的“蓝纸”，虽然我们尚无法确定必是后世的蓝黑纸，但很有可能是经过靛蓝染色的纸张。靛蓝的藏语是 རམས，高田时雄教授曾提示笔者，རམས 字或来自汉文“蓝”，“蓝”字的中古音作 lam，而韵母 r 和 l 可互通[27]。再考虑到史书有吐蕃向唐朝请纸墨之匠的记载，另《巴协》记唐朝皇帝曾赐给吐蕃求法的使者书于蓝黑纸的金汁佛经千卷[28]，则吐蕃“蓝纸”的制作工艺很可能与唐朝有关。

据传，赤松德赞曾用其烧焦的头发和靛蓝混合并用山羊的乳酪来调制浆液，抄写了一部《般若波罗蜜多经》[29]。即使这个传说确有其事，也是用这种浆液写字，而非用作纸张的染料。另从《娘氏教法史》（ཉང་རལ་ཆོས་འབྱུང）、《西藏王统记》（རྒྱལ་རབས་གསལ་བའི་མེ་ལོང）、《贤者喜宴》等文献看，松赞干布（སྲོང་བཙན་སྒམ་པོ། ? -649）遣禄东赞（མགར་སྟོང་བཙན་ཡུལ་ཟུང་། ?-667）前往尼婆罗和唐朝分别迎娶墀尊（ཁྲི་བཙུན）公主和文成公主时，携带松赞干布事先写好的答复尼王和唐王问题的书信，谓乃金汁书于蓝黑纸（མཐིང་ཤོག་ལ་

24 དཔའ་བོ་གཙུག་ལག་ཕྲེང་བ། མཁས་པའི་དགའ་སྟོན། 2006: 214.

25 潘吉星：《中国造纸史》，上海人民出版社，2009：175-176。

26 潘吉星：《中国造纸史》，2009：237。

27 2017 年 4 月 19 日，受高田时雄教授邀请，笔者就此文在复旦大学“中古中国共同研究班”做报告，当时高田老师有此提示之语。谨此向高田老师深致谢意！

28 བདེ་སྐྱིད་ཀྱིས་བསྒྲིགས། ཟ་བཞེད་ཕྱོགས་བསྒྲིགས། པེ་ཅིན། མི་རིགས་དཔེ་སྐྲུན་ཁང་། 2013: 6: ཐིང (མཐིང)་ཤོག་ལ་གསེར་ཆུས་པའི་ཆོས་བམ་པོ་སྟོང་གནང། 不过这条记载不见于《巴协》的早期版本《韦协》，当是后人追加的。见韦·囊赛著，巴擦·巴桑旺堆译：《韦协》，拉萨：西藏人民出版社，2011。

29 Dorji Wangchuk 2016: 381.

གསེར་གྱིས་བྲིས་པ）上[30]。不过此事颇具传奇性质，显系经过后世佛教史家的演义[31]，无法用来证明松赞干布时期吐蕃已经使用蓝黑纸。又《嘛呢全书》（མ་ཎི་བཀའ་འབུམ）记载松赞干布的遗训（བཀའ་ཆེམས）是用金银汁写于蓝色丝绸（ཚུ་དར་སྔོན་པོ）之上并作为王室伏藏（ལྷ་གཏེར）藏于昌珠寺（ཁྲ་འབྲུག）[32]。尽管此事也是传说多于事实，但从以上介绍的赤松德赞父子的兴佛诏书来看，用珍贵材料来书写并保存王室诏敕大概是吐蕃时期的习惯作法[33]。不过当时似还不曾用蓝黑纸来抄写佛经，至少从目前发现的吐蕃时期的写经来看，没有见到书写于蓝黑纸的报道。巴桑旺堆老师说，蓝黑纸在吐蕃后期即开始流行[34]。不过他没有举出确凿证据来支持其说，此不取。

对于佛教徒来说，书写佛经的纸墨的质量自然非常重要[35]。必定越是贵重，越表明功德主发心之诚。据称，在深色纸上用金汁书写佛经并用珍贵的宝石加以装饰始于所谓西藏的文艺复兴时期（Tibetan Renaissance），即 10-13 世纪[36]。已知最早的书于经过靛蓝染色纸张之上的藏文写经可能是上世纪 40 年代图齐（G. Tucci）带回意大利、现藏意大利非洲与东方研究所的一部《般若波罗蜜多经》写本（M.81.90.6），它出自阿里托林寺（Tholing），年代为 11 世纪上半叶[37]。不过从现存实物来看，最初并非所有深色纸皆为靛蓝染色，比如美国纽瓦克博物馆（Newark Museum）收集品中有一件《般若波罗蜜多经》写经，共 14 卷，每卷约 322-384 叶，但各卷皆无原始封面，有时且无原始标题页。其纸张厚而柔韧，各纸层之间填以黏土；纸张四周染成深褐色，中间为黑色长方形方框，文字用金汁或金银汁相间而写，每面写 7-8 行，其中两卷的标题页绘有佛像，另一卷中有 10 页纸绘有佛像；写经年代据测约在 1195 年[38]。这件写经纸张的底色为深褐色，看来不是蓝黑纸。

---

30 Per K. Sørensen, *Tibetan Buddhist Historiography: The Mirror Illuminating the Royal Genealogies*, Wiesbaden: Harrassowitz Verlag, 1994: 203, 217; 索南坚赞著，刘立千译：《西藏王统记》，北京：民族出版社，2000：54，61。参见次旺仁钦：《藏纸考略》，《西藏研究》2002（1）：83；Agnieszka Helman-Ważny 2014: 81; Dorji Wangchuk 2016: 373-374.

31 关于此，参见 Thomas Kerihuel, “The Early History of Mgar: When History Becomes Legend,” *Revue d'Études Tibétaines* 21, 2011: 113-116.

32 R. A. *Stein, Stein's Tibetica Antiqua*, trans. and ed. A. P. McKeown, Leiden: Brill, 2010: 229, note 58.

33 R. A. *Stein, Stein's Tibetica Antiqua*, 2010: 228-229.

34 巴桑旺堆：《关于古藏文写本的研究方法的再探索》，《中国藏学》2009（3）：64。

35 Kurtis R. Schaeffer, *The Culture of the Books in Tibet*, New York: Columbia University Press, 2009: 8-9.

36 Agnieszka Helman-Ważny 2014: 79.

37 Agnieszka Helman-Ważny 2014: 103, 111.

38 V. Reynolds, A. Heller, J. Gyatsho, *The Newark Museum. Tibetan Collection III. Sculpture and Paintings*, Newark Museum, 1986: 139-141 and pl. 7.

《青史》记载，达隆噶举派的创始人达隆 · 唐巴扎西贝（སྟག་ལུང་ཐང་པ་བཀྲ་ཤིས་དཔལ། 1142-1210 年）曾向帕木竹寺（ཕག་མོ་གྲུ）献供蓝纸经函（པོ་ཏི་སྔོན་པོ）。从其行文可见，蓝纸写经是非常贵重的供品：

> [达隆 · 唐巴扎西贝] 共三次前往帕木竹，其末次供献金银佛像难以数计、蓝纸与白纸经帙（པོ་ཏི་སྔོ་སྐྱ）五百五十函、金块与玉团四十、茶砖六十、上缎三千、犏牛与马百匹、黄金百余两所造之明灯、大氅与铠甲等物。他共在帕木竹安置明灯二百八十三盏，临终前供蓝纸经帙（པོ་ཏི་སྔོན་པོ）七百、白纸经帙难以数计、金块与玉团五十、上缎二千五百等物。[39]

པོ་ཏི་སྔོ་སྐྱ 和 པོ་ཏི་སྔོན་པོ,郭和卿译作“经函（涂青纸及白纸）”和“经函青色纸函”[40]；王启龙、还克加的译文与之接近，作“经函青白两种（涂青纸及白纸）”和“经函青色纸函”[41]。其中 སྔོན་པོ 和 སྐྱ 当是以颜色来指称纸张。与此类似的表述有 སྔོ་ཚོས 和 སྐྱ་ཚོས，意为蓝纸经论和白纸经论，是以其所用的蓝纸和白纸来代称文本[42]。看来，所谓 པོ་ཏི་སྔོན་པོ 或为蓝黑纸写经的另一种表述。《后藏志》记载,后藏热隆（ར་ལུང）地方的卓库列寺（འབྲོག་ཁུ་ལེ）有“用蓝琉璃汁书写的经函、纯金写于蓝色纸（གན་ཤོག་མཐིང་ཤུན）的《甘珠尔》《大般若经》（འབུམ）《华严经》（?ཕལ་མོ་ཆེ）等数百函白纸经帙”[43]。所谓“监色纸”（གན་ཤོག་མཐིང་ཤུན）可能是蓝黑纸的一种。

蓝纸或蓝黑纸因其珍贵，常人获得不易。《青史》记载，息解派（ཞི་བྱེད་པ）上师嘉哇登纳（རྒྱལ་བ་ཏེན་ནེ། 1127-1217 年）曾从北方获得两函蓝纸（ཤོག་སྔོན）和六头雌犏牛，并将之献给上师金侠热沃（སྨྱན་ཤྭ་རེ་བོ），作为求法的顺缘[44]。第三世噶脱司徒 · 确吉嘉措

39 འགོས་ལོ་གཞོན་ནུ་དཔལ། དེབ་ཐེར་སྔོན་པོ། ཆེང་དུ། སི་ཁྲོན་མི་རིགས་དཔེ་སྐྲུན་ཁང་། 1984: 728-729. 参见郭和卿译：《青史》第 2 卷，台北：华宇出版社，1988：230-231。

40 郭和卿译：《青史》第 2 卷，1988：230-231。

41 管 · 宣奴贝著，王启龙、还克加译：《青史》，北京：中国社会科学出版社，2012：528。

42 Dorji Wangchuk 2016: 372-373.

43 ཇོ་ནང་ཏཱ་ར་ནཱ་ཐ། མྱང་ཡུལ་སྟོད་སྨད་བར་གསུམ་གྱི་ངོ་མཚར་གཏམ་གྱི་ལེགས་བཤད་མཁས་པའི་འཇུག་ངོགས། ལྷ་ས། བོད་ལྗོངས་མི་དམངས་དཔེ་སྐྲུན་ཁང་། 2002: 15: རིན་པོ་ཆེ་བཻཌཱུརྻ་སྔོན་པོས་བྲིས་པའི་གླེགས་བམ། གན་ཤོག་མཐིང་ཤུན་ལ་གསེར་བཟང་པོས་བྲིས་པའི་བཀའ་འགྱུར། འབུམ་ཤོག་མོ་ཆེ་ལ་སོགས་པའི་སྐྱ་པོད་བརྒྱ་ཕྲག་མང་པོ་དང་། 佘万治译作：“有用蓝琉璃粉末书写的经函、用纯金粉在厚纸和蓝黑色皮革上书写的《甘珠尔》《广般若》等数百函墨写经籍”，似不够确切，见佘万治译：《后藏志》，拉萨：西藏人民出版社，2002：10。

44 འགོས་ལོ་གཞོན་ནུ་དཔལ། དེབ་ཐེར་སྔོན་པོ། 1984: 1087: བྱང་དུ་བྱོན་ནས་རྙེད་པ་ཤོག་སྔོན་པོ་ཏི་གཉིས་དང་མཛོ་མོ་དྲུག་བླ་མ་ལ་ཕུལ། 参见郭和卿译：《青史》第 3 卷，1988：191；王启龙、还克加译：《青史》，2012：751。

（ཀཿཐོག་ཆོས་ཀྱི་རྒྱ་མཚོ། 1880-1923/1925 年）所著《圣迹志》[45] 记述了卫藏及部分康区的 221 个圣迹，其中 74 个地方提到存有大藏经，总共 169 部。这些大藏经虽有多部为金汁所写，但明确记载写在蓝黑纸之上者（མཐིང་ཤོག་ལ་བྲིས་པ）则仅有一处，是康区的类乌齐寺（རི་བོ་ཆེ་དཔལ་གྱི་རི་བོ་ཆེ）[46]。虽其记录必有缺漏之处，但仍说明不是一般寺院皆可拥有蓝黑纸写经，而且可能不是所有金银汁写经所用的纸张都是蓝黑纸。

13 世纪时，阿里芒域贡塘（མང་ཡུལ་གུང་ཐང）的统治者墀杰·本德衮（ཁྲི་རྒྱལ་འབུམ་ལྡེ་མགོན། 1253-1280 年）曾修造一座佛塔，塔中放入一部八千颂《般若波罗蜜多经》作为装藏，这部经书是蓝黑纸金汁写经（མཐིང་ཤོག་ལ་ཇམ་བུ་གསེར་གྱིས་བྲིས་པ）[47]。

1275 年，八思巴从元朝启程返回萨迦寺，太子真金（ཇིམ་གྱིམ། 1243-1286 年）等出资抄写大量佛经，这些佛经后来皆保存在萨迦寺，八思巴为此作诗颂之曰：

མཐིང་ཤོག་མཐོན་ཐིང(མཐིང)་སྣེགས་བུ་ལྷ་བུའི་གཞིར། །
འཛམ་བུ་ཆུ་བོའི་གསེར་མཆོག་བཙོ་མ་ལས། །
འཕྲུལ་ཡིག་ཡིག་མཁན་ད་རིགས་ལ་སོགས་ཀྱིས། །
གསེར་ཕྲེང་ལྷ་བུར་ཡིད་རབ་འཕྲོག་པ་བཀོད། །
སྣ་ཚོགས་བཟོ་རིག་མཁས་པའི་ཚོགས་རྣམས་ཀྱིས། །
དྲས་དང་སྣེགས་ཤིང་སྣེགས་ཐག་ན་བཟའ་སོགས། །
འགྲོ་བ་ཡིད་འཕྲོག་ཕུལ་དུ་བྱུང་བ་ཡི། །
མ་པར་བཀྲ་པ་ཕུན་སུམ་ཚོགས་པ་བསྒྲུབ། །
……
གསེར་གྱི་ཡིག་ཕྲེང་གིས་སྤྲས་པའི། །
མཐིང་ཤོག་མཐོན་ཀ་ཆེན་པོའི་མདངས། །
གསལ་བ་རྣམ་གསལ་ཉི་མ་ཡི། །
གཟི་བརྗིད་ཟིལ་གྱིས་གནོན་པ་བཞིན། །
ཡང་ན་མཐིང་ཤོག་མཐིང་གའི་མདངས། །
ནམ་མཁའ་དྭངས་པའི་ཁ་དོག་བཞིན། །

45 ཀཿཐོག་ཆོས་ཀྱི་རྒྱ་མཚོ། སི་ཏུ་པ་ཆོས་ཀྱི་རྒྱ་མཚོའི་གནས་སྐོར་དབུས་གཙང་གནས་བསྐོར་ལམ་ཡིག་ནོར་བུ་ཟླ་ཤེལ་གྱི་སེ་མོ་དོ། BDRC: W21611, W9668, W27524. 本书著成于 1918-1920 年。

46 Orna Almogi, “Guides to Holy Places as Sources for the Study of the Culture of the Book in the Tibetan Cultural Sphere: The Example of Kaḥ Thog Si Tu Chos Kyi Rgya Mtho’s *Gnas Yig*,” 载《西域历史语言研究所集刊》第 5 辑，北京：科学出版社，2012：505-530。

47 Dorji Wangchuk 2016: 400-401.

གསེར་ཡིག་ཕྲང་དུ་སྦྲངས་པ་ནི།།

རྒྱུ་སྐར་ཕྲང་དུ་དངར་བ་བཞིན།།

深蓝色蓝黑纸之上，

用赡部州最好之纯金，

由今善写幻化文字之书手，

镌录文字如金色花鬘迷人。

诸多善巧工匠，

精心制作袍袱、经板、经绳与经衣，

令其殊胜而夺目悦意，

装帧精美，功德圆满。

……

由金色文字所装饰，

深蓝色蓝黑纸之光泽，

赫赫明亮，

犹如制胜了日华威光。

深蓝色蓝黑纸之光泽，

犹如澄澈苍天之色；

金色文字排列成行，

如同群星灿烂。[48]

看来，真金等出资修造的佛经是用金粉书于深蓝色 མཐིང་ཤོག 之上。八思巴分别用 མཐིང་ཤོག་མཐོན་ཐིང(མཐིང)、མཐིང་ཤོག་མཐོན་ཀ、མཐིང་ཤོག་མཐིང་ག 来形容这种纸，མཐོན་ཐིང(མཐིང)、མཐོན་ཀ 和 མཐིང་ག 意为深蓝色；看来这种纸不是用墨汁或黑色染料制作，否则应呈黑色。笔者推测，因为这次写经是皇室出资，所用材料当十分贵重，很可能就是靛蓝染色的瓷青纸。

从八思巴的诗文看，这些写经所用的袍袱、经板、经绳与经衣亦皆十分考究，精美异常。《萨迦世系史》记载，1265 年八思巴第一次返回萨迦寺时，即用金汁写造了

48 འཕགས་པ་བློ་གྲོས་རྒྱལ་མཚན། "བདེ་བར་གཤེགས་པའི་གསུང་རབ་འགྱུར་རོ་འཚལ་བཞེངས་པའི་སྐལ་བྱེད་སྤེལ་སྦྱོར་གྱི་རྒྱན་རྣམ་པར་བཀྲ་བ།" 见 ཆོས་རྒྱལ་འཕགས་པའི་གསུང་རབ་དཔེ་བསྡུར་མ་པོད་བཞི་པ། ས་སྐྱ་བཀའ་འབུམ། པེ་ཅིན། ཀྲུང་གོའི་བོད་རིག་པ་དཔེ་སྐྲུན་ཁང་། 2007: 409. Cf. Kurtis R. Schaeffer 2009: 131-132.

大量显密经典和《般若经》，共计 200 余部[49]。又称八思巴生前曾在朵甘思书写金汁佛经 115 部；在达托细莫切（སྟག་ཐོག་གཞིས་མོ་ཆེ）书写金汁佛经 40 部[50]。学者研究表明，元代藏文佛经的刊刻曾受到王室成员的大力资助[51]；《元史》中也不乏“书金字”“书西天字”“金书西番字经”等抄写藏文佛经的记载[52]，不知西藏于蓝黑纸或瓷青纸上泥金书写佛经传统的形成与盛行是否有元朝王室推波助澜的作用。有学者指出，从明代宫廷主持缮写的泥金佛经均以瓷青纸为地这个特征来推断，“元明时期金银书佛经应基本采用磁青纸及其他深色纸为书写材料，以便很好地烘托出金、银字迹，在色彩上形成对比，不仅适于阅读，而且更显华贵。”[53] 此论似基本可从。

据研究，在 14-15 世纪的卫藏地区，人们有用白纸墨汁和蓝纸金银汁书写《甘珠尔》和《丹珠尔》的做法[54]，其中有一些明确记载乃书于蓝黑纸之上。比如 1314-1334 年间，止贡替寺（འབྲི་གུང་མཐིལ）第九任堪布多杰结波（རྡོ་རྗེ་རྒྱལ་པོ། 1284-1351 年）曾修造了许多用金粉写在蓝黑纸之上的律和经等佛典[55]。1431 年，司徒·饶丹衮桑帕巴（སི་ཏུ་རབ་བརྟན་ཀུན་བཟང་འཕགས་པ། 1389-1442 年）曾于江孜修造一套白纸墨书和蓝黑纸金粉书写的《甘珠尔》及一套白纸墨书《丹珠尔》[56]。1435-1468 年间，止贡替寺第 13 任堪布仁钦贝桑（རིན་ཆེན་དཔལ་བཟང་། 1421-1469 年）用三个月时间修造了一部用金粉写在蓝黑纸上的《甘珠尔》[57]。从现存的藏文泥金银写经来看，西藏金银写经的传统直至近代未曾中断[58]。事实上，藏文

---

49 ངག་དབང་ཀུན་དགའ་བསོད་ནམས། ས་སྐྱའི་གདུང་རབས་ངོ་མཚར་བང་མཛོད། པེ་ཅིན། མི་རིགས་དཔེ་སྐྲུན་ཁང་། 1986: 173: མདོ་རྒྱུད་དང་ཞེར་ཕྱོགས་སོགས་རྒྱལ་བའི་བཀའ་གསེར་གྱི་པོ་ཏི་ཉིས་བརྒྱ་ལྷག་པ་བཞེངས། 参见陈庆英等译注：《萨迦世系史》，拉萨：西藏人民出版社，2002：135-136。

50 ངག་དབང་ཀུན་དགའ་བསོད་ནམས། ས་སྐྱའི་གདུང་རབས་ངོ་མཚར་བང་མཛོད། 1986: 219: གཞན་ཡང་མདོ་ཁམས་སྨད་དུ་གསེར་གྱི་པོ་ཏི་བརྒྱ་དང་བཅོ་ལྔ་དང་། སྟག་ཐོག་གཞིས་མོ་ཆེར་མདོ་མང་པོ་ཏི་བཞི་བཅུ་གསེར་ལས་བཞེངས། 参见陈庆英等译注：《萨迦世系史》，2002：167。恰白·次旦平措称，据《萨迦世系史》，八思巴时，曾在“蓝色纸上”用金汁书写六套完整的《甘珠尔》，总数达 2157 函（恰白·次旦平措等著：《西藏通史简编》，北京：五洲传播出版社，2000：114)。可惜笔者遍查《萨迦世系史》，未见此条记载。

51 西热桑布：《藏文“元版”考》，《中国藏学》2009（1）：41-50；熊文彬：《元代皇室成员施刊的藏文佛经》，《中国藏学》2009（3）：91-103。

52 参见王启龙：《藏传佛教对元代经济的影响》，《中国藏学》2002（1）：74-55；吴明娣、杨鸿蛟：《元明时期西藏佛经在内地的流传及其对装帧艺术的影响》，《美术观察》2006（11）：101，104，注 3。

53 吴明娣、杨鸿蛟：《元明时期西藏佛经在内地的流传及其对装帧艺术的影响》，《美术观察》，2006（11）：103。

54 Kurtis R. Schaeffer 2009: 27.

55 བསྟན་འཛིན་པདྨའི་རྒྱལ་མཚན། འབྲི་གུང་གདན་རབས་གསེར་ཕྲེང་ལྷ་ས། བོད་ལྗོངས་བོད་ཡིག་དཔེ་རྙིང་དཔེ་སྐྲུན་ཁང་། 1989: 130. Cf. Kurtis R. Schaeffer 2009: 27.

56 འཇིགས་མེད་གྲགས་པ། རྒྱལ་རྩེ་ཆོས་རྒྱལ་གྱི་རྣམ་པར་ཐར་པ་དད་པའི་ལོ་ཐོག་དངོས་གྲུབ་ཀྱི་ཆར་འབེབས། ལྷ་ས། བོད་ལྗོངས་མི་དམངས་དཔེ་སྐྲུན་ཁང་། 1987: 169, 173, 181. Cf. Kurtis R. Schaeffer 2009: 27-28.

57 སྟན་འཛིན་པདྨའི་རྒྱལ་མཚན། འབྲི་གུང་གདན་རབས་གསེར་ཕྲེང་།1989: 150. Cf. Kurtis R. Schaeffer 2009: 176, note 30.

58 参见拙稿《关于藏文蓝黑纸（མཐིང་ཤོག）写经的初步考察：以实物为中心》，待刊。

文献中有关金银汁及其他珍贵材料写经的记录非常之多[59]；近代宗教融合运动（རིས་མེད）大师迷旁·南杰嘉措（མི་ཕམ་རྣམ་རྒྱལ་རྒྱ་མཚོ། 1846-1912 年）曾言，纯金应书于蓝黑纸之上[60]；但我们目前仍无法判断，是否所有藏文金银汁写经皆用蓝黑纸；或其中特别贵重的写经、尤其是皇室出资修造的佛经要用瓷青纸。因为，如果所有金银汁写经都用蓝黑纸，则前述第三世噶脱司徒喇嘛就无需特别指出，类乌齐寺的大藏经乃书于蓝黑纸之上。另一例证是法国吉美博物馆（Musée Guimet）富尼耶收集品（Fournier collection）中一部五世达赖喇嘛的作品集《所见及其义》（མཐོང་བ་དོན་ལྡན）。它修造于 1674-1681 年，金汁写于炭黑色纸张之上，共 108 叶，其中 61 叶上画有图像，共计 886 幅。经叶长 29 厘米，宽 6 厘米，每叶写 4-5 行文字。据称，这部写经的纸张很脆，多数纸张为单独的一页纸，仅其中第二种文献（Text II）的纸张似由两张纸粘合而成，因此比其他纸张略厚且大[61]。如前所述，蓝黑纸一般由数层纸粘合而成，涂以特制的墨汁、颜料或染液，再经研磨打光而成，吉美博物馆这部金汁写经的纸张多为单独的一层纸，似非蓝黑纸。

三、蓝黑纸与瓷（磁）青纸

汉堡大学的多杰旺秋教授将用贵重材料如金汁和深蓝色纸制作的佛教经论称作“豪华版”（Deluxe Edition），并指出对此进行研究所面临的一个挑战是文献中所用相关语言的简洁和术语的模糊[62]。在考察藏文蓝黑纸写经的过程中，笔者确实面临同样难题。藏文文献在记录珍贵写经时，一般会记录其文字所用的材料，特别是金汁和银汁，但对于纸张则很少着墨，偶尔才提到是蓝黑纸或蓝纸，因此我们无法确定是否所有金银写经都用蓝黑纸作为书写载体。另一方面，对于考古出土和现存的珍贵写经，相关报道则往往非常简要地记录是瓷青纸或仅概略地描述其纸张的颜色（蓝色、黑色），但从刊布的少量图片来看，所谓瓷青纸者似乎未必就是瓷青纸，所谓蓝色纸或黑色纸者也无法一眼断定就是蓝黑纸，导致这种情况的主要原因是概念的混淆不清，当务之急无疑是要先梳理基本概念。

---

59 参见如 Orna Almogi 2012: 505-530; Dorji Wangchuk 2016: 378-381, 390-399.

60 མི་ཕམ་རྒྱ་མཚོ། བཟོ་གནས་ཉེར་མཁོའི་ཟ་མ་ཏོག 载 མི་ཕམ་རྒྱ་མཚོའི་གསུང་འབུམ། ཁྲིང་ཏུའུ། གངས་ཅན་རིག་གཞུང་དཔེ་རྙིང་མྱུར་སྐྱོབས་ལྷན་ཚོགས། 2007: f. 91.1-2: གཞན་གསེར་དངོས་ཀྱི་ཡི་གེ་བྲི་ན་གསེར་འདུལ་ཞིགས་པས་མཐིང་ཤོག་ལ་བྲི་བ་དེ་ནི་དེར་ཟད།

61 Samten Karmay, *Secret Vision of the Fifth Dalai Lama: The Gold Manuscript in the Fournier Collection Musée Guimet, Paris*, London: Seindia Publications, 1988.

62 Dorji Wangchuk 2016: 371-372.

本文以传世文献为中心，考察蓝黑纸藏文写经的情况。从上可见，西藏使用蓝黑纸有非常悠久的历史，且其工艺延续至今。很有可能，西藏在 8 世纪末即已开始使用经过靛蓝染色的蓝纸（ཤོག་བུ་མཐིང་ག）。从现存实物与文献记载看，至少在 11 世纪，西藏即开始用靛蓝染色的纸张来抄写佛经，特别是金银汁佛经。至于 མཐིང་ཤོག 一词，我们不知它最早何时出现，但它无疑指经过墨汁或颜料染色的纸张，其中包括汉地所谓的瓷青纸，主要用来抄写金银汁佛经。

笔者认为，就藏文书写载体而言，瓷青纸当属蓝黑纸的一种，元明以后中土抄写的藏文佛经，特别是明清宫廷写经，应主要采用经过靛蓝染色的瓷青纸，但西藏及其他藏族文化圈地区的情况可能较为复杂，从第三世噶脱司徒喇嘛的记录及其他资料来看，似非所有金银写经都用蓝黑纸或瓷青纸。

我们知道，汉地的瓷青纸是指一种经过靛蓝染色的纸张。因其色看起来如同瓷器的青釉，故称瓷青纸，又因瓷、磁相通，故也称磁青纸[63]。靛蓝是一种从蓝草中提取的植物染料，性质较为稳定，可用于油性和水性溶液。作为一种着色剂，靛蓝可能源自印度，据载印度公元前 4 世纪即开始用靛蓝给写本染色[64]。尽管对颜色的观感取决于不同的文化、时间与个人偏好，但许多文化利用不同的方法取得相同的美学效果。靛蓝就是如此，它以其华丽的蓝色光泽而成为贵重物品，曾价如黄金，被许多地方的人们用来装饰神圣书籍[65]。

汉地使用植物靛蓝染色的历史非常悠久，《荀子 · 劝学篇》有“青出于蓝而胜于蓝”之佳句，其中的“蓝”即指提取靛蓝的蓝草。据潘吉星，汉地用靛蓝给纸张染色并制作瓷青纸始于五代至宋。1978 年苏州瑞光寺塔出土有五代大和辛卯（931 年）泥金书瓷青纸《妙法莲华经》，同塔还出土了北宋雍熙年（984-987 年）刻本《妙法莲华经》，卷轴引首为瓷青纸[66]，另外还有《佛说阿弥陁经》一卷，瓷青纸泥金写本，年代在北宋初至天禧元年（1017 年）以前[67]。敦煌文献中也有少量瓷青纸泥金书写本，如敦煌研究院藏“敦

63 潘吉星：《中国造纸史》，2009：280。

64 Helman-Ważny 2014: 103.

65 Elena Pakhoutova and Agnieszka Helman -Ważny, 2012: “Indigo.”

66 潘吉星：《中国造纸史》，2009：280。关于苏州瑞光寺塔出土写经，参见孙同德：《苏州瑞光塔云岩寺塔碧纸金书唐代宋初写经》，《中国书法》2014（9）：80-85。

67 苏州博物馆，名录 07182，见国家图书馆、国家古籍保护中心编：《楮墨芸香：国家珍贵古籍特展图录》，国家图书馆出版社，2010：202。

研附 073”号《妙法莲华经》写经即是 [68]。用墨在瓷青纸上写字，字迹不易显现，但如果将金粉散于胶水中写成金字，经瓷青纸衬托，则颜色鲜明亮丽。据传宋徽宗赵佶（1082-1135 年）和金章宗完颜璟（1168-1208 年）都很喜欢在瓷青纸上用泥金写字，“殊臻壮伟之观” [69]。不过瓷青纸或磁青纸作为一种纸张的专名最早出现在明代，因此有学者认为应将明以前经过靛蓝染色的纸张称作“青纸”，因为唐宋文献常如此称之 [70]。另外苏州瑞光寺塔天宫出土《法华经》卷尾后周显德三年（956 年）发愿文则称为“碧纸”：“时显德三年岁次丙辰十二月十五日，弟子朱承惠特舍净财，收赎此古旧损经七卷，备金银及碧纸请人书写……。” [71] “青纸”或“碧纸”这种称谓，与我们前述 13 世纪以前西藏主要以“蓝纸”（ཤོག་བུ་མཐིང་ག ; པོ་ཏི་སྔོན་པོ ; གན་ཤོག་མཐིང་ཤུན）来称呼经靛蓝染色的纸张正好一致。

从藏文文献来看，西藏确实熟知可从蓝靛提取蓝色染料 [72]。敦煌藏文写本 P.t.1290 正面第 9 行有这样一行字：གསེར་ལེ་མཐོན་གོང། གཡུ་ལེ་བྱང་ཕངས། བཙོད་ལེ་སྣར་གོང། རམ་ལེ་སྔོན་གོང། དུང་ལེ་དཀར་གོང，学者译作“比黄金更纯，比玉石更艳，比‘佐’更美，比‘然’更蓝，比海螺更白。” [73] 其中 རམ 字，今通行作 རམས，即靛蓝。从此行文看，当时已知 རམ(ས) 是一种蓝色颜料。14 世纪成书的《西藏王统记》记载禄东赞去唐都长安为松赞干布迎娶文成公主时，经历唐皇设计的种种考验，其中有这样的句子：དེར་བློན་པོས་ཛ་དེ་ལ་སྐྱོན་ཅན་དུ་གོ་ནས་བློན་པོ་རྣམས་ཁྲིད། སྒོ་རེ་རེ་བཞིན་འདྲེན་གིན། སྒོ་ལ་རམས་དང་ཚོས་ཀྱི་ཁུ་བུས་མཚན་མ་འདེབས་གིན་ཕོ་བྲང་དུ་ཕྱིན་ནོ། “于是使臣（按指禄东赞）知道此次击鼓必有原故，便率领众僚，每进一门，皆在门上涂抹蓝靛和染料之汁液，以作标记，[如是] 抵达宫中。” [74] 另外后世西藏的唐卡也多用靛蓝来做颜料 [75]。从现存实物看，保存下来的藏文瓷青纸写经的数量非常之多。但是，我们不知道瓷青纸所对应的藏文是什么，而且对于西藏利用靛蓝制作瓷青纸的历史，我们亦不清楚。藏族学者次旺仁钦介绍说，瓷青纸的藏文是“汀梭”；其制法，是把数张纸

68 甘肃藏敦煌文献编委会、甘肃人民出版社、甘肃省文物局编《甘肃藏敦煌文献》第 1 卷，兰州：甘肃人民出版社，1999，彩图。——此承敦煌研究院王惠民老师教示，谨此致谢！

69 潘吉星：《中国造纸史》，2009：280。

70 刘仁庆：《论瓷青纸——兼羊脑笺》，《纸与造纸》2012（2）：59-64。

71 张建宇：《克利夫兰藏金书〈法华经〉扉画研究》，《故宫博物院院刊》2017（2）：81，注 2。

72 Christoph Cüppers, “On the Manufacture of Ink,” *Ancient Nepal* 113, 1989: 2, 4.

73 班玛更珠、黄维忠：《P.T.1290 小邦邦伯家臣表译释（下）》，《西藏民族学院学报》2016（5）：73-74。“佐”（btsod）指一种赤黄色染料。

74 བསོད་ནམས་རྒྱལ་མཚན། རྒྱལ་རབས་གསལ་བའི་མེ་ལོང་། པེ་ཅིན། མི་རིགས་དཔེ་སྐྲུན་ཁང་། 2008: 104. 译文参见刘立千译：《西藏王统记》，北京：民族出版社，2000：64。

75 David Jackson and Janice Jackson, “A Survey of Tibetan Pigments,” *Kailash* 4, 1976: 285-287.

迭合，用浆糊粘贴在一起，然后涂一种称为“汀”的染料，再经过研磨打光而成[76]。所谓“汀梭”，显然是 མཐིང་ཤོག 的音译，“汀”即 མཐིང。若按此说，མཐིང་ཤོག 即瓷青纸，མཐིང 指靛蓝。但从藏文文献记载和 Helman-Ważny 博士及 Canary 博士所介绍的制作工艺来看，许多物质都可用作 མཐིང་ཤོག 的染液，靛蓝主要是给汉地的纸张染色；མཐིང་ཤོག 也可用墨汁或其他颜料制作。看来，次旺仁钦所述瓷青纸的制作方法，只是前文介绍的 མཐིང་ཤོག 的制作工艺之一。瓷青纸是 མཐིང་ཤོག 的一种，而且应是非常贵重的一种，但 མཐིང་ཤོག 不等于瓷青纸。

四、结语

近年来，国际藏学界逐渐兴起对西藏书写文化的研究，特别书写材料日益引起学者的关注。其中最著名的当属德国汉堡大学的纸张专家 Agnieszka Helman-Ważny 博士，她的一系列论著分析藏纸的纤维构成，描述藏纸的制作，讨论藏文写本和刻本的装帧，藏文书籍的装订，藏文大藏经的产生等各方面问题，并进而分析其年代学意义，极大地推进人们对西藏书写文化、特别是其物质方面的认识[77]。正如 Helman-Ważny 博士所指出，在蓝色纸上用金汁书写所产生的色彩对比亮丽悦目，并非只有西藏这么做，中原地区、日本、南亚、伊斯兰世界、欧洲等地皆有相似的写木留存下来。但是，西藏的蓝纸或蓝黑纸泥金写本的数量非常之多，影响及于周边地区。在世界上的许多博物馆、图书馆及私家收藏中皆可见到这类写本，或整卷，或单独数叶，其装饰性外观别具匠心，成为一

---

76 次旺仁钦：《藏纸考略》，《西藏研究》2002（1）：83。次旺仁钦文称 མཐིང 是蓝色矿物颜料，不确。实际为植物性染料。

77 Agnieszka Helman-Ważny, “The *Diamond Sutra* in the Collection of the Pomeranian Library of Szczecin in the Historical and Artistic Context of Buddhist Books from Central Asia,” *Biuletyn Informacyjny Konserwatorów Diel Sztuki* 14.3-4 (54-55), 2003: 49-57, 161-166; Idem, “Asian Paper in Works of Art: A Comparative Fiber Analysis,” *Hand Papermaking* 21.2, 2006: 3-9; Idem, “Historical, Art-Historical, and Natural Science Approaches to Dating Tibetan Books-Possilities and Limitations,” in Saadet Arslan and Peter Schwieger ed., *Tibetan Studies: An Anthology*, Internaltional Institute for Tibetan and Buddhist Studies GmbH, 2010: 279-295; Marek Mejor, Agnieszka Helman-Ważny and Thupten Kunga Chashab, *A Preliminary Report on the Wanli Kanjur Kept in the Jagiellonian Library, Kraków*, Warsaw: Research Centre of Buddhist Studies, Faculty of Oriental Studies, University of Warsaw, 2010; Agnieszka Helman-Ważny, “A Preliminary Study of the Paper of the Diamon Sutra (Or.8210/P.2),” *IDP News* 38, 2011-12: 6-7; Elena Pakhoutova and Agnieszka Helman -Ważny, *Illuminated: The Art of Sacred Books*, New York: Rubin Museum, 2012; Helman-Ważny, Agnieszka and Sam van Schaik, “Witnesses for Tibetan Craftsmanship: Bringing Together Paper Analysis, Palaeography and Codicology in the Examination of the Earliest Tibetan Manuscripts,” *Archaeometry* 55 (4), 2013: 707-741; Agnieszka Helman-Ważny, *The Archaeology of Tibetan Books*, Leiden: Brill, 2014; etc.

种独特的工艺[78]。甚至在刻本成为图书的主要形式后，西藏仍然大量抄写佛经，其中金银书佛经往往装帧华丽，用料考究，其目的主要在于作供养，积功德，而非流通[79]。

对于蓝黑纸，我们仍有许多不明之处。比如蓝黑纸的起源、用途及其与金银写经的关系究竟如何，以及 མཐིང 作为一种染料的确切配方、特别是靛蓝在其中的使用情况。正如多杰旺秋教授所说，传世藏文文献中有关蓝黑纸制作的资料很少[80]，而现代学者的相关描述又不完全一致[81]。综合看来，似乎把几张纸粘合，在其表面涂一层特制的墨汁、颜料或染液，再经过研磨打光，这样生产出来的黑色或蓝色纸张即可称作 མཐིང་ཤོག。

学者在介绍现存的贵重藏文写经时，往往用“蓝纸”或“黑纸”来描述其纸张，这单纯是从颜色着眼，我们由此无法得知其所用颜料，也难以判断这种写经是否采用蓝黑纸或瓷青纸作为书写载体。另一种情况是很多珍贵写经的纸张用了两种染液，比如四周为蓝色，中间书写文字的部分为黑色；再者除靛蓝之外，许多其他原料也可用来制作蓝色染液，因此对于有些所谓的瓷青纸写经，可能更合适的名称是蓝黑纸写经，或者分别其部位（四周与中间）做更准确的介绍。笔者在撰写本文过程中，深感概念的混乱，希望纸张专家以后扩大其研究领域到藏文写经纸张的颜料分析，从而进一步丰富我们对藏文书写文化的认识。

◆ 朱丽双　兰州大学敦煌学研究所教授

78 Agnieszka Helman-Ważny 2014: 80.

79 吴明娣、杨鸿蛟：《元明时期西藏佛经在内地的流传及其对装帧艺术的影响》，《美术观察》2006（11）：103；Agnieszka Helman-Ważny 2014: 76; Dorji Wangchuk 2016: 399-401.

80 Dorji Wangchuk 2016: 403.

81 比如前述 Helman-Ważny 博士和 Canary 博士所述之制作方法即很不一样。

西藏夏鲁寺“介尊·喜饶琼乃”壁画释读 *

贾玉平

内容摘要：西藏夏鲁寺三门佛殿现遗存中有一铺以其创建者介尊·喜饶琼乃为主要题材的彩绘壁画，图像及题记完整地折射出 11-14 世纪初夏鲁寺的传承和介氏家族的历史。结合《夏鲁系谱》及相关文献分析，可以清晰看到隐藏在壁画背后的夏鲁寺诸多不为人知的历史，如：夏鲁寺传承情况，夏鲁寺早期在藏地的影响及其与上路传承的联系等。同时，介氏家族承接吐蕃遗风创建夏鲁寺，并在管理模式方面形成最早的家族式政教合一制，成为西藏政教合一制度中早期典型之一。

一

夏鲁寺三门佛殿现遗存中有一铺描绘该寺创建者介尊·喜饶琼乃（图一）的壁画，壁画中介尊所坐莲座台面上有题记“ལྕེ་བཙུན་ཤེས་རབ་འབྱུང་གནས”（介尊·喜饶琼乃）。20 世

* 本文为国家社科基金一般项目“西藏夏鲁寺美术遗存调查与研究”（14BF060）阶段性成果；中国藏学研究中心重点课题“元代夏鲁寺艺术与汉藏文化交流研究”阶段性成果。

图一 “介尊”肖像壁画（出自：金维诺主编,《中国美术分类全集 - 中国壁画全集 34-藏传寺院 4》，天津人民美术出版社，1993）

图二 “介尊”壁画人物排布构图（作者制图）

纪 80-90 年代前后该大殿壁画就被镜头不断地记录过[1]，但以往学者多倾心于三门佛殿北壁的五方佛壁画的精美，少见对西壁这铺“介尊·喜饶琼乃”壁画深入细致地关注。

该壁画位于殿内西壁北段，高约 2.6 米，宽约 1.7 米。介尊绘制最为详细，而且居中几乎占整个画面一半。可以说，这是一幅“介尊·喜饶琼乃”祖师像。壁画为红色调，画面中未被遮蔽的蓝色背景均匀点缀细碎的白色小花朵，前景物象兼以黄、蓝、绿、白色颜料绘制而成。从主尊背屏及两侧装饰物象等众多信息及绘画技巧可以看出该壁画属

1 a. 金维诺主编：《中国美术分类全集·中国壁画全集 34·藏传寺院 4》，天津人民美术出版社，1993：图一六。b. 西藏自治区文物管理委员会编：《西藏佛教寺院壁画艺术》，成都：四川人民出版社，1994：199。c. Kreijger, Hugo, "Mural Styles at Shalu." In *Tibetan Art: Towards a Definition of Style*. eds. J. C. Singer and P. Denwood. London: Laurence King Publishing, 1997: 170-177. d. Franco Ricca and Lionel Fournier, "The Paintings in the Zhwa lu sGo gsum lha khang and bSe sgo ma lha khang: Stylistic Differences." In *The Tibet Journal*, vol.26, nos.3 and 4, 2001: 103-148. e. Munneke Roelof and Ronald Poelmeijer eds, *Shalu: De herontdekking van een Tibetanns klooster*. Leiden: Rijksmuseum voor Volkenkunde, 1992: 24. f. 谢斌：《西藏夏鲁寺建筑及其壁画艺术》，北京：民族出版社，2005：108。

图三 “介尊”壁画局部 - 夏鲁寺的吐蕃风格传承

图四 “介尊”壁画局部 - 夏鲁寺的印度风格传承

图五　“介尊”壁画局部 - 部分介氏家族族人

于典型的尼泊尔风格。

壁画中介尊右上方、左上方各绘三人，莲座下方绘八人，各人下方均附藏文题记，标识其身份、名字。右上方三位由上至下顺时针排列为：2. ལྗེ་ཁྲི་འབྲུག་ལོ་ཙྪ་བ（介 · 赤珠译师），3. ཡང་དེའི་ནུ་བོ་ལྗེ་ཁྲི་འབྲུག་བཀྲ་ཤིས་བརྩེག་པ（其弟介 · 赤珠扎西则巴），4. ཡང་དེའི་ནུ་བོ་ལྗེ་གཡུ་རྩེ་རྩེགས་པ（其弟介 · 玉泽则巴）。左上方三位由上至下顺时针排列为：5. བླ་མ་རྡོ་རྗེ་གདན་པ་ཆེ་བ（喇嘛多杰丹巴且哇），6. བླ་མ་རྡོ་རྗེ་གདན་པ་ཆུང་བ（喇嘛多杰丹巴琼哇），7. མཁན་པོ་མགོ་བ་ཡེ་ཤེས་གཡུང་དྲུང（堪布郭瓦 · 益西雍仲）。下方八位由北自南分别为：8. མཁན་པོ་ལྗེ་ཆུང་བ（堪布介 · 琼哇），9. ལྗེ་གཡུ་ཐོག（介 · 宇妥），10. ལྗེ་འབུམ་པ（介 · 邦巴），11. ལྗེ་འབུམ་མེ（介 · 邦枚），12. ལྗེ་འབུམ་དར（介 · 邦达），13. ལྗེ་འབུམ་བསྙེན（介 · 邦丹），14. ལྗེ་ཨ་མེས་སངས་རྒྱས（介 · 阿枚桑杰），15. ལྗེ་ཛ་སྒྲ་འབུམ（介 · 阿扎邦）（图二至图五）。

这幅祖师像是目前夏鲁寺建筑壁画中所见尺幅最大、人物最多的关于介氏家族的形象再现，而且是对介尊少有的精彩记录，其艺术水准堪称夏鲁寺美术的典范。

二

我们注意到画面描绘的十五位人物中，有十二位介氏家族成员，其中包括介尊。那么，这些人物是什么身份？他们与介尊有什么关系？这些人物与夏鲁寺传统有何联系？这铺壁画创作年代是什么时候？这些问题的水落石出，可以帮助我们进一步了解壁画更多深层信息。通过对该壁画信息及其图像次序分析，可以唤起传统文献对夏鲁寺重要赞助者——介氏家族历史的记忆。

介尊 · 喜饶琼乃出生于 973 年[2]，系介氏家族第十六代。

> （当时）反对介氏家族统治的起义爆发，介氏家族几乎被灭族，介尊逃过劫难，出家为僧，追随洛顿 · 多吉旺秋。洛顿为其受戒，介尊正式拜洛顿 · 多吉旺秋为师。[3]

喜饶琼乃后来成为洛顿 · 多吉旺秋八位弟子之一[4]，并协助洛师建造坚贡寺（རྒྱན་གོང）。在后弘期兴佛背景下，介尊欲建一寺，请师父为其选址，洛师金箭在“青苗之地”（ཞྭ་ལུ，汉译“夏鲁”）落下，始建夏鲁寺[5]。之后，介尊接受洛师建议，去印度金刚座大觉寺迎请圣者羯沙流波泥身像，遂将夏鲁僧团及寺院托付给郭瓦 · 益西雍仲[6]，他到达印度金刚座大觉寺后，师从阿萨雅噶热（ཨ་ས་ཡ་ག་ར）[7]。

义净《大唐西域求法高僧传》中也多次提及“金刚座”这座寺院[8]。《南海寄归内法传》卷上记述玄照、大乘灯二法师巡礼菩提伽耶时，也分别用‘到金刚座’、‘向金刚座’语句[9]。索南孜摩（བསོད་ནམས་རྩེ་མོ）《喇嘛巴哩译师仁钦扎传记》也称该寺为“金刚座”[10]。波罗王朝时期（8-12 世纪），印度佛教寺院建设空前高涨，其中菩提迦耶的金刚座

---

2 དཔལ་ལྡན་ཞྭ་ལུ་པའི་བསྟན་པ་ལ་བཀའ་དྲིན་ཆེ་བའི་སྐྱེས་བུ་དམ་པ་རྣམས་ཀྱི་རྣམ་ཐར་ལོ་རྒྱུས་ངོ་མཚར་དད་པའི་འཇུག་ངོགས། TBRC: W3CN5288, 1971: 178. 下文再次引用该书时简称 ZNT。

3 Bkra shis don grub, "From The Genealogies Ža Lu." In Giuseppe Tucci, *Tibetan Painted Scrolls II*, Rome: Orchid Press, 2006: 656-662: 12b.

4 ཇོ་ནང་ཏཱ་ར་ནཱ་ཐ། མྱང་ཡུལ་སྟོད་སྨད་བར་གསུམ་གྱི་ངོ་མཚར་གཏམ་གྱི་ལེགས་བཤད་མཁས་པའི་འཇུག་ངོགས། ལྷ་ས། བོད་ལྗོངས་མི་དམངས་དཔེ་སྐྲུན་ཁང་། 1983: 155-156.

5 ཇོ་ནང་ཏཱ་ར་ནཱ་ཐ། མྱང་ཡུལ་སྟོད་སྨད་བར་གསུམ་གྱི་ངོ་མཚར་གཏམ་གྱི་ལེགས་བཤད་མཁས་པའི་འཇུག་ངོགས། 1983: 160.

6 ཇོ་ནང་ཏཱ་ར་ནཱ་ཐ། མྱང་ཡུལ་སྟོད་སྨད་བར་གསུམ་གྱི་ངོ་མཚར་གཏམ་གྱི་ལེགས་བཤད་མཁས་པའི་འཇུག་ངོགས། 1983: 161.

7 ཇོ་ནང་ཏཱ་ར་ནཱ་ཐ། མྱང་ཡུལ་སྟོད་སྨད་བར་གསུམ་གྱི་ངོ་མཚར་གཏམ་གྱི་ལེགས་བཤད་མཁས་པའི་འཇུག་ངོགས། 1983: 160-163.

8 义净 ：《大唐西域求法高僧传》《大正藏》第 51 册 ：5 中。

9 义净 ：《大唐西域求法高僧传》《大正藏》第 51 册 ：2，4 。

10 བསོད་ནམས་རྩེ་མོ། བླ་མ་བ་རི་ལོ་ཙཱ་བ་རིན་ཆེན་གྲགས་ཀྱི་རྣམ་ཐར། ས་སྐྱ་བཀའ་འབུམ་མ་ཕྱི་གསར་རྙེད་ཕྱོགས་བསྒྲིགས། TBRC: 20751, vol.1: 256.

寺（Vajrasana）在 10-11 世纪以金刚乘佛教而闻名 [11]。该寺院就是《后藏志》提及的金刚座大觉寺。此外，TBRC 扫描本《介氏系谱》称夏鲁寺为藏地“第二金刚座” [12]，一则表明夏鲁寺在西藏的重要，二则强调其与菩提迦耶的关系。

图齐本《夏鲁系谱》14a 也记载：

> 介尊去印度菩提迦耶（Bodhgaya）师从大阿阇黎阿坝雅迦罗笈多（Abhayakara-gupta，藏译 འཇིགས་མེད་འབྱུང་གནས་སྦས་པ，汉译：吉美琼乃泊巴），学习了律法原理和许多学说，并带了一尊卡萨巴尼观音像回到西藏。

《后藏志》所载阿萨雅噶热应该即阿阇黎阿坝雅迦罗笈多的缩简。“阿坝雅迦罗笈多”是梵文音译，“吉美琼乃泊巴”则是对梵文原名的藏文意译，该藏文名字又被汉译作“无畏生护”或“护无畏”或“无畏笈多”。

“介尊”壁画中介尊左上方的人物 5 喇嘛多杰丹巴且哇（汉译“大金刚座”）即阿阇黎阿坝雅迦罗笈多，曾在波罗王朝末期做金刚大觉寺住持，其师承胜诸怨敌节达哩巴上师（ཛོ་ཏཱ་རི་དགྲ་ལས་རྣམ་པར་རྒྱལ་བ）[13]。多杰丹巴且哇生于东印度西孟加拉邦高尔（Gaur），生活在罗摩波罗王（Rāmapāla，约 1075-1120 年）时代，殁于 1125 年 [14]，系摩揭陀刹帝利种姓，其原名啰怛那菩提阿噶热（意为：含摄觉智摩尼宝）[15]，其受居士戒的名字是功德祥（Puṇyaśrī），出家时的法名是功德生密（Puṇyākaragupta）[16]，曾受尼耶波罗王（Neyapāla）供养。他被认为是大乘和密宗佛教最伟大的导师之一，尤其是在西藏受到崇拜，被当作阿弥陀佛的化身。布顿大师在其《夏鲁祖拉康无量宫东西南北四方所置坛城目录》叙述四座无量宫殿曼陀罗壁画的题材依据时，多处引用其传统。

介尊、尚那囊 · 多吉旺久（ཞང་སྣ་སྣམ་རྡོ་རྗེ་དབང་ཕྱུག）[17] 和巴哩译师（བ་རི་ལོ་ཙཱ་བ）正是

11 Ronald M. Davidson, *Tibetan Renaissance*, New York: Columbia University Press, 2005: 39.

12 ཆོས་གྲྭ་ཆེན་པོ་དཔལ་ཞྭ་ལུ་གསེར་ཁང་གི་བདག་པོ་རྗེ་བོ་ལྡེའི་གདུང་རབས། TBRC: W30349: 55a.

13 བསོད་ནམས་རྩེ་མོ། བླ་མ་བ་རི་ལོ་ཙཱ་བ་རིན་ཆེན་གྲགས་ཀྱི་རྣམ་ཐར། TBRC: W20751: 255-266.

14 Hajime Nakamura, *Indian Buddhism: A Survey with Biographical Notes*, Delhi: Motilal Barnasidass, 1987: 335. 渥德尔著、王世安译：《印度佛教史》，北京：商务印书馆，1987：449-450。

15 བསོད་ནམས་རྩེ་མོ། བླ་མ་བ་རི་ལོ་ཙཱ་བ་རིན་ཆེན་གྲགས་ཀྱི་རྣམ་ཐར། TBRC: W20751: 255-266. 亦见渥德尔著、王世安译：《印度佛教史》，1987：232。

16 渥德尔著、王世安译：《印度佛教史》，1987：449-450。

17 恰白 · 次旦平措等：《西藏通史——松石宝串》（上），拉萨：西藏古籍出版社，2004：276。

当时赴金刚座大觉寺学法的重要人物[18]。索南孜摩《喇嘛巴哩译师仁钦扎传记》载，1073年巴哩译师到该寺院求法并拜师于“小金刚座”[19]。“小金刚座”正是“介尊·喜饶琼乃”壁画中人物6喇嘛多杰丹巴琼哇（汉译为“小金刚座”），八思巴称其为“金刚座第二”[20]，他作为大金刚座主的弟子后来继任金刚大觉寺住持。在此，“大、小金刚座”出现在介尊画像上方，说明他们均是介尊在印度金刚大觉寺求法的重要师承，后世将此誉为介尊四大功德之一[21]。这也是此阶段藏传佛教传承上师制度的体现；同时，施主通过艺术家的创作向观者展示了夏鲁寺宗教传承的印度传统。

关于人物7郭瓦·益西雍仲，文献记载略有出入。《布顿佛教史》载“由他的传徒杰准·协迥修建了夏鲁阿谟寺后，他到印度重受戒律仪，后来由廓哇·耶喜雍珠住持夏鲁寺”。[22] 如果郭瓦·益西雍仲是介尊的老师，其阅历应与“卫藏十人”相近，然目前未见史载。图齐本《夏鲁系谱》恰相反，记载其为介尊的主要门徒，曾住持孜（རྩིས）寺[23]。《后藏志》记载郭瓦·益西雍仲是洛师二十四门徒之一，并曾主持泽乃萨（རྩིས་གནས་གསར། 简称 རྩིས་གསར）寺[24]。泽乃萨寺最早是介·赤桑拉巾（介氏家族第七代）建造，该寺供奉介氏家族的护法神[25]。显然，郭瓦与介尊关系密切。前文述洛师初建坚贡寺前后有八个弟子，其中介尊·喜饶琼乃作为洛师近住弟子曾协助建造坚贡寺，最初八弟子中没有郭瓦·益西雍仲。因此，郭瓦·益西雍仲应该是晚于介尊拜师于洛顿·多吉旺秋[26]。《青史》《布顿佛教史》《后藏志》等记载“卫藏十人”以弟子和寺院为扩张其宗教势力的主要手段，介尊所建夏鲁寺作为洛顿的“夏鲁”支系[27]，属于坚贡寺重要属寺。笔者判断介尊赴印度时，寺院更有可能由洛顿弟子代为管理，而郭瓦·益西雍仲可能是最合适人选。

由以上“介尊·喜饶琼乃”壁画中人物5、6、7与介尊关系分析，应证了《后藏志》

18 a. ཇོ་ནང་ཏཱ་ར་ནཱ་ཐ། མྱང་ཡུལ་སྟོད་སྨད་བར་གསུམ་གྱི་ངོ་མཚར་གཏམ་གྱི་ལེགས་བཤད་མཁས་པའི་འཇུག་ངོགས། 1983: 161. b. བསོད་ནམས་རྩེ་མོ། བླ་མ་བ་རི་ལོ་ཙཱ་བ་རིན་ཆེན་གྲགས་ཀྱི་རྣམ་ཐར། TBRC: W20751: 255-266.

19 བསོད་ནམས་རྩེ་མོ། བླ་མ་བ་རི་ལོ་ཙཱ་བ་རིན་ཆེན་གྲགས་ཀྱི་རྣམ་ཐར། TBRC: W20751: 255-266.

20 八思巴：《巴哩法类传承启请文》《萨迦全集（六）· 法王八思巴全集》，东京：东洋文库，1968: 21/2/6-22/1/6。转引自：徐华兰：《巴哩译师传略》《中国藏学》2012（2）：76-86。

21 a. ZNT: 356. b. Giuseppe Tucci, *Tibetan Painted Scrolls II*, 2006: 657. c. སྤེལ་བཟང་དང་རྒྱལ་པོ། ཞྭ་ལུ་དགོན་གྱི་ལོ་རྒྱུས། ལྷ་ས། བོད་ལྗོངས་མི་དམངས་དཔེ་སྐྲུན་ཁང་། 1987: 13.

22 布顿大师著、郭和卿译：《佛教史大宝藏论》，北京：民族出版社，1986：185。

23 Giuseppe Tucci, *Tibetan Painted Scrolls. II*, 2006: 657.

24 ཇོ་ནང་ཏཱ་ར་ནཱ་ཐ། མྱང་ཡུལ་སྟོད་སྨད་བར་གསུམ་གྱི་ངོ་མཚར་གཏམ་གྱི་ལེགས་བཤད་མཁས་པའི་འཇུག་ངོགས། 1983: 102.

25 Giuseppe Tucci, *Tibetan Painted Scrolls. II*, 2006: 657.

26 ཇོ་ནང་ཏཱ་ར་ནཱ་ཐ། མྱང་ཡུལ་སྟོད་སྨད་བར་གསུམ་གྱི་ངོ་མཚར་གཏམ་གྱི་ལེགས་བཤད་མཁས་པའི་འཇུག་ངོགས། 1983: 155-157.

27 ཇོ་ནང་ཏཱ་ར་ནཱ་ཐ། མྱང་ཡུལ་སྟོད་སྨད་བར་གསུམ་གྱི་ངོ་མཚར་གཏམ་གྱི་ལེགས་བཤད་མཁས་པའི་འཇུག་ངོགས། 1983: 157-158. 布顿大师著、郭和卿译：《佛教史大宝藏论》，1986：185。

对夏鲁寺初建戒律不纯的说法，与后弘期佛教传承的基本情况吻合。

介尊右上方的人物 2 介 · 赤主译师与图齐本《夏鲁系谱》中 ཁྲི་འབྲུག 和 TBRC 扫描本《介氏系谱》中 ལྗེ་ལོ་ཙྪ་བ་ཁྲི་འབྲུག 吻合。

图齐本《夏鲁系谱》7a-8b 记载 :

> 介 · 旺钦（ལྗེ་བང་ཆེན）后来成为赞普松赞干布的囊伦（ནང་བློན། 内相）。他有五子 : 长子名纳拉禅惧赤（ནག་ལ་ཆན་གཡུ་ཁྲི），次子名蒙德日努达（སྨོན་ཏོ་རེ་ནུ་མདའ），三子名札巴（གྲགས་པ），四子因拥有自己的盐湖和盐矿（位于现拉堆〈ལ་སྟོད〉地区）而得名擦哇（ཚ་བ）。
>
> 第五子即介 · 赤主译师。……这五子又各生五子，因此被称为“介氏五父”。

这里提到的介 · 赤主和前文提及“介 · 赤桑拉巾”都是介氏家族有建树的译师。介 · 赤主是赤松德赞（ཁྲི་སྲོང་ལྡེ་བཙན）和塞纳勒（སད་ན་ལེགས། 即赤德祖赞）赞普的囊伦。他还翻译了《般若波罗蜜多经》，起草了《声明八品》（སྒྲའི་གནས་བརྒྱད）等文书[28]。《布顿佛教史》也提及此译师，汉译为“犬龙师”，说明他在后弘佛教复兴过程中具有一定影响。贵族高僧大德和译师的出现，是西藏家族势力进一步深入参与政教的表现，介氏家族是其中的代表之一。

壁画题记明示人物 3 介 · 赤主泽西则巴和人物 4 介 · 玉泽则巴均为赤主的弟弟。图齐本《夏鲁系谱》与 TBRC 扫描本《介氏系谱》中记载介 · 旺钦三子札巴和四子擦哇，གྲགས་པ་བྲག་ལ་སྒྲ་ལྷུར་གཟུར་བས（简称 གྲགས་པ）和 ཚ་ཁ་ཚ་སྒོ་ལ་དབང（简称 ཚ་བ）吻合。由此推断人物 3 和人物 4 应该分别对应“介氏五父”之札巴和擦哇。

介尊莲座下方的八位人物名字在图齐本《夏鲁系谱》也可以对应，其中人物 8 堪布介 · 琼哇（汉译 : 介氏小堪布）应该是介尊弟弟西饶耶协。

> 介尊 · 喜饶琼乃之后，其胞弟介 · 西饶耶协（ཤེས་རབ་ཡེ་ཤེས）任堪布。之后，宇妥扎赛桑（གཡུ་ཐོག་སྒྲ་གསེར་བཟང་། 介尊 · 西饶琼乃的叔叔）和玉本（གཡུ་འབུམ། 介尊 · 西饶琼乃之父）之兄，拜见介尊并且请求做他的徒弟，以便皈依佛门。曾传给他的弟弟介尊 · 西饶耶协的夏鲁堪布一职，由宇妥扎赛桑取得。[29]

28 Giuseppe Tucci, *Tibetan Painted Scrolls. II*, 2006: 657.

29 Giuseppe Tucci, *Tibetan Painted Scrolls. II*, 2006: 657.

《后藏志》《夏鲁寺史》有类似记载[30]。人物 9 介·宇妥在《后藏志》为 གཡུ་ཐོག་སྒྲ་གསེར་བཟང[31]，与图齐本《夏鲁系谱》、TBRC 扫描本《介氏系谱》中拼写相同。后来，宇妥违背了介尊的教律，还俗成为夏鲁寺的世俗首领——“本”（དཔོན）[32]，并将寺院堪布职位移交给琼波扎巴僧格（ཁྱུང་པོ་གྲགས་པ་སེང་གེ）。

从介尊到介 · 宇妥，夏鲁寺世俗权力和宗教权力——即“本”和“堪布”基本集于一人，形成一种典型的家族式政教合一，也是目前所知西藏政教合一制度最早的雏形之一。后来，萨迦政权很好地借鉴发扬了这种模式。此外，12 世纪蔡巴噶举政权和 13 世纪的帕竹政权都应该借鉴了夏鲁寺的这一模式。从社会统治阶层的大力支持建寺到赐封土地庄园等政府保障，到全体农户的集体供养，西藏政教合一模式由萌芽时期世俗和宗教两方面的领主相对分离，发展为介 · 宇妥后期的夏鲁寺模式。因此，夏鲁寺成为西藏政教合一模式的重要转折；这种政教合一模式的转变，为另外一种政教合一模式——13 世纪出现的活佛转世制走向成熟，提供了最早的范例。

这种家族式政教合一制[33]的核心是家族豪强政教权力世袭。其现实表现是，后弘初期卫藏地区众多宗教势力为争夺各寺院的经济财产和收入所进行的战争。在此背景下，夏鲁与曲（密）（ཚུ〈མིག〉）发生了对抗[34]。更为重大的是，宇妥任“本”期间，挑起反对坚贡寺的战争；琼波认为坚贡寺就好比诸寺之母，试图阻止他。然而，宇妥不听劝阻，将坚贡寺全部圣物搬至夏鲁寺。这种宗教僭越成为夏鲁寺历史上最冒险的一次势力扩张。

13 世纪，介氏家族与昆氏家族的联姻成为夏鲁寺另一次重要的势力扩张。这一阶段的重要人物便是本壁画人物 10 介 · 邦枚。

图齐本《夏鲁系谱》21b-24a 载：

宇妥扎赛桑之子是介 · 邦巴（ལྕེ་འབུམ་པ）；介 · 邦巴之子是介 · 邦枚（ལྕེ་འབུམ་མེ）和介 · 邦达（ལྕེ་འབུམ་ར）。当时，夏鲁还没有受封万户，但它的权力却相当于万户。当吐蕃王权崩溃的时候，（22a）王国依附于蒙古；夏鲁的四柱八梁，若算上北方的带鬃狮子则为九梁，以及七十椽，各守其势力，开始变得显赫。

介 · 邦枚（ལྕེ་འབུམ་མེ）之子是阿枚 · 格顿桑波（ཨ་མེས་དགེ་འདུན་བཟང་པོ）；

30 a. ཇོ་ནང་ཏཱ་ར་ནཱ་ཐ། མྱང་ཡུལ་སྟོད་སྨད་བར་གསུམ་གྱི་ངོ་མཚར་གཏམ་གྱི་ལེགས་བཤད་མཁས་པའི་འཇུག་ངོགས། 1983: 161-163. b. ZNT: 356.

31 ཇོ་ནང་ཏཱ་ར་ནཱ་ཐ། མྱང་ཡུལ་སྟོད་སྨད་བར་གསུམ་གྱི་ངོ་མཚར་གཏམ་གྱི་ལེགས་བཤད་མཁས་པའི་འཇུག་ངོགས། 1983: 162.

32 张云：《萨迦本钦与乌思藏宣慰使关系问题再探讨》《中国边疆史地研究》1997（1）：35-45。

33 戴发望：《后弘期西藏的政教合一制度》《中国藏学》2006（3）：48-52。

34 Giuseppe Tucci, *Tibetan Painted Scrolls. II*, 2006: 658.

介 · 阿枚邦达（ལྕེ་ཨ་མེས་འབུམ་འདར）之子是阿枚 · 邦丹（ཨ་མེས་འབུམ་བསྟན）和他的兄弟。阿枚 · 邦丹和娘莫绰羌结婚后生阿枚钦波 · 桑结益西（ཨ་མེས་ཆེན་པོ་སངས་རྒྱས་ཡེ་ཤེས）和释迦罗追。

（24a）阿枚钦波 · 桑结（ཨ་མེས་ཆེན་པོ་སངས་རྒྱས）和擦擦尊结婚，生古相 · 阿扎（སྐུ་ཞང་ཛ་སྐྱ），古相·衮波贝（སྐུ་ཞང་མགོན་པོ་དཔལ）[35]、古相·贡嘎本（སྐུ་ཞང་ཀུན་དགའ་འབུམ）及三个女儿，即喀卓本、觉沃达本，觉沃协本，共六个子女。

壁画题记中介 · 邦枚与 TBRC 扫描本《介氏系谱》记载相同，与图齐本《夏鲁系谱》差别不大。人物 11 介 · 邦巴、人物 12 介 · 邦达亦如此。人物 13 介 · 邦丹称为阿枚 · 邦丹。人物 14 介 · 阿枚桑杰即阿枚钦波 · 桑结益西，在洛桑加措《吉祥夏鲁色康祖拉康殊胜所依目录·雪域白花瓣》中载为“阿枚桑杰益西”（ཨ་མེས་སངས་རྒྱས་ཡེ་ཤེས）[36]。人物 15 介 · 阿扎邦即古相 · 阿扎，洛桑加措《吉祥夏鲁色康祖拉康殊胜所依目录 · 雪域白花瓣》记载相同[37]。

介 · 阿枚钦波桑杰益西（介氏家族第十九代）时期[38]，其女儿玛久坎卓本嫁与萨迦白兰王恰那多吉（1239-1267 年），与萨迦的联姻可以看作是介氏家族重新登上西藏上层政治舞台的预演；因此，阿枚 · 桑杰益西之子阿扎、衮波贝、贡嘎本获得了“古相”称号。之后不久，古相 · 阿扎接受了忽必烈汗（1215-1294 年）的封任，成为“夏鲁万户”。

古相 · 阿扎之后，1290 年[39]阿枚 · 桑结益西次子古相 · 衮波贝继任夏鲁“本”职，同年被“国师”益西仁钦宣诏封以“夏鲁万户”，执掌夏鲁寺。衮波贝在任时主持在夏鲁金殿北面建造了三门佛殿[40]，并在殿内塑造了释迦牟尼金像。佛像背光俱全，身着紫红色绸缎袈裟，并在其上饰珍珠。与此同时，缮写了广、中、略三种文集。以此作为其父

35 ཆོས་གྲྭ་ཆེན་པོ་དཔལ་ཞྭ་ལུ་གསེར་ཁང་གི་བདག་པོ་ཇོ་བོ་ལྕེའི་གདུང་རབས། TBRC: W30349: 47, 亦为 སྐུ་ཞང་མགོན་པོ་དཔལ.

36 བློ་གསལ་རྒྱ་མཚོ། དཔལ་ཞ་ལུ་གསེར་ཁང་གཙུག་ལག་ཁང་གི་ངོ་མཚར་རྟེན་དང་བརྟེན་པར་བཅས་པའི་དཀར་ཆག་གངས་དཀར་གྱི་འདབ་མ། དཔལ་ཞ་ལུ་གསེར་ཁང་གཙུག་ལག་ཁང་རྩོམ་སྒྲིག་ཁང་། TBRC: W3CN5306: 27.

37 བློ་གསལ་རྒྱ་མཚོ། དཔལ་ཞ་ལུ་གསེར་ཁང་གཙུག་ལག་ཁང་གི་ངོ་མཚར་རྟེན་དང་བརྟེན་པར་བཅས་པའི་དཀར་ཆག་གངས་དཀར་གྱི་འདབ་མ། TBRC: W3CN5306: 27.

38 1227 年，阿枚 · 桑结益西已经退出夏鲁“本”的职位。参见 ZNT: 360。

39 Giuseppe Tucci, *Tibetan Painted scrolls II*, 2006: 670, 747. 帝师益西仁钦（1286-1291 年在任）于狗年（1290 年）七月一日在元上都颁布的法旨中提到的衮波贝已经是夏鲁的“本”；衮波贝至少任职至 1303 年，因为帝师仁钦坚赞（1303-1305 年在任）于龙年（1304 年）五月二十三日在元上都颁布的法旨中还提到他的儿子多吉旺秋在位。

40 ཇོ་ནང་ཏཱ་ར་ནཱ་ཐ། མྱང་ཡུལ་སྟོད་སྨད་བར་གསུམ་གྱི་ངོ་མཚར་གཏམ་གྱི་ལེགས་བཤད་མཁས་པའི་འཇུག་ངོགས། 1983: 166. Giuseppe Tucci, *Tibetan Painted scrolls II*, 2006: 658-659. ZNT: 19.

阿枚钦波桑结益西的内依怙圣物。《夏鲁系谱》《布顿·仁钦珠传》《夏鲁寺志》也有相同的记载[41]。

大卫·杰克逊依此判定这铺“介尊”壁画年代断为1290-1303年[42]。实地调查中，笔者发现三门佛殿北正壁壁画宝生佛莲座下方西端绘有两位世俗人物，其中一位女性人物题记为སྲས་མོ་པ（萨摩巴，意即“女儿”，应该是嫁于萨迦的“玛久坎卓本”），男性人物题记为དཔོན་པོ་བ（本波哇），后者应该是对衮波贝的尊称，因为他当时是夏鲁地方长官——即“本”(西藏地方官员的俗称)。这两位人物以赞助人的身份出现在三门佛殿。另由大殿壁画风格判断[43]，三门佛殿其他壁画也应为同期创作。

三

通过“介尊”壁画图像及相关史籍信息互证，我们清晰地看到10-14世纪初介氏家族传承对夏鲁寺乃至整个西藏宗教文化传统影响之深。该壁画中人物身份及其关系清晰展现了介氏家族与夏鲁传承的关系演变，让我们看到夏鲁寺传统既保留吐蕃传统，也有正统的印度传统。其次，史载夏鲁寺第四任堪布琼波扎森、俄译师受古格王哲德邀请参加1076年大法会活动[44]，展示出夏鲁寺在后弘期佛教复兴进程中的重要价值——它是积极参与上部和下部弘传的重要寺院。再次，从介尊依附宗教保存家族势力并创建西藏最早的家族式政教合一制度，到介·宇妥的政教改革再到介·阿枚与萨迦联姻，进而与蒙元皇室达成联盟，使介氏家族在西藏的影响达到辉煌之颠；并最终在14世纪开始为夏鲁寺宗教和艺术的繁荣带来了重要契机。

附记：感谢洛萨加措主任、尼玛扎西、于小冬教授给予帮助！感谢熊文彬教授就藏文部分人名音译和部分观点给予指教！感谢郑岩教授对本文存在的拓展性给出十分有益的赐教！

◆ 贾玉平　成都大学美术与设计学院副教授

41 Giuseppe Tucci, *Tibetan Painted scrolls II*, 2006: 658-659. བསོད་ནམས་གྲུབ། སྒྲ་ཚད་པ། ཆོས་རྗེ་ཐམས་ཅད་མཁྱེན་པ་བུ་སྟོན་ལོ་ཙཱ་བའི་རྣམ་པར་ཐར་པ་སྙིམ་པའི་མེ་ཏོག། 1366: 14b. ZNT: 19.

42 David Jeckson, *The Nepalese legacy in Tibetan painting*, New York: Rubin Museum of Art. 2010: 105-106.

43 Franco Ricca and Lionel Fournier, "The Paintings in the Zhwa lu sGo gsum lha khang and bSe sgo ma lha khang: Stylistic Differences." In *The Tibet Journal*, vol.26, nos.3 and 4, 2001: 103-148.

44 ZNT: 359. 管·宣努贝著、王启龙译：《青史》，北京：中国社会科学出版社，2012：298。

夏鲁寺一层集会大殿回廊中的佛传壁画研究 *

孟瑜

内容摘要：夏鲁寺一层集会大殿回廊的第101铺壁画是一铺佛传壁画，它绘出了佛陀一生中具有典型意义的20个场景，涵盖了佛陀自诞生直至涅槃的内容。本文对每幅场景的细节进行深入分析，认为其依据的文本是《神通游戏》(*Lalitavistara*)等几部文献。佛传是藏传佛教中常见的题材，除《一百本生传》中的佛传之外，藏地也产生了许多关于佛传的著述。同时，佛传壁画作为佛教艺术中经常表现的主题，除夏鲁寺外，也见于西藏其他地方。因此，本文在这幅佛传壁画的基础上，初步探讨藏地佛传故事的模式，认为至迟在16世纪时，藏地的佛传无论是在文献上还是图像上都已经呈现出明显的相似性。

夏鲁寺一层集会大殿回廊绘有101铺壁画，时间大致为14世纪初期。这些壁画是依据元代西藏噶玛噶举派黑帽系第三世活佛让琼多吉（རང་བྱུང་རྡོ་རྗེ། 1284-1339年）的《佛陀一百本生传》(སངས་རྒྱས་བཅོམ་ལྡན་འདས་ཀྱི་སྐྱེས་རབས་བརྒྱ་པ། 下文简称《一百本生传》སྐྱེས་རབས་བརྒྱ་པ)[1] 所绘制。虽被称为“一百本生”，但是该著作共包含101品，其中前100品

* 本文是中国藏学研究中心西藏文化博物馆承担的中心重点课题“元代夏鲁寺艺术与汉藏文化交流研究”阶段性成果。

1 སངས་རྒྱས་བཅོམ་ལྡན་འདས་ཀྱི་སྐྱེས་རབས་བརྒྱ་པ། པེ་ཅིན། མི་རིགས་དཔེ་སྐྲུན་ཁང་། 1995.

为佛陀生前的故事，即佛本生；第 101 品《一切义成菩萨本生》（བྱང་ཆུབ་སེམས་དཔའ་དོན་ཐམས་ཅད་གྲུབ་པའི་སྐྱེས་པའི་རབས）虽被称作“本生”，然而却涵盖了佛陀自诞生直至涅槃的内容，因此实则是一篇佛传故事。

一、壁画内容识读

这铺壁画（图一）位于东壁北部。它依据《一百本生传》中的第 101 品[2]，采用分格绘制的方式，绘出了佛陀一生中具有典型意义的 20 个场景。现结合文献依次分析如下：

1. 佛陀于兜率天宫为弥勒授冠[3]（图二：1）

这是整幅佛传故事的第一个情节。根据壁画下方内容相对简略的榜题以及榜题所依据的源文本《一百本生传》中的内容[4]，佛陀在降生人间之前居于兜率天宫，为诸天神讲法；由于悲悯众生并记起了燃灯佛的授记，因而他决定离开兜率天宫；他向众神阐明了原由后，决定弥勒菩萨为自己的继任者并为之授冠；他考察了降生的时间、地点、国家、族系、父母等因素，最终决定降生于印度中部迦毗罗卫城的释迦族，其国王和王后分别为净饭王和摩耶夫人。从这些细节来看，与榜题和源文本最接近的典籍应当是《神通游戏》（*Lalitavistara*）[5]。

画面中佛陀坐在右侧宝座之上，身着菩萨装，他的面前是一个鞠躬礼敬的菩萨，双手捧冠，这是被授冠的弥勒菩萨；佛陀双手持壶，浇水在弥勒头上，这意味着赠予；此二人被其他三个天神围绕，但是其身份并不能一一确定。需要注意的是，佛陀在兜率天宫为弥勒授冠的场景并不是早期佛传中常见的题材，在印度和中亚未曾见过类似的画面，其出现的时间相对较晚。目前所知最早的一个案例是一幅位于印度尼西爪哇岛中部的婆

2　སངས་རྒྱས་བཅོམ་ལྡན་འདས་ཀྱི་སྐྱེས་རབས་བརྒྱ་པ། 1995: 694-725.

3　这 20 个标题为笔者根据画面内容所加，壁画及下方榜题并不包含标题。

4　Kurt Tropper 已对第 101 铺的榜题转写并翻译。参考其论文 "The Buddha-vita in the *skor lam chen mo* at Zha lu monastery"，载 *Pramāṇakīrtiḥ, Papers Dedicated to Ernst Steinkellner on the Occasion of his 70th Birthday*, Part 2, eds. Birgit Kellner, Helmut Krasser, Horst Lasic, Michael Torsten Much and Helmut Tauscher, Wien: Arbeitskreis Für Tibetische und Buddhistische Studien Universität Wien, 2007: 941-973. 另参考 Sarah Richardson 的博士论文 *Painted Books for Plaster Walls: Visual Words in the Fourteenth-Century Murals at the Tibetan Buddhist Temple of Shalu I-III*. Ph.D Thesis, University of Toronto 2016.

5　*Lalitavistara* 的古代汉译本主要是竺法护译《普曜经》和地婆诃罗译《方广大庄严经》。为避免名称混乱，本文将统一使用黄宝生校注的《梵汉对勘神通游戏》（以下简称《神通游戏》）来指代该经。《神通游戏》最终完成时代大约为 7 世纪末或 8 世纪初，其藏文译本大约也在 8 世纪，见黄宝生校注：《梵汉对勘神通游戏》，北京：中国社会科学出版社，2012。榜题参见 Tropper 2007: 946-948, 译文参见 Tropper 2007: 961-962.

图一　夏鲁寺一层集会大殿回廊东壁佛传壁画（中国藏学研究中心提供图片）

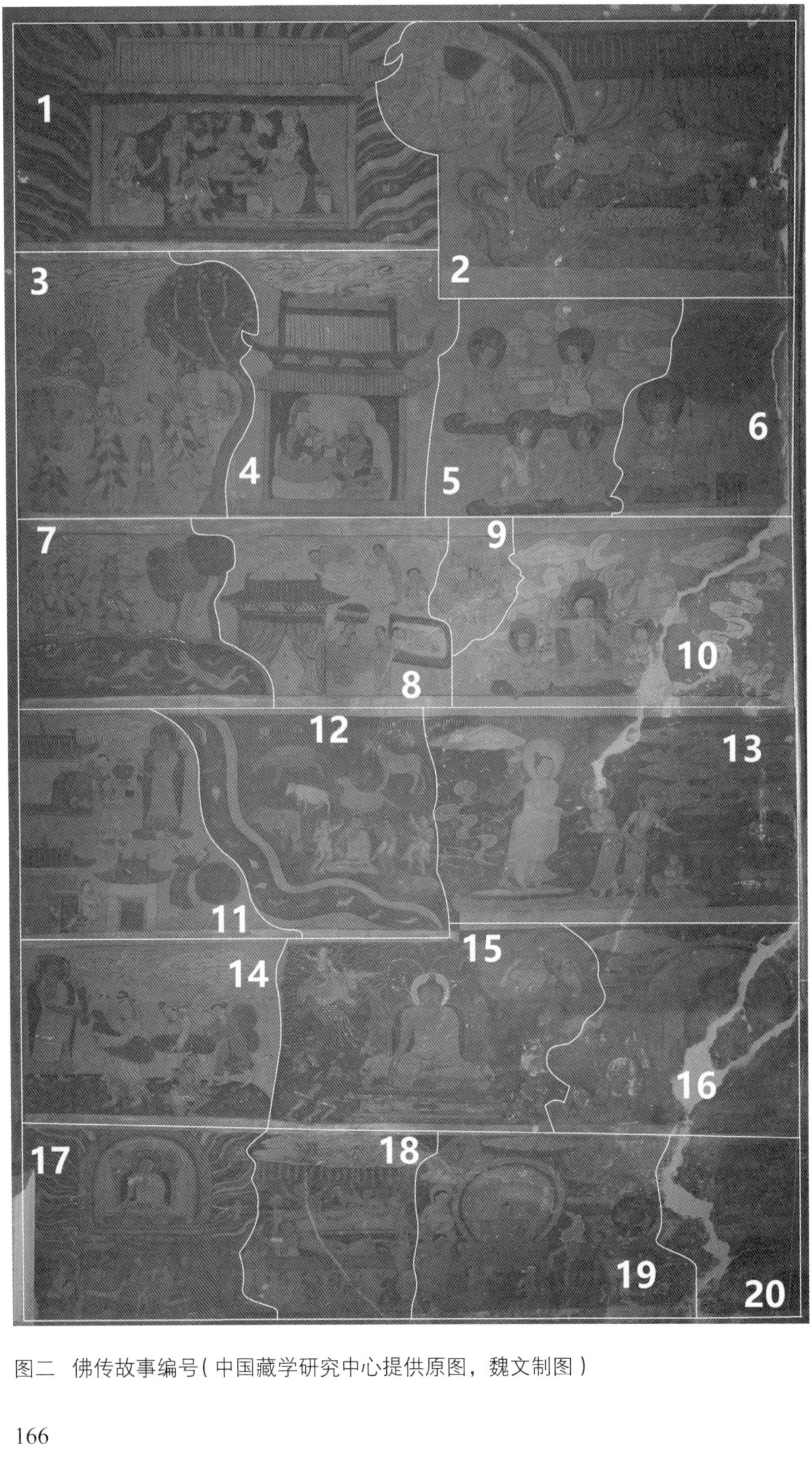

图二　佛传故事编号（中国藏学研究中心提供原图，魏文制图）

罗浮屠塔（Borobudur）塔基的浮雕，时间约为 10 世纪[6]。这个场景的出现应当与佛教在如爪哇岛和西藏等地的传播和建立有密不可分的关系[7]。

2. 入胎 (图二 ：2)

壁画下方的榜题相对简略，仅提到：春天的最后一个月里，满月且伴随 རྒྱལ (puṣya) 星之时，众神之主即因陀罗洁净了摩耶夫人的子宫[8]。源文本则包含更多细节：摩耶夫人梦到一头白象，六牙、红头、装饰精美、步态优雅 ；王后向国王讲述了她的梦之后，国王询问众婆罗门 ；他们都认为这是一个非常惊人的梦，并且预言这个孩子将来会成为转轮王或者佛陀 ；在佛陀入胎之时，众神保护着他 ；因陀罗和梵天也向佛陀献供，并且装饰了房间 ；佛陀入胎时的子宫洁净无尘 ；摩耶也不疲惫，并且感到满足和愉悦[9]。文本中大部分情节与《神通游戏》中的内容相符。唯有因陀罗洁净摩耶夫人子宫这个细节并不见于该经典，这个可以参考根本说一切有部律部的破僧事（*Saṃghabhedavastu*）部分[10]。可见在入胎这个情节上，《一百本生传》吸收了多个文本内容。

在该场景中，摩耶夫人右侧卧于榻上，正在酣睡，床边围绕着三个侍女。一头装饰精美的白象从天而降，准备从夫人左侧入胎。由于入胎是佛传的标志性情节，因此常被绘出，在印度、中亚等地都可以找到很多类似的图像。

3. 诞生（图二 ：3）

壁画下方的榜题仅提到：在蓝毗尼园中，佛陀于第八日出生[11]。而源文本则包含更多细节 ：摩耶夫人预感到自己将要分娩，因此对国王表达想去蓝毗尼园的意愿。国王下令打扫干净蓝毗尼园，尔后众人前往。她右手攀着一根娑罗树树枝，佛陀从她的右胁出生。因陀罗和梵天用柔软的布给佛陀接生。佛陀立刻走了七步，步步生莲并且立誓。随后，那伽给他沐浴。王子被命名为 དོན་ཐམས་ཅད་གྲུབ་པ（意为“一切义成”，即 Siddhārtha，悉达多）；摩耶夫人去世并重生于三十三天；佛陀由摩诃波阇波提和 16 位女子抚养[12]。从这

6 Nicolaas Johannes Krom, *Barabudur, Archeological Description*, 5 vols., New Delhi: Gyan Publishing House, Plate III, 1986[1927].

7 Christian Luczanits, "Prior to Birth, the Tuṣita episodes in Indian Buddhist literature and art." In *The Birth of the Buddha: Proceedings of the Seminar Held in Lumbini, Nepal, October 2004,* eds. Christoph Cüppers, Max Deeg and Hubert Durt. Lumbini International Research Institute: 2010: 41-91, 387-392.

8 榜题参见 Tropper 2007: 948, 译文参见 Tropper 2007: 962-963.

9 源文本的内容可参考 Richardson 2016. 2: 136.

10 *Saṃghabhedavastu. The Gilgit Manuscript of the Saṅghabhedavastu*, 2 vols., ed. R. Gnoli,. Roma: Istituto italiano per il Medio ed Estremo Oriente, 1977-1978.

11 榜题参见 Tropper 2007: 948-949, 译文参见 Tropper 2007: 963.

12 源文本的内容可参考 Richardson 2016. 2: 136.

些细节来看，与榜题和源文本最接近的典籍应当是《神通游戏》。

在画面中，摩耶夫人站一课树下，右手攀着树枝，佛陀从其右胁出生，侍女在摩耶左侧服侍；摩耶右侧的因陀罗和梵天给佛陀接生；佛陀站在一个七层莲台之上；在画面左上方，天神那伽手持水壶，正准备给佛陀沐浴。根据《神通游戏》的内容，佛陀一落地，地上便涌出一朵大莲花，于是佛陀立在莲花上，观察四方[13]。这个细节并未在源文本中提及。而源文本中七步生莲的细节也未在画面中明确绘出。也许画面中的七层莲台正是将这两方面的内容融合在一起，既表现了佛陀出生时站立的那朵莲花，又表示他周行七步。另外，王子命名、摩耶去世以及摩诃波阇波提等女子的形象在画面中未被绘出。

4. 婆罗门观相（图二：4）

这个情节在榜题中缺省，仅在源文本中简略提及：婆罗门预言这个孩子将来要么成为转轮王，要么成为佛陀[14]。由于情节简略，我们无法确定源文本所依据的文本。这个情节在多种经典中均有提及，在此，我们仅援引《神通游戏》这一部文献。根据其内容，佛陀出生后，正在雪山修行的五通大仙阿私陀及其外甥那罗达多立刻飞往迦毗罗卫净饭王处。国王抱着王子向阿私陀展示。阿私陀观察王子有三十二相和八十种好，因而预言这个孩子的两种归宿——转轮王或者佛陀[15]。

这个情节的画面表现十分简略：国王居于宫殿之内，手持襁褓之中的婴儿向给婆罗门展示。婆罗门伸出手掌，指向不同方向，预言王子的两种命运。

5. 王子习学（图二：5）

根据榜题和源文本的内容，王子长大后，接受学业培养。事实上，王子早具诸能，因此他入学只是为了利益众生[16]。这个情节在多种经典中均有提及。

这个情节用上下两个分镜头表示出来。在上面的场景中，王子正在学习藏文三十字母。但藏文是不符合文献记载的[17]。藏文这一因素的加入应当是是佛传故事在西藏本土化的体现。下面的场景描绘了两个正在交谈的人，并没有具体所指习学内容，因而只是象征性的表现。

13 黄宝生校注：《梵汉对勘神通游戏》2012: 152。

14 源文本的内容可参考 Richardson 2016. 2: 136.

15 黄宝生校注：《梵汉对勘神通游戏》2012: 179-196。

16 榜题为参见 Tropper 2007: 949，翻译参见 Tropper 2007: 963.

17 根据文献内容，王子虽入学堂学习文字，但是王子在老师尚未教授的情况下，便已经知晓世上诸多文字（例如《神通游戏》中是 64 种文字，参考黄宝生校注：《梵汉对勘神通游戏》2012: 218-219），然而，藏文并不在其中。

6. 树下观禅（图二：6）

这个情节在榜题中缺省，仅在源文本中提到。有一次，王子去了一个村庄。在一个环境宜人的地方，王子结跏趺坐并观禅。由于王子禅定的力量，仙人们飞到这个树林时，不能从王子上空越过[18]。画面十分简单，仅描绘了一棵树并树下禅定的王子。

虽然文本和图像都十分简略，但是这却是一个非常重要的情节，因为这是王子的"第一次禅定"。这个情节应当是依据《神通游戏》绘出，因为只有在这个版本中，王子的"第一次禅定"发生在少年时期，并且源文本提到的奇异现象也符合该经的内容[19]。

7. 比赛（图二：7）

这个画面展现的是王子与同伴之间射箭和游泳的比赛。这个情节在榜题中提到，并且榜题中包含更多的比赛项目，如算数、文字等[20]。比赛是为了结婚，但是这个原因[21]却在榜题中省去，仅在源文本中提及[22]。该情节可对照《神通游戏》中的《技艺示现品》[23]。

8. 出游四门（图二：8）

在这个画面中，我们可以看到王子坐在车上，右侧有三个裸体的人和一个僧人模样的人（站立和躺卧应当是同一个人的两种姿态）。按照情节发展，这应当表现的是王子出游四门并且遇到老人、病人、死人以及僧人的场景。然而这一情节却在榜题中缺省。榜题中仅提到：王子坐在精美华丽的宫殿里，宫女们在演奏音乐。忽然一些声音传来，劝王子记起前世的事情，放弃尘世生活并成为众生的保护者[24]。但这些内容在壁画中未绘出。榜题中提到的内容可参考《神通游戏》中的《鼓励品》[25]。

与画面对应的内容出现在源文本中：众神向王子依次展现了老、病、死的景象，王子问有什么办法可以逃离这些，众神因而又向他展示了一个受戒的修行者形象，王子对这个身着橘黄色袍子的、平静安详的人赞叹不已，并且也想成为这样的人[26]。该情节可参

18 源文本的内容可参考 Richardson 2016. 2: 136.

19 黄宝生校注：《梵汉对勘神通游戏》2012: 224-225; Ernst Waldschmidt, *Die Legende vom Leben des Buddha*, Hamburg: Tibetisches Zentrum e. V., 1991: 10 [Volksverband der Bucherfreunde Wegweiser Verlag 1929].

20 榜题参见 Tropper 2007: 949-950，翻译参见 Tropper 2007: 963.

21 关于这场比赛的原因，不同的文献记述不同。Dieter Schlingloff, *Ajanta: Handbuch der Malereien/Handbook of the Paintings. Part 1: Erzählende Wandmalereien/Narrative Wall-paintings*. 3 vols. Wiesbaden: Harrassowitz, 2000: 349。

22 略去的源文本的内容可参考 Richardson 2016. 2: 136.

23 黄宝生校注：《梵汉对勘神通游戏》2012: 237-276.

24 榜题参见 Tropper 2007: 950-951，翻译参见 Tropper 2007: 964.

25 黄宝生校注：《梵汉对勘神通游戏》2012: 277-339.

26 这些内容可参考 Richardson 2016. 2: 137.

考《神通游戏》中的《感梦品》[27]。

9. 出家逾城（图二：9）

在这个画面中，王子骑马腾空而去，这表现的是佛传中重要的几个情节之一——出家逾城，然而这个情节却被十分简单地绘出。但是榜题中包含更多的细节：王子命令仆人牵来马；之后四位天神抱住马蹄，因陀罗打开大门，四天王及其随从保护王子，梵天及其随从向王子献供，最终王子成功离家[28]。源文本中还提到：那伽等众神将地方打扫干净；王子离宫六由旬后，于破晓时分与众神和仆人告别，并将马和饰物还给仆人；仆人回到宫中[29]。

画面简略至此，我们其实很难判断其文本依据，并且榜题和源文本中提到的内容见于多种经典，因而也并不能给出一个相当确切的文本来源。我们权且可以参考《神通游戏》中的《出家品》[30]。

10. 削发（图二：10）

在这个画面中，王子居中，用剑削发，在他的两侧各有一个天神形象的人用钵一类的容器接住落发，在他们的后面有一座塔。这个情节在榜题中仅简略提及：王子用双手拔掉自己的头发并弃之[31]。而在源文本提到，王子将割下的头发给了因陀罗，随后因陀罗将头发带到了兜率天宫[32]。因此两个之一极有可能是因陀罗，但是另外一位身份尚不能确定。从画面表现上看，这个情节是王子形象的转折点，因为从此以后，王子便以常见的佛陀形象出现。

值得注意的是，无论是榜题还是源文本都没有提到王子背后的塔。关于塔这个细节，我们可以参考《神通游戏》中《出家品》[33]：在王子削发时，两侧的忉利天神（Trāyastriṃśa）供养王子的落发，并树立了一座名为“接受顶髻（cuda-pratigrahana）”的塔。图像和榜题间的这个差异表明，二者并非依据同样的文本来源。

另外，源文本中还提到了一些情节，但是在画面中没有体现。例如，王子与一个天神伪装的猎人交换衣服，他将华服赠予猎人并穿上猎人的橘黄色粗布衣；再如，王子仆

27 黄宝生校注：《梵汉对勘神通游戏》2012: 340-363.

28 榜题参见 Tropper 2007: 951-952，翻译参见 Tropper 2007: 964-966.

29 这些内容可参考 Richardson 2016. 2: 137.

30 黄宝生校注：《梵汉对勘神通游戏》2012: 364-413。

31 榜题参见 Tropper 2007: 952，译文参见 Tropper 2007: 966.

32 这些内容可参考 Richardson 2016. 2: 138.

33 黄宝生校注：《梵汉对勘神通游戏》2012: 413.

人回到宫中，宫里所有人都十分悲伤；又如，王子遍访老师求道等等[34]。

11. 见频毗沙罗王（图二：11）

这个场景发生在苦行之前，表现的是菩萨在一个城中乞食。这个场景并未在榜题中提及。根据源文本的内容，我认为这个情节表现的是菩萨入王舍城乞食，遇见频毗沙罗王（Bimbisāra）并受到他的礼遇[35]。与菩萨相对而立、手持食物且着俗装的人也许就是频毗沙罗王；另外的人或许是王舍城中的居民，他们看到菩萨到来，纷纷出门礼敬或带来食物。但是由于文本中情节简略，我们无法准确判断场景中每一个人的身份。该情节可参考《神通游戏》中的《频毗沙罗来访品》[36]。

12. 苦行（图二：12）

在这个场景中，菩萨在尼连禅河边的草地上苦行，几个牧人用木棍戳他的耳朵，然而菩萨不为所动。这个情节的画面表现与榜题表现不一致。榜题的内容为：在菩萨苦行之时，几个牧牛的孩子朝他身上扔脏东西；尽管如此，菩萨岿然不动；他每天只吃一粒芝麻；无论环境多么艰苦，他毫无动摇；就这样，他经历了六年的苦行[37]。榜题中的内容可参考《神通游戏》中的《苦行品》[38]。而木棍戳耳朵的细节应当来自一些较为古老的文本，例如《中部》（*Majjhimanikaya*）[39]等。

13. 接受乳糜供养（图二：13）

这个场景展现的是菩萨接受苏迦塔的乳糜供养。苦行了六年之后，菩萨意识到这样无法得到觉醒，于是放弃苦行并且开始吃真正的食物。随后他去了鹿野苑，开始接受人们的供养。苏迦塔正是在此时向佛陀献乳糜。情节从右到左发展：牛奶挤出后盛在奶牛旁边的两个桶中；接着，苏迦塔（配有头光）和她的朋友一起用锅（奶牛前方的方形容器）熬制乳糜；最后，苏迦塔（她被第二次绘出）将乳糜献给菩萨；菩萨喝了乳糜后，身体恢复。这个情节在榜题中缺省，仅在源文本中提及。源文本还包含这之后许多情节，例如菩萨喝完乳糜之后，将杯子扔到水中，那伽王将它拿出，随后因陀罗将它带回天上

34 见 Richardson 2016. 2: 138.

35 Richardson 认为这个场景是菩萨寻找教法，见 Richardson 2016. 1: 236.

36 黄宝生校注：《梵汉对勘神通游戏》2012: 439-455.

37 榜题参见 Tropper 2007: 952-953，译文参见 Tropper 2007: 966.

38 黄宝生校注：《梵汉对勘神通游戏》2012: 456-483.

39 Schlingloff 2000: 369.

并供养[40]。这部分内容可以参考《神通游戏》中的《尼连河品》[41]。

14. 吉祥施草（图二：14）

这个场景展现的是草商吉祥（བཀྲ་ཤིས། Svastika）向菩萨献草。情节从右下方的割草人开始，转至右上方的背草人，接着吉祥用双手抱着草，最后吉祥（他被第二次绘出）将草献给菩萨。该场景在下方榜题中提及，但榜题包含更多细节，诸如菩萨接受献草之后，敷草作座于菩提树下并誓得证悟等等[42]。这部分内容可以参考《神通游戏》中的《前往菩提道场品》[43]。

15. 降魔成道（图二：15）

这个场景展现的是降魔，它标志着佛陀的觉醒。画面中佛陀居中结跏趺坐；两侧的魔众用各种手段向他发起进攻；佛陀右手持触地印击退魔军——我们可以看到，在画面左下方的一个魔罗所执的武器顶部已变成了花。

相对于榜题和源文本，该场景的画面表现十分简略。榜题中提到：魔军向菩萨发起各种各样的进攻；他们的力量使山峰和大地震动；到了夜里，他们又显现出各种恐怖的模样；而菩萨通过禅定完全击溃了魔军，并且在世间建立了法的国度[44]。源文本中则包含更多的细节：魔军来到菩提树前，菩萨却保佑众人既看不到他们的样子，也听不到他们的声音；随后魔军向菩萨投掷武器，而武器变成了花；菩萨以手触地，地神和一千个追随者出现，他们为菩萨作证，证明菩萨已经积累了上千次的功德；魔王的女儿们到菩萨跟前展示了三十二种幻术，而菩萨将她们变成了很丑的老妇；她们恳请菩萨将其复原，随后菩萨恢复了她们原来的样子；最终，菩萨战胜了魔军，觉醒成佛，转动了法轮[45]。

降魔成道是佛陀传记中重要的情节，在多种经典中均有提及[46]。由于这个情节榜题内容和图像表现都很简略，因此我们并不能准确判断其文献来源。

40 这些内容可参考 Richardson 2016. 2: 138.

41 黄宝生校注：《梵汉对勘神通游戏》2012: 484-502。源文本中还包含一些情节，并不见于该经典，例如由于菩萨的福祉，水中一条失明的蛇恢复了视力，因而赞美菩萨。这个情节出现在很多其他的文本中。这说明源文本的来源也并不统一。由于这个情节和画面无关，因此不放在文中讨论。

42 榜题为参见 Tropper 2007: 953，译文参见 Tropper 2007: 966.

43 黄宝生校注：《梵汉对勘神通游戏》2012: 503-534.

44 榜题参见 Tropper 2007: 954-955，译文参见 Tropper 2007: 967.

45 这些内容可参考 Richardson 2016. 2: 139.

46 关于降魔的文献可参考张丽香博士的相关研究。参见 Zhang Lixiang, *Der Sieg über Māra im Leben des Buddha in den literarischen und bildlichen Überlieferungen von Indien bis Zentralasien*, PhD Dissertation, Ludwig-Maximilians-Universität München, 2008.

16. 初转法轮（图二：16）

这个场景接在降魔之后，展现的应当是佛陀在鹿野苑的初转法轮，但是画面保存状况不佳。我们可以看到佛陀居中结跏趺坐，双手有可能持说法印，他的座前有一个不完整的法轮；画面右侧有五个模糊的比丘形象——这是最早的出家僧团；画面左下方有一个女子，她双手捧物礼敬佛陀。画面大部分内容均与榜题相符，但是女子的细节在榜题及源文本中均未提及，因此其身份尚不能确定。该场景可以参考《神通游戏》中的《转法轮品》[47]。

在“降魔成道”和“初转法轮”这两个情节之间，榜题和源文本还提到了一些情节，但这些情节在壁画中未被绘出，例如商人帝履富娑（ག་གོན། Trapuṣa）和婆履（བཟང་ཚོ། Bhallika）对佛陀献供，四天王献钵；梵天劝请等等[48]。这些内容可以参考《神通游戏》中的《帝履富娑和婆履品》和《劝请品》[49]。

17. 舍卫城神变（图二：17）

这个情节在榜题中仅被简略提及，即为降伏外道，佛陀在舍卫城示现大神变[50]。但是画面包含更多细节，例如佛陀居中，被波浪条纹所围绕，这代表他放出的光明；光明中有四个或立或坐的佛陀，这是佛陀示现的化身；下方的六个人应当是被降服的六师外道；水和树（可能是芒果树[51]）也是佛陀示现的神变。

舍卫城神变是一个常见的题材，而画面所表现出的内容在文献中一般均有提及，因此我们并不能准确判断其文献来源。

18. 涅槃（图二：18）

这个场景展现的是佛陀涅槃。佛陀右侧卧于画面中央的榻上，弟子们围绕在榻边痛哭哀号，上方还有两个飞舞撒花的天神。该情节所对应的榜题和源文本内容为：四月十五日，佛陀意识到生命将尽，于是宣布将入涅槃。佛陀“狮子卧”于床，而后入涅槃。此时，世间六种震动[52]。由此可见，壁画表现较文本内容简略。但是由于无论画面表现还是文字内容，都没有可以判断版本的具体的细节，因此我们无法确定其文献来源[53]。

47 黄宝生校注：《梵汉对勘神通游戏》2012: 753-817.

48 榜题参见 Tropper 2007: 955-957，译文参见 Tropper 2007: 967-968.

49 黄宝生校注：《梵汉对勘神通游戏》2012: 683-752.

50 榜题为参见 Tropper 2007: 957，译文参见 Tropper 2007: 968.

51 Schlingloff 2000: 488, 498.

52 榜题参见 Tropper 2007: 957-958，译文参见 Tropper 2007: 968.

53 “涅槃”一节在多种经典中均有提及，可参考宫治昭相关研究。参见宮治昭：涅槃と弥勒の図像学：インドから中央アジアへ，博士論文，名古屋大学，1991。

19. 荼毗（图二：19）

这个情节表现的事佛陀肉身的火化。佛陀居于画面中央，背后绘出火焰，此时他的身量要比之前场景中的小很多，这象征着逐渐缩小的佛身。该场景与榜题内容相符：火焚烧佛身，佛身逐渐缩小，直至芥子大小[54]。但是由于榜题内容简略，画面中的一些细节无法确定，例如佛陀周围的天神和弟子等。

20. 分发舍利（图二：20）

这是夏鲁寺一层回廊佛传的最后一个情节——分发舍利。该情节所对应的榜题和源文本内容为：佛陀涅槃之后，比丘阿那律（མ་འགགས་པ། Aniruddha）收集起佛陀的舍利；四枚智慧佛牙被献供给因陀罗、龙王、犍陀罗和羯陵伽（ཀ་ལིང་། Kaliṅga）国王；婆罗门徒卢那（ཟྲེ་བོ། Droṇa）将佛舍利均分为八份，分往八处；随后，人间建立了七座塔，龙宫建了一座；后来，阿育王的儿子建了各种各样的塔，因而佛塔遍布世间[55]。

该幅情节画面漫漶不清，可辨识出的细节有限：中央为一佛座；佛座下方有一个僧人，这也许是收敛佛骨的比丘阿那律；佛座上方是一个婆罗门形象，这应该是分舍利的徒卢那；佛座周围分散着八个袋子（佛座右侧三个，左侧五个），这应该是等分的舍利；最外层围绕着九个（？）人物，但是由于画面不清晰，尚不能准确判断他们的身份。

通过上述分析可知，这幅佛传壁画的榜题来源并不统一。前16个情节除个别细节外，基本上可以参考《神通游戏》；最后四个情节来自多种其他文献，但由于内容简略，我们并不能准确判断其文献来源。壁画图像和榜题内容基本相符，但是在某些细节上，图像明显依据其他文本传统。这表明，艺术家并非完全按照文本内容绘制壁画，而且从壁画中某些程式化的表现可知，他们极有可能遵循着自己的粉本传统进行创作。

二、藏地佛传模式略探

从上述题记和画面的内容来看，第101品《一切义成菩萨本生》是让琼多吉以《神通游戏》为基础，融合其他多种文献而成。虽然在文章的末尾让琼多吉提到了 དཔའ་བོ，这似乎暗指作者圣勇（Āryaśūra, སློབ་དཔོན་དཔའ་བོ）[56]，但是在圣勇所著《本生鬘》（*Jātakamālā*）中并未见这样一则佛教故事，所以第101品应当是让琼多吉自己的撰述。

54 榜题参见 Tropper 2007: 958-959，译文参见 Tropper 2007: 969.

55 榜题参见 Tropper 2007: 959，译文参见 Tropper 2007: 969-970.

56 榜题参见 Tropper 2007: 960，译文参见 Tropper 2007: 970.

这篇佛传虽然包含了20个情节，但是让琼多吉对佛陀生平事迹的总述仍然回到了藏地独特的佛传叙事传统中，即十二宏化。这部分内容位于整篇榜题的末尾部分，但不幸地是，很多文字已经残损。根据Tropper的识读，让琼多吉对佛陀一生的总结共计十二个事业，即降临、入胎、诞生、学习、游戏、出家、苦行、前往菩提道场、降伏魔王、觉醒、转动法轮和涅槃[57]。

对十二宏化进行明确阐述的当属布顿大师（1290-1364年），但是他在《佛教史大宝藏论》提到的十二宏化体系事实上来自《究竟一乘宝性论》中的偈颂，即从兜率天退（དགའ་ལྡན་ནས་ནི་འཕོ་བ），入胎（ལྷུམས་སུ་འཇུག），生（བལྟམས་པ），习学诸伎艺（བཟོ་ཡི་གནས་ལ་མཁས་པ），厌离诸欲相（བཙུན་མོའི་འཁོར་གྱིས་དགྱེས་རོལ），出家（ངེས་འབྱུང），行苦行（དཀའ་བ་སྤྱོད་པ），往诣于道场（བྱང་ཆུབ་སྙིང་པོར་གཤེགས་པ），降伏诸魔众（བདུད་སྡེ་འཇོམས），成大妙觉尊（རྫོགས་པར་བྱང་ཆུབ），转无上法轮（ཆོས་ཀྱི་འཁོར་ལོ）和入无余涅　（མྱ་ངན་འདས་པར་གཤེགས་མཛད）[58]。与这个体系相比，榜题中这部分的内容也是根基于这个体系，但仅是一个略写，例如以 འཕོ 表示 དགའ་ལྡན་ནས་ནི་འཕོ་བ, བཟོ 表示 བཟོ་ཡི་གནས་ལ་མཁས་པ 等等。

《究竟一乘宝性论》并没有对这个纲要铺陈，《佛教史大宝藏论》中有关佛陀十二事业细致描写是布顿在这个纲要之上，融汇各种经典中的内容合缀而成。同样的情形也出现在让琼多吉的所编纂的《一切义成菩萨本生》中。但是，对比让琼多吉和布顿有关佛陀生平的撰述，二者虽然都基本上选材于《神通游戏》《涅槃经》等几部经典，但是两人的叙事并不完全一致，让琼多吉的撰述较之布顿要简单得多。

像让琼多吉和布顿这样，用《神通游戏》等几部经典来组合汇编佛陀生平的作者在藏地不乏少数。尤其是伴随着布顿所述十二宏化在藏地的广泛流传，后世对于佛陀生平的再叙述也大多采用这样的框架。这种情形的出现与《神通游戏》自身特点有直接关系，因为这部经典中的佛传终结于佛陀的初转法轮，因此作者为了叙述一个完整的生平必须要借鉴其他经典中的内容。

另外，在这种叙事传统的大背景下，藏地的佛传图像也逐渐趋同。因此，集会大殿回廊中的这幅佛传壁画无论在情节选择还是在画面表现上在藏地都并不特殊，我们可以发现很多来自不同时期的类似图像。比如，夏鲁寺般若佛母殿内还有另外一铺绘制于14

57 榜题参见 Tropper 2007: 960，翻译参见 Tropper 2007: 970-971. Tropper 认为，让琼多吉是按照布顿所归纳的十二宏化事迹对佛陀生平进行总结，但是题记中实际辨别出的不足九个。

58 བུ་སྟོན་རིན་ཆེན་གྲུབ། བུ་སྟོན་ཆོས་འབྱུང། པེ་ཅིན།། ཀྲུང་གོའི་བོད་ཀྱི་ཤེས་རིག་དཔེ་སྐྲུན་ཁང་། 1991：82-117. 汉译本见布顿大师著，郭和卿译：《佛教史大宝藏论》，北京：民族出版社，1986：69-101。另参考萨尔吉：《佛传叙事演变略探——从四相成道到十二宏化事迹》《藏学学刊》第15辑，北京：中国藏学出版社，2018：18-19。

世纪的佛传壁画[59]。其中很多情节的表现形式与前述回廊中的佛传壁画相同，如削发、涅槃等；还有一些情节，其细节表现虽略有不同，但是大体相仿，如入胎、婆罗门观相等。除此之外，我们还可以参考东嘎1号窟（11世纪）[60]、贡嘎曲德寺（15世纪）[61]等地的佛传壁画及大量的唐卡作品，此处不再赘言。

至迟在16世纪时，藏地的佛传无论是在文献上还是图像上都已经呈现出一种强烈的模式化倾向。这样的叙事方式曾被多罗那他（1575-1634年）旗帜鲜明地反对。在他看来，如此叙事，是将"大乘"和"小乘"经典混为一谈，因此多罗那他在他自己编写的佛传著作《信仰之日》（དད་པའི་ཉིན་བྱེད）中用125章的篇幅详述佛陀的一生，且完全采用了所谓"小乘"经典中的语料[62]。

多罗那他的批判反而使人思考他所批判的对象——从文献上来看，藏地很多佛传的内容都是以《神通游戏》等几部文献为依据，尤其是《神通游戏》似乎总是被使用，但是以现在我们掌握的材料来看，我们还无法准确归纳出《神通游戏》究竟被使用到何种程度；从图像上看，藏地的佛传图像有很大的相似性。因此，处理这些佛传内容时，不仅需要细致的图文互证的工作，还需要在此基础之上对文献和图像这两方面材料各自的相似和差异之处进行标注，同时还应深入考察藏地早期的佛传内容的表现形式和形成原因，从而才能更好地揭示藏地的佛传模式。

◆ 孟瑜　中国人民大学国学院讲师

59 Verena Ziegler, *A preliminary report on the life of Buddha Śākyamuni-In the murals of the circumambulatory of the Prajñāpāramitā chapel in Zha lu*. https://www.asianart.com/articles/ziegler/index.html, 2009, accessed on 10.06.2019.

60 关于东嘎1号窟的佛传故事，参见四川大学中国藏学研究所、四川大学历史文化考古学系、西藏自治区文物事业管理局编：《皮央·东嘎遗址考古报告》，成都：四川人民出版社，2008：46-59。Kurt Tropper, *The Buddha-vita in Cave 1 of Dung dkar (Mnga' ris)*，载[奥]恭特朗·哈佐德、沈卫荣主编：《西藏宗谱：纪念古格·次仁加布藏学研究文集》，北京：中国藏学出版社，2018：649-677。另见Christiane Kalantari在"第七届西藏考古与艺术国际学术讨论会"上的会议报告*The Visual and Textual Narrative of the Life of the Buddha at Dungkar, Ngari: Preliminary Attempt at a Reconstruction and Interpretation of the Complete Wall-painting Cycle*，成都，2018年10月20日。

61 罗文华、格桑曲培主编：《贡嘎曲德寺壁画——藏传佛教美术史的里程碑》，北京：故宫出版社，2015：34-38。

62 Andrew Quintman & Kurtis Schaeffer, "The Life of the Buddha at Rtag brtan Phun tshogs gling Monastery in Text, Image, and Institution: A Preliminary Overview."《藏学学刊》第13辑，2016：32-73、36-37。

Art Historical Evidence for a Cult of the Triloknāth Lokeśvara in Zangskar

Rob Linrothe

Abstract: The Triloknāth Mandir (temple) has been of enduring interest to historians of religion, anthropology, art history and architecture since the nineteenth century. It is located in Tunde (Tib. Ras phag) Village along the Chandrabhaga River valley in Himachal Pradesh, on the periphery of the Western Himalayan Buddhist horizon. The Drukpa Kagyu monk Taktsang Repa (Stag tshang ras pa, 1574-1651) visited it in the seventeenth century, and the account of his pilgrimage to what he seems to have assumed was Uḍḍīyana, attracted the attention of Giuseppe Tucci. Part of Triloknāth's fascination is the fact that contemporary villagers in the region identify and revere the white marble image of Sugatiśaṃdārśana Lokeśvara as Śiva, while Buddhist visitors from Lahul, Zangskar, and other areas recognize it as Buddhist. In recent years, a Buddhist monk and a Hindu *pujārī* are deputed to assist both types of visitors. Another alluring issue is that a temple with a *śikhara* in the Nāgara style usually associated with north Indian Brahmanical architecture houses a Buddhist sculpture, and that too carved in white marble, a highly unusual material in Himalayan Buddhism. No overwhelming consensus has been arrived at about either the date of the temple, or the sculpture installed within it, or whether the architecture was "originally" Brahmanical and then adapted to house a Buddhist image, or was Buddhist from start. Rather than taking up those well-rehearsed if unresolved matters, here I focus on the iconography of the image in question, Sugatiśaṃdārśana Lokeśvara, its association with Kashmir, and the appearance in neighboring Zangskar of images that appear to be copies of the particular white marble sculpture now in Triloknāth. Most of the Zangskari images are relatively late, and so this study may indirectly contribute some evidence to

Fig. 1 Triloknāth Mandir in Tunde Village, Himachal Pradesh, India
(Photograph attributed to Henry Cousens, Snr, ca. 1865-1870. The Hugh A. Rayner Collection, Bath, England).

the issue of the date of white marble sculpture in the Triloknāth Mandir and when it replaced an earlier, smaller grey stone image of the same deity also preserved there.

The Triloknāth Mandir (temple) has been of enduring interest to historians of religion, anthropology, art history and architecture since the nineteenth century (Figs. 1, 2, 3).[1] It is located in Tunde (Tib. Ras phag) Village along the Chandrabhaga River valley in Himachal Pradesh, on the periphery of the Western Himalayan Buddhist horizon (Fig. 4). The Drukpa Kagyu monk Taktsang Repa (Stag tshang ras pa; 1574-1651) visited it in the seventeenth century, and the account of his pilgrimage to what he seems to have assumed was Uḍḍīyana, attracted

1 Vogel 1902: 35-41; Maxwell 1980: 9-74; Young Drukpa Association 2011: 41-46, 134-137; Widorn and Kozicz 2012: 15-35; Cousens 2014; Cousens 2015: 241-262; Widorn 2015: 189-235; Kozicz and Grimm in press.

Fig. 2 Triloknāth Mandir in Tunde Village, Himachal Pradesh, India (Photo: Rob Linrothe, 2018).

Fig. 3 Upper part of Triloknāth Mandir *śikhara* in the Nāgara style (Photo: Rob Linrothe, 2018).

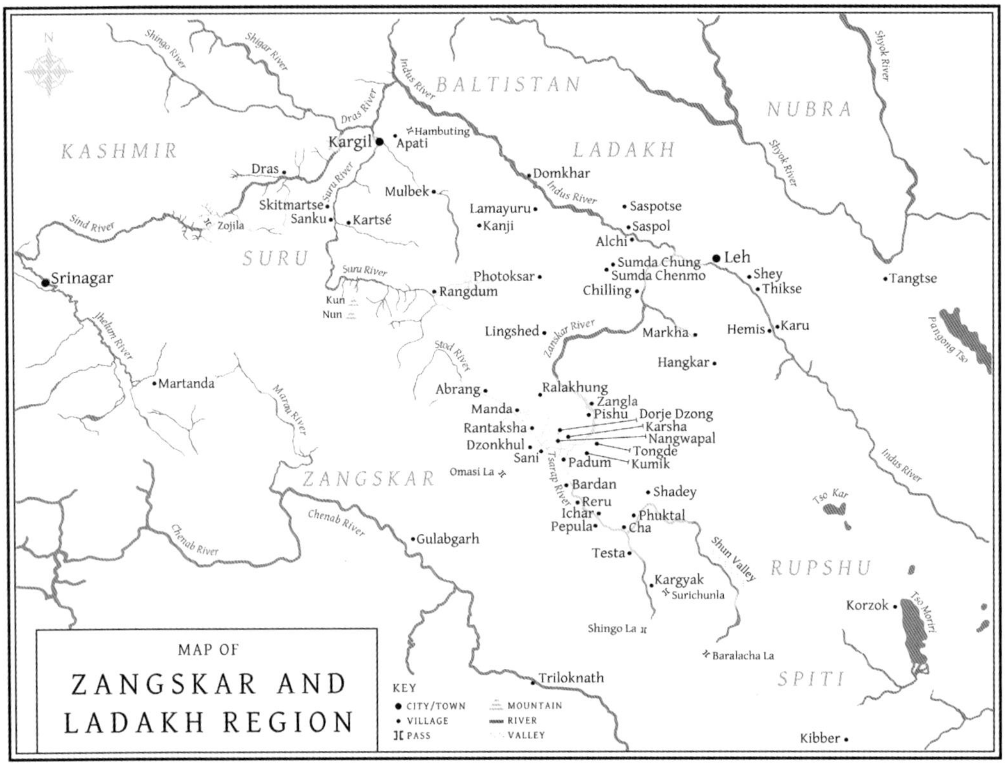

Fig. 4 Map of Ladakh, Zangskar and northern Himachal Pradesh (Map prepared by Mel Keiser).

the attention of Giuseppe Tucci.[2] Part of Triloknāth's fascination is the fact that contemporary villagers in the region identify and revere the white marble image of Sugatiśaṃdārśana Lokeśvara as Śiva, while Buddhist visitors from Lahul, Zangskar, and other areas recognize it as Buddhist (Fig. 5). In recent years, a Buddhist monk and a Hindu *pujārī* are deputed to assist both types of visitors. Another alluring issue is that a temple with a *śikhara* in the Nāgara style usually associated with north Indian Brahmanical architecture houses a Buddhist sculpture, and that too carved in white marble, a highly unusual material in Himalayan Buddhism.[3] No overwhelming consensus has been arrived at about either the date of the temple, or the sculpture installed within it, or whether the architecture was "originally" Brahmanical and then adapted to house a Buddhist image, or was Buddhist from the start. Rather than taking up those

2 Tucci 1971: 369-418.

3 Mahesh Sharma argues that rare marble images in north India have been misdated much earlier than they should be; see Sharma 2013: 161-175. Vogel also highlights the medium's rarity, noting that white marble is "a material, which I did not find used anywhere else in the Kullū sub-division". Vogel 1902: 36.

Fig. 5 Sugatiśaṃdārśana Lokeśvara, date and origin unknown, white marble, approx. 90 cm (Photograph by unknown photographer; purchased by the author in a commercial framing shop in Manali, Himachal Pradesh, 2018).

well-rehearsed if unresolved matters, in what follows I focus on three tangential issues.

They are: the iconography of the image in question, Sugatiśaṃdārśana Lokeśvara, its association with Kashmir, and the appearance in neighboring Zangskar of images that appear to refer to the particular white marble sculpture now in Triloknāth. Most of the Zangskari images are relatively late, and so this study may indirectly contribute some data relevant to the issue of the date of the white marble sculpture in the Triloknāth Mandir and when it replaced an earlier, smaller grey stone image of the same deity also preserved there, though their dating is not the main focus here.

As for the iconography of Sugatiśaṃdārśana Lokeśvara, in the *Sādhanamālā*, this form appears under the title of Bhaṭṭāraka Sugatiśaṃdārśana Lokeśvara,[4] which translated means the Great Lord (Bhaṭṭāraka) Lokeśvara who blissfully looks on all things with impartial eyes (Sugatiśaṃdārśana).[5] Its precise form is prescribed in the text as a white, one headed, six-armed form of Avalokiteśvara. The text provides a quite specific set of attributes and gestures and with one exception they correspond surprisingly well to surviving images from Kashmir, Zangskar and the two at Triloknāth. Most distinctive is the so-called *tridaṇḍa* held in the upper proper left hand. This is a forked wooden stick or branch.[6] It is quite different than a Śaivite *triśūla* which, as its name implies, also has three tips, but which are arranged symmetrically, while the *tridaṇḍa* is a natural-looking branch of a tree with asymmetrical forks.[7] In Zangskar the *tridaṇḍa* is known as *klu shing*, or the *nāga* tree-branch.[8] Sugatiśaṃdārśana Lokeśvara is not the only deity to hold it: it is mentioned in the *Sādhanamālā* as one of the attributes of Bhṛkuṭī[9] and has been observed in a Bhṛikūṭī sculpture in the Bharat Kala Bhavan and in Nepalese

4 Bhattacharyya 1968 [1958]: 141. See also de Mallmann 1986: 110. Although as discussed at the 7th International Conference on Tibetan Archaeology and Art (Chengdu, China, 20 October, 2018), Bhattacharyya's version of the *Sadhanamālā* is sometimes unreliable and must be used with caution, de Mallmann's careful compilation of the text is more dependable, though in the case of Sugatiśaṃdārśana Lokeśvara, both versions coincide and closely relate to many surviving sculptures. I thank Jeff Watt and Ulrich von Schroeder for sharing their perspectives with me at the conference.

5 Taktsang Repa refers to the sculpture as *'gro drug yes she sgrol*, or "Liberator of the Six Realms of Being," which seems to be related to the name Trilokanātha, "Lord of the Three Realms"; Young Drukpa Association 2011:134 n. 30. The latter usually refers to Śiva. On the other hand, an inscription in proto-*śāradā* script of Kashmir found in the entrance of the inner cella of Triloknāth refers to it as Avalokiteśvara; Young Drukpa Association 2011:135 n. 32. According to the learned historian of Zangskar, Karsha Lonpo Sonam Wangchuk, the literal Tibetan translation of Triloknāth used in the *nyung gnas* fasting ritual associated with Lakṣmīṅkarā is Jigten Sumgyi Gonpo Chogla ('jig rten gsum rgyi mgon po mchog la); personal communication 22 June, 2018.

6 See de Mallmann, 1986: 22 and pl. III.8.

7 Maxwell, who argued that the marble image was actually Śiva-Maheśvara, misidentifies this attribute as a *triśūla*, which lends itself better to his argument; Maxwell 1980: 66. Vogel, who understood it as Avalokiteśvara, also read it as a *trisūla*; Vogel 1902: 36.

8 Information provided by Karsha Lonpo Sonam Wangchuk, personal communication, 22 June, 2018.

9 Bhattacharyya 1968 [1958]: 152.

sculptures of two other forms of Lokeśvara (Amoghapāśa and Harihariharivāhana Lokeśvara) in the same collection.[10] I have also recently identified it as held by Maitreya Buddha in an 18th century painting by the Zangskari artist Zhedpa Dorje (Bzhad pa rdo rje) in the village of Relagong (Fig. 6). In that case it may relate to the *nāgakesara* tree, the *nāgāpuspa* flower of which is associated with Maitreya,[11] just as the *utpala* is associated with Mañjuśrī and Tārā and the *padma* with Avalokiteśvara.

Fig. 6 Zhedpa Dorje, detail of a painting of Vajrapāni depicting Maitreya holding a *tridaṇḍa*, ca. late 18th C., overall 56 × 42.5 cm; painted portion 49 × 37 cm (Photo: Rob Linrothe, 2018).

Other attributes of Sugatiśaṃdārśana Lokeśvara are more standard for Avalokiteśvara and are frequently met with in his various forms: the just-mentioned *padma* also on his left, the stem of which is held in the middle left hand, the *akṣamālā* (prayer beads) held by the top or middle right hand, and *dāna* (or *varada*) *mudrā* made by the lower right hand. The *kuṇḍīka* (alt. *kamaṇḍalu, amṛtakalasa*) or water pot (Tib. *spyi blugs*), also held by Maitreya, is frequently found in early images of Avalokiteśvara, and is consistently held in the lower left hand of Sugatiśaṃdārśana Lokeśvara. Most images of him also feature a seated Amitābha on top of the crown, larger than usual for other Avalokiteśvaras.

The one inconsistency between the *Sādhanamālā's* description of Bhaṭṭāraka Sugatiśaṃdārśana

10 Biswas 1989: 175-180.

11 Bhattacharya 1980: 100. It is under this kind of tree that he will be enlightened.

Fig. 7 Sugatiśaṃdārśana Lokeśvara, ca. 10th C., Bihar, h. 72 cm. Ashutosh Museum, Kolkata, 2002.1148 (Photo: Rob Linrothe, 2016).

Lokeśvara and the Kashmiri and Triloknāth images is that the latter are all depicted sitting on what often appears as a stool with his proper left leg pendant, and his right knee bent at the knee and parallel to the top of the seat. This posture is known as *vāmārdhaparyaṅkāsana*, which is related to the more common *lalitāsana* in the sense that in the latter, the right leg hangs down off the throne, and left leg lies along the top of the seat.[12] The *sādhana*, however, states that the bodhisattva stands. As we will see, most of the Zangskari examples also show him seated, but a few seem to construe *vāmārdhaparyaṅkāsana* into a standing pose.

Claudine Bautze-Picron analyzed 26 works (3 paintings and the rest sculptures) of 6-armed Avalokiteśvara from Bihar and Bengal dating to between the 9th and 12th century, many of which had been provisionally identified as either Sugatiśaṃdārśana or Amoghapāśa.[13] Only 3 of the 26 hold the *tridaṇḍa*, and all of them are standing in *samadasthānaka* or *ābhaṅga*.[14] One example is in the Ashutosh Museum, Kolkata (Fig. 7). Thus there are a small number of sculptures from eastern India which follow the *Sādhanmālā* even more closely in this regard. Kashmir and the regions in its cultural sway in the early period (i.e. Ladakh, Zangskar, Kullu, Chamba, Spiti, etc.), however, consistently follow the seated type, a well-established variant that is distinct from the eastern Indian standing type of Sugatiśaṃdārśana which does not seem to have had a significant impact even in eastern India, much less in the Western Himalayas.[15]

In the most elaborate early examples from Kashmir, the bodhisattva is accompanied

12 De Mallmann 1986: 10 and pl. I.2. I am grateful to Ulrich von Schroeder for pointing this out to me at the 7th International Conference on Tibetan Archaeology and Art, Chengdu, China, 20 October, 2018.

13 Bautze-Picron 1989: 35-50, figs. 7-13.

14 Bautze-Picron 1989: nos. 3, 6, and 7. According to Bautze-Picron's Panel I-A, no. 15 also holds the *tridaṇḍa* but in the central right hand, instead of the upper or central left hand, something not seen in the many Western Himalayan examples. However, in examining the drawing of the sculpture in question in an 1838 publication, in fact, it represents not a *tridaṇḍa* but an *utpala* or some other type of flower. Bautze-Picron's no. 22, one of only 7 of the 26 that are seated, is illustrated in von Schroeder 1981: 57B, and identified by him there as Sugatiśaṃdārśana Lokeśvara. Von Schroeder's image and caption is cited, in turn, in Widorn and Kozicz 2012: n. 35, as an example of the iconographic type shared by the Triloknāth sculpture — all the other ones they cite are Kashmiri. However, as Bautze-Picron's analysis shows, this metalwork image excavated at Nālandā and now in the Indian Museum, Kolkata, does not hold the *tridaṇḍa*. Moreover, it is the right foot, not the left that is pendant. It may be one of the many other related forms of Lokeśvara described in the *Sādhanamālā*. Another example cited by Widorn and Kozicz from the same source is also too different from the others to be accepted as iconographically identical to the Triloknāth Sugatiśaṃdārśana Lokeśvara (von Schroeder 1981: 16G): he stands and has a book instead of the *tridaṇḍa*.

15 It also seems not to have been transmitted to China or Japan along with other forms of Avalokiteśvara, such as Amoghapāśa, Ekadaśamukha (11-headed), and Sahasramukhasaharanetra (1000-armed 1000-eyed), the latter three forms which by contrast have whole texts devoted to them in the East Asian Buddhist canons. Sugatiśaṃdārśana Lokeśvara does not appear in the index volumes of the Tantric section of the *Taishō Tripiṭaka* (Takakusu et al. 1924-1935:vols. 10 11); in the Hobogirin index volume (Paul Demiéville et al 1978), nor the Korean Buddhist Canon (Lancaster with Park 1979). The name did not even merit an entry in Soothill and Hodous 2003 [1937], nor in the Sanskrit index to the ten-volume *Bukkyo Daijiten* (Buddhist Dictionary) (Mochizuki and Tsukamoto 1954 1958 [1932-1936]).

Fig. 8 Sugatiśaṃdārśana Lokeśvara, datable to 989 from an inscription mentioning Queen Didda (d. 1003), Kashmir, metal, h. 25 cm. Sri Pratap Singh Museum, Srinagar (Photograph courtesy of American Institute of Indian Studies, no. 112-4).

Fig. 9 Sugatiśaṃdārśana Lokeśvara, late 10th-early 11th C., Kashmir, metal. Musée Guimet, MA 6266 (Photo: Rob Linrothe, 2013).

by two female figures, both two-armed in the case of the Queen Didda (Fig. 8) and Museé Guimet (Fig. 9) examples. Neither of the two-armed female retinue figures is mentioned in the *Sādhanamālā*, though as Bautze-Picron points out, the "presence/absence of the attendants is not bound to a specific form of the bodhisattva."[16] All three of the identified eastern Indian examples of the standing bodhisattva also have two female retinue figures, but the one on the deity's proper left is four-armed: thus the 2-armed figure is Tārā and the 4-armed is Bhṛkuṭī (Fig. 7).[17] Other retinue figures also accompany the bodhisattva in eastern India such as a *preta* (hungry ghost), Hayagrīva and Sudhanakumāra, but not in Kashmir. To be sure, not all of the Kashmiri examples show a triad of the large male bodhisattva at center with two female figures

16 Bautze-Picron 1989: 36.

17 Bautze-Picron 1989: nos. 3, 6, and 7.

Fig. 10 Sugatiśaṃdārśana Lokeśvara, ca. 10th C., Kashmir or Kulu, stone. Triloknāth Mandir, Himachal Pradesh (Handa, *Buddhist Art & Antiquities of Himachal Pradesh*, fig. 64).

(at least as they are preserved today),[18] and most of the Zangskar paintings and sculptures follow the Triloknāth white marble (as well as an older grey stone sculpture preserved there) in depicting only the central figure, not the two female or any other retinue or sponsor figures such as are seen on some of the Kashmiri examples.[19]

To summarize this examination of the iconography, there are two slightly differing but easily distinguishable forms of Sugatiśaṃdārśana Lokeśvara: the eastern Indian variant and the Kashmiri variant, the former standing and usually accompanied by one or more retinue figures of the standard set accompanying various forms of Lokeśvara (Fig. 7), and the latter seated and sometimes accompanied by two 2-armed females (Figs. 8, 9).[20] It is notable that the Triloknāth examples, to which we now turn, follow the Kashmiri variant, while the Zangskari images follow the Triloknāth iconography almost without exception.

Indeed, to date it has not been sufficiently emphasized that the white marble sculpture at Triloknāth (Fig. 5) replaced a considerably older and smaller grey stone image which is now displayed next to the larger white marble (Fig. 10). In terms of the grey stone sculpture's formal

18 For example, the ones in the Brooklyn Museum, the Jokhang, and the Potala; for the Brooklyn Museum work, see Linrothe et al, 2014: fig. 1.56; for the ones in Tibet, see von Schroeder 2001: 51D-E and 54A-C, respectively.

19 For example, the Skitmartse (see below), "Queen Didda," Brooklyn Museum and Musée Guimet examples.

20 As Bautze-Picron wisely observes, "A rough classification of the artistic material shows that (i) the number of deities is large, (ii) within the iconography of one specific deity, multiplication of forms exists, (iii) within the iconography of each of these forms, variations exist"; Bautze-Picron 1989: 35.

Fig. 11 Sugatiśaṃdārśana Lokeśvara, ca. 9th C., low-relief carving on stone. Skitmartse, Suru Valley Ladakh (Photo: Rob Linrothe, 2018).

characteristics, as Widorn observes, "the narrow waist and sharply cut belly clearly display an 8th century Kashmiri style."[21] Although the white marble sculpture does not have Kashmiri formal characteristics, the iconographical form itself suggests Kashmir is in the background, directly or indirectly. The older grey stone and the white marble are iconographically quite similar, yet there are enough slight differences — such as the *akṣamālā* held in a different hand as well as the relative positions of the *padma* and the *tridaṇḍa*, not to mention the size and formal traits — to conclude that the latter is not simply a "copy" of the former.

Two of the early Kashmiri examples are found in or near Zangskar. In the Suru Valley,

21 Widorn 2015: 218. Speaking more generally, Goetz writes that "a strong Kashmīrī style developed . . . . [and] spread also towards the East, and its influence is felt in many places [including] in the sculptures of . . . Triloknāth and Maylang in Lāhul"; Goetz 1969: 79.

Fig. 12 Sugatiśaṃdārśana Lokeśvara, ca. 10th C., Kashmir, metal, h. approx. 28 cm. Nangwapal Shrine, central Zangskar near Karsha (Photo: Rob Linrothe, 2018).

between Zangskar and Kashmir proper, at a site known as Skitmartse, is a low-relief stone carving, the largest of the known sculptures of Sugatiśaṃdārśana Lokeśvara (Fig. 11).[22] It includes the pair of female deities and, in addition, two pairs of sponsor couples appearing below. In central Zangskar, at a location known as Nangwapal, near Karsha, a Kashmiri metalwork Sugatiśaṃdārśana Lokeśvara was found at some point in the twentieth century by someone digging for clay (Fig. 12).[23] While knowledge of the earlier Kashmiri versions

22 INTACH and Devers 2017: 130; an excellent photograph of the Skitmartse rock carving is published in Snellgrove and Skorupski 1980: fig. 2. The caption identifies it as "Padmapāṇi Avalokitesvara flanked by two goddesses."

23 Linrothe 2006: 167-79 and Linrothe et al 2014. This past summer (2018), the small shrine in which it has been housed for the last few decades was renovated.

Figs. 13, 14 *Thangka* depicting and close-up of Sugatiśaṃdārśana Lokeśvara of Triloknāth Mandir, ca. 19th C. Dukhang at Phugtal Monastery, eastern Zangskar (Photo: Rob Linrothe, 2018).

might have prepared Zangskaris for the acceptance of this iconography at Triloknāth, the Nangwapal example is a relatively recent discovery and so is unlikely to have been the model for the paintings and sculptures in some of the major and minor shrines of Zangskar that I am about to discuss. In other words, Kashmiri art from the ca. 9th to the 12th century was surely the inspiration for the Triloknāth sculptures, the older grey one being most likely itself Kashmiri or a close derivative, whilst the later images in Zangskar are, I argue, based directly on the white marble image, not the earlier grey stone image or other Kashmiri examples.

One of the clearest examples of a painting in Zangskar of Sugatiśaṃdārśana Lokeśvara that is meant to represent not just the deity but the Triloknāth icon in particular, is found in Phugtal Monastery in eastern Zangskar's Lungnak Valley (Figs. 13, 14). That it is the six-armed deity in question is unmistakable: note the *tridaṇḍa* in the upper left hand and the other attributes. The main variant is the posture which looks as if it is meant to represent a half-dancing pose. This can be explained as due to the fact that the lower part of the Triloknāth sculpture is usually covered by clothes and scarves, so that the precise posture is rarely clear to visitors — for example see figures 22, 24. But note that the white deity is housed within a

Fig. 15 Painted clay sculpture of Sugatiśaṃdārśana Lokeśvara, ca. 19th C. Tonba Lhakhang at Phugtal Monastery, eastern Zangskar (Photo: Rob Linrothe, 2018).

Fig. 16 *Thangka* depicting Sugatiśaṃdārśana Lokeśvara of Triloknāth Mandir, ca. 19th C. Lhakhang at Dorje Dzong Nunnery, central Zangskar (Photo: Rob Linrothe, 2018).

Fig. 17 Close up of *thangka* depicting Sugatiśaṃdārśana Lokeśvara holding *tridaṇḍa*.

distinctive white *śikhara* that closely resembles the Nāgara temple at Triloknāth (Fig. 3). The painting is hung near the ceiling of the Dukhang at Phugtal, so it was not possible to examine it closely or to see if any inscriptions are to be found on the front or back. I was able to discuss it with the former abbot of Phugtal, Zurba Angdus (Dbang 'dus), who in my experience going back to his time as abbot, is particularly knowledgeable and interested in art. Like every other Zangskari monk or nun I spoke to about its resemblance to the Triloknāth icon, he was unaware of any particular association with Triloknāth.

Also in Phugtal, but in the Tonba (Ston pa) Lhakhang is a sculpture of the same deity, with a slightly silvery look (Fig. 15). Only the head of Amitābha emerges from the top of the hair, instead of the whole body. Nevertheless, the *padma, tridaṇḍa*, and *kamaṇḍalu* in the left hands, the *akṣamālā* — in this case, two of them — in the right hands, and the particular form of the seated pose, all correspond to the Triloknāth Sugatiśaṃdārśana Lokeśvara.

Another relatively recent painting in Zangskar that closely resembles the Triloknāth icon is found in the nunnery named Dorje Dzong near Karsha in central Zangskar (Figs. 16, 17). It does not have the distinctive Trilokāth *śikhara* in the background, but the figure is more intelligible as sitting. It does have an inscription on the back, which appeared to me at the time

Fig. 18 Painted clay sculpture of Sugatiśaṃdārśana Lokeśvara, early 21st C. (?). Lhakhang at Dorje Dzong Nunnery, central Zangskar (Photo: Rob Linrothe, 2018).

Fig. 19 Painted clay sculpture of Sugatiśaṃdārśana Lokeśvara, early 20th C. (?). Gonkhang at Karsha Monastery, central Zangskar (Photo: Rob Linrothe, 2018).

of viewing to consist of *dhāraṇī*-prayers, not discursive documentation, but unfortunately the nun in charge of the shrine (the *dkon gnyer*) did not allow me to take the painting down from the wall in order to photograph the back.

Likewise, in the same *lhakhang* of Dorje Dzong is a sculpture that is either very new or newly repainted (Fig. 18). The *tridaṇḍa* in the bodhisattva's upper left hand is discernible, but the posture is obscured by the cloths and objects placed in front of it. It is also behind glass, making it even more difficult to photograph. The same constraints — objects in front of it, covered with cloths, and behind glass — are in play for a sculpture in the Gonkhang at Karsha Monastery (Fig. 19). Moreover, it has lost its attributes, which were, apparently, made separately and then placed in the hands. The position of the arms, the large Amitābha on the crown, and the fact that it has the left leg down and the right bent inwards, strongly suggests that it was meant to be understood as Sugatiśaṃdārśana Lokeśvara, and probably the Triloknāth

Figs. 20, 21 *Thangka* depicting and close-up of Sugatiśaṃdārśana Lokeśvara of Triloknāth Mandir, ca. 19th C. In shrine room of Amchi Nordan in Shadey Village, Shun Valley, eastern Zangskar (Photo: Rob Linrothe, 2018).

icon in particular.[24] The fact that it was painted silver instead of white is intriguing, silver being a more precious variant of white. As is well known, there are many Tibetan Buddhist paintings in which the exposed bodies of the deities are painted with gold pigment, regardless of their iconographically prescribed color, as a way to honor them.[25] Artists in Zangskar seem to have used silver in a similar way.

Indeed, in Shadey Village in the family shrine of Amchi Nordan (nor 'dzom) in the Shun Valley a few days walk east of Tongde (stong sde) Monastery over the Tongde La, one painting

24 So far I have only discussed images from Zangskar that I have personally seen. One that I have not yet seen is published in Snellgrove and Skorupski 1980: fig. 23, of a clay sculpture painted white in Tongde (Stong sde) Monastery. Although it too appears to have lost all the objects the hands should hold, the hands and feet are in the appropriate positions. The caption identifies it only as "Lokesvara," but describes the "small surmounting image of the Buddha Amitābha [as] shaped so as to compose the whole pointed headdress. Although we would hesitate to give an early date to the image, the face is remarkably Indian in its features and the whole effect is more Śiva-like than Buddha-like."

25 See, for example, the central triad of Mañjuśrī with two bodhisattvas in the 15th-century painting from the western Himalayas, on loan to the Art Institute of Chicago, illustrated in Linrothe, et al 2014: fig. 3.21.

Fig. 22 Interior shrine room of Triloknāth Mandir with white marble sculpture and large butter lamp visible (Photo: Rob Linrothe, 2016).

depicts a dark Sugatiśaṃdārśana Lokeśvara (Figs. 20, 21). The only plausible explanation for the dark color of the deity is that it was painted with a pigment that was originally white or silver in color but has turned very dark over the decades. The large butter lamp at the bottom center of the *thangka* (Fig. 20) is also the same dark color as the body of the main deity. Butter lamps in Zangskar are almost invariably silver, as is the very large one placed below the white marble in the Triloknāth shrine visible in my photograph of 2016 (Fig. 22),[26] so the fact that

26 Maxwell mentions that "[i]n the foreground [of the Triloknāth inner shrine] stands a very large butter lamp with a bulbous stem set in a lotus base"; Maxwell 1980: 63. It is still there, placed directly below the white marble sculpture and is featured in a photograph taken in 2007 published in Widorn 2015: fig. 3. However, in the text, it is described as "a large brass [sic] vessel functioning as a huge butter lamp" (2015: 20).

Fig. 23 Framed black-and-white photograph (photographer unknown) of Triloknāth white marble Sugatiśaṃdārśana Lokeśvara in Satak hamlet, Shun Valley, eastern Zangskar (Photo: Rob Linrothe, 2018).

Fig. 24 Unframed color photograph (photographer unknown) of Triloknāth white marble Sugatiśaṃdārśana Lokeśvara in Satak hamlet, Shun Valley, eastern Zangskar. According to the label on the back it was distributed by the "District Administration, Lahaul-Spirit and Triloknath Temple Committee" at the "Triloknath Fair 1991" (Photo: Rob Linrothe, 2018).

it is so dark in the painting confirms the hypothesis that the skin of the deity was originally painted silver — "white as silver plate."[27] It shares with the Phugtal painting (Figs. 13, 14) the conceit of the placement of the deity within a white Nāgara-style *śikhara*.

At an abandoned hamlet named Satak in the Shun Valley of Zangskar, among a large number of discarded photographs in the shrine room of one of the two large houses, I found two photographs of the Triloknāth Sugatiśaṃdārśana Lokeśvara (Figs. 23, 24). The cultic reverence held for the Triloknāth icon is unmistakable: the two were found among photographs of the 14th Dalai Lama, the recently deceased 19th Bakula Rinpoche, the 18th Karmapa, and other revered teachers. The black-and-white photograph of the white marble (Fig. 23) was in a simple frame

27 The phrase is found in an English translation of a *jataka* in Cowell 1895-1907, quoted in Goswamy with Agrawal 2018: 10.

Fig. 25 Sugatiśaṃdārśana Lokeśvara of Triloknāth Mandir, page of an illuminated manuscript in Kumik Village, ca. 17th C. Central Zangskar (Photo: Rob Linrothe, 2012).

whereas almost all of the other photographs were unframed, including a color photograph that was distributed in 1991 by the Triloknāth Temple Committee according to a printed caption on the back of the photograph (Fig. 24).

To the best of my knowledge, the oldest example of an image made in Zangskar that appears to refer to the Triloknāth image is found in a ca. 17th century manuscript owned by a family in Kumik Village of central Zangskar (Fig. 25).[28] Like some of the other Zangskari examples, the bodhisattva appears to be dancing, not sitting, the proper left foot supported by a lotus. Only the head of Amitābha instead of the whole body emerges from the turban. Despite these variations, it depicts the *tridaṇḍa* clearly, and even shows a trilobed arch backdrop[29] found on the white marble sculpture and the older darker stone as well (Figs. 5, 10).

Although many local Zangskaris know about Triloknāth Mandir, today, as already mentioned, few of the people I questioned recognize the painted and sculptural representations in Zangskar as related to the icon of that site. They recognize it only as Phagspa Chenrezig

28 On this manuscript and its date, Linrothe 2016: 169-202.

29 What Maxwell called "a gilt trilobite *toraṇa*." (1980: 64).

(phags pa spyan ras gzigs), a form of Avalokiteśvara, but not that of Triloknāth in particular. This suggests to me that although the cult of the Triloknāth white marble sculpture found expression in the relatively recent paintings and sculptures, the cult might have been stronger in previous generations than it is today. In fact, the cult of the Triloknāth Phagpa in Zangskar may go back as far as the 17th century, when the Kumik manuscript (Fig. 25) was made and Taktsang Repa visited Triloknāth before his renowned activities with the royalty of Ladakh.[30]

More than a century ago, Triloknāth Mandir was, according to Vogel, "[o]ne of the most famous *tīrthas* of the Western Himālayas," one that, he noticed at the time, was visited and honored by, among others, Buddhists of Ladakh.[31] We should probably see the cult as having cyclical importance in Zangskar, one peak reached in the 17th century during the reign of Sengge Namgyal (seng ge rnam rgyal, 1570-1642) who expanded Ladakh's borders southwards,[32] during which Taktsang Repa traveled to both Triloknāth and Zangskar. While Ladakh's rule over Spiti and Ngari ended by the late seventeenth century, its connections with the regions to the south, to Lahul and Kulu extended into the early 19th century, particularly among the Drukpa Kagyu including Zhedpa Dorje (Fig. 6) and Lama Karma of Dzonkhul Monastery. Such trans-Himalayan connections were disrupted by the armed conflicts with and invasions by the Dogra armies aided by the people in the villages of the Paldar region (its main seat is Chatargarh, now known as Gulabgarh) in the 1830s and 1840s.[33] Another crest in the intensity of the Triloknāth cult in Zangskar was reached in the early to mid-20th century, aided by the British encouragement of travel and taxable trade across the Himalayas.[34]

On the other hand, the decline in awareness of the Triloknāth image as a source for the Sugatiśaṃdārśana Lokeśvara images of Zangskar that I am positing in the last quarter of the 20th and early 21st century may have to do with contemporary travel routes to and from Zangskar. Historically, the Omāsi La pass from southern Zangskar leading to Paldar and then to Udaipur and Triloknāth was an important route for Zangskaris leading to Lahul and

30 See for example, Schwieger 1996: 81-107 and Petech 1977: 40-49, 54-63.

31 Vogel 1902: 35, 36.

32 Halkias discusses Ladakh's "expansionist cravings." (2009: 63).

33 See Handa 2001: 178, 189, 192 for military expeditions across Omāsi La to and from Zangskar to Paldar.

34 Stutchbury writes of the importance of Karzha (Lahul) as a whole for Himalayan Buddhism and of a "resurgence of Tibetan Buddhist influence in Karzha . . . at about the turn of the [20th] century" (Stutchbury 1994: 160). It also probably helped when in the late 19th century, "Zangskari newcomers......settled in Paldar," and Zangskar and Paldar "formed a single subsdistrict referred to as 'Padar Jaskar;'" Riaboff 2002: 328. Halkias mentions "British political agents assessing geopolitical risks across the north-western sectors of the Indian Himalayas and aspiring for uniform taxation for traders from British India in Tibet," as well as "a keen interest in securing safe passage of goods and regulating taxation along the main Himalayan trading routes." Halkias 2009: 73, 74.

beyond.[35] Zangskar's Karsha and Bardan Monasteries established branches in the area, and a number of Drukpa Kagyu sites in Lahul maintained connections with Zangskar, particularly with Dzongkhul, over that route.[36] For the last fifty years or so, the motorable road connecting Zangskar to Lahul was instead built to the east, via the Shingo La and Kyelong. Now it is the much more common and convenient route, but it bypasses Triloknāth. As Widorn and Kozicz point out, "Due to the lack of accessible roads, today the Chandrabhaga Valley [in which Triloknāth is situated] has become remote, and the former traversing routes are only of minor importance — only the tribal peoples, the Gaddis [shepherds], use the passes [anymore]."[37] Riaboff points to a similar decline of trade relations between Zangskar and Paldar over the Omāsi La since the 1980s.[38]

If I am correct that a considerable number of paintings and sculptures found in Zangskar refer to the Triloknāth white marble image, this would expand the known area of the Triloknāth cult, which to date has been recognized as extending only as far as the Kulu Valley and to India proper.[39] Even while it was increasingly seen as a Śaivite shrine by local caretakers and visitors from central and northern India, the northern extension of the cult of Triloknāth to Zangskar ensured an audience among Buddhists who rightly recognized the enshrined white marble sculpture as a Buddhist deity, prepared as they were by familiarity with considerably earlier images from Kashmir.

Appendix

Yannick Laurent recently brought to my attention three images of Sugatiśaṃdārśana Lokeśvara in Spiti and Kinnaur, southeast of Lahul. One of them is a wall mural at the *stūpa* at Tashigang,

35 Riaboff 2008: 101-115. Kozicz and Grimm report that in an interview with a monk, the latter stated that one can leave Sani Monastery in the early morning and reach Triloknāth in a single day (in press). Having in September 2018 made the trek from Dzonkhul Monastery over Omāsi La, I feel confident that this is an exaggeration; perhaps locals could do it in three days, but I doubt it. "The main route [from Paldar to Zangskar] through the Omasi Pass (around 5,300 metres) took several days" (Riaboff 2008: 109).

36 The former abbots of Dzongkul, Ngawang Tsering and Lama Karma, for example, had strong connections to Omāsi La and Triloknāth; see Widorn 2015: 218, confirmed by Karsha Lonpo Sonam Wangchuk as well; personal communication, September 2018.

37 Widorn and Kozicz, "The Temple of Triloknath," 18. In September 2018, there were both Bakkerwallahs (Muslim herders) and Hindu Gaddis from Himachal in the valleys on the Kishtwar-Kashmir and Himachal side of the Omāsi La pass.

38 Riaboff 2008: 112.

39 Maxwell 1980: 70. For the extension of the cult into Spiti and Kinnaur, see "Appendix," below.

Fig. 26 *Thangka* depicting Mañjuśrī and, below center, Sugatiśaṃdārśana Lokeśvara of Triloknāth Mandir, ca. 19th or 20th C. A Sakya monastery in Tenggyu (steng rgyud), Spiti (Photo: Yannick Laurent).

Fig. 27 Close-up of Sugatiśaṃdārśana Lokeśvara of Triloknāth Mandir in Mañjuśrī *thangka*.

near Kibber Village, a photograph of which has been published.[40] A second is a relatively recent wall mural found in Thangi temple in Kinnaur (Bashahr); the white figure holds the *tridaṇḍa, akṣamālā*, and *kuṇḍīka*, makes the *varada mudrā* with the lower right hand, and bears a large seated Amitāyus on the crown of his head. However, rather anomalously, he is clearly *standing* on a round pedestal, wears a curious skirt that appears to be formed of blue leaves, and holds a green snake in his central proper left hand. The third example is clearly a representation of the Triloknāth image since, like the Phugtal and Shadey paintings (Figs. 13, 14, 20, 21), the bodhisattva sits within a trilobed niche below a white *śikhara* vaguely resembling the Triloknāth Nāgara temple architecture (Figs. 26, 27). It depicts a walled court around the temple, with a very large yellow butter lamp below the seated bodhisattva. Laurent found the painting in the Sakya-affiliated monastery of Tenggyu (steng rgyud) in Spiti. Sugatiśaṃdārśana Lokeśvara is not the central image of the *thangka* — which instead features a four-armed form of Mañjuśrī-but appears directly beneath the main figure. A three-line Tibetan inscription has been deciphered and translated by Laurent. It identifies the painter as "Ananpune" (a nan pu

40 Kozicz 2017: fig. 8. Identification of the deities depicted in the mural is not mentioned in the article, but the Sugatiśaṃdārśana Lokeśvara appears next to Uṣṇiṣavijayā in the second register of the wall painting.

ne), and includes the following verse referring to Sugatiśaṃdārśana Lokeśvara in Laurent's translation:

> From a manifestation of Amitābha,
> The One and only Lord of Tibet is the glory of all migratory beings,
> Liberating the six kinds of beings without exception,
> I take refuge in Avalokiteśvara.[41]

Although it appears obvious that the image refers to the sculpture in the Triloknāth Mandir in Tunde, the inscription does not directly refer to it, only recognizing it as a form of Avalokiteśvara, the compassionate bodhisattva revered for its special connection Tibetans. If that unspecific, generalized recognition was regularly the case in Zangskar as well, it might explain the current lack of awareness of the association of images in Zangskar with Triloknāth referred to above. At any rate, Laurent's observations of such images in Spiti extend the area of what I have referred to as the "cult of Triloknāth Lokeśvara" into Buddhist regions to the southeast of Lahul, into Spiti and Kinnaur, as well north into Zangskar.

Bibliography

Asian Civilisations Museum. 2015. *Treasures from Asia's Oldest Museum: Buddhist Art from the Indian Museum, Kolkata*. Singpapore: Asian Civilisations Museum.

Bautze-Picron, Claudine. 1989. "'Identification' or 'Classification' in Buddhist Iconography: The Case of the Six-handed Avalokiteśvara Images in Bihar and Bengal, 8th to 12th Century." In *Shastric Traditions in Indian Arts*, ed. Anna Libera Dallapiccola, with Christine Walter-Mendry and Stephanie Zingel-Avé Lallemant, Stuttgart: Steiner Verlag Wiesbaden, 35-50, figs. 7-13.

Bhattacharya, Biswanath. 1976. *Aśvaghoṣa: A Critical Study*. Santiniketan: Bidyut Ranjan Basu.

Bhattacharya, Gouriswar. 1980. "Stūpa as Maitreya's Emblem." In *The Stupa: Its Religious, Historical and Architectural Significance*, ed. Anna Libera Dallapiccola, Wiesbaden: Steiner, 100-111.

——1989. "Deva: Caturmukha-Pañcamukha: Brahmā and Śiva: Śilpa-śastras and Art-objects." In *Shastric Traditions in Indian Arts*, ed. Anna Libera Dallapiccola with Christine Walter-

41 *'od dpag med kyi rnam sprul las/ bod [k]yi lha [g]cig 'gro kun dpal/ 'gro drug ma lus sgrol mdzad pa'i/ spyan ras gzigs la bdag skyabs so/*. Transcription and translation by Yannick Laurent, used with permission and gratitude. Personal communication, October 2018.

Mendry and Stephanie Zingel-Avé Lallemant, Stuttgart: Steiner Verlag Wiesbaden, 51-70, pls. VII-XVII.

Bhattacharyya, Benoytosh. 1968 [1958]. *The Indian Buddhist Iconography Mainly Based on the Sādhanamālā and Cognate Tāntric Texts of Rituals*. 2nd edition, Calcutta: Firma K. L. Mukhopadhyay.

Biswas, T. K. 1989. "Certain Rare Aspects of Avalokiteśvara in Bharat Kala Bhavan." In *Buddhist Iconography*, 175-180.

Cousens, Diana. 2014. *The Triloknath Temple of Lahaul: A study of the self arising image of Triloknath and the veneration of self arising objects in Tibetan Buddhism*. Saarbrücken: Scholar's Press.

——2015. "Mapping the Buddhist Sacred Status of Triloknāth." In *Asia Horizons: Giuseppe Tucci's Buddhist, Indian, Himalayan and Central Asian Studies*, ed. A.A. Di Castro and D. Templeman. Melbourne: Monash University, 241-262.

Cowell, E. B. ed. 1895-1907. *The Jataka*. 6 vols. Cambridge: Cambridge University Press.

Demiéville, Paul, Hubert Durt, and Anna Seidel. 1978. *Repertoire du Cannon Bouddhique Sino-Japonais*. Paris: Librairie d'Amérique et d'Orient; and Tokyo: Maison Franco-Japonaise.

Director General, Archaeological Survey of India. 2012. *Rediscovering India 1961-2011*. New Delhi: Archaeological Survey of India.

Goetz, Hermann. 1969. *Studies in the History and Art of Kashmir and the Indian Himalaya*. Wiesbaden: Otto Harrassowitz.

Goswamy, B. N. with Vrinda Agrawal, eds. 2018. *Oxford Readings in Indian Art*. New Delhi: Oxford University Press.

Halkias, Georgios T. 2009. "Until the Feathers of the Winged Black Raven Turn White: Sources for the Tibet-Bashahr Treaty of 1679." In *Mountains, Monasteries and Mosques: Recent Research on Ladakh and the Western Himalaya, Proceedings of the 13th Colloquium of the International Association for Ladakh Studies*. ed. John Bray and Elena De Rossi Filibeck. Pisa/Rome: Università di Roma Dipartimento di Studi Orientali, 61-86.

Handa, O. C. 1994. *Buddhist Art & Antiquities of Himachal Pradesh Up to 8th Century A.D.* New Delhi: Indus Publishing Company.

—— 2001. *Buddhist Western Himalaya, Part 1: A Politico-Religious History*. New Delhi: Indus Publishing Company.

Indian National Trust for Art & Cultural Heritage (INTACH), and Quentin Devers. 2017. *Historical Sites of Purig: Kargil, Ladakh, Jammu & Kashmir*. New Delhi: INTACH.

Kozicz, Gerald. 2017. "One Stūpa and Three *Lha thos*: The Monuments of Tashigang." In *Revue d'Etudes Tibétaines* 41: 226-248.

Kozicz, Gerald, and Ludwig Grimm. In press. "Triloknath Revisited: Recent Results from Field Research and the IAM Digital Lab."

Lancaster, Lewis R., with Sung-bai Park. 1979. *The Korean Buddhist Canon: A Descriptive Catalogue*. Berkeley: University of California Press.

Linrothe, Rob. 2006. "Two Fieldnotes from Zangskar: A Kashmiri Sculpture in a Personal Shrine and The Etymology of 'Kankani' Chorten." In *Mei shou wan nian (Long Life without End): Festschrift on the Occasion of Roger Goepper's 80th Birthday*, ed. Jeong-hee Lee-Kalisch, Antje Papist-Matsuo, and Willibald Veit. Frankfurt: Peter Lang Verlag, 167-179.

—— 2016. "Siddhas and Sociality: A Seventeenth-Century Lay Illustrated Buddhist Manuscript in Kumik Village, Zangskar (A Preliminary Report)." In *Visible Heritage: Essays on the Art and Architecture of Greater Ladakh*, ed. Rob Linrothe and Heinrich Pöll. New Delhi: Studio Orientale, 169-202.

Linrothe, Rob, with Melissa R. Kerin and Christian Luczanits. 2014. *Collecting Paradise: Buddhist Art of Kashmir and Its Legacies*. New York: Rubin Museum of Art and Mary and Leigh Block Museum of Art.

Lunsingh Scheurleer, P.C.M. 1989. "The Tridaṇḍa of the Main Image of Candi Jago." *Southeast Asian Archaeology Newsletter* 2: 14-19.

de Mallmann, Marie-Thérèse. 1986. *Introduction a l'Iconographie du Tântrisme Bouddhique*. Paris: Librairie d'Amérique et d'Orient.

Maxwell, T. S. 1980. "Lākhamaṇḍal and Trilokināth: The Transformed Functions of Hindu Architecture in Two Cross-Cultural Zones of the Western Himalaya." *Art International* 24, nos. 1-2: 9-74.

Meisezahl, R.O. 1967. "Amoghapāśa: Some Nepalese Representations and Their Vajrayānic Aspects." *Monumenta Serica* 26: 455-497.

Mochizuki Shinko and Zenryu Tsuka. 1954-1958 [1932-1936]. *Bukkyo Daijiten* (Buddhist Dictionary). Tokyo: Sekai Seiten Kanko Kyokai,

Petech, Luciano. 1977. *The Kingdom of Ladakh c.* 950-1842 A.D. Serie Orientale Roma, 51. Rome: Istituto Italiano per il Medio ed Estremo Oriente.

Riaboff, Isabelle. 2002. "The Bod of Kabön (Jammu and Kashmir, India): How To Be a Buddhist in a Hindu Land?" In *Territory and Identity in Tibet and the Himalayas* (PIATS 2000), ed. Katia Buffetrille and Hildegard Diemberger. Leiden: Brill, 325-340.

—— 2008. "Distant Neighbours Either Side of the Omasi La: The Zanskarpa and the Bod Communities of Paldar." In *Modern Ladakh : Anthropological Perspectives on Continuity and Change*, ed. Martijn van Beek and Fernanda Pirie. Leiden: Brill, 101-115.

Sankrtyayana, Rahula. 1938. "Search for Sanskrit Mss. In Tibet." In *Journal of the Bihar and Orissa Research Society* 24 no. 4: 137-163.

von Schroeder, Ulrich. 1981. *Indo-Tibetan Bronzes*. Hong Kong: Visual Dharma.

—— 2001. *Buddhist Sculptures in Tibet, Volume 1: India & Nepal*. Hong Kong: Visual Dharma.

Schwieger, Peter. 1996. "Stag-tshang Ras-pa's Exceptional Life as a Pilgrim." *Kailash* 18, nos. 1-2: 81-107.

Sharma, Mahesh. 2009. *Western Himalayan Temple Records: State, Pilgrimage, Ritual and Legality in Chambā*. Leiden and Boston: Brill.

—— 2013. "The Lakṣmī-Nārāyana Image and Vaiṣṇavism in Chamba: Evidence, Context and Chronology." In *Legacy of Indian Art: Continuity and Change*, ed. Ashvini Agrawal. New Delhi: Aryan Books International, 161-175.

Snellgrove, David L. and Tadeusz Skorupski. 1980. *The Cultural Heritage of Ladakh, Vol. 2: Zangskar and the Cave Temples of Ladakh*. New Delhi: Vikas Publishing.

Soothill, William Edward, and Lewis Hodous. 2003[1937]. *A Dictionary of Chinese Buddhist Terms*. Delhi: Motilal Banarsidass.

Stutchbury, Elisabeth. 1994. "The Making of Gonpa: Norbu Rinpoche from Kardang and Kunga Rinpoche from Lama Gonpa." In *Tantra and Popular Religion in Tibet*, ed. Geoffrey Samuel, Hamish Gregor, and Elisabeth Stutchbury. New Delhi: Aditya Prakashan, 155-204.

Takakusu Junjiro, Watanable Kaigyoku, and Ono Gemmyo, eds. 1924-1935. *Taishō Shinshū Daizōkyō* (Taishō Tripiṭaka). Tokyo: Taishō Shinshū Daizōkyō Kanko Kai.

Tucci, Giuseppe. 1971. "Travels of Tibetan Pilgrims in the Swat Valley." In *Opera Minora, Parte II*. Rome: Università di Roma, 369-418.

Vogel, Ph. 1902. "Triloknāth." *Journal of the Asiatic Society of Bengal* 71, no. 1: 35-41.

Widorn,Verena. 2015. "Traversing the Land of *siddhas* and *ḍākinīs*: Art Historical Evidence along the Buddhist Pilgrimage Routes through Lahul." In *Cultural Flows across the Western Himalaya*, ed. Patrick McAllister, Cristina Scherrer-Schaub and Helmut Krasser. Vienna: Österreichische Akademie der Wissenshaften, Wien, 189-235.

Widorn, Verena and Gerald Kozicz. 2012. "The Temple of Triloknath: A Buddhist Nāgara Temple in Lahul." In *South Asian Studies* 28, no. 1: 15-35.

Young Drukpa Association. 2011. *Garsha: Heart Land of the Dakinis*. Keylong: Young Drukpa Association Garsha (Lahaul).

◆ Author: Rob Linrothe, Associate Professor and Chair of the Department of Art History at Northwestern University.

明朝颁赐西藏印章的初步研究 *

李帅

内容摘要：明朝中央政府颁给西藏地方的印章类型多样，至少包括宗教名号印、封爵印、官印及图章这四类，不同类型印章在颁赐对象、印章特征以及所选择的印章制度方面都有所不同，是明朝治藏政策灵活性和多样性的体现。明朝颁给西藏地方人员的印章不只是作为一种政治象征品，而且在西藏地方被实际使用，被用来发布公告、处理地方事务等，甚至部分印章一直使用到清代，成为受赐者在西藏地方享有政治地位和行使统治权力的重要凭证。

明朝建立后，为继承元朝对西藏的统治，采取了一系列举措来经略西藏，其中之一便是对相关僧俗人员进行封授，予以官职名号并颁以诏敕印章。因此，印章不仅是明朝治藏措施的体现，也是明廷与西藏地方之间管理与被管理关系的凭证，更是西藏人员获得进入内地并与明廷开展朝贡贸易资格的重要凭信，故备受西藏地方政教人员珍视。通过对明朝颁赐西藏地方印章及其在西藏使用情况的考察，既可以了解明朝治藏策略及其在西藏地方的效果和影响，也可以窥探西藏方面对明朝的态度。目前有关明朝颁赐西藏

* 本文为四川大学创新火花项目库项目（2018hhs-12）和中国博士后科学基金第 64 批面上资助项目（2018M643461）的阶段性成果。

地方的印章材料已经被逐步刊布出来[1]，但学界开展的研究还比较有限，大部分成果仍是对资料及其历史的简要介绍[2]，仅极少文章专门对明朝颁赐西藏地方印章的相关方面进行过考察[3]。鉴于此，本文尝试以明朝颁赐西藏地方印章为研究对象，对这些印章的类型、特征、印制选择、使用情况等进行考察，并就其中反映出的明朝治藏策略进行认识。

一、明朝颁赐西藏印章的类型

西藏保存有不少直接由明朝中央政府颁赐的印章[4]，按质地可分玉印、镀金银印、银印、铜印及象牙印，不同质地印章的颁赐对象有所不同，代表着不同的等级地位。现按照性质的不同，可将这些印章分为宗教名号印、封爵印、官印及图章四类。

（一）宗教名号印

宗教名号印主要是明朝颁给高等级藏僧的印章，通常以明朝封授藏僧的名号作为印文。这类印章与明朝建立的一套藏僧等级体系相关联[5]，目前可见玉印、镀金银印和银印三种类型（图一），它们的颁赐对象主要是法王、大国师及国师等级的藏僧。

1. 如来大宝法王之印

该印为白玉印，双龙纽，高 8.3 厘米；方形印面，边长 12.8、印台厚 3.5 厘米。印文为九叠篆汉字，内容为“如来大宝法王之印”[6]（图一：1）。此印为玉印中之上乘佳品。这枚印章是永乐五年（1407 年）明成祖颁给噶玛噶举派黑帽系活佛得银协巴（དེ་བཞིན་

1　相关代表性著作如欧朝贵、其美：《西藏历代藏印》，拉萨：西藏人民出版社，1991：18-50。西藏自治区档案馆编：《西藏历史档案荟萃》，北京：文物出版社，1995：图三一～三三。西藏博物馆编，何晓东著：《历史的见证——西藏博物馆藏历代中央政府治藏文物集萃》，成都：四川美术出版社，2015：76-96。甲央、王明星主编：《宝藏——中国西藏历史文物 3》，北京：朝华出版社，2000：88-93、138-147。《西藏自治区志·文物志》编纂委员会编撰：《西藏自治区志·文物志》，北京：中国藏学出版社，2012：963。西藏博物馆编：《西藏博物馆》，北京：中国大百科全书出版社，2001：33、140、143 等。

2　相关代表性论文如西藏自治区文物管理委员会：《明朝封授西藏地方官员的印章》，《文物》1981（11）：38-41。文竹：《西藏地方明封八王的有关文物》，《文物》1985（9）：89-94。陈金钟：《元以来中央政权颁授西藏地方首领印章举要》，《中央民族学院学报》1988（3）：16-17。

3　彭晓静、戴子佳：《从狮钮象牙僧印看明代的民族与宗教关系》，《青海民族大学学报》2013（4）：63-67。李帅：《明朝颁赐藏僧象牙图章研究》，《西藏大学学报》2015（3）：91-99。朱德涛：《两枚明清中央政府颁赐西藏地方官员印章考释》，《藏学学刊》第 15 辑，北京：中国藏学出版社，2017：174-184。

4　西藏还有不少明朝所颁印章的复制印，因与原印有所差别。参见李帅：《论西藏地方的明代复制官印》，《西藏大学学报》2019（3）：113-120。

5　《明英宗实录》卷一七，正统元年五月丁丑，台北，“中研院历史语言研究所”校印本，1962：333。

6　甲央、王明星主编：《宝藏——中国西藏历史文物 3》，2000：138-139，图 49。

གཤེགས་པ། 1384-1415 年）的印章。

2. 正觉大乘法王之印

该印为墨玉印，双龙纽，高 13.5 厘米；方形印面，边长 12.8 厘米。印文为九叠篆汉字，内容为“正觉大乘法王之印”（图一：2)。这是永乐十一年（1413 年）明成祖颁发给萨迦派首领贡噶扎西坚赞贝桑布 (ཀུན་དགའ་བཀྲ་ཤིས་རྒྱལ་མཚན་དཔལ་བཟང་པོ། 1349-1425 年，汉文写作昆泽思巴) 的印章 [7]。

3. 灌顶国师之印

该印为青玉印，螭纽，高 8.8 厘米；方形印面，边长 10.2 厘米。印文为汉字九叠篆，内容为“灌顶国师之印”（图一：3）[8]。以灌顶国师之号敕封藏僧始于元代，明朝承袭之，明太祖时期在西藏封授了几位灌顶国师并赐以玉印 [9]。到永乐时期灌顶国师之地位已经有所下降，不再赐予玉印。故推测这枚灌顶国师玉印应是明太祖时期颁赐给某位国师的印章。

4. 灌顶净慈通慧国师印

该印为二台镀金银印，如意纽，高 7.4 厘米；方形印面，边长 9.5 厘米。印文为汉字九叠篆，内容为“灌顶净慈通慧国师”。印背有汉文款识，右上为“灌顶净慈通慧国师印”，左上为“永乐九年二月日礼部造”，边沿为“智字九十四号”（图一：4）[10]。据文献记载，该印主人为端竹斡薛儿巴里藏卜，他是噶玛噶举派主寺楚布寺（མཚུར་ཕུ）的掌寺僧人 [11]。

5. 灌顶广善慈济国师印

该印为二台镀金银印，如意纽，高 9 厘米；方形印面，边长 9.6 厘米。印文为汉字九叠篆，内容为“灌顶广善慈济国师印”。印背有汉文款识，右侧为“灌项广善慈济国师印”，左侧为“景泰七年六月日礼部造 泰字九百四十二号”（图一：5）[12]。该印主人应为藏僧葛藏 [13]。

7 甲央、王明星主编：《宝藏——中国西藏历史文物 3》，2000：144、145，图 52。

8 西藏博物馆编，何晓东著：《历史的见证——西藏博物馆藏历代中央政府治藏文物集萃》，2015：83。

9 《明太祖实录》卷七三，洪武五年夏四月丁酉，1962：1342。《明太祖实录》卷七九，洪武六年二月癸酉，1962：1438。《明太祖实录》卷九一，洪武七年七月己卯，1962：1596。

10 西藏博物馆编，何晓东著：《历史的见证——西藏博物馆藏历代中央政府治藏文物集萃》，2015：84。

11 《明太宗实录》卷一三七，永乐十一年二月己未，1962：1665。

12 欧朝贵、其美：《西藏历代藏印》，1991：35。

13 《明英宗实录》卷二二三，景泰三年十一月乙亥，1962：4831-4832。

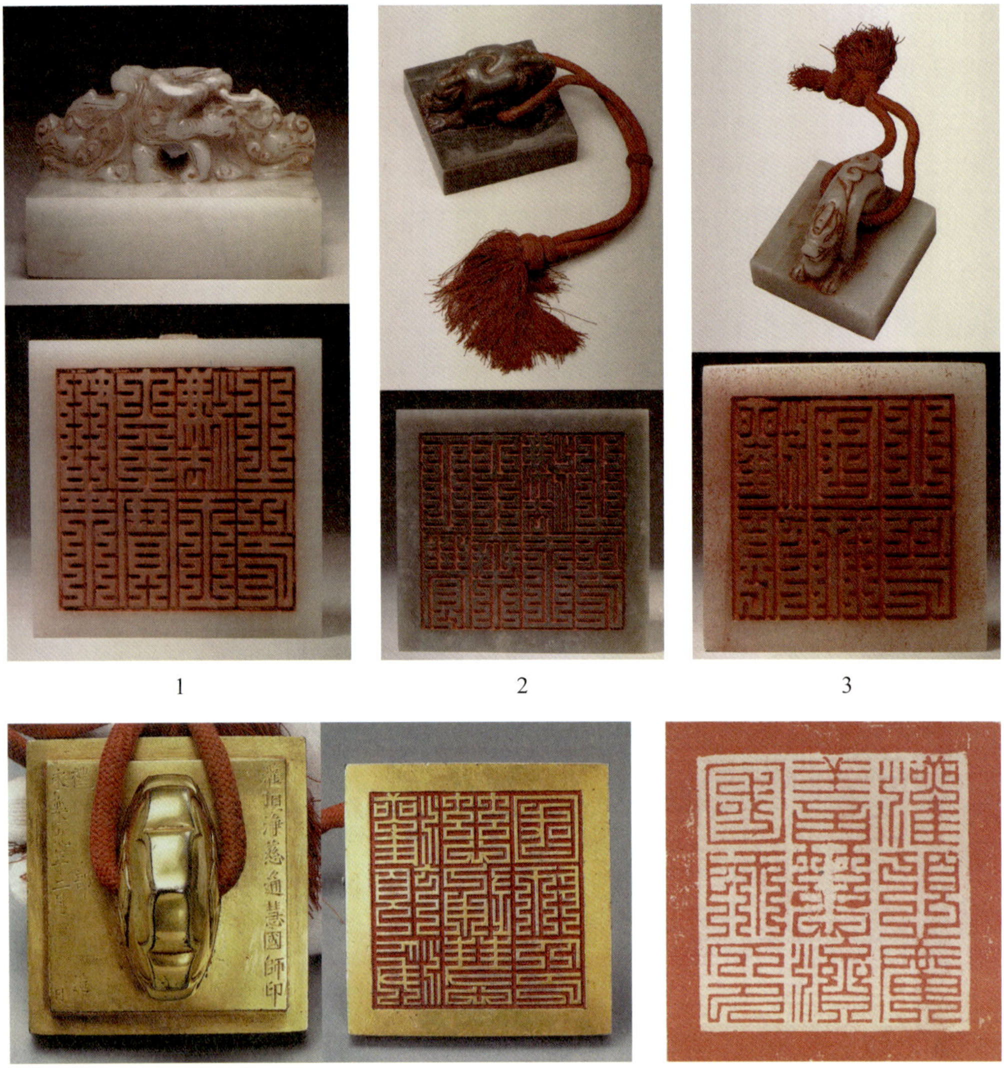

图一　宗教名号印
（1. 如来大宝法王之印　2. 正觉大乘法王之印　3. 灌顶国师之印
4. 灌顶净慈通慧国师印　5. 灌顶广善慈济国师印）

6. 戒定善悟灌顶国师

该印为镀金银印，如意纽，高 9.1 厘米；方形印面，边长 9.6 厘米。印文为汉文九叠篆，内容为“戒定善悟灌顶国师印”；印背有汉文款识，右侧为“戒定善悟灌顶国师

6

7

8

图一　宗教名号印

（6. 戒定善悟灌顶国师　7. 弘慈妙觉灌顶大国师印　8. 灌顶净觉广慧国师印）

印”，左侧为“成化二十一年九月 日 礼部造”（图一：6）[14]。该印主人不详。

7. 弘慈妙觉灌顶大国师印

该印为二台银印，如意纽，高 9.7 厘米；方形印面，边长 9.5 厘米。印文为汉文九叠篆，内容为“弘慈妙觉灌顶大国师印”；印背有汉文款识，右侧为“弘慈妙觉灌项大国师”，左侧为“正德十年（1515 年）十一月 日 礼部造 天字五百九十四号”（图一：7）[15]。据《明英宗实录》记载，正统十三年（1448 年），“礼部奏乌思藏灌顶国师赞善王遣人奏保番僧绰吉坚粲（ཆོས་ཀྱི་རྒྱལ་མཚན）为灌顶弘慈妙觉大国师及求大藏经并护持敕，上从之，寻赐绰吉坚粲诰命及镀金银印、僧帽袈裟”[16]。可知“弘慈妙觉灌顶大国师”名号最初出现于明英宗时期，当时所颁印章为“镀金银印”。现存这枚银印应该是明武宗

14　西藏博物馆编，何晓东著：《历史的见证——西藏博物馆藏历代中央政府治藏文物集萃》，2015：85。

15　欧朝贵、其美：《西藏历代藏印》，1991：38。

16　《明英宗实录》卷一六六，正统十三年五月丁酉，1962：3212。

时期二次颁赐的，故与原印已经不同。

8. 灌顶净觉广慧国师印

该印为镀金银印，如意纽，高 9.2 厘米；方形印面，边长 9.7 厘米。印文为汉文九叠篆，内容为“灌顶净觉广慧国师印”（图一：8）[17]。此印较为特别，从印质、尺寸等特征来看应为明朝官方颁赐的印章，但却不见纪年款识和印章编号等内容，其主人待考。

（二）封爵印

这类印章在明朝颁给西藏的印章中较为特殊，从印文及颁赐对象来看，既不同于前文的宗教名号印，又与后文的官印有区别，可单独作为一种印章类型。目前西藏可见的封爵印有三枚，包括镀金银印和银印两种（图二：1-3）。

1. 阐教王印

该印为镀金银印，驼纽，高 8.5 厘米；方形印面，边长 10.2 厘米。印文为汉文九叠篆，内容为“阐教王印”（图二：1）[18]。这枚印章是永乐十一年（1413 年）明成祖封西藏必力工瓦地方政教首领领真巴儿吉监藏（རིན་ཆེན་དཔལ་གྱི་རྒྱལ་མཚན）为阐教王时所颁。阐教王是明朝在藏区封授的五大教王之一，除帕木竹巴（ཕག་མོ་གྲུ་པ）阐化王获“赐螭纽玉印”外，其余四位教王应获赐金印（实为镀金银印）[19]。

2. 司徒之印

该印为银印，二台直纽，高 11.9 厘米；方形印面，边长 9.4 厘米。印文为九叠篆汉字，内容为“司徒之印”。印背有汉文款识，右侧为“司徒之印”，左侧为“永乐十年二月 日礼部造”，边沿有“智字一百六号”（图二：2）[20]。司徒（སི་ཏུ）本为中国古代掌管教化、土地和民政等事务之官，到元代已经成为虚衔，无实际职务。据文献记载，明永乐十一年（1413 年），明成祖“授锁巴头目刺昝肖、掌巴头目扎巴、八儿土官锁南巴、仰思都巴头目公葛巴等俱为司徒。各赐银印、诰命、锦币”[21]。现存这枚司徒之印可能就与明朝对西藏的这次大规模封授事件有关。

3. 赏巴国公之印

此印为银印，二台直纽，高 11.4 厘米；方形印面，边长 9.5 厘米。印文为九叠篆汉

17 欧朝贵、其美：《西藏历代藏印》，1991：37。

18 西藏博物馆编，何晓东著：《历史的见证——西藏博物馆藏历代中央政府治藏文物集萃》，2015：82。

19 《明史》卷三三一《西域三》，北京：中华书局，1974：8580、8582-8585。

20 甲央、王明星主编：《宝藏——中国西藏历史文物 3》，2000：142-143，图 51。

21 《明太宗实录》卷一三七，永乐十一年二月己未，1962：1666。

1

2

3

图二　封爵印

（1. 阐教王印　2. 司徒之印　3. 赏巴国公之印）

字，内容为“赏巴国公之印”。印背有汉文款识，右侧为“赏巴国公之印”，左侧为“礼部造永乐十二年正月 日”，边沿“礼字一百七十四号”（图二：3）[22]。赏巴为地名，在今西藏日喀则南木林县一带[23]；《明实录》中也写作赏司巴，其头领名为公哥列思监藏巴藏卜。该人为故元国公（གུ་གུང་）、司徒，洪武时期派人入贡，永乐十二年（1414 年）被明成祖续封为赏巴国公[24]。

（三）官印

明朝在经营西藏过程中设立了一批机构，封授了一批职官，因此有不少官印传世。这些官印可分为官司印、官职印，质地有银印和铜印两种（图三：1-5）。

1. 朵甘卫都指挥使司印

该印为银印，直纽，高 9.4 厘米；方形印面，边长 9.4 厘米。印文为九叠篆汉字，内容为“朵甘卫都指挥使司印”；印背右侧款识为“朵甘卫都指挥使司印赐南葛监藏”，左侧为“礼部造永乐五年二月 日”，侧边有“智字三十七号”字样（图三:1）[25]。这枚印章是永乐五年（1407 年）明成祖“命馆觉头目南葛监藏、阿屑领占俱为朵甘卫行都指挥使司都指挥使”时颁给南葛监藏（ནམ་མཁའ་རྒྱལ་མཚན་）的印信。

2. 乌思藏宣慰司分司印

该印为铜印，如意纽，高 6.2 厘米；方形印面，边长 8.4 厘米。印文为汉字九叠篆，内容为“乌思藏宣慰司分司印”，边沿有款识“大字一十三号”（图三:2）[26]。据《明太祖实录》记载：“洪武六年二月癸酉，诏置乌思藏、朵甘卫指挥使司，宣慰司二…宣慰使同知、副使、元帅、招讨、万户等官”[27]。可知明初应承袭元朝旧制而设有乌思藏宣慰司这一机构。该印与目前常见的明代官印不同，未刻出颁赐部门和年月，纽形也较为特殊，亦不为明廷规定的柱纽；但从印章编号、印面及印文特征来看，其应当是明朝颁赐的印章原物。至于此印与标准的明代官印不同的原因，可能与其颁赐年代较早而相关制度未严有关。

22 甲央、王明星主编：《宝藏——中国西藏历史文物 3》，2000：146-147，图 53。
23 陈庆英、高淑芬主编：《西藏通史》，郑州：中州古籍出版社，2003：272。
24 《明太祖实录》卷八五，洪武六年九月己卯，1962：1518。
25 甲央、王明星主编：《宝藏——中国西藏历史文物 3》，2000：140-141，图 50。
26 欧朝贵、其美：《西藏历代藏印》，1991：21。
27 《明太祖实录》卷七九，洪武六年二月癸酉，1962：1437。

1

2

3

4

5

图三　官印
（1. 朵甘卫都指挥使司印　2. 乌思藏宣慰司分司印
3. 必力公万户府印　4. 多笼僧纲司印　5. 都纲之印）

3. 必力公万户府印

该印为铜印，直纽，高 9.7 厘米；方形印面，边长 8.2 厘米。印文为九叠篆汉字，内容为“必力公万户府印”；印背款识为“必力公万户府印”及“洪武十八年 正月日礼部造”，侧边有“兰字七十号”字样（图三：3）[28]。必力公，亦作必力公瓦，其势力范围在今拉萨以东墨竹工卡县止贡区一带，故史家也称止贡（འབྲི་གུང）。公元13世纪止贡势力强大，为元代在西藏设立的十三万户之一。明承元制，仍置必力公万户府并颁发此印。

4. 多笼僧纲司印

该印为铜印，直纽，高7.3厘米；方形印面，边长6厘米。印文为汉字九叠篆，内容为“多笼僧纲司印”。印背和印边有汉文款识，印背右侧为“多笼僧纲司印”，左侧为“永乐十二年正月 日 礼部造”；侧边上“礼字一百七十八号”（图三：4）[29]。印中“多笼”疑即“朵陇（སྟོད་ལུང）”或“朵垄”的异译，该地位于今堆龙德庆区德庆镇[30]。僧纲司是明廷于地方各府设置的佛教事务机构[31]，此印是明朝在藏区亦设置此类宗教机构的证明。

5. 都纲之印

此印为铜印，直纽，高7.6厘米；方形印面，边长5.8厘米。印文为汉文九叠篆，内容为“都纲之印”。印背和印边有汉文款识，右侧为“都纲之印”，左侧为“礼部造”；左边为“景泰四年三月日”，右边为“泰字六百七十三号”（图三：5）[32]。都纲是明朝于僧纲司下所设的宗教职官，等级较低。

（四）图章

图章也称为“图书”或“图记”，一般为象牙质，是明朝颁赐西藏印章中比较特殊的一类印章，目前已有专文对其进行研究。目前西藏发现的图章有“妙缘清净”“妙智崇善”“圆修般若”“静修觉道”“如如自在”“朵儿只唱”“果累千户所印”等，这类印章主要颁给喇嘛这一等级较低的藏僧（图四）[33]。其中“果累千户所印”从印文来看似为官司印，但据印背“钦赐大觉禅师图记”的款识可知其应该为一枚图章。西藏还发现过以名字作为印文的图章，收藏在西藏昌都统战部，该印印背左、右两面分别阴刻汉文款识“赐剌麻钻竹罗古鲁”和“宣德二年月日”，印面则为阳文的八思巴字“德来钻竹扎西若印”[34]。另一枚是西藏博物馆收藏的“夹实坚赞”印，印文为汉字九叠篆；印背有汉

---

28 甲央、王明星主编：《宝藏——中国西藏历史文物3》，2000：90-91，图46。

29 欧朝贵、其美：《西藏历代藏印》，1991：45。

30 欧朝贵、其美：《西藏历代藏印》，1991：45。

31 《明史》卷七五《职官四》，1974：1853。

32 西藏博物馆编，何晓东著：《历史的见证——西藏博物馆藏历代中央政府治藏文物集萃》，2015：96。

33 李帅：《明朝颁赐藏僧象牙图章研究》，《西藏大学学报》2015（3）：97。

34 《西藏自治区志·文物志》编纂委员会编撰：《西藏自治区志·文物志》，2012：963。

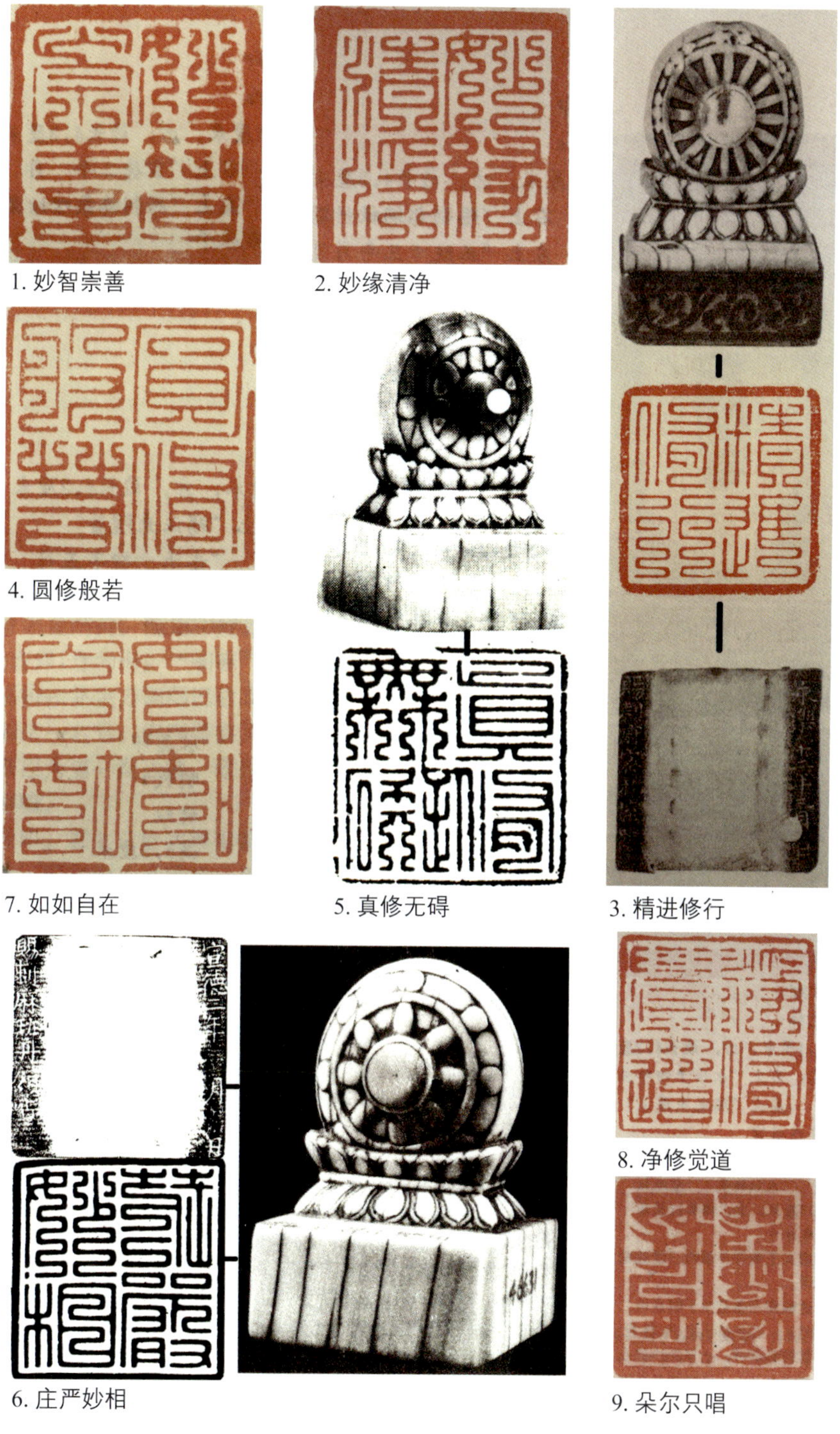

1. 妙智崇善　2. 妙缘清净　4. 圆修般若　7. 如如自在　5. 真修无碍　3. 精进修行　6. 庄严妙相　8. 净修觉道　9. 朵尔只唱

图四　明代图章

（图片摘自李帅：《明朝颁赐藏僧象牙图章研究》，《西藏大学学报》2015（3）：92，图1）

文款识，右侧为“永乐十三年五月日”，左侧为“赐思褁般领葛剌”[35]。

二、明朝颁赐西藏印章的印制选择

如前所述，明朝颁给西藏的印章至少有四种类型，不同类型的印章具有不同的特征，各自所选择的印章制度也有所不同。宗教名号印是明朝颁赐给法王、大国师及国师这三个等级藏僧的印信，质地有玉印和镀金银印及银印三种，其中玉印等级最高，受赐者包括洪武时期的几位国师、明成祖封授的三大法王以及阐化王等。现存玉印包括二位法王之印和一枚灌顶国师之印，其中法王的玉印为双龙纽，与元朝颁给西藏萨迦帝师和国师的“大元帝师统领诸国僧尼中兴释教之印”（图五：1)、“统领释教大元国师印”（图五：2）[36]在印质及印纽方面相同。灌顶国师玉印为螭纽，与元朝颁给藏僧的一枚玉质“灌顶国师之印”（图五:3）[37]也非常相似。由此可知，明代早期颁给西藏少数宗教上层人物的玉印在质地、印纽方面应该受到了元代印制的影响，但印文发生了重大改变，元代使用的是八思巴字，而明代使用汉字。洪武之后明朝颁给大国师及国师的印章通常按照如意纽的镀金银印之规范来制作，等级已经有所降低。据现存一枚明正德时期的银质弘慈妙觉灌顶大国师印显示，该制度到明代中后期已经出现松动。

明朝官方玺印可分为皇族用印、百官用印及藩属赐印等类型，不同类型的印章在颁赐对象、印质、尺寸、印文乃至称呼等方面都有差别。其中皇族用印包括帝、后、妃、太子、亲王、公主、世子及郡王等人的印章，为首的皇帝使用玉印，郡王使用镀金银印，其余则使用金印[38]。明朝颁给高等级藏僧的宗教名号印主要为玉印和镀金银印，这与明朝皇族用印和藩属赐印有诸多相似之处，如玉印与皇帝玺印质地一致，但皇帝的玉印尺寸更大，称“宝”，而颁给西藏宗教首领的玉印尺寸稍小，称“印”[39]，这应是有意进行的等级区分。镀金银印与明朝颁给皇室郡王及安南、占城等外藩国王的印章质地一致[40]，但印纽等又有不同。综上所述，明朝颁给西藏高等级藏僧的宗教名号印在印制的选择上既承袭了元朝印制的传统，同时也借鉴了明朝皇族用印、藩属赐印的部分因素。如此安排一

35 欧朝贵、其美：《西藏历代藏印》，1991：44。

36 甲央、王明星主编：《宝藏——中国西藏历史文物 3》，2000：22-23，图 9；36-37，图 14。

37 甲央、王明星主编：《宝藏——中国西藏历史文物 3》，2000：38-39，图 15。

38 《明史》卷 68《舆服四》，1974：1657-1660。

39 张金梁：《明代朝廷玺印研究》，《中国历史文物》2008（5）：26。

40 《明史》卷六八《舆服四》，1974：1660，1663。《明史》卷三二四《外国五 · 暹罗》，1974：8398。

图五　元代印章

（1. 大元帝师统领诸国僧尼中兴释教之印　2. 统领释教大元国师印　3. 灌顶国师之印　4. 白兰王印　5. 大司徒印　6. 门国公印）

是出于更顺畅快捷的接收元朝在西藏的统治权，二是考虑到西藏作为神权社会，宗教地位要高于世俗权力这一社会现实。此举反映了明初统治者对西藏部分宗教人士超规格的“崇敬”和优待，是明朝“因俗治藏”策略在印章上的体现。

封爵印是明代颁赐西藏印章中较为特殊的印章类型，颁赐对象多为地方头领，从质地来看有镀金银印和银印两种。其中镀金银印为明朝颁给阐教王的印章，印面边长10.2厘米，印文为汉文叠篆，采用驼纽。该印与元朝颁给西藏的“白兰王（སའོ་ཞིན་དབང）印”（图五：4）[41]及明朝赐给安南、占城、暹罗等外藩国王的印章在印质和印纽方面一致[42]，但尺寸较明朝颁给上述外藩国王之印章略大[43]。这说明明廷按藩属王之印制来颁赐阐教王印章，但视其较外藩国王为尊。银印有赏巴国公之印和司徒之印，二印均为二台直纽，印面边长分别为9.5、9.4厘米。据《明史》记载，洪武时期“乃者摄帝师喃加巴藏卜率所举故国公、司徒、宣慰、招讨、元帅、万户诸人，自远入朝…已授国师及故国公等为指挥同知等官，皆给诰印…初，元尊番僧为帝师，授其徒国公等秩，故降者袭旧号。”[44]又《明成祖实录》载：“司徒者，其俗头目之旧号，因而授之”[45]。可见，赏巴国公和司徒之印应该是明朝承袭元朝旧制所颁。值得注意的是，元代司徒、国公的等级按规定应使用银印[46]，但目前所见元代颁给西藏人员的“大司徒印”（图五：5）[47]和“门国公之印”（图五：6）[48]均为三台直纽的铜印，明显与元朝印制不符。现存明朝颁给国公和司徒的印章为直纽二台银印，与前述两枚元代印章的质地和形制不同，采用的是明朝正、从二品官印的规制[49]。因此本文认为，明朝颁给西藏的封爵印既受到了元朝印制的影响，同时又遵循了明朝的印制规定。

明朝颁赐西藏的官印分为官司印和官职印，这类印章特征比较一致。从印质来看，除朵甘卫都指挥使司印为二台银印外，其余均为铜印。从印纽来看，以直纽为主，仅见

41 甲央、王明星主编：《宝藏——中国西藏历史文物3》，2000：30-31，图12。

42 《明史》卷三二一《外国二·安南》，1974：8309。《明太宗实录》卷一七，永乐元年二月甲寅，1962：304。

43 明朝颁给安南、占城、暹罗的印章方三寸，按明尺一寸约2.9-3.2厘米算，这些印章尺寸均不及10厘米，较现存的“阐教王”尺寸小。参见《明史》卷六八《舆服四》，1974：1663。《明史》卷三二四《外国五·暹罗》，1974：8398。

44 《明史》卷三三一《西域三》，1974：8588。

45 《明太宗实录》卷一三七，永乐十一年二月己未，1962：1666。

46 陈高华、张帆、刘晓、党宝海点校：《元典章》卷二十九《礼部卷二·印章》，天津：天津古籍出版社，北京：中华书局，2011：1039。

47 王毅：《西藏文物见闻记（二）》，《文物》1960（Z1）：56，58。

48 西藏博物馆编，何晓东著：《历史的见证——西藏博物馆藏历代中央政府治藏文物集萃》，2015：54。

49 《明史》卷六八《舆服四》，1974：1661-1662。

乌思藏宣慰司分司印为如意纽。印面均呈方形，尺寸的大小与机构和职官的品秩高低相关。现存的朵甘卫都指挥使司印为直纽，二台银印，是明朝颁给朵甘卫都司的官司印，属于“六部、都察院并在外各都司”的范畴，其印制规定为“银印二台，方三寸二分，厚八分”[50]。按明代一寸约相当于现在的2.9-3.3厘米[51]，三寸二分大约等于9.28-10.56厘米，这枚朵甘卫都指挥使司印的印面边长为9.4厘米，在上述尺寸范围内。由此可见，朵甘卫都指挥使司印在印质、印形及尺寸方面均符合明朝官印制度的规定[52]。明朝规定乌思藏宣慰司为正三品机构，必力公瓦万户为正四品机构[53]，与此对应的官印分别是正三品“俱铜印，方二寸七分，厚六分”，正四品机构“俱铜印，方二寸五分，厚五分”[54]。现存的乌思藏宣慰司分司印和必力公万户府均为铜印，印面边长分别为8.4和8.2厘米，亦基本符合印制规定的印章尺寸。僧纲司是明廷于地方各府设置的佛教事务机构，都纲是该机构下的职官，均为从九品[55]。明代印制规定从九品的官印“俱铜印，方一寸九分，厚二分二厘”[56]。现存的多笼僧纲司印和都纲之印均为铜印，边长分别为6、5.8厘米，亦与此类印章的规制相符。基于上文分析，我们注意到明廷颁给西藏的官印比较严格的遵循了明朝的官印制度，在质地、尺寸、印形等方面基本没有逾制，这表明明朝经营西藏的部分制度与内地一致。

明朝颁赐西藏的图章通常为象牙质，印面较小，呈方形，边长多在4厘米左右，较明代标准的官印和封号印都小。印纽形制较多样，具有明显的宗教特色，包括法轮纽、如意纽、狮纽、佛光纽等。此类印章的印文比较多样，可见汉文、梵文及八思巴文，内容包括宗教“赞词”、人名及称号[57]。这类印章在印质、印纽、印文等方面具有多样性，是明朝根据藏区情况而新创制的一类印章类型，已经脱离了明代官方玺印制度的约束。

通过对明朝颁赐西藏印章的特点以及其所依据的印制规范来看，除图章这类特殊的印章外，其他三类印章基本遵循了明朝玺印制度下玉、金、银、铜的等级序列，但针对不同的颁赐对象而选取不同的印章类型，不同印章类型所选择的印制规范也不同，各具

50 《明史》卷六八《舆服四》，1974：1661。

51 林哲：《桂林明代靖江王陵营造尺初探》，《桂林工学院学报》2004（3）：294，注释④。

52 印台厚度亦为印章等级的重要标志，等级越高，厚度越厚。但目前大部分描述只有高，缺乏印台厚度的数据，故无法考察。

53 《明太祖实录》卷一七　，洪武十八年正月丁卯，1962：2582。

54 《明史》卷六八《舆服四》，1974：1662。

55 《明史》卷七五《职官四》，1974：1853。

56 《明史》卷六八《舆服四》，1974：1662。

57 李帅：《明朝颁赐藏僧象牙图章研究》，《西藏大学学报》2015（3）：91-99。

特点。其中宗教名号印和封爵印在承袭元朝印制的基础上，又借鉴了明朝部分印章类型的要素，在印章的规格和等级上都有意提高，体现了明朝对这批印章颁赐对象的重视和优待。明朝颁给西藏的官印主要遵循了明朝的官印制度，既能体现明朝在西藏推行的新制度，亦可见到元朝旧制的延续。象牙图章是明朝新创制的一类印章类型，加入了不少佛教和西藏的因素，符合西藏社会的宗教传统，应该是明廷根据藏僧心理和宗教文化背景所做的“因俗”之举，是明朝治藏政策灵活性和多样性的反映。

三、明朝颁赐印章在西藏的使用

作为政治物品的印章是明廷与西藏之间建立政治关系的凭证，对这类物品在西藏使用情况的考察不仅能了解明朝政治文明在西藏所达到的效果，而且也能窥探西藏人员对明廷的政治态度。下面就结合文物和文献材料就明朝颁赐印章在西藏的使用情况进行初步探讨。

宗教名号印是目前西藏保存较多的一类印章，这类印章的使用方式与藏僧的身份和地位密切相关。法王之印作为明朝颁赐西藏等级最高的印章，目前虽不见与之使用相关的文物材料，但据《贤者喜宴》记载：“大明皇帝授予得银协巴永久性的官印，因此便不需要再次确认了。由于不清楚上述的原因，出现了用朱砂制成的印章和官印。因此，法王心生恐惧，历代法王均为元、明中央朝廷做了有关事情并盖有印章等，此只为满足皇帝之心愿，其他小官员们见如此，便也心生畏惧”[58]。这段表述说明噶玛巴将明廷颁给他的印章视作获得明廷认可和授予权力的凭证，并且使用该印章在西藏为中央政权办理相关事务。

西藏博物馆收藏有一件明代西藏地方的档案，写于黄色丝绸之上，内容是呼吁全藏区，特别是多（ཨ་མདོ）、康（ཁམས）地区的活佛、头人、达官和普通百姓要敬重、爱戴和供养红帽尊者曲吉旺秋（ཆོས་ཀྱི་དབང་ཕྱུག 1584-1635 年，即第六辈红帽噶玛巴），同时也要求上师本人要继承和弘扬教证二法[59]。在文告顶部及末尾各有一方朱色印痕，其中顶部印文略小，印文为藏文“ཞྭ་དམར་ཅོད་པན་འཛིན་པ”。该藏文小印与布达拉宫收藏的一枚木质宝珠纽印在印文格式和内容上均一致，印文可译为“红帽系持冠者（之印）”，应是红

58 巴卧·祖拉陈瓦著，周润年、韩觉贤译：《〈贤者喜宴——噶玛噶仓〉译注（二十六）》，《西藏民族学院学报》2015（3）：55。

59 该文书现藏西藏博物馆，感谢何晓东先生示图，在此致谢。

图六　宣德六年班丹扎释法旨

（图片出处见本文注 62）

帽系噶玛巴的印章[60]。末尾的印痕较大，印文为汉字九叠篆的“灌顶国师之印”，系一枚宗教名号印，这说明明朝颁给西藏地方的印章会被用来发布相关公告。《卫藏通志》中收录有一份清廷查抄噶玛噶举派红帽系活佛的主寺羊八井（ཡངས་པ་ཅན）寺的奏折，其内提到的查抄之物“有灌顶国师镀金铜印一颗，系属元明封赐”[61]。这枚收藏在羊八井寺中的“灌顶国师之印”从质地和印文来看应该是明朝颁赐的印章，或许与上述文告上的“灌顶国师之印”系同一枚。

甘肃岷县近来发现两件由明代著名藏僧班丹扎释（དཔལ་ལྡན་བཀྲ་ཤིས）从北京大隆善寺发往岷州大崇教寺的法旨，其中一件法旨年代为宣德六年（1431 年），涉及大崇教法脉传承的事情，在法旨下部有一大一小两方朱色印痕，小印痕内容已不可考，大印痕呈方形，边长 10 厘米，印文为汉字九叠篆的“净觉慈济大国师之印”（图六）[62]。从印痕尺寸及印文格式和内容来看，上述法旨上的“净觉慈济大国师之印”印痕应该是由明朝颁给班丹扎释的宗教名号印之原印所盖，这是藏僧在处理藏区相关事务时使用明廷所颁印章的又一证明。

灌顶国师阐化王是明代西藏帕木竹巴地方政权的首领，明廷颁给他的印章在西藏之使用情况最能反映明朝治藏之成效。西藏档案馆有一件与阐化王相关的藏文档案，其上共有五处朱色方形印痕，其中首、尾各二处，中间一处（图七）。五处印痕中有四处内容相同，应为同 印章所盖，印文为汉字九叠篆，内容为“灌顶国师阐化王印”。最末尾的一枚印痕较小，印文亦为汉字，内容似为“大阐佛宗”[63]，应该是一枚图章。据藏文内容显示，这是一件与税收条款相关的文书，由灌顶国师阐化王旺秋扎巴坚赞（ངག་གི་དབང་ཕྱུག་བཀྲ་ཤིས་གྲགས་པ་རྒྱལ་མཚན་དཔལ་བཟང་པོ་ཀོན་དིང་ཀུ་ཤྲི་ཆེན་ཏྭ་ཤང）于土龙年（1568 年）从乃东（སྣེ་གདོང）大殿发出。该文书上的“灌顶国师阐化王印”之印文十分规整，印痕边长约 10 厘米，应该是明廷颁给阐化王的印章原物所盖，这是明朝颁赐阐化王的印章在西藏实际使用的证明。

作为西藏帕木竹巴地方政权首领的阐化王同时也是明代大部分时期内西藏名义和实际上的统治者，明廷颁给阐化王的印章也自然成了西藏地方最高统治权的象征，被五世

60 欧朝贵、其美：《西藏历代藏印》，1991：50。

61 （清）松筠撰：《卫藏通志》卷一三下《纪略下》，拉萨：西藏人民出版社，1982：416。

62 李志明、洲塔：《新发现的两件班丹扎释法旨及相关史实考述》，《中国藏学》2016（3）：21-30，附图 1。

63 参见德国波恩大学数字化西藏档案材料（Digitized Tibetan Archives Material at Bonn University），Document0122-1/#/1/1(until/1d)/3；http://www.dtab.uni-bonn.de/php/sct_show.php?groupid=101；http://www.dtab.uni-bonn.de/php/p_show.php?dokid=989&pageid=4；http://www.dtab.uni-bonn.de/php/m_show.php?dokid=989。

图七　西藏档案馆藏明代藏文档案及其上印痕

（图片采自德国波恩大学数字化西藏档案：Digitized Tibetan Archives Material at Bonn University, Document0122-1/#/1/1(until/1d)/3: http://www.dtab.uni-bonn.de/php/sct_show.php?groupid=101; http://www.dtab.uni-bonn.de/php/p_show.php?dokid=989&pageid=4; http://www.dtab.uni-bonn.de/php/m_show.php?dokid=989）

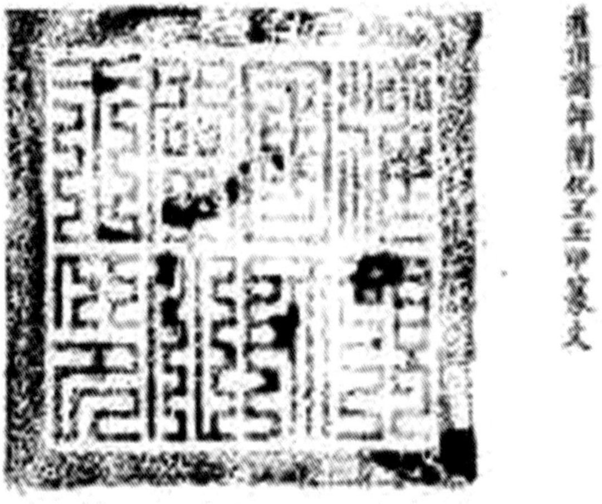

图八　灌顶国师阐化王玉印篆文
（图片采自台北史语所藏明代档案：档案登录号：035998-001。
网址：http://catalog.digitalarchives.tw/item/00/26/da/3d.html）

达赖喇嘛称为“大明皇帝赐给的在吐蕃称为珍宝的水晶印”[64]。这枚玉印（水晶印）实物现已不存，仅在台北史语所藏明清内阁大库档案中一件顺治二年（1645年）的档案上有其印痕，为方形，印文为汉文篆字“灌顶国师阐化王印”，旁有“灌顶国师阐化王玉印篆文”题名（图八）[65]。上述这件与阐化王有关的档案中还提到阐化王一方向清廷请求“换新敕、玉印回藏，弹压地方”[66]。从西藏人员向清廷上缴明代阐化王旧印并请求换取新印的这一事件来看，明朝颁给西藏人员的印章在清朝建立后不仅被西藏人员作为向清朝表示归附和忠诚的信物，而且还被他们作为向清朝求取继续享有明代已获权力和地位的凭证。据邓锐龄先生研究，清初西藏的第巴势力曾试图以阐化王名义向清朝请求换取新的敕书和玉印，以期利用前明所封阐化王的名义获得西藏的统治权，但被清廷识穿，故不再续封阐化王[67]。由此看来，明朝颁给西藏帕木竹巴地方政权首领阐化王的印章在西藏极具权威性，被视作在西藏行使统治权力合法性的重要凭证，甚至在中央政权发生更替时仍能以此作为从新朝继续获得政治资本的凭据。

64 五世达赖喇嘛著、陈庆英、马连龙、马林译：《五世达赖喇嘛传》，北京：中国藏学出版社，2006：326。
65 台北史语所藏明代档案：档案登录号:166471-001；网址：http://catalog.digitalarchives.tw/item/00/28/d7/f1.html。
66 台北史语所藏明代档案：档案登录号：035998-001。网址：http://catalog.digitalarchives.tw/item/00/26/da/3d.html。http://catalog.digitalarchives.tw/item/00/26/da/3d.html。
67 邓锐龄：《清初阐化王入贡请封始末及其意义》，《中国藏学》1998（1）：64-74。

虽然国公和司徒等称号在明代已经属于荣誉性的勋爵和虚衔，通常不具有实质性职权，但明承元制继续在西藏封授司徒和国公并颁给印章，这些印章仍然被西藏人员视作权力和地位的凭证。据藏文文献《协噶尔教法史》记载，拉堆洛家族的拉赞加玛（ལྷ་བཙན་སྐྱབས་མ）“从皇帝那里得到了治理从素尔措（ཟུར་མཚོ）以南至曲堆（ཆུ་འདུས）一带地方的诏书，被封为大司徒，并获赐水晶印”一事[68]。这位拉赞加玛即汉文献中的锁巴头目刺昝肖，明朝皇帝敕封他为司徒的诏书现在仍然保存在西藏[69]。结合内地官方文献来看，明朝赐给刺昝肖的司徒印章不是水晶印而是银印，这是他在西藏素尔措以南至曲堆一带行使统治权力的重要依据。

不仅如此，明朝颁给西藏人员的封爵印在明朝灭亡以后仍继续在西藏使用，相关档案材料在西藏保存不少。桑结嘉措（སངས་རྒྱས་རྒྱ་མཚོ）是五世达赖喇嘛的第巴（སྡེ་པ），曾长期主持西藏政务，他在向西藏地方周围诸地区颁发公函时使用过一枚“司徒之印”，该印为汉文篆体字，印面边长 9.5 厘米[70]；从印文及尺寸来看应该就是前述那枚永乐十年由明廷颁发的银质司徒之印。由此可见，明廷颁给西藏的印章被受赐者用于处理西藏地方的具体社会事务，不仅在当时备受重视，甚至到清代仍在继续使用，成为清初西藏地方用印的重要内容。

四、小结

明朝中央政府颁给西藏的印章类型比较多样，不同类型印章在颁赐对象、印章特征以及所依据的印章制度方面有所不同，是明朝治藏策略的体现。其中宗教名号印主要是颁给高等级藏僧的印章，在印制上既延续了元朝印制的影响，同时亦参考了明朝皇室用印及藩属赐印的相关制度，体现了明朝对西藏宗教人士的重视和优待。封爵印主要是明朝颁给西藏地方僧俗头领的印章，该类印章在许多方面受到了元朝印章的影响，是明承元制在印章方面的体现。明朝颁给西藏的官印可以分为官司印和官职印，这类印章比较严格的遵循了明朝的官印制度，是明朝在西藏地方设立世俗军政机构和职官的证明。图章是明朝颁给西藏人员的一类特殊印章，这类印章的颁赐对象比较多样，但主要为等级较低的藏僧，在特征上表现出浓厚的佛教特色，是明朝因俗治藏的体现。明朝颁给西藏

68 转引自熊文彬、陈楠主编：《西藏通史·明代卷》，北京：中国藏学出版社，2015：185。

69 西藏自治区档案馆编：《西藏历史档案荟萃》，1995：图二五。

70 陈金钟：《西藏第司历任世系之印》，《西藏研究》1995（1）：119。

的印章不只是作为一种政治象征品，而且在西藏地方被实际使用，包括发布公告、处理地方事务等。尤其是作为明代西藏地方政权首领的帕木竹巴第司（སྡེ་སྲིད）之灌顶国师阐化王印，更是被视作在西藏行使统治权力的凭证，引起了相关势力的争夺。这些现象表明明朝对西藏施政起到了具体的成效，西藏也认同明朝及其在西藏推行的相关政策。

附记：本文使用的藏文档案材料由朱德涛博士帮助翻译，感谢杨天雪博士指正英文翻译，在此一并致谢。

◆ 李帅　四川大学历史文化学院考古系专职博士后

清代四川藏区土司官印初探

刘莎

摘要：文章结合文献材料，对作者搜集到的17枚清代四川藏区土司官印的性质、特点、来源、颁授和功用等情况进行了探讨，认为土司所用官印主要是来自清朝中央政府的颁赐，按清廷官方印制，这些印章的质地、形制、尺寸、印文和款识都有专门的规定。清政府对四川藏区各土司颁授官印主要有承袭明朝旧例和清朝因功新赏两类事由形式，这些官印作为政治信物，除具有实用功能外，还在地方社会发挥多方面的功用，并受到历代土司的高度重视。文章通过比较还发现，四川藏区土司所用官印在诸多方面都与西藏的官印系统有非常明显的差异，而与清朝内地省份的官印系统相一致，表明清王朝在四川藏区的行政建置和制度划分都有别于西藏。对土司官印的研究能补清代印制之阙，还可窥探清朝治理边疆地区的政策与特点，具有重要的意义。

土司是元、明、清三朝在边疆地区授予少数民族首领的一种官职，其所用官印不仅是研究古代政治与官制的重要史料，还是中央王朝与地方政治关系的历史物证。有关清代四川藏区的土司官印资料，因限于研究材料和视角，尚未引起学界的足够重视。据笔者陋见，这类研究以往主要是在部分著作中有过简要的文字介绍，且过去的资料公布与相关考释亦有不完备或不准确之处[1]。笔者因工作之便，近来集中搜得一批清代四川藏区土司的官印资料，其中8枚官印为四川博物院馆藏一级文物，且图片资料为首次公布。本文首先对这些印章进行介绍和考释，并在此基础上，对这类印章的性质、特点、来源、颁授和意义等相关问题进行初步探讨，诚望相关方家指正见教。

一、土司官印考释

根据馆藏文物和以往公布的文献著作与玺印著录，笔者共搜集到17方清朝四川藏区土司的官印资料。兹分别介绍考释如下。

1. 瞻对安抚司印（图一）

该印章为铜印，纽残，方形，边长7.7厘米，残高2厘米，西藏博物馆藏。印文为满、汉双语，楷体满文在左，篆体汉文“瞻对安抚司印”在右。印背款识为满汉对照“康熙四十一年七月 礼部造”，边款为“康字八千六十九号”[2]。瞻对在昌都以东，今四川省甘孜藏族自治州中部新龙县一带，分上、中、下三部分，史书称为“三瞻”，地处雅砻江上游，纵横数百里。据史书记载，明朝中央政府已在瞻对设土官，给有印信。康熙四十一年（1702年），瞻对地方首领策冷滚布同喇滚地方喇嘛布木一道，带领所属人民向清朝投诚，“缴明代印信，请授为五品安抚使之职，换给印信。”仍令其管辖瞻对地方。清廷从其所请，并换给“瞻对安抚司印”[3]。

2. 喇滚安抚司印（图二）

该印章为铜印，椭圆形柱纽，方形，边长7.3厘米，高9.5厘米，西藏博物馆藏。印文为满、汉二体合璧，楷体满文在左，篆体汉文在右。印背款识为满汉文对照“喇滚安抚司印 礼部造”，边款“康熙四十一年七月 日”和“康字八千七十号”[4]。喇滚大致在四川甘孜藏族自治州雅砻江流域，清初其首领“带领所属人口投诚，缴明代印信。请授

1 欧朝贵、其美：《西藏历代藏印》，拉萨：西藏人民出版社，1991：51-55。四川文物管理局编：《四川文物志》（下册），成都：巴蜀出版社，2005：1136-1139。阿坝藏族羌族自治州地方志编纂委员会编：《阿坝州志》，北京：民族出版社，1994：2184-2185。张孝忠、毛万良：《金川发现清乾隆年间土司印章》，《四川文物》，1987（4）：38。四川省地方志编纂委员会编：《四川省志·文物志》，成都：四川省地方志编纂委员会，1999：433。金川县地方志编委：《金川县志》，北京：民族出版社，1994：877。王晓春：《梭磨宣慰司印》，《四川文物》1991（1）：51-53。王晓春：《清乾隆梭磨宣慰司铜印：见证清政府有效管理嘉绒藏区》，《中国档案报》2016年3月18日第4版。

2 欧朝贵、其美：《西藏历代藏印》，1991：51。

3 《清实录·清圣祖实录》卷二零八，康熙四十一年五月十三日，北京：中华书局，1985：119。

4 欧朝贵、其美：《西藏历代藏印》，1991：52。

图一　瞻对安抚司印

图二　喇滚安抚司印

图三　瞻对安抚司印

图四　霍尔东科长官司印

图五　嘉克杜特述长官司印

图六　绰倭安抚司印

为五品安抚使之职，换给印信”[5]，“康熙四十年（1701 年），归附，授职”[6]，并赐给“喇滚安抚司印”，即今存之印。

3. 瞻对安抚司印（图三）

该印章为铜印，椭圆形柱纽，方形，边长 7.5 厘米，高 12 厘米，西藏博物馆藏。印文为满、汉双语，都使用篆体，满文在左，汉文“瞻对安抚司印”在右。印背款识为满文和汉文对照“瞻对安抚司印 礼部造”，边款“嘉庆十三年六月 日”和“嘉字七百四十三号”[7]。该印与前一枚印章同属瞻对土司印，但年代有所不同。

4. 霍尔东科长官司（图四）

该印章为铜印，直纽，方形，边长 7 厘米，高 15 厘米，西藏博物馆藏。印文为

5　《清实录 · 清圣祖实录》卷二零八，1985：119。

6　赵尔巽等撰：《清史稿 · 列传三百 · 土司二》卷五百十三，北京：中华书局，1996：14243。

7　欧朝贵、其美：《西藏历代藏印》，1991：54。

满、汉双语，篆体满文在左，右侧篆体汉字，文曰“霍尔东科长官司”。印背款识为满汉文对照“霍尔东科长官司印 礼部造”，边款“乾隆二十七年三月 日”和“乾字一万二千五百九十九号”[8]。霍尔东科是四川甘孜藏族自治州所属道孚、炉霍、朱倭、甘孜、东谷“霍尔五地”之一。

5. 嘉克杜特述长官司印（图五）

该印章为铜印，椭圆形柱纽，方形，边长 7.3 厘米，高 10.5 厘米，西藏博物馆藏。印文为满、汉双语，印文右一半为汉字篆文，文曰“嘉克杜特述长官司印”，左为相应满文。印背款识为满汉对照“嘉克杜特述长官司印 礼部造”，边款“乾隆肆拾陆年叁月 日”和“乾字壹万伍千贰百玖拾叁号”[9]。嘉克杜特述长官司是乾隆四十六年设置。现存铜印，即为当时所授。

6. 绰倭安抚司印（图六）

该印章为铜印，椭圆形柱纽，方形，边长 7.5 厘米，高 10 厘米，西藏博物馆藏。印文为满、汉双语，印文右一半为汉字篆文，文曰“绰倭安抚司印”，左为相应满文。印背款识为满汉对照楷体“绰倭安抚司印 礼部造”，边款“乾隆肆拾陆年贰月 日”和“乾字壹万伍千贰百捌拾壹号”[10]。绰倭是四川甘孜藏族自治州所属道孚、炉霍、朱倭、甘孜、东谷“霍尔五地”之一。

7. 卓克基长官司印（图七）

该印章为铜印，椭圆形柱纽，方形，边长 7.1 厘米，通高 10.6 厘米，其中纽高 8.5 厘米，印台高 2.1 厘米，四川博物院藏。印文为满、汉双语，印右一半为汉字篆文，文曰“卓克基长官司印”，左为相应篆体满文。印右边款为“乾隆十四年十一月 日”。左边款为“乾字二千五百三十九号”。印背右阴刻“卓克基长官司印 礼部造”，左背为相应满文[11]。卓克基，其地在今马尔康县东。据文献记载，卓克基长官司“其祖良尔吉，系杂谷土舍。乾隆十三年，随征大金川有功。十五年，颁给长官司印信号纸，寻以通匪伏诛”[12]。

8. 松冈长官司印（图八）

该印章为铜印，椭圆形柱纽，方形，边长 7.1 厘米，通高 10.5 厘米，其中纽高 8.7 厘米，印台高 1.8 厘米，四川博物院藏。印文为满、汉双语，印文右一半为汉字篆文，

8 欧朝贵、其美：《西藏历代藏印》，1991：56。
9 欧朝贵、其美：《西藏历代藏印》，1991：55。
10 欧朝贵、其美：《西藏历代藏印》，1991：53。
11 四川文物管理局编：《四川文物志》（下册），2005：1136。
12 《清史稿 · 列传三百 · 土司二》卷五百十三，1996：14235。

图七　卓克基长官司印

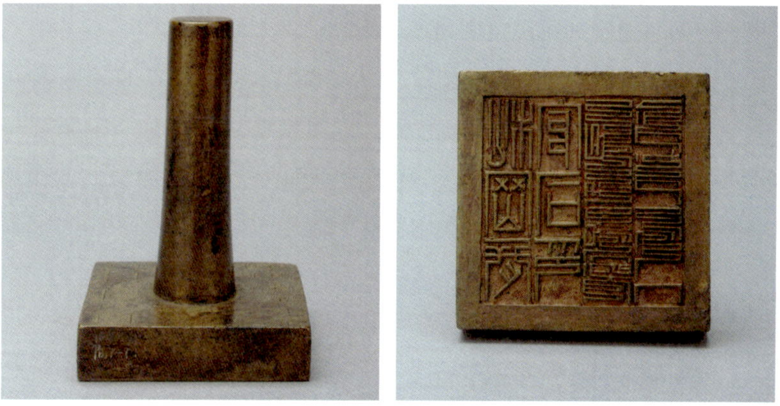

图八　松冈长官司印

图九　党坝长官司印

文曰“松冈长官司印”，左为相应篆体满文。左边款为“乾隆一万一千七百四十号”。右边款为“乾隆十八年五月 日”。印背右阴刻“松冈长官司印 礼部造”，左背为相应满文[13]。松冈，其地在马尔康县。据文献记载，松冈长官司“其祖系杂谷土目，自唐时安设。康熙二十二年（1683年），颁给安抚司印信号纸”[14]。

9. 党坝长官司印（图九）

该印章为铜印，椭圆形柱纽，方形，边长7厘米，通高10.5厘米，其中纽高8.7厘米，印台高1.8厘米。印文为满、汉双语，右一半为汉字篆文，文曰“党坝长官司印”，左为相应篆体满文。左边款为“乾隆一万二千四百十二号”。右边款为“乾隆二十六年二月 日”。印背右阴刻“党坝长官司印 礼部造”，左背为相应满文[15]，四川博物院藏。党坝长官司，其地在今理县西、马尔康境内大渡河上游。据文献记载，“其曾祖阿丕，系杂谷土舍。乾隆十三年（1748年），土舍泽旺随征大金川有功，颁给长官司印信号纸”[16]。

10. 四川长河西鱼通宁远军民宣慰司印（图一〇）

该印章为铜印，椭圆形柱纽，方形，边长8.7厘米，通高11.4厘米，其中纽高9.3厘米，印台高2.1厘米，四川博物院藏。印文为满、汉双语，印面右一半为汉字篆文，文曰“四川长河西鱼通宁远军民宣慰司印”，左为相应满文。印侧边款“道字四百八十七号”和“道光五年七月 日”。印背右刻阴“四川长河西鱼通宁远军民宣慰司印 礼部造”，左为相应满文[17]。长河西鱼通宁远地在今甘孜藏族自治州境内。四川长河西宁远鱼通宣慰使，亦即明正宣慰使司，宣慰司始于元代，明清沿袭。在世袭土司中以宣慰司、宣慰使为最高官职，从三品。据文献记载，“明正宣慰使司，其先系木坪分支。明洪武初，始祖阿克旺嘉尔参随征明玉珍有功。永乐五年，授四川长河西宁鱼通宁远宣慰使。康熙五年，丹怎札克巴归附。乾隆三十六年（1771年），甲木参德侵随征金川有功，赏赐‘佳穆伯屯巴’名号，并二品顶戴花翎”[18]。

11. 盐源县瓜别安抚司印（图一一）

该印章为铜印，椭圆形柱纽，方形，边长7.7厘米，通高10.5厘米，其中纽高9.2厘米，印台高1.6厘米，四川博物院藏。印文为满汉、双语，印面右一半为汉字篆文，

13 四川文物管理局编：《四川文物志》（下册），2005：1136。
14 《清史稿·列传三百·土司二》卷五百十三，1996：14235。
15 四川文物管理局编：《四川文物志》（下册），2005：1137。
16 《清史稿·列传三百·土司二》卷五百十三，1996：14235。
17 四川文物管理局编：《四川文物志》（下册），2005：1138。
18 《清史稿·列传三百·土司二》卷五百十三，1996：14242。

图一〇　四川长河西鱼通宁远军民宣慰司印

图一一　盐源县瓜别安抚司印

图一二　绰斯甲布宣抚司印

文曰“盐源县瓜别安抚司印”，左为相应满文。右边款为“乾隆三十九年十月 日”。左边款为“乾字一万二千八百十五号”。印背右阴刻“盐源县瓜别安抚司印 礼部造”，左背为相应满文[19]。据文献记载，“瓜别安抚司系麽些夷人。其先玉珠迫，于康熙四十九年（1710年）归附”[20]，并颁给印信号纸。

12. 绰斯甲布宣抚司印（图一二）

该印章为铜印，椭圆形柱纽，方形，边长 8.4 厘米，通高 12.3 厘米，其中纽高 10.1 厘米，印台高 2.2 厘米，四川博物院藏。印文为满、汉双语，印文右一半为汉字篆文，文曰“绰斯甲布宣抚司印”，左为相应满文。右边款为“乾字壹万肆千陆佰捌拾肆号”。左边款为“乾隆肆拾年叁月 日”。印背右阴刻“绰斯甲布宣抚司印 礼部造”，左背为相应满文[21]。绰斯甲布位于今阿坝藏族自治州金川县北，观音桥乡。据文献记载，绰斯甲布“始祖资立，康熙三十九年（1700 年），归附。四十一年，颁给宣抚司印信号纸，随将旧印呈缴[22]。

13. 四川穆坪董卜韩胡宣慰司印（图一三）

该印章为铜印，椭圆形柱纽，方形，边长 8.8 厘米，通高 10.3 厘米，其中纽高 7.7 厘米，印台高 2.6 厘米，四川博物院藏。印文为满、汉双语，印面右一半为汉字篆文，文曰“四川穆坪董卜韩胡宣慰司印”，左为相应满文。左边款为“乾隆五十七年三月日”。右为相应满文。印背右刻阴文“四川穆坪董卜韩胡宣慰司印 礼部造”，左背为相应满文[23]。与印章同时保存下来的还有一件印盒，银质，中空，外形与印章一致。印盒底部可以打开，旁边设有锁具，印章便是从印盒底部盛装。穆坪董卜韩胡宣慰司，简称穆坪土司。其地在今四川宝兴县城城关镇。据文献记载，穆坪董卜韩胡宣慰司“其先於明世袭土职。至康熙元年（1662 年），坚参喃喀归附，仍授原职，请领宣慰司印信。乾隆十年（1745 年）颁给号纸”[24]。

14. 瓦寺宣慰司印（图一四）

该印章为铜印，椭圆形柱纽，方形，边长 8.9 厘米，通高 12.3 厘米，其中纽高 9.8 厘米，印台高 2.5 厘米，四川博物院藏。印文为满、汉双语，印面右一半为汉字篆文，

19 四川文物管理局编：《四川文物志》（下册），2005：1138。
20 《清史稿 · 列传三百 · 土司二》卷五百十三，1996：14238。
21 四川文物管理局编：《四川文物志》（下册），2005：1137。
22 《清史稿 · 列传三百 · 土司二》卷五百十三，1996：14236。
23 四川文物管理局编：《四川文物志》（下册），2005：1138。
24 《清史稿 · 列传三百 · 土司二》卷五百十三，1996：14241-14242。

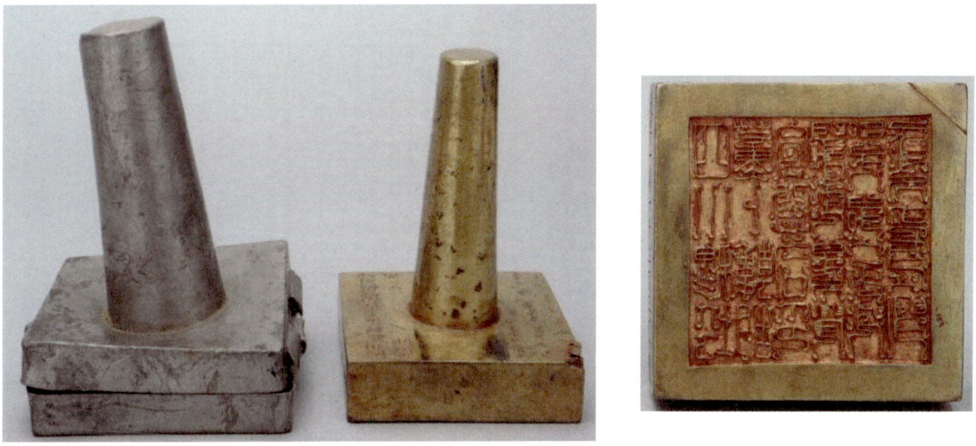

图一三　四川穆坪董卜胡宣慰司印

图一四　瓦寺宣慰司印

文曰“瓦寺宣慰司印”；左为相应满文。右边款为“嘉字四百六十八号”。左边款为“嘉庆九年四月 日”。印背右阴刻楷体“瓦寺宣慰司印 礼部造”，左背为相应满文[25]。与印章同时保存下来的也有一件印盒，铜质，造型和设计与前一件印盒相同。瓦寺宣慰司，其地在今汶川县玉龙乡涂禹山。据文献记载，“顺治九年（1652年），土司曲翊伸归附，授安抚司。康熙五十九年（1720年），征西藏，土司桑郎温恺随征有功，加宣慰司衔。乾隆二年（1737年），加指挥使职衔。乾隆十七年及三十六年，征剿杂谷土司苍旺并金川

25　四川文物管理局编：《四川文物志》（下册），2005：1137。

图一五　梭磨宣慰司印

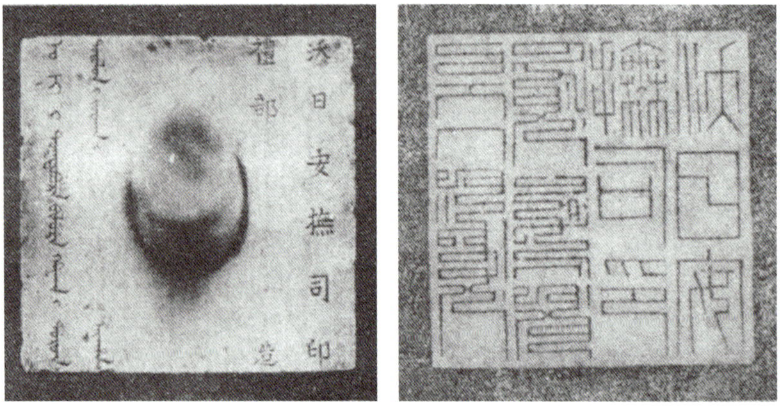

图一六　沃日安抚司印

等处，土司桑郎雍中随征出力，赏戴花翎。嘉庆九年（1804 年），随征达州教匪，经四川总督勒宝奏升宣慰司，换给印信号纸”[26]。

15. 梭磨宣慰司印（图一五）

该印章为铜印，椭圆形柱纽，方形，边长 9 厘米，印台高 2.2 厘米，阿坝州藏族档案馆藏。印面为满、汉双语，印文右一半为汉字篆文，文曰“梭磨宣慰司印”，左为相应满文。印右侧面阴刻楷书汉文“梭磨宣慰司印 礼部造”，印背两侧款识为汉文“乾字壹万肆千柒百肆拾伍号”和“乾隆肆拾年拾壹月日”，印背左侧为相同意思的满文[27]。梭磨地区是川西北嘉绒藏族四土族姓的发源地。据文献记载，梭磨宣慰司“始祖囊素沙甲

26 《清史稿 · 列传三百 · 土司二》卷五百十三，1996：14234-14235。

27 王晓春：《梭磨宣慰司印》，《四川文物》1991（1）：51-53。王晓春：《清乾隆梭磨宣慰司铜印：见证清政府有效管理嘉绒藏区》，《中国档案报》2016 年 3 月 18 日第 4 版。

布，原系杂谷土目，自唐时归附。雍正元年（1723年），征缴郭克贼番有功，颁给副长官司印信号纸。乾隆十五年（1750年），换给安抚司印。三十六年（1771年），进剿大小金川，土司随征，经将军阿桂奏赏宣慰司职衔并花翎，换给印信号纸”[28]。

16. 沃日安抚司印（图一六）

该印章为铜印，椭圆形柱纽，方形，边长7.6厘米，印台高1.2厘米，金川县文化馆藏。印文满、汉双语，印文右一半为汉字篆体，文曰“沃日安抚司印”，左为相应的篆体满文。印侧边款“乾隆十九年十二月 日”和“乾字一万一千八百八号”。印背右刻汉文“沃日安抚司印 礼部造”，左侧为相应的满文 。沃日位于今天四川省阿坝藏族羌族自治州小金县。沃日安抚司亦称鄂克什安抚司，授职于清初，乾隆四十四年（1779年）后，受懋功直隶厅同知及懋功协副将辖。据文献记载，沃日土司“始祖巴碧太。顺治十五年（1658年），归附，颁发沃日贯顶净慈妙智国师印信号纸。乾隆二十年（1755年），颁给土司色达拉安抚司印信号纸，随将旧印呈缴。二十九年，随征金川有功，赏二品顶戴花翎。沃日地名更为鄂克什，原系维州协所辖。乾隆五十年（1785年），改隶懋功协管辖。宣统三年（1911年），改流”。[29]

17. 霍尔白利长官司印

该印章为铜印，坐狮纽，方形，边长7.5厘米，通高5.9厘米，其中印纽高3.8厘米，印台高2.1厘米，西南民族大学博物馆藏。印文为汉、满双语，印文右一半为篆体汉字，文曰“霍尔白利长官司”，左一半为相应满文 。此印没有颁发机构、编号和年号，狮纽制作较细，印体制作厚薄不均，铸造工艺较为粗糙。霍尔白利长官司，简称白利土司，为霍尔七部之一，兴起于清雍正年间，其官寨所在地在今甘孜藏族自治州甘孜县生康村白利乡。据《清史稿 · 土司传》载："霍尔白利土司，其先隆溥特查什，雍正六年（1728年），归附，授职。宣统三年改流”。

二、土司官印性质与特点

通过对目前已搜集到的清代四川藏区土司所用官印资料的观察和分析，我们可以对这类印章的性质和特点进行初步的认识与归纳。

按照官职类型划分，目前所见的清代四川藏区土司官印可分作宣慰司印、宣抚司印、

28 《清史稿 · 列传三百 · 土司二》卷五百十三，1996：14235。

29 《清史稿 · 列传三百 · 土司二》卷五百十三，1996：14235-14236。

安抚司印和长官司印等四类。这些印章都为铜质，一般都是椭圆形柱纽（直纽），印面呈方形，尺寸略有差别，其中宣慰司印尺寸略大，边长在8-9厘米之间，高10-13厘米；其余三类印的边长一般都在7-8厘米之间，通高多在10-12厘米之间不等。从印章整体特征看，土司所用官印主要来自中央政府的颁赐，有个别印章为地方自制。按照清朝官方印制，朝廷颁授给地方官员的印信，都是在中央统一制作，具体是由礼部铸印局承担。清朝的铸印局（或称印铸局），由“汉员外郎、满洲署主事、汉大使各一人”组成，“题销铸印，掌铸宝玺，凡内外诸司印信，并范冶之”[30]，这与上述印章款识中的“礼部造”字样正相吻合。需要注意的是，并非土司使用的所有印章都由中央直接铸造，前文介绍的“霍尔白利长官司印”，无论是从其有无边款、尺寸大小，还是纽式设计等特征，都不符合清廷官印的规制，因此可推测它应是地方上的自制印章，但该印在制作过程中，其质地和满汉双语合璧的特点，以及印文的官职内容等，都参照了朝廷封印的特点，所以，这枚的性质属于一枚复制印。

从印文特点来看，土司印章的印面文字都是以阳文刻成，由满、汉两种文字构成，其中汉字都使用篆体，而满文则因时代不同，既有楷体，又有篆体。据《清史稿•职官》记载，土司印章中等级最高者为宣慰使司和指挥使司，“清、汉文殳篆，方二寸七分、厚九分”；宣抚司副使、安抚使司用“清、汉文悬针篆，方二寸四分、厚五分五厘”；长官司用“清、汉文悬针篆，方二寸二分，厚四分五厘”[31]。关于清代印章满文的用篆问题，清廷曾专门出台过政策。乾隆十三年（1748年），因交泰殿贮藏的皇家宝玺“向兼清、汉文。汉文皆用篆体，清文则有专用篆体者，亦有即用本字者”。对此，清高宗认为不妥，令儒臣“广搜载籍，据援古法，成三十二类”，将篆体做一全面性的整理，并以乾隆皇帝东巡盛京祭祖时创作的《盛京赋》为本，缮成满汉篆文，以广为流传[32]。乾隆帝先是下令将二十一枚御宝改铸为新篆体，到乾隆十四年，因“印信关防所关甚重，篆文既经钦定，理应普给颁发，以昭画一”，又从三十二种新定篆体中另选七种，将文武百官的印信全数改铸[33]。这种变化，在四川藏区土司所用的官印中也得到体现。如前文介绍的两枚康熙四十一年七月“瞻对安抚司印”和“喇滚安抚司印”，它们的印文中满文并未用篆，其余乾隆十三年以后的土司印章，都使用了乾隆朝新创制的满文篆体。

30 《清史稿 · 志八十九》卷一一四，1996：3280。

31 《清史稿 · 志八十九 · 职官一》卷一百十四，1996：3281。

32 中国第一历史档案馆编：《乾隆朝上谕档》第2册，乾隆十三年九月十二日，北京：档案出版社，1991：238。

33 允祹等撰：《钦定大清会典》（乾隆朝）卷二八，台北：台湾商务印书馆，1983：13。

关于土司印章的款识，按照清朝官印规制，印章之“印文清、汉本字镌于印背，年、月、号数镌于印旁”[34]，其目的是便于印文快速、准确地识别，以及确认颁发机关的可信性，而制造时间与编号，则是便于登记管理。从上述印章实物可知，印章款识通常用汉满两种文字，且都用楷体字刻写，款识内容包括印名、铸印机构、时间和序号。以前述四川博物院收藏的“瓦寺宣慰司印”为例，该印印背右侧的“瓦寺宣慰司印 礼部造”为印名和铸印机构；两侧边款“嘉庆九年四月 日”和“嘉字四百六十八号”分别为该印章的铸造时间和序号，其中“嘉庆九年四月”为铸印时间，“嘉”字表明该印是嘉庆朝所颁官印的标志，而“四百六十八号”则是“嘉字”的编号。

综上所述，我们可以看出，清代四川藏区土司所用官印主要是来自中央政府的颁授，另有少数是地方官员仿照朝廷封印复制而成。中央王朝对地方土司用印的质地、形制、尺寸、印文和款识都有专门的规定。具体来说，四川藏区土司所用官赐封印俱为铜印，椭圆形柱纽（直纽），印面方形。土司的职级高低会直接体现在其所用官印的尺寸和用篆等方面。此外，标识有印章年、月、号数的行款，是官赐封印最重要的特征，地方上虽然有少数自制印，但都是以朝廷封印为参照。

三、土司官印的封授与意义

从文献记载和现存文物材料看，清朝中央政府在四川藏区封授的土司均属武职，其职衔依次为宣慰司、宣抚司、安抚司、招讨司、长官司，等级从三品至正六品，各级土司之间虽有等第，但并不相统率，皆属世袭职衔[35]。清政府封授四川藏区土司印章的事由形式大致可以归纳为两类，即承袭明朝旧例和清朝因功新赏。清朝定鼎中原之初，制度草创，多因袭明代旧制。清政府对西部少数民族采取羁縻之策，规定凡明代旧封喇嘛缴回诰敕、印信、札符者，由理藩院查验注册后均予换给清之诰敕、印信[36]。因此承袭明朝旧例的做法主要出现在清朝初期，例如穆坪董卜韩胡土司“其先於明世袭土职。至康熙

34 《光绪朝大清会典》卷三四，见任万平：《清代官印制度研究综论》，载朱诚如、王天有主编：《明清论丛》第一辑，北京：紫禁城出版社，1999：298-316。

35 《钦定大清会典》卷四六，武选清吏司，第1-2页；卷四七，第22-23页。吴玉章：《中国土司制度渊源与发展史》，成都：四川民族出版社，1988：159-161、213-216。周伟洲：《清代川康藏区土司建制及其社会组织》，《西北民族论丛》，2013（00）。

36 《大清会典事例》卷八七五，见张羽新：《清朝治藏典章研究》（中卷），北京：中国藏学出版社，2002：628。

元年（1662 年），坚参喃喀归附，仍授原职，请领宣慰司印信”[37]；瓦寺宣慰司“顺治九年（1652 年），土司曲翊伸归附，授安抚司”[38]；瞻对和喇滚土司都是在清初先“缴明代印信，请授为五品安抚使之职，换给印信”，后朝廷仍令其管辖原有地方，并赐给安抚司印[39]。因功犒赏是清廷封授土司首领印信中更为常见的一种方式。因为清政府所封土司都是武职，所以地方土司跟随清军出征剿乱，是他们建立功勋最普遍的做法，如瓦寺土司“康熙五十九年（1720 年），征西藏，土司桑郎温恺随征有功，加宣慰司衔。乾隆二年（1737 年），加指挥使职衔。乾隆十七年及三十六年，征剿杂谷土司苍旺并金川等处，土司桑郎雍中随征出力，赏戴花翎。经四川总督勒宝奏升宣慰司，换给印信号纸”[40]；梭磨宣慰司因“雍正元年（1723 年），征缴郭克贼番有功，颁给副长官司印信号纸。乾隆十五年（1750 年），换给安抚司印。三十六年，进剿大小金川，土司随征，经将军阿桂奏赏宣慰司职衔并花翎，换给印信号纸”[41]。

在弄清楚了清朝政府对四川藏区土司印信的颁授问题后，我们进一步再考察这些印章对于地方土司首领所具有的功能意义。一般来说，在日常行政事务中钤盖使用，是印章最基本的功能属性。在现存的档案文书中，有不少能反映土司官印在日常事务中被使用的材料，如阿坝藏族羌族自治州红原县江宫寺收藏的由梭磨土司水虎年颁发的“梭磨杰布关于保护辖区内嘉西嘉和曼扎拉二寺的文令”、马尔康县松岗镇直波村私人收藏由松冈土司土鼠年三月七日颁发的“松冈杰布关于给无地者划拨份地的文令”，以及小金县私人收藏由沃日土司于土龙年十二月五日颁发的“沃日杰布关于给嘎罗格西根尕等人减免粮税的文令”[42]等。除此以外，从相关文献记载来看，中央政府颁授给土司的印章，其所承载的意义并不只是单纯的实用功能，而是具有更加广泛和深刻的政治蕴涵。关于这个问题，我们可以从以下几方面进行考察。

首先，清朝颁授土司印信时要举行隆重的授印仪式。清朝土司职衔的封授被当作土司政治和社会生活中的重大事件，往往以隆重的仪式活动迎请新授土司印信，并加以庆祝。如乾隆二十八年（1763 年）四川总督阿尔泰描述了大金川新任土司郎卡接去印信的场景：“三月初六日，至该酋交界地方，土司郎卡带领大小头人百姓约五百余人，焚香

37 《清史稿 · 列传三百 · 土司二》卷五百十三，1996：14241-14242。

38 《清史稿 · 列传三百 · 土司二》卷五百十三，1996：14234-14235。

39 《清实录 · 清圣祖实录》卷二零八，1985：119。

40 《清史稿 · 列传三百 · 土司二》卷五百十三，1996：14234-14235。

41 《清史稿 · 列传三百 · 土司二》卷五百十三，1996：14235。

42 阿坝州藏族历史文化古籍研究协会编：《嘉绒地区杰布和文书档案》，成都：四川民族出版社，2017：227、240-241、242-243。

跪道叩接，并排列旗伞鼓乐，焚香抬请新印至官寨。土司郎卡三跪九叩头领受新印，请在经堂佛龛上供养，又望东三跪九叩头谢恩”[43]。再如乾隆十六年（1751年）杂谷土司苍旺因随征金川有功，从安抚司升任宣慰司。为示庆祝，苍旺组织戏班，以《格东特传》为基础编演祭祀“长寿六仙”的《则让兰芝》，并在祭年大典“斯格仁真”上表演。到乾隆十八年（1753年），杂谷事件以后，党壩由杂谷分出，正式被封授长官司职衔。为此，土司泽旺斯旦真举行长达十三天的“斯格仁真”庆典，编排藏戏演出[44]。

其次，地方土司要设专人保管中央政府颁赐的官印。从文献记载看，土司官印都由拥有权势者保管。在土司之位悬空或土司年幼期间遂有“护印舍人”或“护印土舍”之说。待土司及冠之年，方由成年的土司视印。如光绪十六年（1890年）松冈土妇的藏文承袭奏折中就声称，“泽旺龙珠土司因年幼不能掌管土司印章，故由老土妇索郎卓玛代管土司印章，泽旺龙珠成年后，由其管理土司印章”[45]。再如大金川促浸土司甚至专设“扎勒达克”，为掌印信之职，该职位由掌握政治实权者担任。所以大金川呈递清朝的禀文中有“莎罗奔及扎勒达克并我等二人”之说，将掌印信者同土司并列。莎罗奔直接自称“掌印土司”[46]。

最后，清朝颁授的官印是权力、身份和地位的象征，是各土司之间权力斗争焦点。据文献记载，在地方土司阶层内部的权力争夺中，印章常具有重要价值。例如清代初期沃日纳吉儿、泽儿吉与朗金初围绕土职继承问题发生纠纷时，纳儿吉之姑泽儿吉长期把持印章，“每有文书必白于泽，可行则请印，印扃于庙中，泽章其钥”[47]。由此可知，印章既被土司阶层恭敬地供奉于庙中，足证印章在其观念中的神圣性和重要性。

综上所述，我们可以知道，清朝中央政府在四川藏区封授的土司印章，主要有两种事由形式，一是延续前朝旧例，一是清朝因功犒赏。这些印章除了基本的实用功能以外，还具有重要的象征意义，并受到地方土司的高度重视。具体表现在三方面，即四川藏区的土司在接受朝廷赐印时要举行隆重的授印仪式；地方上要设专人保管朝廷颁赐的

---

43 第一历史档案馆藏宫中朱批奏折民族类，10006卷8号件，转引自刘源：《从清代档案看清政府对金川土司的政策》，《中国藏学》1993（4）：123-128。

44 刘志群：《嘉绒藏戏》，载《四川省嘉绒地区藏戏问题研讨会资料汇编》，四川省民族事务委员会、《中国戏曲志·四川卷》编辑部编印，1993年，转引自邹立波：《明清时期嘉绒藏族土司关系研究》，2017：210。

45 《松岗土妇呈报土司世系及辖区官民情况之折子》，原件存于阿坝州阿坝县卓格寺。见红音：《嘉绒藏族土司藏文档案的内容与价值分析》，《青海民族研究》2015（3）：28。

46 《清高宗实录》卷九零四、九零五、九二五，乾隆三十七年三月上、乾隆三十七年三月下、乾隆三十八年正月下，北京：中华书局，1986：76、102-103、435。

47 吴羹梅、周祚峄：《理番厅志·边防志七·夷事》卷四，同治五年刻本，转引自邹立波：《明清时期嘉绒藏族土司关系研究》，2017：212。

官印；官赐封印是权力、身份和地位的象征，各土司间会围绕官印展开权力斗争。总之，对地方土司来说，有了朝廷封印，他们便可以在地方的政治事务中行使中央政府赋予的权力，这也将会为他们在地方社会中带来受人尊敬的崇高的身份和地位。

四、余论

上文通过对清代四川藏区土司印章的梳理和研究，使我们对清代土司的用印情况有了初步的了解与认识。为了更全面和深刻地认识清代四川藏区土司用印的特点与内涵，还有必要对四川藏区土司与西藏地方官员的用印制度进行比较观察。笔者注意到，根据清代官方印制，清朝政府颁授给西藏地方的宗教首领和行政官员的印章，都与四川藏区的土司印章有明显的区别。

首先，掌理四川藏区土司官印颁授的官员与机构不同。从文献来看，负责四川藏区土司印章颁授事宜的官员主要是四川总督，如乾隆三十六年，梭磨土司因随清军征伐大小金川有功后，经四川总督阿桂奏赏梭磨宣慰司职衔和印信[48]；嘉庆九年，瓦寺土司在随清军征缴达州教匪过程中立功以后，是经四川总督勒宝向朝廷奏升其瓦寺宣慰司印信号纸[49]。但掌理西藏僧俗官员印章颁授的官员与机构，则更为复杂。据文献记载，朝廷在封授西藏首领时，一般会涉及到理藩院、礼部和户部等重要机构的参与[50]，有时清廷还要派遣由中央僧俗官员组成的钦差队伍赍送印信到西藏[51]。其次，清朝颁授给四川藏区土司的官印与西藏地方的印章在形制特点等方面也有较大差别。据文献记载，清廷颁授给西藏的印章“喇嘛、呼图克图，或金质，或银印，扎萨克大喇嘛，铜质，并云纽”[52]，印面文字包括满、汉、藏、蒙等语种；而四川藏区则没有藏语和蒙语，其所用满、汉双语合璧的组合形式，与内地省份的官印系统相一致。最后，清政府在四川藏区封授的土司主要以武职为主，文职和宗教首领所占比重较轻，因此，中央政府在管理和统治四川藏区的过程中，其宗教因素比较微弱；相反，清朝中央政府的直接统治权力相对更强。总地来

48 《清史稿 · 列传三百 · 土司二》卷五百十三，1996：14235。

49 《清史稿 · 列传三百 · 土司二》卷五百十三，1996：14234-14235。

50 《西藏研究》编辑部编：《清实录藏族史料》（一），拉萨：西藏人民出版社，1982：25-26。西藏自治区档案馆、中国藏学研究中心等合编：《元以来西藏地方与中央政府关系档案史料汇编》，北京：中国藏学出版社，1994：601-602。

51 西藏自治区档案馆、中国藏学研究中心等合编：《元以来西藏地方与中央政府关系档案史料汇编》，1994：1711、1713、1716、1718。

52 《清史稿 · 志八十九》卷一一四，1996：3282。

说，通过对清代四川藏区土司用印的研究，我们能发现，四川藏区土司所用官印在诸多方面都与西藏的官印系统有非常明显的差异，而是与清朝内地省份的官印系统相一致，表明清王朝在四川藏区的行政建置和制度划分都有别于西藏。

附记：本文在资料收集、撰写以及修改过程中得到四川大学历史文化学院朱德涛博士、四川博物院典藏部主任彭代群老师、张丽华老师等师友的帮助，谨致谢忱。

◆ 刘莎　四川博物院文博馆员

乾隆御用嘎巴拉鼓研究

林欢

内容摘要：本文从两岸故宫现存的几件清宫旧藏嘎巴拉鼓出发，结合乾隆朝造办处档案，对其来源、改制、艺术特征等问题进行了探究。有资料表明，乾隆帝要求造办处对这些嘎巴拉鼓进行了局部加工改制，并命令苏州织造利用玉、象牙等材质进行仿制。现存清宫御用嘎巴拉鼓融合了藏、汉、蒙古等地多元文化因素，反映了乾隆帝的审美趣味。内地对于嘎巴拉法器加工并进行仿制的史实证明：无论内地还是边疆，在大一统格局下，随着手工业技术的传播，边疆与内地之间相关文化理念，也在相互交流中得到融合与升华。

嘎巴拉鼓，又写作“噶布拉鼓”“嘎布拉鼓”等，原本是由人骨制成的无柄鼗鼓、手鼓。藏文称ཌ་མ་རུ（达玛茹），清宫依藏文称“札（扎）嘛噜”，为梵文“ḍamaru”音译。达玛茹最早起源于古印度，多由人骨、象牙、玉以及木料等制作而成。在印度教嘎巴拉派中，天杖、达玛茹和嘎巴拉碗分别瑜伽母的三大器物。这三大器物后来被密宗佛教成就大师所吸纳，代表着神的身、语、意。它属于藏传佛教中的称赞类法器，同时也是修行密乘四部之无上瑜伽部时不可缺少的乐器，经常被用在宗教法会、仪式、诵经活动和宗教舞蹈等场合，平时也陈供于香案之上。嘎巴拉鼓的具体形态通常为以两个头盖骨黏合成的鼓腔，并束以金属腰箍。其作为伴奏用乐器，在法事演奏时常与金刚铃等并用，是人与神之间进行沟通或者建立特殊亲密关系的重要器具。人们以食指套执鼓腰部位上面的活环，用中指、无名指、小指持握活环上面的彩色缎带，迅速转动腕部，使鼓坠左右摆动，来回撞击鼓面而发出声响。用来击鼓的两个鼓坠在敲击鼓面时，会因时间差发出清脆的双击声。其发音方式与内地使用的拨浪鼓相同。鼓声会起到召唤一切佛、菩萨和空行母的作用，用大乐激励他们[1]，同时也可以驱除一些恶魔。对此，学术界早对其来源、使用习俗、符号意义、现实功用等内容进行过一些探讨。故本文拟从工艺制作角度，在前辈学者研究的基础上，结合清宫内务府造办处档案，对于故宫现存一些御用嘎巴拉鼓的加工、来源及艺术历史价值等内容试作进一步阐述。

一、故宫藏嘎巴拉鼓

按照故宫博物院现存御用嘎巴拉鼓的来源，基本可分为藏地进献、造办处改制、苏州织造承造三类。尽管每一类别的缺类断档较多，无法形成系列，但是仍可反映出乾隆御用达玛茹的基本面貌，能够为探讨清宫御用嘎巴拉法器的情况提供一定的参考依据。

1. 镶金串珠嘎巴拉鼓（文物号：故 11373）（图一），长 13、宽 12.5、高 8 厘米，飘带长 70 厘米。手鼓由两个头骨相背黏合而成。鼓腔两端蒙以绿色鼓面，中绘穿海金龙一，周围饰莲纹。接合之处束以金质嵌松石花朵累丝腰箍一个。金圈腰箍饰有缠枝莲纹，上设活环，附有红色鼓锤软球左右各一以及镶红色珊瑚珠、白色砗磲珠等纽带两根。纽带另接白、蓝、绿、红、黄五色镶青边缂丝八宝纹飘带。此鼓另附圆形漆皮盒一个。盒盖内衬有长方形白绫签，从右至左上有墨书汉、蒙古、满、藏四体铭文。其汉文曰："济隆胡土克图世世功课所持大利益嘎布拉鼓。"藏、满及蒙古文意与汉文相同。铭文中的"济隆胡土克图"，当为八世济隆呼图克图益西洛桑丹贝贡布（1760-1811 年）。据清宫造办处档案记载：此鼓修改于乾隆五十五年。当年二月十八日，清宫造办处"油木作"接得"嘎布拉鼓一件（银线带腰箍松石结子、五色片金飘带、珊瑚珠一个、坠角一个、松石珠一个、坠角一个、催生石珠一个、坠角一个、砗磲珠一个，坠角一个、蜜蜡珠二个、坠角二个、鞔皮画金套，系萨穆诸布德臣凌庙密藏供奉，济隆胡图克图辈辈手内常执）"，要求将其与阿嘉胡图克图、德穆胡图克图二件嘎布拉鼓与香山宗镜大昭之庙白台南楼下经桌上一件、白台北楼上经桌上一件、楼下经桌上一件象牙嘎布拉鼓三件（各随镀金镶

1 ［英］罗伯特·比尔著、向红茄译：《藏传佛教象征符号与器物图解》，北京：中国藏学出版社，2007：114。

图一　八世济隆进镶金串珠嘎巴拉鼓

图二　六世班禅进金嵌宝石嘎巴拉鼓

松石腰箍、三角云头、松石结子、五色绦子飘带、珊瑚、松石、蜜蜡、砗磲、催生石珠各二个，五彩鞔皮画金套）上的腰箍、飘带进行“迁换”[2]。

2. 金嵌宝石嘎巴拉鼓（故 11693）（图二）。长 13、宽 12、高 9 厘米，飘带长 65 厘米。双颅骨手鼓，绿色鼓面，满绘金色缠枝莲纹。金质腰箍，其上满嵌松石以及猫眼石两块、大紫宝石一块，小紫宝石两块。金环左右各系有红黄两色小软槌一枚。金箍上另设活环，系有穿孔红色蜜腊、珊瑚佛头珠纽带一根，其下另附五色丝绦飘带。飘带以蓝

2　中国第一历史档案馆主编：《清宫内务府造办处档案总汇（52）》，北京：人民出版社，2005：217-218。

图三　镶金嘎巴拉鼓

底包红绒云头纹“三角”为首，其上缀有米珠305粒，另有蜜腊珠、珊瑚珠等各色宝石坠角，其下饰以十色丝穗。此鼓附圆形漆皮盒一个。盒盖内衬有长方形白绫签，从右至左上有墨书汉、蒙古、满、藏四体铭文。其中汉文曰：“乾隆四十五年八月初二日班禅额尔德呢（尼）恭进嵌宝石嘎布拉鼓一件。”铭文中的“班禅”为六世班禅额尔德尼班丹益西（1738-1780年）。他于乾隆四十五年（1780年）进京庆贺乾隆帝七十寿辰。此前曾在热河逗留。据清宫造办处档案记载：此鼓修改于乾隆四十五年。

3. 镶金嘎巴拉鼓（故11694）（图三）：长14、宽12.5、高8厘米，飘带长75厘米。颅骨鼓身，色泽较白，质地温润。鼓面罩绿色金莲纹，色泽鲜艳。金质腰箍，上饰累丝缠枝莲纹及松石花朵镶嵌。腰箍上附活环，另有黄色鼓锤软球左右各一对，共四只。其上另设活环，系有穿孔紫红色蜜腊佛头珠纽带两根。纽带下缀白、蓝、绿、红、黄镶青边缂丝八宝纹飘带五根。此鼓同样附有圆形漆皮盒一个。盒盖内衬有长方形白绫签，从右至左上有墨书汉、蒙古、满、藏四体铭文。其汉文曰：“大利益嘎布拉扎穆噜鼓。”

4．乾隆款青玉嘎巴拉鼓（故102229）（图四）：口径11-12.3厘米，高7.7厘米。青玉质，取整块材料，模仿人头骨的形状雕制成形。鼓面失粘，可见鼓腔相接处中有一空。鼓面髹绘绿地描金云龙纹。中腰束以镀金嵌松石箍圈及各色飘带，鼓壁另有阴文填金“乾隆年造”四字楷书。手鼓附圆形漆皮盒，盒盖内有白绫签一，上有墨书汉、蒙古、满、藏四体铭文：“乾隆五十九年五月二十日交利益新造青玉嘎布拉鼓一件”。据清宫造办处档案记载：乾隆五十九年五月二十日，苏州进青玉嘎布拉鼓、铃、杵一分（计三件）。皇帝降旨将其中的手鼓“交造办处配腰箍飘带”，具体要求为“配银镀金腰箍五

图四　乾隆款青玉嘎巴拉鼓

图五　青玉嘎巴拉鼓

色香片金飘带”。当年八月初三日及十一月十一日，苏州方面曾两次将样品呈览。乾隆较为满意，遂下令从内库领取松石珠一个“将松石珠在鼓上做结子用”[3]。此鼓最终于乾

3　中国第一历史档案馆主编：《清宫内务府造办处档案总汇（54）》，2005：401。

图六　乾隆款青玉嘎巴拉鼓

隆六十年四月二十一日得以完成并由造办处呈交热河行宫[4]。

5. 青玉嘎巴拉鼓（故 102230）（图五）：通高 8.2，口径 10.4-11.3 厘米。青玉质鼓腔，绿色鼓面。银镀金嵌绿松石镂花腰箍。腰箍活环坠一条明黄色丝绦，中穿红色珊瑚珠。黑色金丝“云头”，下缀红、蓝、黑、绿、黄五色飘带。其中红、黄两色另缀三串各色宝石六粒。

6．乾隆款青玉嘎巴拉鼓（故 102231）（图六）：通高 7.5，口径 10.9-12.3 厘米。青玉质。整材雕刻而成。饰银镀金镂花嵌松石腰箍，手鼓另坠丝质绳柄一个。鼓面绿色素面。腰箍另缀蒙古卫拉特式十色带穗飘带，坠松石佛头、三角结子。

7. 嘎巴拉鼓（故 186709）（图七）：通高 8.8，口径 14.1 厘米。颅骨鼓身，色泽较黄。绿色鼓面。铜镀金腰箍，坠有丝质绳柄一个。绳柄下穿红色珊瑚珠一粒，另附六字真言飘带一。附鞔皮圆盒一。盒盖内有白绫签，题曰：“利益嘎布拉鼓一件”。

4　中国第一历史档案馆主编：《清宫内务府造办处档案总汇（54）》，2005：406。

图七　嘎巴拉鼓

二、清宫御用嘎巴拉鼓的制作步骤

关于清宫嘎巴拉鼓较为详尽的制作过程，可以参见清宫造办处《各作成做活计清档·记事录》乾隆四十一年四月十七日的记载[5]。此段文字是了解乾隆时期嘎巴拉骨器制作活动的重要资料之一。具体而言，这段文字记录了从嘎巴拉骨器（包括嘎巴拉碗、嘎巴拉鼓以及胫骨号等）的选材、造办处精心制作到乾隆皇帝亲自审定并陈列于重要佛堂的过程。

（一）材料的选择

嘎巴拉骨器的制作，首先需要由专人进行初步的制坯、挑选，并对骨料进行整体切

5　中国第一历史档案馆主编：《清宫内务府造办处档案总汇（39）》，2005：410-420。

割。按密宗经典规定，手鼓的制作要求很苛刻：由于制作材料的特殊性，由人头骨制成的达玛茹被视作具有强大镇伏威慑力量的法器。因而必须要用 16 岁男童和 12 岁女童的颅骨各一，或者是由高僧坐化时自愿献出。不过从档案记载来看，清宫还有一些达玛茹的鼓坯是由战俘的头颅制作而成。据说被谋杀（或被处决）之人的颅骨最具法力，是修怒相神时不可多得的中介物[6]。另外，有人认为达玛茹的两个鼓腔是由小孩头盖骨做的，或者是猴头颅骨做成的，例如四川西南地区散居藏民将这种鼓腔称为“敏杂库”，字面意思是猴子碗[7]。之所以如此，是因为小型达玛茹的鼓面直径大约为 8-10 厘米，其大小与小孩或猴头头盖骨大小相似。

（二）制作的过程

1. 鼓坯的制作

造成有人认为达玛茹的两个鼓腔是由少年头盖骨或者是猴头颅骨做成的原因，可能与鼓面的大小有关。据清宫档案记载，造办处工匠曾实际使用大小金川首领七图阿甲、山塌尔萨木坍、七图甲噶尔斯甲布、僧格桑、莎罗奔冈达克、索诺木六个成年人的颅骨制作嘎巴拉鼓。此举与一般传言中所谓选取少年或猴子颅骨的标准有所不同，很有可能是进行了二次切割，并视使用者、制作者的具体要求而定。如做碗，选其宽大且深者，故切割过程到此为止；如需做鼓，工匠们则会进行再次切割。之所以作如上推断，在于目前所见清宫御用达玛茹的鼓面直径皆在 10 厘米左右。无论是真正的人头盖骨达玛茹，或是象牙、玉、珐琅或各类木材制成的仿制鼓，其鼓面形状大多是按照人类颅骨的环切面呈自然莲花瓣状的椭圆形而衍变。这种独特的椭圆形，被称之为头盖骨形[8]。这与同时期造办处工匠所制嘎巴拉碗的碗坯尺寸（即正常人的颅骨宽度）差距不小。由此可知，人们对于头骨原料的加工，主要是进行整体平行切割，仅仅保留其头盖骨正中一小部分以充鼓坯。事实操作是否如此，待考。

2. 鼓坯的连接

空心鼓体象征着法身[9]。在其制作时，工匠们利用两块头盖骨的天然弧面底部的中间位置钻孔（图八），并进行顶对顶的反向固定。固定时，需用木制的环形连接体作为固定物，再以胶或漆加以粘连。李心衡《金川琐记》：“土僧喇嘛，……有小鼓如䥫者，截

6　[英]罗伯特·比尔著、向红笳译：《藏传佛教象征符号与器物图解》，2007：118。

7　古涛、王轩、王德和：《川西南杂散居藏族民间信仰与法器研究》，《西昌学院学报》2014（3）：101-104。

8　格多：《试论藏族传统乐器之膜鸣乐器——鼓》，《西藏艺术研究》2009（4）：23-31。

9　[英]罗伯特·比尔著、向红笳译：《藏传佛教象征符号与器物图解》，2007：116。

图八　象牙质嘎巴拉鼓料坯的穿孔

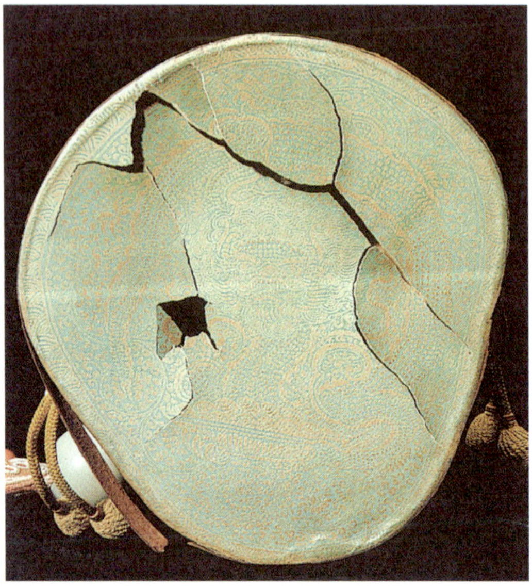

图九　班禅额尔德尼进嘎巴拉鼓（台北故宫藏）

两骷髅，以胶漆粘连自门骨……”[10] 这种组合体从内部形状来看，中间的孔腔极为明显，起到了共鸣腔的作用，利于声波的共振与传导。当然，由于粘连部位的影响，两个鼓面并非平行，故而这种组合呈“V”形字。从象征的角度讲，人们常将其竖放，以示“阴阳”对合，进而印证了“空乐双运”的实践，其音不仅极乐，且能震慑恶魔。

3. 蒙皮与鼓皮的装饰

据清宫造办处“档案”，蒙皮与鼓皮的装饰工序多在造办处的“皮作”中完成。鼓的两面均需蒙皮。对于皮子和木质材料的选择种类较多。通常是动物皮，如羊皮、猴皮等，另外还有蒙人皮的记载。清代官员李心衡在考察金川地区时记载：“……两面蒙人鞟（用背肋皮）。取阅之，色微黄，薄似羊皮，而腥秽特甚，令人森寒植毛发。”鼓皮多被染为墨绿色。在蒙皮之前，颅骨内壁还用红色颜料书写梵文咒语。例如台北故宫藏班禅所进鼓的鼓皮两面“似皆经锐器蓄意击破，破裂处得见头骨内满布血书梵文经咒。”[11] 而在蒙皮活动结束之后，还需要对鼓面进行额外的装饰。图案的选择要根据鼓宗教用途来决定，如绘有莲瓣、双身佛等内容。除此以外，鼓面还绘有穿花龙纹、祥云等。事实的确如此，例如现存宫廷实物的鼓面外侧多用金色绘以莲瓣纹或龙纹（图九），另外还

10 （清）李心衡：《人皮鼓》，《金川琐记》卷三，北京：中华书局丛书集成初编本，1985：24。

11 蔡玫芬：《皇权与佛法——藏传佛教法器特展图录》，台北故宫博物院，1999：142。

图一〇　未装饰前的象牙质嘎巴拉鼓腰身部位

图一一　装饰后的象牙质嘎巴拉鼓腰身部位

有花鸟、法轮和摩尼珠[12]等内容。金、绿对照，色彩鲜明。除此以外，在清宫造办处“档案”中还有画“云香露”内容的记载。其具体样式尚待考证。

4. 腰箍的装饰

(1) 腰箍的基本情况

一件制作精美的嘎巴拉鼓，须在两个鼓坯的粘合部位进行掩饰和遮盖（图一〇）。从实用角度而言，腰箍源于人们日常所用的腰带。在封建时代，腰带既作服饰，又是显示人们权利高下、地位尊卑的象征。清宫御用手鼓的鼓腰部位通常更为讲究，常常束以累丝镂花金质或镀金银片的金属腰箍，嵌有松石、珊瑚、玛瑙等大颗的珠宝装饰。另外在腰箍上有固定位置的环座。这些固定环座用于拴系鼓槌软绳及活环。鼓槌环则有两个，左右对称，与手柄活环呈三足鼎立，不仅便于使用，而且具有强烈的稳定感和对称美（图一一）。

据清宫档案记载，乾隆帝曾不断下令对其进行改制，以求满足自己所中意的装饰效果。造办处曾有多次对原有“例样”鼓进行改造的例子。例如早在利用金川首领头颅制作嘎巴拉鼓之前，乾隆帝便四处寻访合适的“例样”以备工匠参考。四十一年夏六月，身在热河行宫的乾隆皇帝曾传旨将热河（布达拉庙）供奉嘎布拉鼓一件(随五色片金飘带、密蜡结子、珊瑚并松石等珠六个)带进京内，要求新收三件嘎巴拉鼓坯（六人）俱照此样仿做。除此之外，他还要求新做之鼓的腰箍、宝盖、飘带皆仿照热河殊像寺嘎巴

12　蔡玫芬：《皇权与佛法——藏传佛教法器特展图录》，1999：141。

图一二　镀金银手镯

图一三　宝石包镶

拉鼓上镶松石腰箍、宝盖、飘带一样进行制作。某些关键部分的配饰零件会被工匠们拆下，以另外一种组合形式重新配置在新做的嘎巴拉鼓上。如若拆下的配饰在材料和数量上不足，则会随时填补[13]。

（2）腰箍的等级分类

清宫御用嘎巴拉鼓按照鼓腰配饰的不同可以大致分为三个等级。而这也是区分嘎巴拉鼓等级的关键。头等鼓：鼓坯由重要“钦犯”的头骨制成，如金川首领山塌尔萨木坍、僧格桑等。此类手鼓的鼓腰处配金镶松石腰箍，另用鞔皮画金套盛装。此鼓在举办佛事活动时，需与达赖喇嘛进贡的铜铃杵进行配合使用。二等鼓：其材质是人骨，可能也会用到象牙材质。其配饰与头等鼓基本类似，同样配金镶松石腰箍，用鞔皮画金套盛装。在举办佛事活动时，此鼓与班禅额尔德尼进贡的铜铃杵进行配合使用。三等鼓：仅配得银镀金腰箍一件。其装饰与象牙胎、玉胎等材质的嘎巴拉鼓并无特殊之处。

（3）腰箍的装饰

从制作工艺角度而言，腰箍属于由一定宽度的金皮制成的金箍环（多为累丝镀金嵌宝石圈）。其制作与清宫手镯、戒指等御用金属首饰的加工制作有类似之处：即腰箍是一个由环形金片合围而成的圆箍（图一二）。其宽度依照两个鼓腔之间的实际距离而定，正好覆盖两个鼓腔的结合部，首尾结合处由嵌松石宝石托座连接固定。工匠按照皇帝的设计要求，在包好的金皮上进行各种图案的加工。在制作上主要使用花丝工艺，进行掐、

13　中国第一历史档案馆主编：《清宫内务府造办处档案总汇（39）》，2005：415。

图一四　红色鼓坠

堆、填、垒、攒、焊等一整套技法，以构成各种不同纹样的装饰图案。

在腰箍部分的装饰上，内廷工匠除了针对贵金属使用的花丝工艺外，还使用了镶嵌工艺。可以说，大量使用宝石镶嵌是清宫御用嘎巴拉鼓的一大装饰特点。此举可将人们的目光吸引到宝石上，起到画龙点睛的作用。清宫御用首饰的包镶工艺的制作技法在很大程度上借鉴了蒙古族和藏族的传统首饰工艺品中的包镶、光圈镶、齿钉镶、组合镶以及插镶等制作方法。这些方法使用的目的便是将各种宝石固定在托架上，使之不易损坏和脱落。其技术要求十分精细。例如鼓 1 和鼓 2 皆使用了包镶技法（图一三）。这也是是清宫首饰镶嵌工艺制作中经常用到的手段。

（4）鼓槌

腰箍上的鼓槌环左右有一至两个，各系丝绳，绳尖系有用红色织物包裹的球状骨质鼓槌（图一四）。鼓槌环左右对称，与手柄活环呈三角形对峙，不仅便于使用，而且具有强烈的稳定感和对称美。两个鼓槌象征着相与空的结合[14]。据说使用尸陀林里的人发织成的细绳，系以用水鸟之腿骨关节制成的鼓槌，效果最好。目前所能看到的几乎是左

14 ［英］罗伯特·比尔著、向红茄译：《藏传佛教象征符号与器物图解》，2007：116。

图一五　手柄活环

图一六　手柄活环上的黄色绳柄与珊瑚“结子”

右各只系一只鼓槌，当然也有各系两支鼓槌的例子。如民族文化宫收藏的六世班禅贡品“班禅额尔德尼恭敬大利益象牙成造嘎巴拉鼓”就是左右各系两只鼓槌的达玛茹，台北故宫藏达赖喇嘛所进之鼓也是鼓槌左右各一对，共四只。当然，二只鼓槌与四只鼓槌在宗教功用上是否有差别，还有待于继续进一步的研究。

(5) 活环

除鼓槌环外，清宫御用嘎巴拉鼓的腰箍上还设有代替鼓柄作用的活环（图一五）。这类活环多装饰为“算盘珠”式样，质地为金或银镀金。另外它们还系有用缠有五色黄色织锦或皮革系结的绳柄，便于执掌人对于鼓的把握与操作。其中自活环引出的上部为飘带的牵引绳索，例如鼓 1 为明黄色丝绳，素面无装饰，起牵引过渡作用（图一六）。绳柄延长处通常再饰有一穿孔宝珠，材质为松石、珊瑚等，档案上称为“结子”。“结子”下继续拴系长短不一的彩色缎带与丝穗等，档案上称其为“飘带”。

5. 飘带的安装

狭义的飘带仅为帐幔而已。不过从广义而言，飘带装饰的范畴可以从腰箍的活环开始算起，即由绦绳（过渡绳）、佛头（宝珠）、云头或镀金“三角结子”、加上帐幔、各类宝石以及流苏丝穗共同组成。其结构从由上到下大致可以分为五部分。配饰内容越多，其等级越发高贵。值得一提的是，“云头”多为五色织锦制作，其上利用缝珠、绣珠等多种表现形式缀有组成如意形的米珠数十粒。在某些飘带上，有三角结子替代了“云头”的作用。人们在对这些“结子”进行加工的过程中，往往涉及錾刻、锤鍱、焊接等技法。例如鼓 6 上的嵌宝石三角结子为模印而成，并有局部錾刻、锤鍱等痕迹（图一七）。

图一七　嵌宝石的三角结子

图一八　故宫藏飘带缺失的嘎巴拉鼓

图一九　飘带缺失的嘎巴拉鼓（北京民族文化宫藏）

结子下面则坠有十个飘带活环，系有色彩艳丽的飘带。其正反面皆有边框，边框内为线条较为简单的连续缠枝莲纹及S形云纹。图案细腻，轻巧生动。

帐幔则为飘带的主体一般为五条，分为五色。最常见的帐幔多为五方形，由丝绸制成，其边由为五段长短不一的蓝色镶边，中间有刺绣图案。这些图案以不同花草装饰的“八宝”图案为主，另有海水江崖等装饰。由于长度较长，保存不易。如故宫有一件手鼓（图一八）有鼓坠二条及黄色绳柄，虽然下坠红珊瑚穿绳珠“结子”一枚，但是其下的飘带部分已有缺失。类似情况在北京民族文化宫所藏嘎巴拉鼓中亦可见到（图一九）。据“档案”，飘带的制作与装饰工序在造办处“裁作”、“玉作”及苏州织造等处完成。

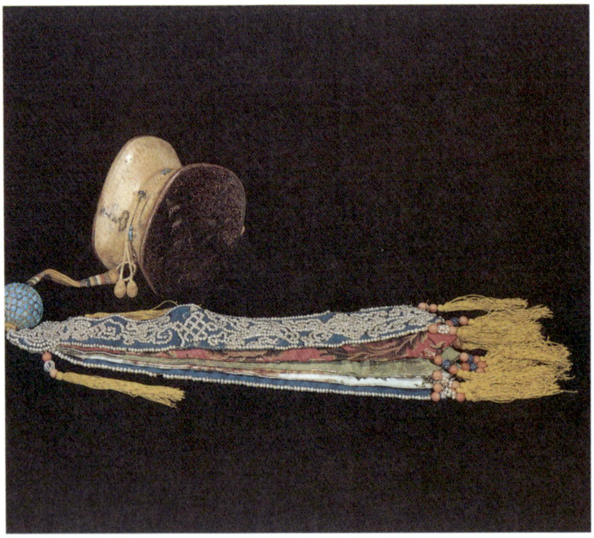

图二〇：1 布达拉庙藏第二、三、五世达赖喇嘛手持嘎巴拉鼓飘带装饰（台北故宫藏）

图二〇：2 用于包装御用嘎巴拉鼓的鞔皮匣

6. 其它

嘎巴拉鼓的制作还有将飘带末端的丝穗进行加工的工序。这个步骤被称为“拈绳”，要求将这些丝穗顶端加工为环状螺旋形，以至于其不易散开，其间不得有断茬出现。有各色流苏或穗子是清宫御用嘎巴拉鼓的另一个鲜明特征（图二〇）。某些流苏占飘带长度 1/3，使飘带整体更显别致光鲜。嘎巴拉鼓制成后，会配合铃杵盛装于以鞔皮画金制成的盒中，皮盒内部题写白绫签。在呈送给皇帝亲自验看并核准之后，会被安放于养心殿、中正殿及热河等处相应佛堂。

三、御用嘎巴拉鼓的特点

（一）鲜明的佛教主题特征

在御用嘎巴拉鼓装饰艺术中，与佛教内容相关的图案纹样扮演着非常重要的角色。它们多以单独形式呈现，或以组合方式出现在法器用具上。这些纹样组合的不同，不仅丰富了清宫手工艺的装饰形式，而且极大地丰富了藏传佛教的文化蕴涵。

莲花的造型与图案在佛教文化中被经常用到。例如鼓 3 是鼓面图案以莲花为主体，极具佛教文化特质（图二一）。具体而言，在其图案中，莲叶表现为单体且非重复图案，

图二一　鼓面上的莲花图案

图二二 腰箍上的莲花图案

图二三　嘎巴拉鼓飘带上的六字真言纹

图二四　嘎巴拉鼓飘带上的八宝纹

整体效果庄重大方，宗教象征色彩直白。类似的还有鼓 1、鼓 2 和鼓 4。虽然它们的鼓面各有不同，但是各自腰箍上饰有的莲花纹样花瓣与花蕊底部皆錾刻为圆珠粒状并作有秩序的排列，再加上大小各不相同的绿松石的合理使用，使得莲花图案在整体上呈现逐层次退晕的效果，更显得富丽华贵（图二二）。

除了本体外，御用嘎巴拉鼓的飘带上还饰有八宝纹、六字真言以及盘肠纹等，如故宫藏一件嘎巴拉鼓的飘带上装饰有金地蓝字“真言”六字（图二三）。同样体现了佛教艺术的丰富多彩。八宝纹又称“八瑞相”，“八吉祥”等，包括金鱼、法轮、宝瓶、宝伞、莲花、盘肠结（吉祥结）、华盖（胜利幢）、白海螺八种法器。这八个图案是最具代表性的标志性图案。即可单独成形，也可组合在一起。如鼓 1 和鼓 3 中，八宝纹在白、蓝、

图二五 嘎巴拉鼓飘带上的盘肠装饰（北京民族文化宫藏）

绿、红、黄五色丝绸飘带上重复展示，色彩搭配大胆、强烈。由于丝绸本身所富有的闪亮光泽，进而形成炫目的装饰效果。不仅如此，工匠在丝织品上加强了对飘带的主体纹样的刻画（图二四）。其所绣八宝纹具有极强的浮雕感，进而使得丝织物的华美和柔顺舒适与八宝的立体感相得益彰。这种纹样的装饰特点决定了它并非单纯的装饰图案，而是起到了不断强调与渲染佛教文化的作用。

盘肠纹也是佛教经常运用的吉祥纹样，又称为吉祥结。从结构上来看，它具有直线样式和曲线相结合的样式。其纹样在佛教中寓意佛法无边，威力无穷，是幸福绵长的象征。例如在鼓 2 以及北京民族文化宫藏品中的吉祥结（图二五）起到了连接绦带与丝穗的关键作用。造型流畅且醒目。其纹样本身重叠盘曲，头尾相连。虽然看起来繁琐、缠绕，但是结构自然有序，既严谨又有节奏感，进而起到连绵不断的信仰理念。不仅如此，这种结构与类似卷草的流苏丝穗相结合，互相交叉，紧密连接，显得活力十足。

总而言之，人们在法器装饰中，通过一系列程式、凝练的图形符号，展现了大量佛教信息和元素。此举不仅构建并传递了特定的文化讯息，激发人的宗教情愫，而且体现出信仰者的宗教情感以及虔诚心理，以此获得文化上的强烈认同感以及内心深处的情感共鸣。这种影响渗透到了皇帝的审美趣味之中，充分说明当时清宫对于佛教信仰的广泛认同。

图二六　布达拉庙第二、三、五世达赖喇嘛手持嘎巴拉鼓（台北故宫藏）

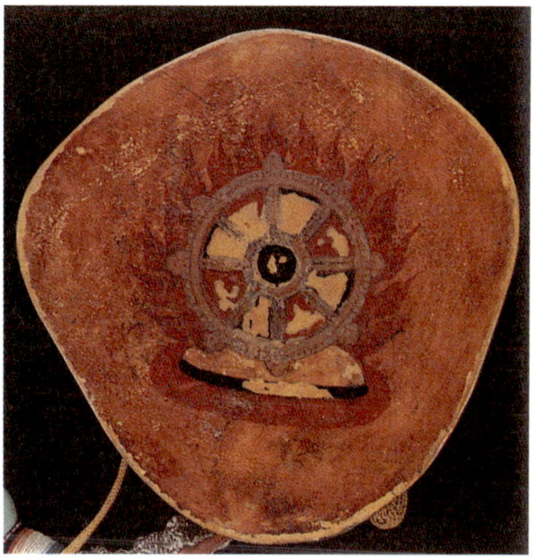

图二七　永宁寺章嘉呼图克图进嘎巴拉鼓（台北故宫藏）

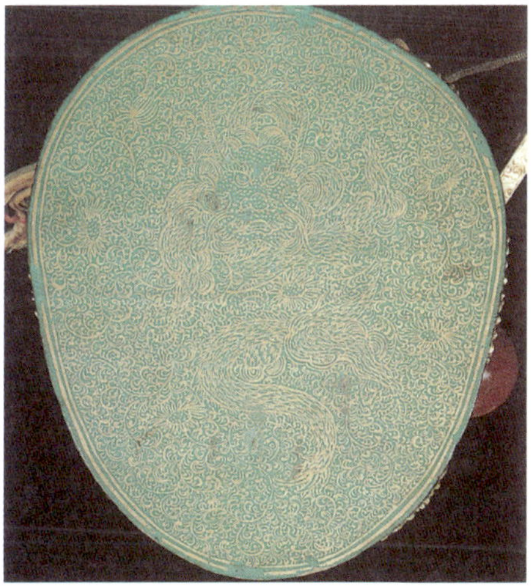

图二八　章嘉呼图克图进嘎巴拉鼓（台北故宫藏）

图二九　乾隆五十八年交青玉手鼓（台北故宫藏）

（二）装饰图案主次分明

清宫御用嘎巴拉鼓在装饰图案的构成上有着主次分明、构图饱满、纹饰繁复、连续规范的特点。

总体而言，其鼓面在构图装饰上基本上可以分为两种组织形式。一是中心突出式。即各种形象以一个中心为支撑点，突出表达了佛教文化的寓意。例如鼓 1 中的蟠龙作为

图三〇　镶金串珠嘎巴拉鼓

图三一　乾隆款黄地青花云龙纹福寿字碗

图三二　金鱼纹夹缬绸袱

图三三　石青色纳纱四团缠枝莲蝠金龙纹单衮服

图三四　乾隆款青花红龙纹双耳背壶

图案主体位于正中，周围辅以火云纹。类似的龙纹主题还可见于台北故宫所藏达赖喇嘛、班禅喇嘛、章嘉呼图克图等高僧所进嘎巴拉鼓之上。如达赖喇嘛所进鼓的鼓面绘有飞龙（图二六）。又有永宁寺章嘉所进鼓的皮面有红黑漆彩绘：一面绘法轮，一面绘摩尼珠（图二七）。班禅与章嘉所进鼓的鼓面则绘有绿地金彩穿花龙纹（图二八）。此类组织形式往往涉及到对圆形画面的充分运用。这是因为在圆形的鼓面上易于找到图案的中心点，并围绕于此绘制繁密、饱满、完整的装饰图案，具有固定化的程序规则。例如台北故宫藏青玉嘎巴拉鼓（图二九），虽然其形仿照上文提到颅骨形，但在实质上仍为圆形，更加利于主题纹样的表现。

这些图案既可以单独使用，又能与许多图案组合应用。比如鼓 1 中的游龙周边祥云

图三五　金嵌宝石嘎巴拉鼓

图三六　乾隆款剔红花卉纹圆盘

图三七　乾隆款七香图御墨

缭绕（图三〇），鼓 3 中的莲花旁边枝叶蔓延。此类装饰的外围被设计为装饰带，形成弧状的连续纹样。从而形成一种主次分明，错落有致的底纹效果。类似的装饰在清宫文物中屡见不鲜（图三一至图三四）。所有这类陪衬纹样与主题纹样相比，不仅独立性较强，充满对称感和节奏感，在形式上不与主题重复，而且其作为独立的形式出现在所装饰的器具上，有效协调了中心图案与周围纹样之间的关系，进而在整体形成闪耀、悦目的视觉效果。

第二种组织形式是满地铺式。鼓面图案空间内部各类物象能按其各自性状被有效地经过穿插、叠合、并列、挪移、复制等手段，将彼此之间的空白尽量填充，进而表现出丰富多彩的意境。形成类似鼓 2 表面的花中套花、叶中套花的效果（图三五）。这些各种草纹以卷曲、盘旋、缠绕的集合形式作 S 状或涡卷状，极尽蔓延之势，给人以委婉多姿的感受。类似的装饰在其它清宫制品中也较为常见（图三六至图三七）。

（三）精湛的宝石镶嵌工艺

御用嘎巴拉鼓中广泛运用了金、银、玉、珊瑚、蜜蜡、玛瑙等各种不同质地、不同色彩的原材料来进行装饰。这些不同的材质在色彩上十分鲜明，与西部边疆民族偏爱使用贵金属和宝石进行装饰的习惯有关。

宝石镶嵌工艺是与金丝加工工艺密切结合在一起的。它们作用在腰箍中，便是有大量以宝相花为装饰主题的内容出现。除此以外，其花卉的枝叶纹样多遵循对称平衡原则，特别是以浮雕式凸花形构成两道卷草云头纹，遍布腰箍一周（图三八）。这种技法将器形与纹饰完美结合，不仅象征着吉祥如意，而且给人以婉转多姿的韵律动感。这种金丝满饰技法在较小的空间里排列均匀、密布，分布均匀，线条流畅。与光亮平滑底面形成

图三八　腰箍光滑底面上的掐丝工艺

图三九　金镶四龙戏珠镯

图四〇　腰箍边缘部位的串珠状装饰

图四一　金镶翠戒指

强烈的对比，既起到了烘托主题的作用，又使得腰箍的装饰效果更具立体感（图三九）。另外，构成卷草纹样的金丝造型，与腰箍左右边缘，皆为细小的金珠颗粒状（图四〇）。这些金珠分为圆形与菱形两种，在档案中常被曾为“算盘珠”。广泛应用于首饰的边缘。此类装饰手法在清宫首饰中也多有出现（图四一）。

珠宝在嘎巴拉鼓腰箍上的镶嵌工艺主要使用了光圈镶和柱镶两种方式。其中光圈镶即是工匠们在腰箍上等距安置若干个花式宝石托座，托座内镶嵌各式大颗宝石，如红、蓝宝石、琥珀或绿松石等。这些宝石除特殊要求外，不加雕琢，基本保持了原有外形，因而宝石托座随其形状而定。又如鼓 2 的腰箍还涉及连珠镶嵌，即以松石作为主要纹饰的例子。其间各种形状、大小不等的蓝色松石互相穿插组合，再配合以各种几何或花瓣

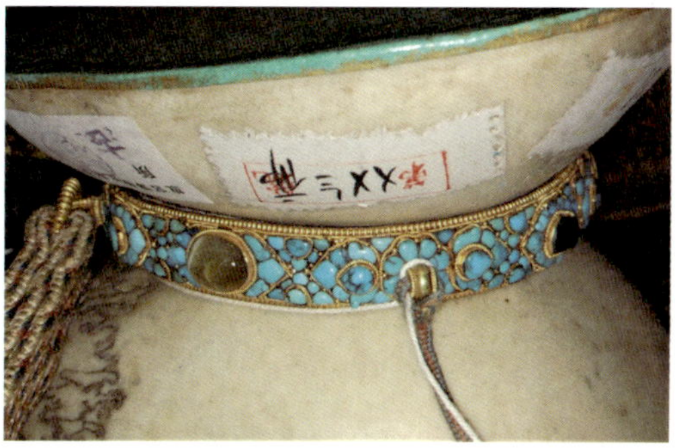

图四二　宝石镶嵌中连珠镶与光圈镶的结合

图四三　银嵌珊瑚石戒指

图四四　柱镶的松石活环底座

图四五　镶嵌有松石、青金石、珊瑚的三角结子

形的托座（图四二），使得腰箍整体的装饰纹样显得简洁而又不失华丽。宝石的外围有一下陷的金属环边，边部由金属包裹嵌紧。光圈镶在宝石周围的光环也具有一定的装饰性，从视觉上起到了增大宝石体积的效果（图四三）。又如在鼓 3 腰箍上的活环底座上，使用了柱镶工艺：柱镶大多选用小颗的松石片，松石片围绕着一个中心点镶嵌，然后把每一颗松石用纤细的金属条分隔开，既华丽又严谨。再配上金黄色的环座，色彩更显协调醒目（图四四）。再如上文提到鼓 6 的三角结子，缠枝纹中均匀分布着红色珊瑚、绿色松石以及蓝色青金石镶嵌（图四五）。总之，就整体效果而言，这些金、银、珠宝、玉石等的色泽交相辉映，给人大气稳重的美感，彰显出清代皇家御用器物独特的艺术表现魅力。

另外，还有一些手鼓的装饰将宝石与刺绣技艺完美结合。例如红珊瑚、玛瑙等宝石用作飘带装饰时，需要进行切割、抛光、打孔等加工。除用金色扁平丝绳进行简单的单行串接固定（图四六）外，还有利用五彩绳将一股变多股等编织方法。丝绳不仅对珠宝无任何遮挡，反而衬托出了珠宝的光莹质朴特征和天然材质美。同时，被贯于飘带两侧

图四六　穿有黄色丝绦的玉珠

图四七　飘带末端的宝石装饰

及末端的珠串，呈对称状分布，起到了对平面化的飘带进行色彩分割，增强立体感和秩序感的作用（图四七）。

（四）色彩丰富艳丽

清宫御用嘎巴拉鼓的色彩较为鲜明，装饰性浓厚。无论是在鼓面、腰箍还是飘带等方面，多有不同明度的色彩进行密集交替、并列和重复，因此在整体上呈现出错落有致的视觉效果。例如在鼓面上，黄色图纹与绿色鼓面之间鲜明色彩的对比运用，体现了其独特的审美趣味。又如腰箍上的金属花卉装饰突出醒目，且配以松石，层次极为分明。金色本身所具有的闪光效果与蓝色松石花朵形成强烈的搭配，具有极强的生命律动感。如果说鼓面原有的绿色与腰箍上的金质缠枝莲纹皆算作陪衬的话，那么鼓面上的金色图案与腰箍上所镶嵌的松石亦可作为高位。低位烘托高位，高位反衬低位，主题明确而又和谐统一。

相对而言，飘带的主题装饰部位的色彩相较于其它等处更要鲜艳的多，无论是色彩的明度、纯度还是绣线的粗细皆有不同程度上的差异。例如在鼓 1、鼓 3、鼓 4 和鼓 5 等飘带的色系中，金（黄）、白、蓝、红、绿等得到最为普遍的应用。这五种色彩的表现是佛教美学思想和抽象色彩观念的表达。从实物观察，飘带面料对比色的使用极为广泛。手工艺人通过或冷或暖色调作底，衬以相对或相反的图案，使得主题纹样在背景单色的衬托下更加熠熠生光，体现出极强的“闪色”装饰效果（图四八）。这种强化主题装饰，弱化附属装饰的手法起到了观赏性与实用性并举的效果，同时形成密中有疏，艳中有净的风格。另外，绣品的主题图案经过了彩色绣线的反复绣缀，不仅具有极高的装

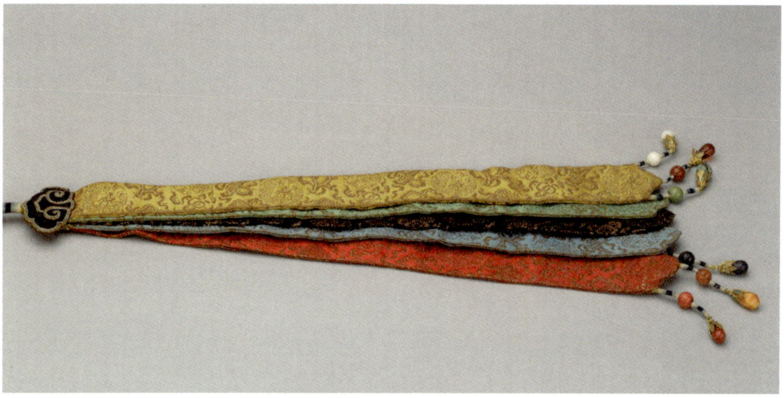

图四八　八宝云纹五色飘带

饰价值，而且还能增加衣物的耐磨度。

另外在清宫档案中，皇帝将某些嘎巴拉鼓上的飘带称之为“厄勒忒绦子”，具有鲜明的民族特征。“厄勒忒”即“厄鲁特”“卫拉特”等，故而“厄勒忒绦子”属于新疆卫拉特蒙古族服饰中的一部分。清人祁韵士《西陲要略》中对西蒙古服饰作了如下描述：

“冠无冬夏之别，但以毛质厚薄为差，白毡为里，外饰以皮，贵者饰以毡或染紫绿色，其顶高，其檐平，谓之哈尔帮，略如内地暖帽，而缀缨止及其帽之半。妇女冠与男子同，带以丝为之，端垂流苏，其长委地。妇人辫发双垂，约发用红帛，在辫之腰帛间，缀以好珠瑟瑟之属，望若繁星。……妇人衣用棉绣，两肩两袖及交襟续衽处，镶以金花，其民妇则以染色皮镶之。……”[15]

由此可见，卫拉特蒙古族服饰纹样丰富多彩。其来源不仅与游牧生活习性密切相关，而且借鉴和吸纳了周边民族各地区不同的服饰文化因素，凸显了同一民族在不同地区审美文化的地域差异性。具体而言，其装饰多在关键之处铆有金属装饰或镀金饰件，并嵌有宝石。尤其是卫拉特蒙古女服，特别注重对称、均衡、调和、节奏等形式美原则。与此同时，卫拉特服饰用色华丽讲究，进而在整体上形成华丽闪耀、富贵的视觉效果。特别是在镶边装饰工艺上，如帽子、服饰、发套（盖）以及如烟袋等配饰的下垂位置上，

15 （清）祁韵士：《厄鲁特旧俗纪闻》，《西陲要略》卷四，北京：中华书局，1985：63。

图四九　色彩丰富的“厄勒忒绦子”

盛行流苏挂饰，只需少量点缀，便会增色不少。

在“厄勒忒绦子”上主体部分的装饰过程中，其色彩选用了各种颜色交替重复并相互对比的形式，例如明黄色过渡绳前后两段皆用两到五种颜色的彩线交叉缠绕而成，呈现出彩虹般绚丽夺目的自然视觉。不仅如此，飘带装饰由彩色织绦组合而成。其刺绣纹样结构紧凑，针脚密实，色彩鲜艳又不失厚重。如鼓 2 主要的装饰部分为彩色波浪纹编织图案，其主体色彩选用了红、绿对比色的形式，其中穿插以黑色，增强了相互之间的对比度，从竖向视觉呈人字纹的色彩排列来说，分别是黑、玫红、桃红、粉红、深绿、浅绿、翠绿，两种对比色明度依次降低，由于不同明度色彩的密集交替、并列、重复给人以穿插错落的视错觉。再以鼓 2 的吉祥结为例，形成两组冷、暖渐变色，其一宝蓝、浅蓝、银白、浅褐，其二为紫、玫红、粉红、浅褐，其三为草绿、浅绿、浅黄、明黄。三组渐变色交替排列，具有强烈的规律性几何视觉彩虹图案（图四九）。它们依次按照每个色系的明度由浅入深地排列，形成极大的对比和色彩反差，呈现出更为紧凑和强烈的节奏美、规律性和趣味性。这种彩色波浪纹具有强烈的秩序感和视觉冲击，充分展现了卫拉特蒙古人丰富而浪漫的想象力和创造力。另外，在飘带末端的装饰上，多坠以各色宝石串珠并配以五彩丝穗。丝穗随需要而灵活变换，可长可短，呈波浪状，飘逸摇曳，给人以优雅神秘、雅致精美之感。

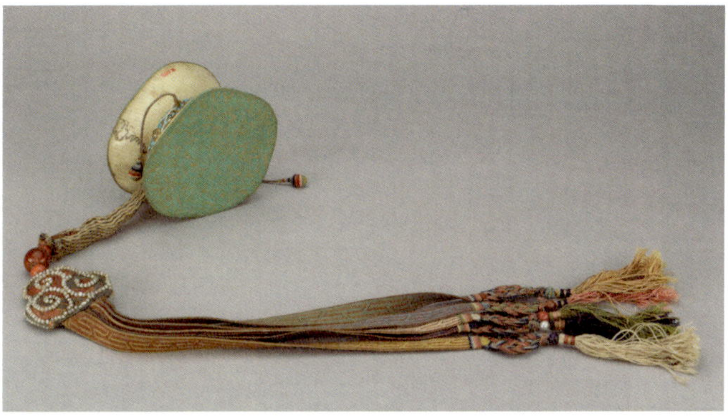

图五〇　金嵌宝石嘎巴拉鼓

图五一　章嘉进嘎巴拉鼓（台北故宫藏）

（五）注重线条对比和协调

就“厄勒忒绦子”的种类而言，可以分为两种形式。除了前面提到的色彩丰富且具有规律性带状图案的第一种花绦形式外（图五〇），还有第二种形式，如鼓 6 和台北故宫所藏章嘉进鼓（图五一）。它的样式是在三角结子之下饰有十条五色直线式绦绳。此类飘带同样为典型的直线式水平条纹图案。其宽度与第一种形式相比较为细窄，属于结子装饰的附属物品。

在飘带的制作中，造办处工匠善于利用几何纹样进行排列。例如在以直线为基本的设计形态中，他们讲点、线、面的元素加以灵活协调，尤其是与圆润的珠宝佩饰进行组合，增强了艺术美感。这样的纹路往往讲单线与双线、粗线和细线、直线与曲线互相配合，同时结合螺旋、波浪等纹路，形成了极具特色的图案色彩表达。例如鼓 2 在有限的利用空间框架内，利用宽度相同的两条或三条不同色彩的毛线混合搓捻而成。其上的工字纹是以空心线条组成二方连续折叠扭转的工字形图案，这种几何纹样是由古代青铜器和陶器上的雷纹变化而来的。这种装饰虽然极其简单，但是整体图案简洁质朴，疏密得当，轮廓清晰且丰富多变，在视觉层次上具有强烈的秩序美感。

图五二　织锦云纹荷包式火㡳

图五三　黄色缎绣花卉荷包式火㡳

为解决花绦直线形式较为单一的问题，工匠在单体花绦上又增添了诸如吉祥结等图式符号。工匠们利用其夸张变形的曲折迂回，交错盘旋，以增强装饰效果。起到类似作用的还有云纹等。其特点是以半圆弧的形式重复连续，在形式上极具美感。仅以“云头”布艺为例，从结构上来说，其造型与清宫火镰包（图五二至图五三）、烟荷包或针线包类似。其上部为灵芝云头状，接以黄色绦绳为吊绳，下部则引出五片飘带。云头主体由内芯与外罩两部分构成。外罩整体线条流畅，圆润丰满，造型较为优美。内芯由各类絮状物填充，针脚平齐。如鼓 1 云朵外部轮廓整体饱满充实，两边角点突出，各缀一珠串，长度基本与云头同宽。珠串上各有三珠，上下有花结固定。云头正面主体以黑色为底，边缘弧线圆滑流畅，饰以网状丝线纹。鼓 2 外部轮廓整体则呈现“品”字三朵云纹。下接五条花绦。三朵云瓣边缘弧线圆滑流畅，正反两面皆以浅蓝色作底，表面附以红绒。上缀由数十颗米珠串联而成的卷云纹，颜色醒目，完全与云头形状相适合。给人以高雅大方的视觉感受。又如鼓 3 外部轮廓整体呈云鼻纹造型。上接黄色绦绳，下接五片五色八宝纹丝绦。云头整体轮廓边缘则以白色曲线纹进行缘边刺绣。此云头整体以蓝色作底，由外向内颜色逐渐变蓝变深。两个云鼻处又以红、粉、白色三色再次锁边。飘带位于云鼻结构的正中位置，酷似灵芝造型。

四、结论

法器指各种佛事活动中使用的器物，由于其功用、形制、材质各不相同。可以分为礼敬、称赞、供养、持验、护身、劝导六大类。虽然其来源各异，但都具有深刻的宗教含义。例如嘎巴拉鼓同样象征了大悲与空性。它是人与神之间进行沟通或者建立特殊亲密关系的重要器具。

综合纹饰与装饰手法来看，乾隆御用嘎巴拉鼓体现了多元文化杂揉的特质。除了蒙、藏民族在地理环境、生活习俗、宗教信仰等诸多领域存在着大量的共同点之外，满、汉民族推崇的“重意尚韵”精神作为指导观念之一，也起到了至关重大的作用。无论是内地还是边疆，藏传佛教的传播，对传统工艺品的形制、装饰纹样、工艺技法乃至民众的精神文化等方面影响深远，各民族又各自以自己特有的方式对传统工艺进行改变和革新，同时发生了某种程度的变形，进而出现了多种结构变体。清宫御用嘎巴拉鼓的制作工艺成熟，造型精巧，纹样丰富，极具有装饰性和浓厚的民族特色。其造型、图形、纹样皆源自日常生活。无论是从嘎巴拉鼓的造型乃至图案的纹样，皆集中展现和强化了对称和平衡这种倾向。例如在整体造型上，从鼓面到绳柄，穿珠到“云头”（或“结子”），从飘带到缀珠、丝穗，无论是纹样造型，还是构图都多为对称式，给人以结构紧凑、庄重美观的感觉，具有稳定对称、简洁柔韧、延续回环的特点。这种富有韵律美的设计，既符合于自然规律，又与人们的心理和视觉机制相适应。同时为了体现自然美，常精心保留木、骨等这些物品本来的颜色，更不随意改变这些本色的性质和淳朴的质地。手工艺人在掐丝和刺绣工艺过程中，常常采用色彩明艳的金属丝或绣线，在纹样上多选择几何抽象化的连续纹样以表现喜庆、圆满、平安等吉祥意义。很好地处理了单独与组合、局部与整体、对比与统一之间的关系，使得图案与颜色有机统一、相得益彰，兼顾了装饰与实用。其线条清晰流畅，整体上呈现出一种强烈的秩序感，进而形成和谐统一的审美特点以及鲜明亮丽的装饰效果，给人以光鲜明亮的视觉感受。不仅如此，时人还将具有宗教意义的元素通过符号化的包装进行表达，以其特有的隐晦、含蓄的手法寓教于美，进而去感化人们的灵魂。不仅如此，创新后的主题图案仍能够完美地体现宗教观念，直接烘托出佛法的高深恢弘。同时也反映了物品持有者对待信仰时的虔诚与执着、痴迷与自律。这是宗教类物品进行造型艺术创作的鲜明特点。

有资料表明，乾隆帝要求造办处对这些嘎巴拉鼓进行了局部加工改制，并命令苏州织造利用玉材进行仿制。现存乾隆御用嘎巴拉鼓融合了藏、汉、蒙古等地多元文化因素，反映了乾隆帝的审美趣味。具体而言，这些手鼓在附件装饰上多运用各种名贵、珍稀材料，在视觉效果上力求突出御用法器的奢华、张扬与独一无二。同时，法器本体及其相应的包装囊匣却并未进行过度修饰，体现了法器本身庄重典雅、高尚质朴的自然内敛之美。这种貌似矛盾的对立，反映了乾隆帝试图将文人的“归隐”修行与皇家威仪的彰显有机统一起来。

内地对于嘎巴拉法器加工并进行仿制的史实证明：在乾隆时代，无论内地与边疆，在“大一统”格局下的清宫法器工艺品具有符号化、程式化的特点，带有普遍通俗的社会认同性。不仅代表了皇室贵族对佛法的领悟，而且还包含了祈福的寓意。蒙藏地区宗教上层和世俗贵族频繁来朝将法器进献给皇帝的行为，更增进了彼此之间的宗教和个人感情。不仅如此，随着手工业技术的传播，其各自成熟的地方手工业绝技也被移植到宫廷，并且被快速掌握和吸收，进而反超原创，达到相当高的水准。边疆与内地之间相关的文化理念，也在相互交流中得到融合与升华。

五、附录（嘎巴拉鼓白绫签题记）

序号	藏文	满文	蒙古文	汉文
鼓 1（图一：2）	rje drung hu thog thu'i skyes rabs su thugs dam du bzung pa'i thod pa'i ḍa ma ru byin chen//	jirung kūtuktu i jalan jalan i tukdam de jafaha amba adistid bisire gebala j'amaru:	ǰirung qutuɣtu-yin töröl üyen-ün(üy-e-yin) tuɣtam-dur bariɣsan yeke adistid-tu kabala damaru	济隆胡土克图世世功课所持大利益嘎布拉鼓
鼓 2（图二：2）	gnam skyong lo zhe lnga pa'i zla ba brgyad pa'i tshes gnyis la paṇ chen el te nis 'gus pas phul ba'i rin po che'i phra rgyan kā pā la'i ḍa ma ru gcig/	abkai wehiyehe i dehi sunjaci aniya jakūn biyai ice juwe de bacan erdeni i ginggulemc jafaha erimbu wehe i kiyamnaha g'abala j'amaro emke:	tngri-yin tedkügsen-ü döčin tabuduɣar on aɣur-un dumdadu sar-a-yin sin-e qoyar-a bančan erdeni-yin kičiyenggüyilen bariɣsan erdeni čilaɣad-iyar sigidkegetu kabala damaru nige:	乾隆四十五年八月初二日班禅额尔德呢恭进嵌宝石嘎布拉鼓一件
鼓 3（图三：2）	thod pa ḍa ma ru byin chen	amba adistid bisire g'abala jamaru:	yeke adistid-tu kabala zhamaru	大利益嘎布拉扎穆噜鼓
鼓 4（图四六）	gnam skyong lo nga dgu pa'i zla ba lnga pa'i tshes nyi shu la gsar bzo g.yang ḍi'i ka pā la ḍa ma ru byin chen gcig/	abkai wehiyehe i susai uyuci aniya sunja biyai orin de afabuha adistid bisire ice weilehe yacin gu g'abala jamaru emke.	tngri-yin tedkügsen-ü tabin yisüdüger on ǰun-u dumdadu sar-a-yin qorin-dur tusiiɣsan adistid-tu sin-e bütügegsen-ü qaraqan qas damaru nige.	乾隆五十九年五月二十日交利益新造青玉嘎布拉鼓一件
鼓 5（图五：2）	gsar bzhengs g.yang ḍi ḍa ma ru byin can	adistid bisire ice weilehe gu i g'abala jamaru:	Adistid-tu sin-e bütügegsen qan(s)-u kabala damaro	利益新造玉嘎布拉鼓
鼓 7（图二〇：2）	ka pā la ḍa ma ru gcig byin can	adistid bisire g'abala jamaru emke:	Adistid-tu kabala damaru nige:	利益嘎布拉鼓一件

◆ 林欢　故宫博物院器物部副研究馆员

故宫博物院藏乾隆皇帝本生故事集
——《法王新胜传》*

李若愚

内容摘要：故宫博物院收藏有一部名为《法王新胜传》的藏文文本（宗 23584），据作者考证，该文本是六世班禅洛桑班丹益西 1780 年在热河陛见乾隆皇帝时为乾隆皇帝所作的本生故事集，整个文本由 11 个传记故事组成，构建了乾隆皇帝的转世体系。在这一体系下，乾隆皇帝的前世分为三个部分：护持佛教的国王，修行的大成就者，噶当派、格鲁派的上师。本文讨论了该文本的创作背景，并首次对部分传记进行了摘译，为学界提供了新的研究资料，有利于促进学界对相关问题的进一步深入研究。

故宫博物院收藏有一部名为《法王新胜传》的藏文朱墨写本（文物编号为：宗 23584），在《北京地区藏文古籍总目》中有收录，但该目录信息简略，无法为进一步研

* 本文系故宫博物院 2018 年度科研课题《故宫博物院藏藏文文献序跋整理研究》（KT2018-04）的阶段性成果。

究所用，并且将该写本拆分为 11 条编目进行介绍，容易让人误以为是 11 部书[1]，有鉴于此，本文再对该文本进行详细介绍并考证其创作年代和创作背景，并对部分传记内容进行翻译，为学界提供新的研究资料，以期加深学界对这一问题的认识。

一、《法王新胜传》介绍

《法王新胜传》为梵夹装，页面 18.8×6.9 厘米，墨框 15.6×5.1 厘米，朱色双栏，左侧框外写有 རྟོགས་བརྗོད、文本序号和藏文叶码，页 4 行，共 108 叶，随经附带紫檀木匣一个，用来盛放经叶。整套写本由 11 个传记故事组成，每个传记藏文名皆有 གླིང་བཞི་ལྷ་དང་བཅས་པའི་འགྲོ་བ་ཡོངས་ཀྱི་གཙུག་རྒྱན་ཆེན་པོ་༄རྗེ་བཙུན་འཇམ་པའི་དབྱངས་༄གོང་མ་བདག་པོ་ཆེན་པོའི་འཁྲུངས་རབས་གསོལ་འདེབས་སུ་གསུངས་པའི་བརྒྱུད་རིམ།（四洲诸天与众生之大顶严 · 讲说至尊文殊大皇帝本生祈愿次第）之语，之后为各个传记的序号与人物名称，如第一份传记全名为 གླིང་བཞི་ལྷ་དང་བཅས་པའི་འགྲོ་བ་ཡོངས་ཀྱི་གཙུག་རྒྱན་ཆེན་པོ་༄རྗེ་བཙུན་འཇམ་པའི་དབྱངས་༄གོང་མ་བདག་པོ་ཆེན་པོའི་འཁྲུངས་རབས་གསོལ་འདེབས་སུ་གསུངས་པའི་བརྒྱུད་རིམ་དང་པོ་ཆོས་ཀྱི་རྒྱལ་པོ་གསལ་རྒྱལ་གྱི་རྟོགས་བརྗོད་བཞུགས་སོ།།（《四洲诸天与众生之大顶严 · 讲说至尊文殊大皇帝本生祈愿次第之第一 · 法王胜光王传》）。笔者认为该部书的封面即是第一部传记的题名，因此有可能以往工作人员即以此作为整部书的命名，并且将 གསལ་རྒྱལ 误作 གསར་རྒྱལ，为避免引起新的混淆，本文仍沿用旧称《法王新胜传》来指代这整部著作（图一至图五）。其 11 个传记故事依次如下：

1. དང་པོ་ཆོས་ཀྱི་རྒྱལ་པོ་གསལ་རྒྱལ་གྱི་རྟོགས་བརྗོད་བཞུགས་སོ།།（图一）
   第一，法王胜光王传（共 13 叶）
2. གཉིས་པ་ཀུ་སཱ་ལིའི་རྟོགས་བརྗོད་བཞུགས་སོ།།（图六）
   第二，孤萨利传（共 4 叶）
3. གསུམ་པ་རྒྱལ་པོ་སངས་རྒྱས་ཕྱོགས་ཀྱི་རྟོགས་བརྗོད་བཞུགས་སོ།།（图七）
   第三，觉方王传（共 9 叶）

1　阿华 · 阿旺华丹主编：《北京地区藏文古籍总目》，北京：中国藏学出版社，2013：253-254。该书在“2. 证道记”这一条目下列举了 11 个条目分别介绍，依次为《四洲众生顶严 · 至尊文殊怙主 · 先祖先师本生传之一胜光王本生传》《赤钦 · 孟兰白哇本生传》《忽必烈本生传》《大成就师旦慈多结本生传》《赤钦 · 金巴嘉措本生传》《至尊嘉却白桑波本生传》《孤萨利本生传》《勒贝希饶本生传》《成道师达恰本生传》《牟尼赞普本生传》《桑结确王本生传》。

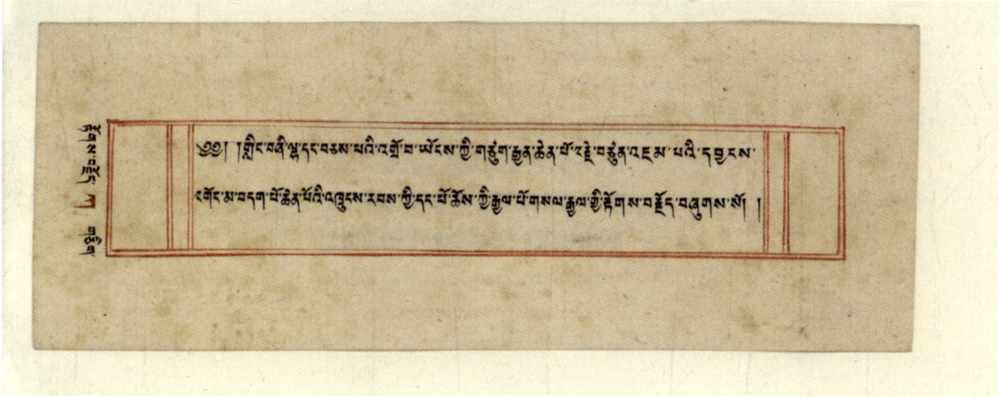

图一 《法王新胜传》封面 (1a)

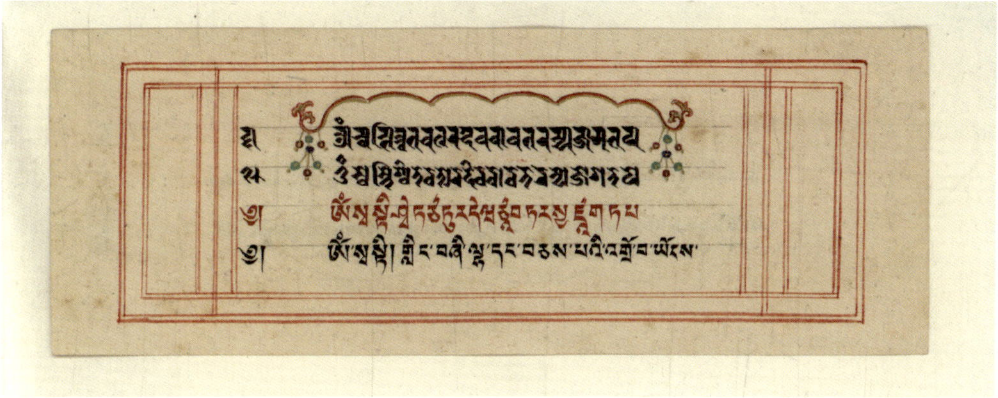

图二 《法王新胜传 · 胜光王传》标题 (1b)

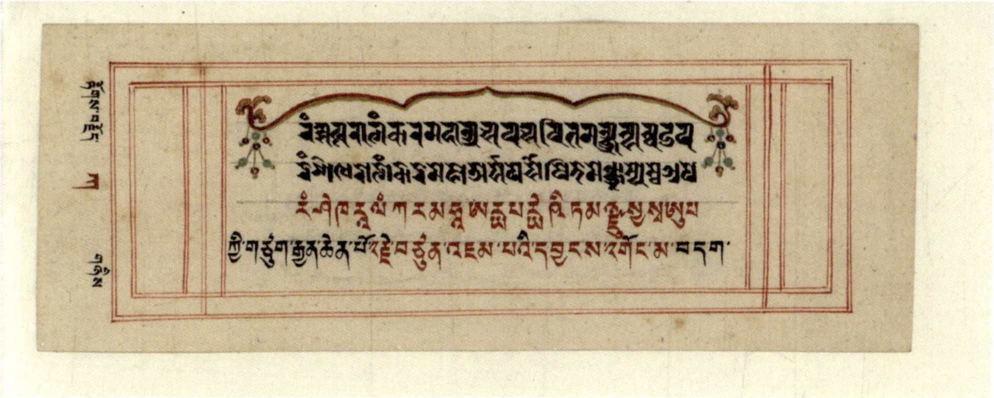

图三 《法王新胜传 · 胜光王传》标题 (2a)

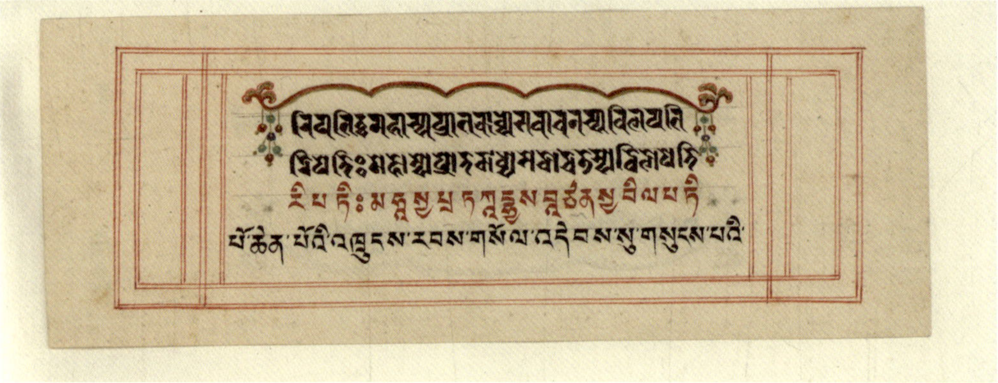

图四 《法王新胜传・胜光王传》标题 (2b)

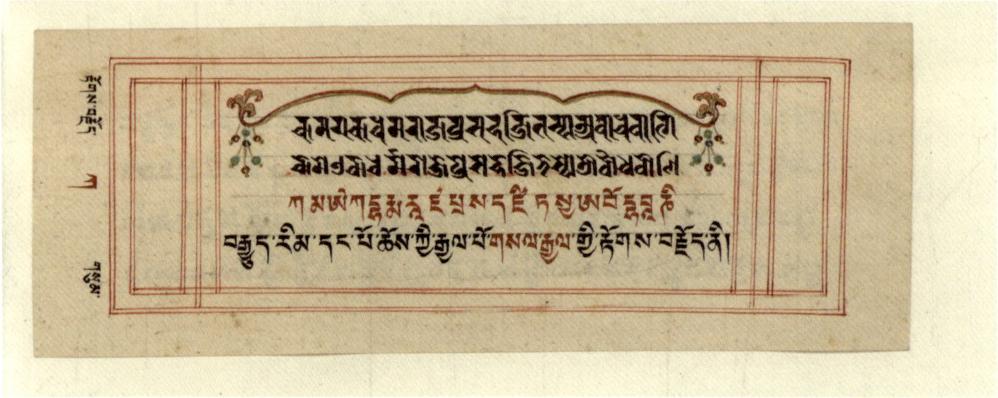

图五 《法王新胜传・胜光王传》标题 (3a)

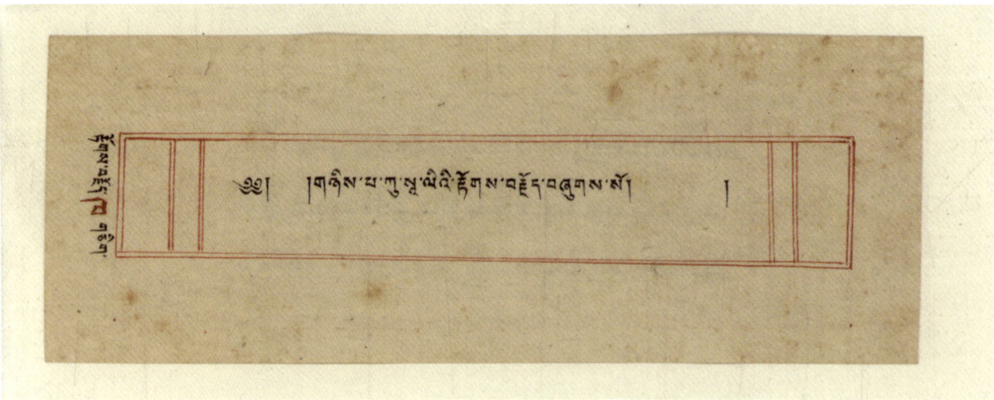

图六 《法王新胜传・孤萨利传》封面

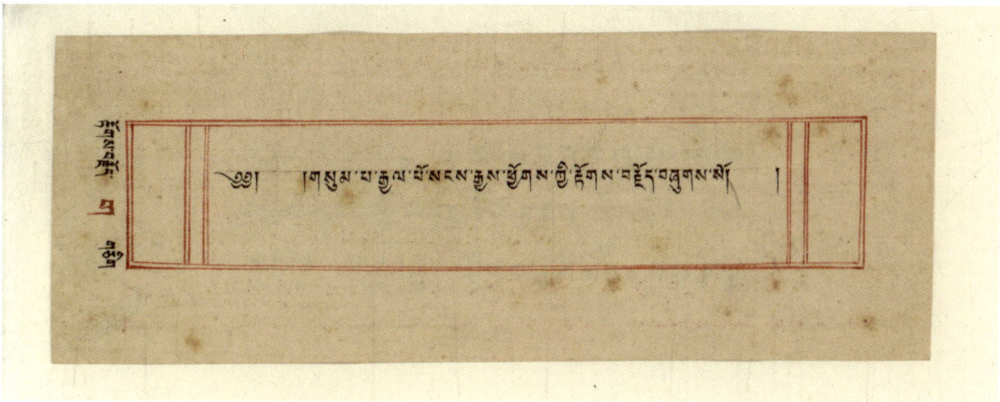

图七 《法王新胜传·觉方王传》封面

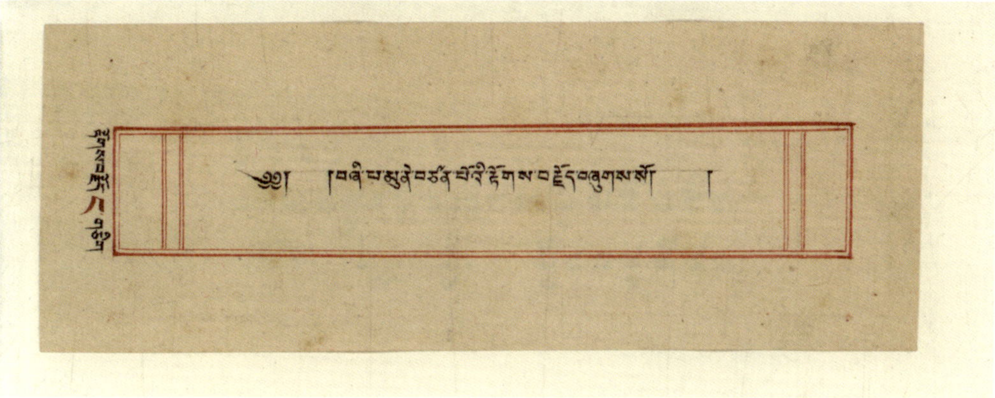

图八 《法王新胜传·牟尼赞普传》封面

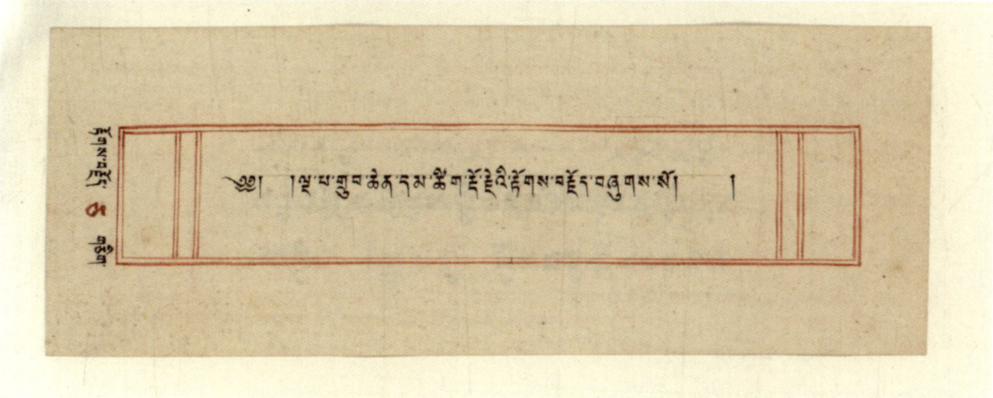

图九 《法王新胜传·旦慈多吉传》封面

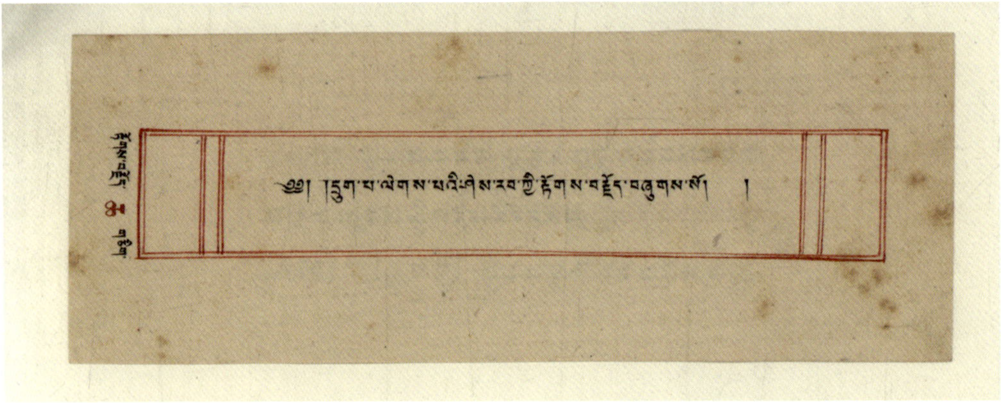

图一〇 《法王新胜传·勒贝喜饶传》封面

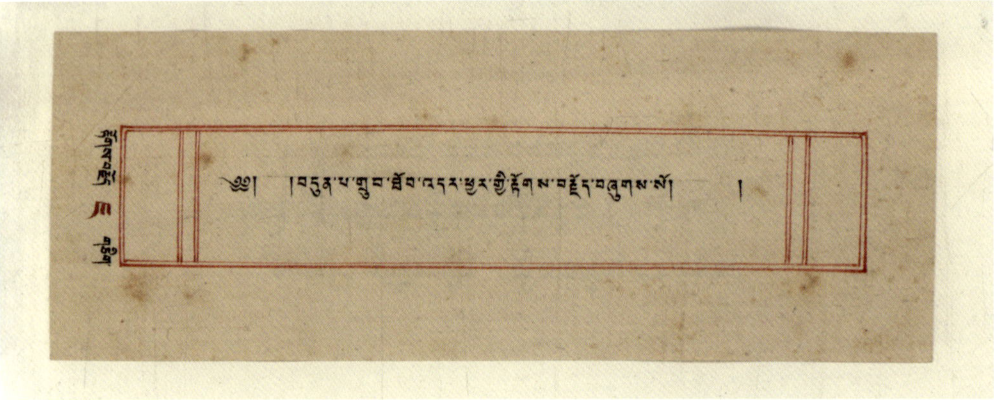

图一一 《法王新胜传·达洽传》封面

4. བཞི་པ་མུ་ནེ་བཙན་པོའི་རྟོགས་བརྗོད་བཞུགས་སོ།། （图八）

第四，牟尼赞普传（共 12 叶）

5. ལྔ་པ་གྲུབ་ཆེན་དམ་ཚིག་རྡོ་རྗེའི་རྟོགས་བརྗོད་བཞུགས་སོ།། （图九）

第五，大成就者旦慈多吉传（共 3 叶）

6. དྲུག་པ་ལེགས་པའི་ཤེས་རབ་ཀྱི་རྟོགས་བརྗོད་བཞུགས་སོ།། （图一〇）

第六，勒贝喜饶传（共 8 叶）

7. བདུན་པ་གྲུབ་ཐོབ་འདར་ཕྱར་གྱི་རྟོགས་བརྗོད་བཞུགས་སོ།། （图一一）

第七，得道者达洽传（共 17 叶）

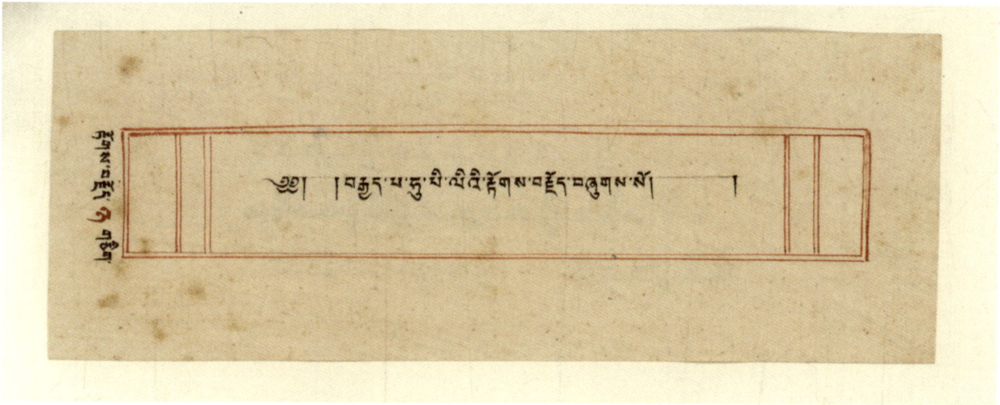

图一二 《法王新胜传・忽必烈传》封面

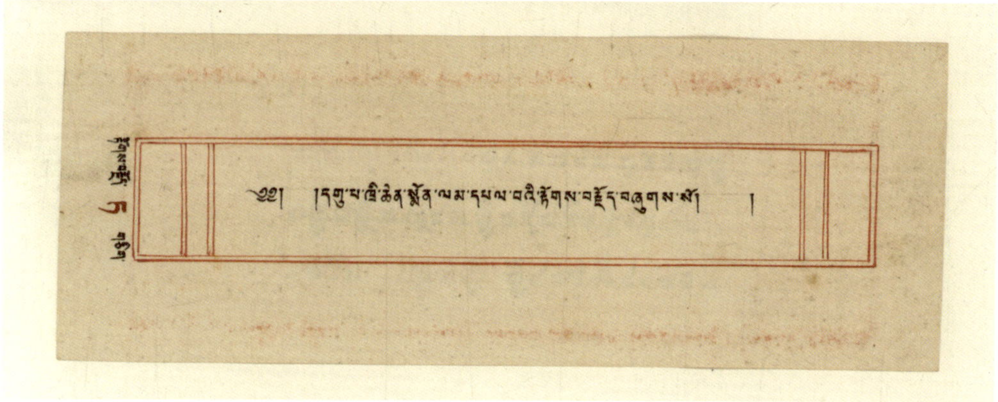

图一三 《法王新胜传・赤钦默朗贝哇传》封面

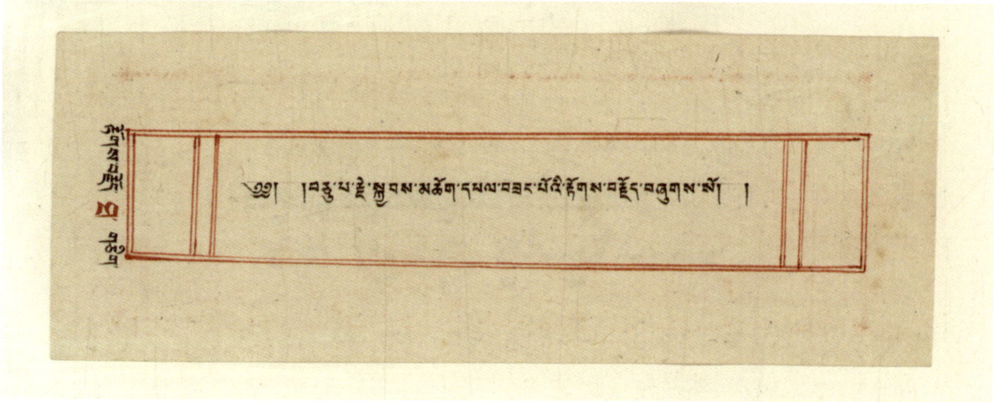

图一四 《法王新胜传・杰却贝桑波传》封面

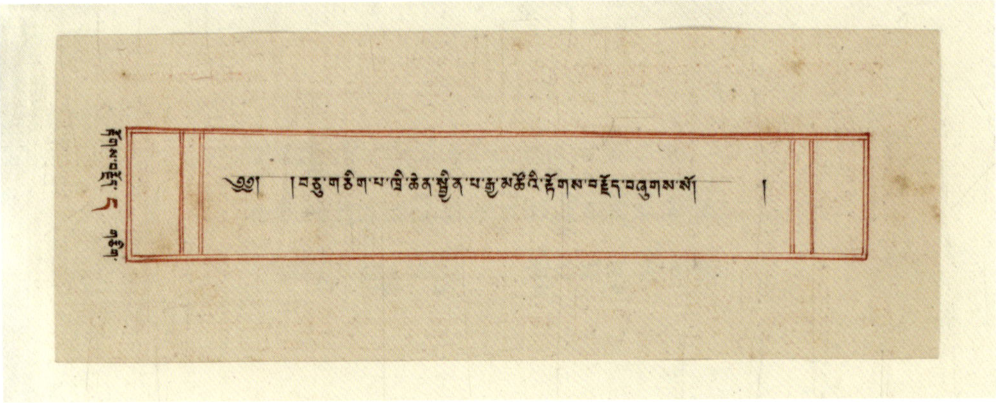

图一五 《法王新胜传·赤钦金巴嘉措传》封面

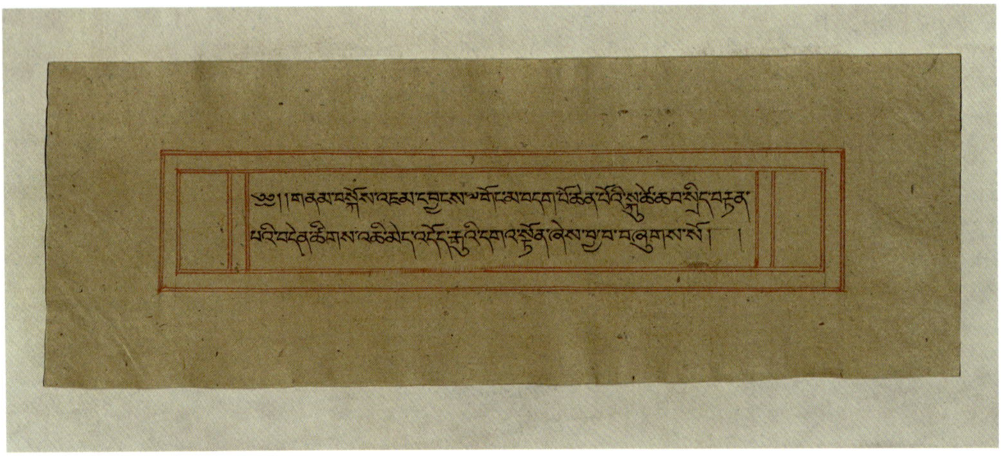

图一六 《皇图永固经》第 1 叶正面

8. བརྒྱད་པ་ཧུ་པི་ལའི་རྟོགས་བརྗོད་བཞུགས་སོ།། （图一二）

第八，忽必烈传（共 5 叶）

9. དགུ་པ་ཁྲི་ཆེན་སྨོན་ལམ་དཔལ་བའི་རྟོགས་བརྗོད་བཞུགས་སོ།། （图一三）

第九，赤钦默朗贝哇传（共 5 叶）

10. བཅུ་པ་རྗེ་སྐྱབས་མཆོག་དཔལ་བཟང་པོའི་རྟོགས་བརྗོད་བཞུགས་སོ།། （图一四）

第十，尊者杰却贝桑波传（共 27 叶）

11. བཅུ་གཅིག་པ་ཁྲི་ཆེན་སྦྱིན་པ་རྒྱ་མཚོའི་རྟོགས་བརྗོད་བཞུགས་སོ།། （图一五）

第十一，赤钦金巴嘉措传（共 5 叶）

འཇམ་པའི་དབྱངས་ཀྱི་གོང་མ་བདག་པོ་ཆེན་པོ（文殊大皇帝）一词在清代往往为皇帝专用，这在清代的藏文文本中屡见不鲜，如第十三世达赖喇嘛土丹嘉措（ཐུབ་བསྟན་རྒྱ་མཚོ། 1876-1933 年）写给宣统皇帝的贺词，标题为 གནམ་བསྐོས་འཇམ་དབྱངས་ཀྱི་གོང་མ་བདག་པོ་ཆེན་པོའི་སྐུ་ཚེ་ཆབ་སྲིད་བརྟན་པའི་བདེན་ཚིགས་འཆི་མེད་འདོད་རྒུའི་དགའ་སྟོན་ཞེས་བྱ་བ་བཞུགས་སོ། །（《天授文殊大皇帝之寿命王政永固之愿言 · 不死所欲之喜宴》）（图一六）[2]，因此，རྗེ་བཙུན་འཇམ་པའི་དབྱངས་ཀྱི་གོང་མ་བདག་པོ་ཆེན་པོའི་འཁྲུངས་རབས（至尊文殊大皇帝之本生），当指清代皇帝的本生故事，而《法王新胜传》，应是一本清代皇帝的本生故事集。

二、《法王新胜传》创作年代

在土观 · 洛桑却吉尼玛（ཐུའུ་བཀྭན་བློ་བཟང་ཆོས་ཀྱི་ཉི་མ། 1737-1801/1802 年）所著的《章嘉国师若必多吉传》中，有如下记载：

> རྗེ་བླ་མ་ཉིད་ནས་སྔོན་འགྲོ་མགོན་ཆོས་རྒྱལ་འཕགས་པས་ཧོར་གྱི་རྒྱལ་པོ་ཧུ་པི་ལས་ཆེ་ཆེན་ཧན་ལ་ཀྱི་ཀྱཻ་རྡོ་རྗེའི་དབང་གནང་བ་ཆུ་མོ་གླང་གི་ལོ་ཡིན། ངེད་ཀྱིས་ཀྱང་གོང་མ་ཆེན་པོར་འཁོར་ལོ་བདེ་མཆོག་གི་དབང་ཕུལ་བ་ཤིང་མོ་གླང་ཡིན། གནམ་ལོ་འདི་གཉིས་ཁམས་མི་འདྲ་བ་མ་གཏོགས་གླང་གི་ལོར་གཅིག་པ་ཡིན་འདུག་ཅེས་གསུང་། འདི་ལྟར་གསུངས་པ་རྗེ་བླ་མ་ཉིད་འཕགས་པ་རིན་པོ་ཆེའི་སྐུའི་སྐྱེ་བར་དོན་གྱིས་ཞལ་གྱིས་བཞེས་སམ་སྙམ་ཞིང་། པཎ་ཆེན་ཐམས་ཅད་མཁྱེན་པས་མཛད་པའི་རྗེ་བླ་མའི་འཁྲུངས་རབས་གསོལ་འདེབས་སུ་འཕགས་པ་རིན་པོ་ཆེ་བཞུགས་པ་དང་། ཡང་དུས་ཕྱིས་ཀྱི་གོང་མ་ཆེན་པོའི་འཁྲུངས་རབས་སུ་ཧུ་པི་ལས་ཆེ་ཆེན་ཧན་ཀྱང་ཡོད་འདུག་པས། སྐུ་སྐྱེ་འཕྲེང་དུ་མར་མཆོད་ཡོན་གྱི་ཚུལ་གྱིས་བསྟན་པའི་བྱ་བ་མཛད་པ་གོར་མ་ཆག་གོ [3]
>
> 师尊（三世章嘉）曾说："在之前，众生怙主法王八思巴为蒙古皇帝忽必烈薛禅汗作喜金刚灌顶是水牛年，而我为大皇帝授胜乐轮灌顶亦是在木牛年，这两个年份仅是天干不同，却都是牛年"。师尊有如此说法，正说明他认为自己是八思巴的化身。在遍知一切班禅大师所作的《上师本生祈愿》中有八思巴的记载，而且在后来所作的《大皇帝本生》中亦有忽必烈薛禅汗的记载，可以肯定的是，在（他们）历辈转世中就曾以供施关系来弘扬教法的事业。[4]

2　《皇图永固经》，第 1 叶正面，故宫博物院藏书。

3　ཐུའུ་བཀྭན་བློ་བཟང་ཆོས་ཀྱི་ཉི་མ། ལྕང་སྐྱ་རོལ་པའི་རྡོ་རྗེའི་རྣམ་ཐར། ལན་ཀྲོའུ། ཀན་སུའུ་མི་རིགས་དཔེ་སྐྲུན་ཁང་། 1989：297。

4　土观 · 洛桑却吉尼玛著，陈庆英、马连龙译：《章嘉国师若必多吉传》，北京：民族出版社，2007：131。笔者在原译文的基础上重新进行了翻译。

根据文意，这里的《上师本生祈愿》（རྗེ་བླ་མའི་འཁྲུངས་རབས）中上师指的是三世章嘉若必多吉，而《大皇帝本生》（གོང་མ་ཆེན་པོའི་འཁྲུངས་རབས）中的大皇帝指的是乾隆皇帝，因此陈庆英、马连龙先生直接将其翻译为《章嘉活佛本生祈愿》和《乾隆皇帝本生传》，显然是十分正确的。由此可知，至迟在土观 · 洛桑却吉尼玛写书的时候，即 1798 年左右[5]就已经有了一本乾隆皇帝的本生传记，并且在这本传记中记载了乾隆皇帝的一个前身为忽必烈薛禅汗，因此土观呼图克图才会将章嘉国师和乾隆皇帝的前世因缘追溯为八思巴和忽必烈。

在《章嘉国师若必多吉传》中略述了章嘉国师先世的转生故事，第八个转世即是八思巴，记载如下：

འོད་གསལ་འཁོན་གྱི་གདུང་རིགས་ཤར་རིའི་རྩེར།
རྒྱལ་སྲས་དཔའ་བོ་སྨྲ་བའི་ཟླ་བ་འཛེགས།
གངས་རིའི་མདངས་ཀྱིས་ཕྱོགས་ཀུན་དཀར་བའི་ལྗོངས།
ཕན་བདེའི་འོད་ཀྱིས་ལྷག་པར་དཀར་བར་བྱས།
མཁྱེན་བརྩེ་ནུས་པས་རྒྱ་བོད་ཧོར་གསུམ་ཀུན།
དབང་དུ་བསྡུས་ཏེ་ཐུ་རམ་ཤིང་པའི་བསྟན།
འཁོར་ལོ་གསུམ་གྱིས་ཕྱོགས་མཐར་རྒྱས་མཛད་པས།
ཆོས་རྒྱལ་འཕགས་པར་གྲགས་པ་དོན་དང་མཐུན།[6]
出自光净天的款氏家族，
像佛法明月升上东山顶，
在这雪山般洁白的地区，
用利乐光芒使它分外素净。
你以智慧和慈悲的力量，
教化汉地吐蕃以及蒙古，
释迦牟尼之教弘遍各方，
尊你为法王八思巴名实相符。[7]

5 ཐུའུ་བཀྭན་བློ་བཟང་ཆོས་ཀྱི་ཉི་མ། ལྕང་སྐྱ་རོལ་པའི་རྡོ་རྗེའི་རྣམ་ཐར། 1989：781；土观 · 洛桑却吉尼玛著，陈庆英、马连龙译：《章嘉国师若必多吉传》，2007：302。

6 ཐུའུ་བཀྭན་བློ་བཟང་ཆོས་ཀྱི་ཉི་མ། ལྕང་སྐྱ་རོལ་པའི་རྡོ་རྗེའི་རྣམ་ཐར། 1989：13。

7 土观 · 洛桑却吉尼玛著，陈庆英、马连龙译：《章嘉国师若必多吉传》，2007：9。

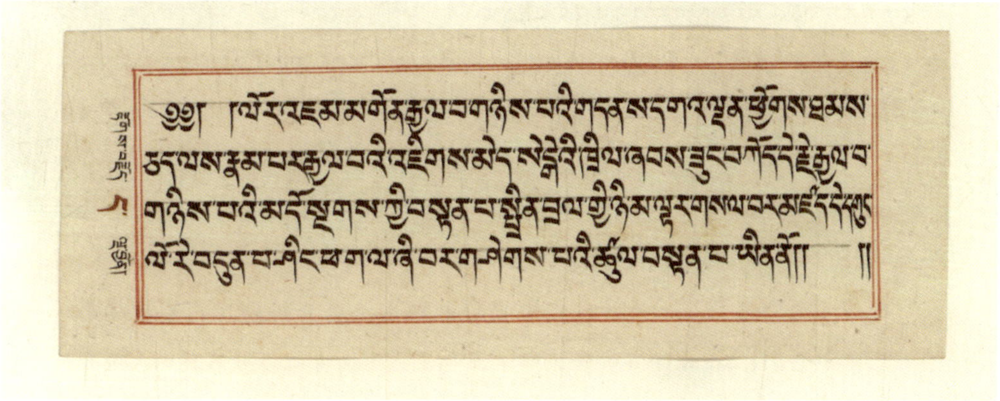

图一七 《法王新胜传·赤钦金巴嘉措传》第 5 叶背面

而《法王新胜传》中的第八个转世，亦恰好为忽必烈。前文所述，《法王新胜传》为清代皇帝的本生故事集，那么显然这个皇帝应为乾隆皇帝。

此外，《法王新胜传》最后一个本生传记为第 46 任甘丹赤巴金巴嘉措（སྦྱིན་པ་རྒྱ་མཚོ། 1629-1695 年），而在其传记末尾也记录了他于 67 岁土猪年（1695 年）圆寂（དགུང་ལོ་རེ་བདུན་པ་ཤིང་ཕག་ལ་ཞི་བར་གཤེགས་པའི་ཚུལ་བསྟན་པ་ཡིན་ནོ）（图一七）[8]，那么《法王新胜传》作为清代某一个皇帝的本生传记，其出生时间应该在 1695 年之后，而乾隆皇帝是在 1711 年出生，时间上来看，也恰好衔接了该本生传记的时间顺序，可以作为一个佐证。

对于乾隆皇帝的本生传记，弗拉基米尔·乌斯宾斯基（Vladimir .L. Uspensky）曾指出，在乾隆皇帝七十寿辰之际，六世班禅洛桑班丹益西（བློ་བཟང་དཔལ་ལྡན་ཡེ་ཤེས། 1738-1780 年）进京陛见乾隆皇帝，为其作《本生祈愿》（འཁྲུངས་རབས་གསོལ་འདེབས），并在文章中给出了该《本生祈愿》的录文与翻译[9]，里面提到的本生世系与《法王新胜传》中的一致。需要指出的是其提到的乾隆皇帝的《本生祈愿》应为六世班禅在热河时所做的丹书克，其全名为 བརྟན་བཞུགས་འཇིགས་མེད་གདོང་ལྔའི་སྒྲ་དབྱངས་བཞུགས་སོ།།（《丹书克·无畏狮子音》），此文本在故宫博物院图书馆有收藏，其末尾有如下序跋：

ཅེས་འཇམ་དཔའི་དབྱངས་མི་ཡི་རྗེ་བོར་རོལ་པ་གནམ་གྱི་ལྷ་གོང་མ་ལྷས་སྐྱོང་བདག་པོ་ཆེན་པོའི་

8 《法王新胜传·赤钦金巴嘉措传》，ད 函第 5 叶背面，故宫博物院藏书。

9 Vladimir. L. Uspensky, “The Previous Incarnations of the Qianlong Emperor according to the Panchen Lama Blo bzang dpal ltan ye shes.” In *Tibet, Past and Present: Proceedings of the Ninth Seminar of the International Association for Tibetan Studies*. ed. Henk Blezer, Leiden: Brill, 2002: 215-228.

འཁྲུངས་རབས་གསོལ་འདེབས་དང་འབྲེལ་བའི་བརྟན་བཞུགས་གསོལ་འདེབས་འཇིགས་མེད་གདོང་ལྔའི་སྒྲ་དབྱངས་ཞེས་བྱ་བ་འདི་ནི་ལྷས་སྐྱོང་ཁྲིར་བཞུགས་སྐབས་ལོ་ཞེ་ལྔ་པའི་དགུང་གྲངས་བདུན་ཅུར་ཕེབས་པའི་བཀྲ་ཤིས་ཁྲི་ཕྲག་ཁྲི་ཕྲག་གི་སྤྲ་ཡེར་ཆེན་པོའི་དུས་སུ་གསེར་གྱི་བཟང་མཇལ་སྐབས་རང་གི་སེམས་ཀྱི་སྣང་བ་ལ་ཇི་ལྟར་ཤར་བ་བཞིན། ཤཱཀྱའི་དགེ་སློང་བློ་བཟང་དཔལ་ལྡན་ཡེ་ཤེས་ཀྱིས་སུམ་རྩེན་གྱི་དགའ་ཚལ་ས་ལ་འཕོས་པ་ལྟ་བུའི་ཡེ་ཧོར་གྱི་ཕོ་བྲང་ཆེན་པོའི་ཉེ་འདབས་བཀྲ་ཤིས་ལྷུན་པོའི་དགོན་གནས་སུ་གུས་པ་ཆེན་པོས་སྦྱར་བའི་ཡི་གེ་པ་ནི་གསོལ་དཔོན་བློ་བཟང་མཁས་མཆོག་གོ། དགེ་ཞིང་བཀྲ་ཤིས་པར་གྱུར་ཅིག།། [10]

此与《文殊化身人主天神乾隆大皇帝的本生祈愿》所分开的《丹书克祈愿·无畏狮子音》，在乾隆皇帝登极四十五年、七十大寿之万分吉祥的大喜乐[11]之际，逢此金美良时，自心升起如此想法。释迦之比丘洛桑班丹益西于天界欢喜林般的热河大宫殿附近的扎什伦布寺[12]，恭敬所作，抄写人岁本洛桑克却，愿吉祥安乐！

可见在热河陛见乾隆之时，六世班禅为乾隆皇帝进献了《丹书克·无畏狮子音》之外，还作了一部《本生祈愿》。著名的蒙古学者吉美日白多吉（འཇིགས་མེད་རིག་པའི་རྡོ་རྗེ། 1761-1835 年）所著的《蒙古教法源流》（ཧོར་གྱི་ཆོས་འབྱུང）更是清楚地记载了六世班禅在热河向乾隆皇帝进献丹书克，作《本生祈愿》的情形，如下：

ཆོས་བཅུ་གསུམ་གོང་མ་ཆེན་པོའི་འཁྲུངས་སྐར་གྱི་པྲ་ཡར་ཆེན་པོ་ལ་རྗེ་ཉིད་ཀྱིས་བརྟན་བཞུགས་ཕུལ་ཏེ་གོང་མའི་འཁྲུངས་རབས་གསོལ་འདེབས་གསར་རྩོམ་མཛད་པ་དེར་ཡོད་པའི་འཁྲུངས་རབས་ཀྱི་རིམ་པ་ནི། སྟོན་པ་སངས་རྒྱས་ཀྱི་དུས་སུ་རྒྱལ་པོ་གསལ་རྒྱལ། དེ་ནས་ཀུ་སྣ་ལི་ཆེ་བ། ས་སྐྱོང་སངས་རྒྱས་ཕྱོགས། བོད་རྒྱལ་མུ་ནེ་བཙན་པོ། ཡང་རྒྱ་གར་དུ་གྲུབ་ཐོབ་དམ་ཚིག་རྡོ་རྗེ། བོད་དུ་རྟོག་ལེགས་པའི་ཤེས་རབ། དཔལ་ལྡན་དར་འཕྱུར་བ། ཆེན་པོ་ཧོར་གྱི་ཆོས་རྒྱལ་ཧོ་པི་ལའི་སེ་ཆེན། འཇམ་དབྱངས་སློན་ལམ་དཔལ་བ། རྗེ་སྐྱབས་མཆོག་དཔལ་བཟང་། པཎ་ཆེན་སྦྱིན་པ་རྒྱ་མཚོ། ཆོས་ཀྱི་འཁོར་ལོས་བསྒྱུར་བ་ལྷས་སྐྱོང་རྒྱལ་པོ་ཆེན་པོ་རྣམས་བཞུགས་སོ།། [13]

（八月）十三日，在大皇帝生日的大喜乐之时，尊者（六世班禅）献丹书克，且为皇帝新作《本生祈愿》，该本生世系依次为：在导师佛陀时代的胜光

10 故宫博物院藏书，宗 23596。

11 喜乐，藏文作 སྤྲ་ཡེར 或 པྲ་ཡར，音译蒙文 bayar（喜乐）。

12 扎什伦布寺，藏文作 བཀྲ་ཤིས་ལྷུན་པོའི་དགོན，即须弥福寿之庙。

13 འཇིགས་མེད་རིག་པའི་རྡོ་རྗེ། ཆེན་པོ་ཧོར་གྱི་ཡུལ་དུ་དམ་པའི་ཆོས་ཇི་ལྟར་བྱུང་བའི་ཚུལ་བཤད་པ་རྒྱལ་བའི་བསྟན་པ་རིན་པོ་ཆེ་གསལ་བར་བྱེད་པའི་སྒྲོན་མེ། ཁྲི་ཞིང་། མཚོ་སྔོན་མི་དམངས་དཔེ་སྐྲུན་ཁང་། 1993: 255-256。

王，孤萨利大士，国王觉方王，藏地国王牟尼赞普，在印度的成就者旦慈多吉，在藏地的鄂·勒贝喜饶，具德的达洽，大蒙古法王忽必烈薛禅汉，文殊默朗贝哇，尊者杰却贝桑波，大班智达金巴嘉措，转轮法王乾隆大皇帝。

考虑到《法王新胜传》藏文名称 གླིང་བཞི་ལྷ་དང་བཅས་པའི་འགྲོ་བ་ཡོངས་ཀྱི་གཙུག་རྒྱན་ཆེན་པོ་༸རྗེ་བཙུན་འཇམ་པའི་དབྱངས་༸གོང་མ་བདག་པོ་ཆེན་པོའི་འཁྲུངས་རབས་གསོལ་འདེབས་སུ་གསུངས་པའི་བརྒྱུད་རིམ། (四洲诸天与众生之大顶严·讲说至尊文殊大皇帝本生祈愿次第) 有“本生祈愿”之语，按照藏族的习惯，故宫博物院所收藏的《法王新胜传》就是这样的一部《本生祈愿》。因此，《法王新胜传》是六世班禅洛桑班丹益西在热河陛见乾隆皇帝时特为乾隆皇帝所作的一份本生故事集，创作的时间为 1780 年。

三、《法王新胜传》部分传记摘译

《法王新胜传》创作的背后有着深刻的政治目的，清朝皇帝继承了元以来西藏地方势力对北京皇帝的称呼“曼殊室利大皇帝”，[14] 即所谓的“文殊皇帝”（འཇམ་དབྱངས་གོང་མ）。这一称号附带有宗教上的额外优势，在众多信徒心中成了神权的来源 [15]。不同于元明两朝皇帝，虽贵为天子，但在西藏喇嘛面前却只能作为一位虔诚的佛家弟子顶礼膜拜，清帝则不同，他们自称本人就是佛子，就是文殊菩萨化身的转轮圣王，他们就是受膜拜的对象 [16]，而《法王新胜传》，正是乾隆皇帝对自己宗教形象的一次构建。

在《法王新胜传》中乾隆皇帝的前世可以分为三个类别：作为护持佛教的国王，其前生为胜光王、觉方王、牟尼赞普和忽必烈薛禅汗；作为修行的大成就者，其前生为孤萨利、大成就者旦慈多吉、得道者达洽；作为噶当派和格鲁派的著名上师，其前生为勒贝喜饶、赤钦默朗贝哇、尊者杰却贝桑波、赤钦金巴嘉措。下面摘译护持佛教国王的事迹予以分析说明：

（一）胜光王传

དཔག་བསམ་གྱི་ལྗོན་པ་ཆེན་པོ་འཛམ་བུ་ཏི་ཤས་མཚན་ཞིང་མཛེས་པའི་ཡུལ་འཛམ་གླིང་ཆེན་པོ་

---

14 罗文华：《龙袍与袈裟·上》，北京：紫禁城出版社，2005：24。

15 孙逊：《包容神性：清朝皇帝的文殊形象与藏传佛教的臣服——正统性传承中主导性虚构的凝聚力作用》，《西藏研究》2013（3）：1-9。

16 罗文华：《龙袍与袈裟·上》，2005：27。

འདིའི་དབུས་ན་གྲོང་ཁྱེར་ཆེན་པོ་དྲུག་ཡོད་པའི་ནང་ནས་ཀྱང་དགེ་མཚན་ཤིན་ཏུ་ཁྱད་པར་ཏུ་འཕགས་པ་མཉན་ཡོད་ཅེས་བྱ་བའི་གྲོང་ཁྱེར་ཆེན་པོའི་རྒྱལ་པོའི་ཕོ་བྲང་དུ་རྒྱལ་པོ་ཆེན་པོ་རྩིབས་ཀྱིས་འཕྱུར་ཚངས་བྱིན་ཞེས་བྱ་བའི་སྲས་སུ་འཁྲུངས་ཏེ། དེའི་ཚེ་དགའ་ལྡན་ནས་ལྷའི་བུ་དམ་པ་ཏོག་དཀར་པོ་གཟིགས་པ་ལྔ་ལ་གཟིགས་ནས་འཛམ་བུའི་གླིང་གི་སེར་སྐྱའི་གནས་སུ་དཔྱིད་ཟླ་ཐ་ཆུང་ས་ག་ཟླ་བའི་ཚེས་བཅོ་ལྔའི་ཉིན་ཡུམ་སྒྱུ་འཕྲུལ་མ་སྐྱིད་མོས་ཚལ་གྱི་གཞལ་མེད་ཁང་ཆེན་པོར་གསོ་སྦྱོང་མཛད་པའི་ལྷུམས་སུ་ཞུགས་ཏེ་དེའི་ཕྱི་ལོ་དཔོ་ཟླ་བའི་ཚེས་བཅོ་ལྔའི་ཉིན་ཡུམ་སྒྱུ་འཕྲུལ་མའི་རྩིབས་ལོགས་གཡས་པ་ནས་བྱང་སེམས་འཁྲུངས་པ་དང་དུས་མཚུངས་པར་གསལ་རྒྱལ་ཡང་ཡུམ་ལས་འཁྲུངས་ཏེ། དེའི་ཚེ་བྱང་ཆུབ་སེམས་དཔའི་མཐུས་འཇིག་རྟེན་ཐམས་ཅད་སྣང་བ་ཆེན་པོས་ཁྱབ་ཅིང་། ཉི་མ་འབུམ་གྱི་འོད་པས་ཀྱང་ཆེས་གསལ་བས་ས་འོག་གི་གཏིང་ཚུན་ཆད་སྣང་བར་བྱས། ལྷ་རྣམས་ཀྱིས་ཤིས་པ་བརྗོད་ཅིང་མེ་ཏོག་གི་ཆར་ཕབ། སྐད་ཅིག་དེ་ལ་སྟོང་གསུམ་གྱི་སྟོང་ཆེན་པོའི་འཇིག་རྟེན་ན་གནས་པའི་སེམས་ཅན་ཐམས་ཅད་ལུས་སེམས་བདེ་བས་ཁྱབ་པ་སོགས་ངོ་མཚར་བའི་ལྟས་བསམ་གྱིས་མི་ཁྱབ་པ་བྱུང་བ་ན་རྒྱལ་པོ་ཆེན་པོ་རྩིབས་ཀྱིས་འཕྱུར་ཚངས་བྱིན་གྱི་བསམས་པ་ལ་ངའི་བུ་འདི་སྐྱེས་པས་འཇིག་རྟེན་ཐམས་ཅད་འོད་ཀྱིས་གསལ་བར་བྱས་པ་སོགས་ངོ་མཚར་བའི་ལྟས་འདི་ལྟ་བུ་བྱུང་ངོ་སྙམ་ནས་བུའི་མིང་དུའང་དགེ་ལེགས་ཀྱི་མཚན་མ་དང་མཐུན་པར་གསལ་རྒྱལ་ཞེས་བཏགས་སོ། །དེ་ནས་རྒྱལ་བུ་གསལ་རྒྱལ་མ་མ་བརྒྱད་ཀྱིས་འཚོ་བར་བྱེད་པ་སོགས་བསྐྱེད་བསྲིངས། རིམ་གྱིས་ནར་སོན་ཏེ་ཡབ་རྒྱལ་པོ་འདས་པ་ན་མཉན་ཡོད་དུ་ཀོ་ས་ལའི་རྒྱལ་པོར་དབང་བསྐུར།

བྱང་ཆུབ་སེམས་དཔའ་གཞོན་ནུ་དོན་ཐམས་ཅད་གྲུབ་པ་ཡང་དགུང་ལོ་ཉི་ཤུ་རྩ་དགུའི་བར་ཁབ་ཏུ་བཞུགས་ཏེ་ལྷ་མི་བགྲང་ཡས་ཀྱི་དོན་མཛད། དེ་ནས་རབ་ཏུ་བྱུང་སྟེ་ལོ་དྲུག་ཏུ་དཀའ་བ་སྤྱད། དེ་ནས་རྡོ་རྗེ་གདན་བྱང་ཆུབ་ཀྱི་ཤིང་དབང་དྲུང་དུ་སངས་རྒྱས་ནས་འགྲོ་བ་ལྷ་དང་བཅས་པ་ཐམས་ཅད་ལ་ཆོས་ཀྱི་འཁོར་ལོ་བསྐོར་བར་མཛད་པ་ན། རྒྱལ་པོ་གསལ་རྒྱལ་འདིས་དེ་བཞིན་གཤེགས་པ་ལ་རྩེ་གཅིག་ཏུ་གུས་པས་མཆོད་ཅིང་རྣམ་པ་ཀུན་ནས་བསྙེན་བཀུར་བ་ལ་བརྩོན་པ་དང་། སྟོན་པའི་འཁོར་རྣམ་བཞི་ཐམས་ཅད་རང་གི་སྲོག་ལས་ཀྱང་གཅེས་པར་སྐྱོང་ཞིང་། གུས་པ་དང་ཕུ་དུད་བླ་ལྷག་ཏུ་བྱས། སྟོན་པ་ཐུབ་པའི་དབང་པོས་ཀྱང་གྲོང་ཁྱེར་ཆེན་པོ་དྲུག་གི་ནང་ནས་ཀྱང་གཙོ་བོར་མཉན་ཡོད་དུ་ཡུན་རིང་བཞུགས་ཤིང་སྐྱེ་འགྲོ་བསམ་གྱིས་མི་ཁྱབ་པ་སྨིན་གྲོལ་ལ་འགོད་པར་མཛད། ལྷག་པར་སྟོན་པས་ཆོ་འཕྲུལ་ཆེན་པོའང་མཉན་ཡོད་དུ་སྟོན་པར་མཛད་དེ། དེའི་ཚེ་འཛམ་བུའི་གླིང་གི་རྒྱལ་ཕྲན་ཕལ་མོ་ཆེས་རང་རང་གི་ཡུལ་དུ་ཆོ་འཕྲུལ་ཆེན་པོ་སྟོན་པར་གསོལ་བ་བཏབ་ཅིང་། དེའི་ཚེ་བསྙེན་བཀུར་བྱ་བར་གསོལ་བ་བཏབ་ཀྱང་གཞན་ཐམས་ཅད་ལ་ཞལ་གྱིས་མ་བཞེས་པར། ང་ཉིད་དུས་མཁྱེན་ནོ་གསུངས་ནས་རིམ་གྱིས་བྱོན་ཏེ་མཉན་ཡོད་དུ་ཕེབས་ནས་ཆོས་ཀྱི་རྒྱལ་པོ་གསལ་རྒྱལ་གྱིས་གསོལ་བ་བཏབ་པ་ན་ཞལ་གྱིས་བཞེས་ཏེ་རྒྱལ་པོ་ཆེན་པོ་གསལ་རྒྱལ་གྱིས་ཆོ་འཕྲུལ་གྱི་འདུན་ཁང་ཆེན་པོ་བཞེངས་ནས། སྟོན་པ་འཁོར་དང་བཅས་པ་ལ་མཆོད་པའི་ཡོ་བྱད་ཁྱད་པར་དུ་འཕགས་པ་མ་ཚང་བ་མེད་པར་སྦྱར་ཏེ་ཐུབ་དབང་དགུང་ལོ་ང་བདུན་ལ་བབ་པ་དཔྱིད་འབྲིང་ཆོ་འཕྲུལ་ཟླ་བའི་དཀར་ཚེས་དགའ་བ་དང་པོའི་ཉིན་རྒྱལ་པོ་ཆེན་པོ་གསལ་རྒྱལ་གྱིས་སྟོན་པ་འཁོར་དང་བཅས་པ་ལ་བསྙེན་བཀུར་མཛད་པ་ན་སྟོན་པས་ཕྱག་དང་། ཞལ་བསིལ་ནས་ཕྱག་གཡས་པས་ཚེམས་ཤིང་ས་ལ་

བཙུགས་པ་ན། ཆོམས་ཤིང་དེ་སྐད་ཅིག་ཉིད་ལ་དཔག་བསམ་གྱི་ཤིང་ཆེན་པོ་ཡལ་ག་དང་ལོ་མས་ས་དང་བར་སྣང་ཐམས་ཅད་ཁྱབ་པ་འབྲས་བུ་ཕུན་སུམ་ཚོགས་པས་ཡོངས་སུ་གང་བ་ཞིག་ཏུ་གྱུར་ཏེ། འབྲས་བུའི་རོས་ལྷ་མི་ཐམས་ཅད་ཚིམས་པ་དང་དཔག་བསམ་གྱི་ཤིང་དེའི་ཡལ་ག་དང་ལོ་མ་རླུང་གིས་བསྐྱོད་པ་ལས་ཀྱང་ཆོས་ཀྱི་སྒྲ་དབྱངས་བྱུང་བས་ལྷ་མི་བགྲང་བ་ལས་འདས་པ་སྨིན་གྲོལ་ལ་བཀོད་པ་སོགས་ཟླ་བ་དེའི་ཚེས་བཅོ་ལྔའི་བར་ཆོ་འཕྲུལ་ཆེན་པོ་བསམ་གྱིས་མི་ཁྱབ་བརྗོད་ཀྱིས་མི་ལང་བ་བསྟན་ནས་བདུད་དང་མུ་སྟེགས་ཐམས་ཅད་ཕམ་པར་བྱས། འགྲོ་བ་ཐམས་ཅད་ཆོས་ཀྱི་བདུད་རྩིས་ཚིམ་པར་མཛད་དེ་མཉན་ཡོད་ཆོ་འཕྲུལ་ཆེན་པོའི་དུས་ཆེན་ཞེས་སྲིད་གསུམ་སྙན་པའི་གྲགས་པས་ཁྱབ་པར་གྱུར་ཏོ།། [17]

在名为赡部大如意树的美丽地方，在南赡部洲中央，有六座大城，其中有一城名为吉祥殊胜舍卫城（མཉན་ཡོད），城内有一座王宫，国王名为辐飞梵施王（རྩིབས་ཀྱིས་འཕུར་ཚངས་བྱིན）。彼时，兜率天内白幢天子[18]观世间五次，在春季氐宿月[19]十五日白昼摩耶夫人在迦毗罗城（སེར་སྐྱའི་གནས）花园内大无量宫时，安住于摩耶夫人母胎之中，次年翼宿月[20]十五日白昼，从摩耶夫人右肋出生，与此同时，胜光王亦从母胎出生。彼时，由于菩萨（出生）的力量[21]，一切世间光明遍显，十万太阳放大光明，地底之下亦光明遍显，诸天众赞叹吉祥，降下花雨，刹那间一切安住三千大千世间之众生身心安乐，显现出种种不可思议的希有征兆。对此辐飞梵施王心想“因为我这个儿子出生，一切世间大放光明，出现如此希有的征兆”，想到这，于是起了一个符合此祥瑞征象的名字，名为胜光。之后，王子胜光由八个保姆抚养，逐渐长大之后，父王逝去，他就在舍卫城登极，为憍萨罗国(ཀོ་ས་ལ)国王。

菩萨童子一切义成[22]此时也二十九岁了，安住王宫之内，利益无量的天人，之后他出家苦修六年，后在金刚座菩提树前成佛，并为一切天众转大法轮。而胜光王由于一心礼敬如来，不断努力做殊胜的侍奉，并对世尊四众弟子中的每一个，都予以无上的恭敬与照顾。导师能仁王[23]长久安住六大城尤其是舍卫城内，使众生安立于成熟解脱，尤其是以神变的方式开示。彼时，南赡部洲大部

---

17 《法王新胜传 · 法王胜光王传》，ཀ 函第 3 叶正面至第 10 叶背面，故宫博物院藏书。

18 白幢天子（ལྷའི་བུ་དམ་པ་ཏོག་དཀར་པོ），释迦牟尼佛的前世，佛在降生之前为一生补处菩萨，于兜率天说法，号“白幢天子”。

19 氐宿月（ས་ག་ཟླ་བ），藏历四月，藏历四月中氐宿出现，故名氐宿月。

20 翼宿月（དབོ་ཟླ་བ），藏历二月，藏历中正月十六日至二月十五日，望在翼宿，故名翼宿月。

21 这里指释迦牟尼，因为此时没有成佛，仍是菩萨果位，故名菩萨。

22 一切义成（དོན་ཐམས་ཅད་གྲུབ་པ），世尊释迦牟尼之幼名。

23 能仁王（ཐུབ་པའི་དབང་པོ），世尊释迦牟尼之异名。

分的王国境内皆祈请世尊以大神变开示，然而即使是祈请侍奉世尊的要求都没有被应允，世尊说“我知道应该什么时候”，说完开始继续巡游。当世尊来到舍卫城内，法王胜光王亦做了祈请，世尊应允了，于是胜光王准备了用于神变的处所，齐备了世尊和其眷属所需要的殊胜资具。在世尊五十七岁仲春上弦月做威猛神变时的第一个喜日[24]白昼，国王胜光王侍奉了世尊及其眷属，世尊沐洗手脸之后，右手将牙签插入地上，牙签瞬间变成大如意树，地上和空中都遍满枝叶，上结圆满之果，其味道让一切天人意足，且彼如意树枝叶随风摇动，发出阵阵法音，使无量的天人成熟解脱，该月十五日内以种种不可思议不可描述大神变开示完后，世尊又击败了一切魔与外道，使一切众生，意足于法之甘露，这就是闻名于三界之中的舍卫城大神变。

（二）觉方王传

སྟོན་ཡུན་རིན་པོ་ནས་ཐུགས་བསྐྱེད་དེ་རྒྱལ་བའི་བསྟན་པ་ཉམས་པ་གསོ་བའི་སྨོན་ལམ་རླབས་པོ་ཆེའི་མཐུ་གྲུབ་པ་ཞིག་སྟེ། བསམས་བཞིན་དུ་རྒྱལ་པོ་ཧྲཱ་ཙནྡྲའི་ཞང་པོའི་བུར་འཁྲུངས། ནར་སོན་པ་ན་རྒྱ་གར་གྱི་གྲོང་ཁྱེར་ཆེན་པོ་དྲུག་གི་ནང་ནས་ཝཱ་ར་ཎ་སི་ཞེས་བྱ་བ་བསྐལ་བཟང་གི་སངས་རྒྱས་སྟོང་པོ་ཐམས་ཅད་ཀྱིས་གང་དུ་ཐོག་མར་ཆོས་ཀྱི་འཁོར་ལོ་བསྐོར་བ་དང་། བསྐོར་བར་འགྱུར་བའི་གནས་ཁྱད་པར་ཅན་ཞིག་ཡོད་པའི་ཡུལ་ཕྱོགས་དེའི་རྒྱལ་པོར་དབང་བསྐུར་རོ། །དེར་རྒྱལ་པོ་ཧྲཱ་ཙནྡྲ་རྒྱལ་སྲིད་བྱེད་པའི་དུས་སུ་ནུབ་ཕྱོགས་ལ་ཧོར་གྱི་རྒྱལ་པོ་ཁུ་ནི་མ་སྟ་ཞེས་པ་མུ་སྟེགས་ཀྱི་རིག་བྱེད་གསང་བའི་མཐའ་པ་ལ་སོགས་པ་ཏུ་རུ་ཀ་སྟེ་སོག་པོའི་རྒྱལ་རིགས་ཀྱི་རྒྱལ་པོ་ཞིག་དང་། རེས་མཛའ་ཞིང་རེས་འཁྲུག་པ་ལས་མཐར་སྐྱེས་བསྐུར་ཚུལ་ཞིག་ལ་ཡིད་འཕྲོས་ཏེ་སོག་རྒྱལ་དེས་དམག་ཡུལ་དབུས་སུ་དྲངས། རྒྱལ་པོ་ཧྲཱ་ཙནྡྲ་གཡུལ་འཕམ་སྟེ་འབངས་སུ་བསྡུས། སངས་རྒྱས་ཀྱི་བསྟན་པ་ལ་སྤྱི་ཞུ་མ་ཡིན་པས་སྡིག་སྤྱོད་ཚད་མེད་པ་བྱས་ཏེ་སངས་རྒྱས་ཀྱི་བསྟན་པ་ཤིན་ཏུ་ཉམས་དམའ་བར་བྱུང་བ་དང་། མུ་སྟེགས་པའི་སྲུང་པོ་ཞིག་གིས་ཀྱང་ཉི་མ་བསྒྲུབས་ཏེ་གྲུབ་ནས་སངས་རྒྱས་པའི་གཙུག་ལག་ཁང་མང་པོའི་བཀའ་དང་བསྟན་བཅོས་ཀྱི་གླེགས་བམ་མང་པོ་བསྲེགས་ཏེ་སངས་རྒྱས་ཀྱི་བསྟན་པ་ཤིན་ཏུ་ཉམས་དམའ་བར་གྱུར་པ་ན། དེའི་ཚེ་ཧྲཱ་ཙནྡྲའི་ཞང་པོ་རྒྱལ་པོ་སངས་རྒྱས་ཕྱོགས་ཞེས་བྱ་བ། ཡུལ་ཀ་ཤིའམ་ཝཱ་ར་ཎ་སིའི་རྒྱལ་སྲིད་ལ་གནས་པ་དེས་བསྟན་པ་ཉམས་པ་ཐུགས་ཀྱིས་མ་བཟོད་ནས་པཎ་གྲུབ་མཁས་པ་ཐམས་ཅད་བསགས་ཏེ་རྒྱལ་བའི་བསྟན་པ་ཚེས་ཆེར་དར་བར་འགྱུར་བའི་རྟེན་འབྲེལ་སྒོ་དུ་མ་ནས་བསྒྲིགས་ཤིང་།

རང་ཉིད་ཀྱིས་སྟོན་ནས་རྒྱ་ནག་ཏུ་ཐང་བཟན་ཏྲ་ཤང་སོགས་བསྐྱེལ་བའི་གྲོགས་བྱས་ཤིང་། མདོ་སྡེ་སླ་བའི་སློབ་དཔོན་དག་བརྫངས་པའི་རྒྱུ་མཚན་གྱིས་གོང་མ་ཅེའུ་འན་དང་འགྲོགས་བཤེས་སུ་ཡོད་པའི་གང་

24 喜日（དགའ་བ），每月的初一、初六、十一、十六、二十一、二十六日。

ཅིའི་རྒྱ་མཚན་གྱི་ཡི་གེ་དང་བཅས་པོ་ཉ་མངགས་ནས་གྲོས་བྱས་པར། རྒྱ་ནག་གི་རྒྱལ་པོ་ནས་སེམས་གསོ་བའི་ཡི་གེ་བཟང་པོ་དང་གསེར་མི་ཁུར་བརྒྱ་ལ་སོགས་པ་ཕོལ་པོ་སྟོབས་ལྡན་སྟོང་ཕྲག་གིས་ཁུར་བའི་ནོར་བཟང་པོ་དག་སྐྱེ་སུ་བསྐུར་བས་སངས་རྒྱས་ཕྱོགས་ནས་དངོས་པོ་དེ་རྣམས་ཀྱིས་ཤར་དང་། འཕགས་བྱེད་རི་བོའི་ཁོངས་ཀྱི་རྒྱལ་པོ་ཆེན་པོ་རྣམས་དང་བོད་དང་ཉེ་བའི་རི་བྲག་གི་རྒྱལ་པོ་གཏུམ་པོ་དག་དང་། དབུས་ཀྱི་མཆོན་ཆས་འཚོ་བ་ཐམས་ཅད་མགུ་བར་བྱས་ཏེ། ཕྱོགས་གཅིག་ཏུ་བསྒྲིལ་ནས་ཏུ་རུ་ཀའི་རྒྱལ་པོ་དང་གཡུལ་བཀྱེ་སྟེ་རྒྱལ་པོ་ངན་པ་དཔུང་དང་བཅས་པ་ཐལ་བར་བརླག། རང་གི་ཆབ་འབངས་སུ་འཕགས་པའི་ཡུལ་ཕལ་ཆེར་བཙུག་ནས་རྡོ་རྗེ་གདན་སོགས་སུ་ཞིག་གསོ་ཆེར་མཛད། བསྟན་པ་ལ་བསྙེན་བཀུར་ཚད་མེད་པ་བསྒྲུབས་ཤིང་ལྷ་ཁང་ཉམས་པ་ཐམས་ཅད་གསར་དུ་གསོས་དགེ་འདུན་གྱི་སྡེ་ཕྱོགས་མཐའ་དག་ནས་སྤྱན་དྲངས། དཔལ་ན་ལེནྡྲ་ལ་མཆོད་གཞི་རྒྱ་ཆེན་པོ་ཕུལ། རྗེ་བཙུན་འཇམ་པའི་དབྱངས་དངོས་སུ་གྲུབ་པའི་པཎྜི་ཏ་ཆེན་པོ་ཞིག་ཀླ་ཀར་ཁ་ཟུང་སྟེ་སྲི་ཞུ་ཤུ་དུད་ཆེན་པོས་མཆོད་ཅིང་རྒྱལ་བའི་བསྟན་པ་ཆེས་ཆེར་སྤེལ་བར་མཛད་དོ། དེ་ནས་རྒྱལ་པོ་སངས་རྒྱས་ཕྱོགས་ཀྱི་སྐུ་ཚེའི་སྨད་ལ་ཨོ་ཏི་བི་ཤའི་ཡུལ་ཞེས་བྱ་བ་རྒྱ་མཚོ་ཆེན་པོ་དང་ཐག་ཉེ་བ་ཞིག་ཡོད་པ་དེར་རིན་ཆེན་རི་བོའི་གཙུག་ལག་ཁང་ཆེན་པོ་གསར་དུ་བཞེངས་རྒྱལ་བའི་བཀའ་དང་བསྟན་བཅོས་འཕགས་ཡུལ་ན་བཞུགས་པ་ཐམས་ཅད་བསྡུས་ཏེ་ཚར་གསུམ་གསར་དུ་བཞེངས་ཏེ་གཙུག་ལག་ཁང་དེར་བཞུགས་སུ་གསོལ། གཙུག་ལག་ཁང་དེར་མཆོད་གཞི་རྒྱ་ཆེན་པོ་ཕུལ་ཏེ་དགེ་སློང་སྡེ་སྣོད་འཛིན་པ་ལྔ་བརྒྱ་རྒྱུན་དུ་འཚོགས་ཏེ་རྒྱལ་བའི་བསྟན་པ་ཆེས་ཆེར་སྤེལ། ཡང་ཤར་ཕྱོགས་ཀྱི་རྒྱ་མཚོའི་འགྲམ་གྱི་རི་ཆུང་ཞིག་ཏུ་རིན་ཆེན་རི་བོ་དང་འདྲ་བའི་གཙུག་ལག་ཁང་ཆེན་པོ་གསར་དུ་བཞེངས་ཏེ་མཆོད་གཞི་རྒྱ་ཆེན་པོ་བཙུགས། དགེ་འདུན་མང་པོ་སྤྱན་དྲངས་ཏེ་དེར་ཡང་སངས་རྒྱས་ཀྱི་བསྟན་པ་ཆེས་ཆེར་འཕེལ་བར་བྱས་སོ།།[25]

从先前过了很久之后，因为有一个要恢复衰落佛教的发心，且由于这个誓愿的力量，国王达摩旃陀罗（ཧརྨ་ཙནྡྲ）舅父的儿子出生了，其长大后，在印度六大城内，有叫做波罗奈斯（ཝཱ་ར་ཎ་སི）的地方，此地曾是一切贤劫千佛首转、续转法轮之地，他成为此殊胜之地的国王。此地在国王达摩旃陀罗统治时期，其北方有一个叫做苦尼摩多（ཁུ་ནི་མ་སྟ）的大食国王，他信奉边地外道的秘密经典，且是突厥和蒙古人的国王，他与达摩旃陀罗屡战屡和，最后因为一次赠送礼物的事件，心生愤怒，发兵攻打摩揭陀（ཡུལ་དབུས），国王达摩旃陀罗战败，只得归拢残余庶民，由于无人侍奉佛的教法，出现了无数的罪行，佛教也极度衰落了。有一个外道乞丐修行太阳法，他做法烧掉了许多佛教寺庙收藏的经论

25 《法王新胜传 · 觉方王传》，ཀ 函第 2 叶正面至第 7 叶背面，故宫博物院藏书。

典籍，至此，佛教更加衰落了。彼时，达摩旃陀罗舅父的儿子觉方王[26]，统治迦尸城（ཀ་ཤི）和波罗奈斯，面对教法衰落，心不能忍，召集了许多班智达与得道者，世尊的教法又开始广为流行起来。

觉方王之前曾派遣和尚、讲经的阿阇梨以及使臣，带着与汉地交好的文书到达汉地，汉地国王回以抚慰的文书、百人负荷的黄金、千名力士负荷的珍宝，觉方王拿这些珍宝交好东方和皮恰（འབིགས་བྱེད）山区的众国王，以及藏地及其附近的威猛国王们，甚至包括中部的雇佣军队，使他们欢喜，并将他们会聚在一起，发兵与大食国王交战，将这个恶毒的国王和他的军队一并化为灰烬。觉方王将大部分庶民迁入圣地，从新修葺了菩提伽耶金刚座等地方，对教法做了无量的供奉，并将毁坏废弃的寺庙修葺一新，从各处迎请僧众，为吉祥那烂陀寺（ན་ལེནྡྲ）献上大量的供品。他亦尊奉一个具有圣者文殊成就的班智达作为自己的上师，并做了无量的侍奉与礼敬，胜者[27]的教法得到了广大的发展。之后，在觉方王晚年之时，他在欧提毗舍（ཨོ་ཏི་བི་ཤ）邻近大海的地方分三次新建了宝山寺（རིན་ཆེན་རི་བོའི་གཙུག་ལག་ཁང），将其收集的一切经论安放于此，并献上了大量的供奉，不断聚集五百比丘、三藏法师等，使胜者的教法大为增益。其又在东方海边的一个小山上，新修了如同宝山寺一样的寺院，献上了大量的供奉，又迎请了许多僧众，使佛教大为增益。

（三）牟尼赞普传

མུ་ནེ་བཙན་པོ་ནི་རྒྱལ་པོ་ཁྲི་སྲོང་ལྡེ་བཙན་གྱི་སྲས་སུ་ཚུ་མོ་སྟག་གི་ལོ་ཟླ་དམར་དུ་སྐུ་འཁྲུངས། ཆོས་རྒྱལ་ཁྲི་སྲོང་ལྡེ་བཙན་ཞིང་གཤེགས་ནས་རྒྱལ་སྲིད་བཟུང་། བྱང་ཕྱོགས་བོད་ཀྱི་རྒྱལ་ཁམས་ཐམས་ཅད་ལ་དབང་བསྒྱུར། སྐྱེ་འགྲོ་ཐམས་ཅད་དགེ་བ་བཅུའི་ཁྲིམས་ལ་བཀོད། ཡབ་ཆོས་རྒྱལ་ཁྲི་སྲོང་ལྡེ་བཙན་གྱི་དགོངས་པ་ཡོངས་སུ་རྫོགས་པར་བྱ་བའི་ཕྱིར་དང་། སྐྱེ་འགྲོ་ཡོངས་ལ་སྙིང་བརྩེ་བ་ཆེན་པོས་ཀུན་ནས་བསླངས་ཏེ་སྡེ་སྣོད་གསུམ་གྱི་ཆོས་འཁོར་རྒྱ་ཆེན་པོ་བཙུགས། གཙུག་ལག་ཁང་རྒྱ་ཆེན་པོ་སྤེལ། མཆོད་རྟེན་ཆེན་པོ་བཞིའི་གདུགས་དང་། དབུ་རྩེའི་བྱ་འདབ་ལྕགས་ཐག་གིས་སྦྲེལ། དར་པོ་ཆེ་དང་། འཕན་ཆེན་པོ་རྣམས་ཕྱར། མཆོད་པ་དཔག་ཏུ་མེད་པ་ཕུལ་ཏེ། རྒྱལ་པོའི་ཞལ་ནས། ངའི་ཡབ་ཀྱི་གཙུག་ལག་ཁང་འདི་རྣམས་ལ། ཁྱོད་བོད་འབངས་ཐམས་ཅད་ཀྱིས་རྟ་ཕྱུགས་དང་། མཆོན་ཆ་མ་གཏོགས། གཞན་གསེར་དངུལ་གཡུ་མུ་

26 此处藏文作 དྷརྨ་ཙནྡྲའི་ཞང་པོ་སངས་རྒྱས་ཕྱོགས་ཞེས་བྱ་བ། （达摩旃陀罗的舅父觉方王），据文意应为 དྷརྨ་ཙནྡྲའི་ཞང་པོའི་བུ་སངས་རྒྱས་ཕྱོགས་ཞེས་བྱ་བ།（达摩旃陀罗舅父的儿子觉方王），似当据改。

27 胜者（རྒྱལ་བ），佛的异名。

ཏིག་ལ་སོགས་པའི་དངོས་པོ་གང་འདུག་ཕུལ་ཅིག། གསུངས་པས། རྗེའི་བཀའ་བཙན་པས། ལ་ལས་ནི་གསེར་དངུལ་རིན་པོ་ཆེ་མང་པོ་ཕུལ། ལ་ལས་ནི་གཡུ་དང་བེར། དར་ཟབ་ཕུལ། ལ་ལས་ནི་གོས་དང་རྒྱན་ཕུལ། ལ་ལས་ནི་གོས་རྩུལ་པོ་དང་རས་སློག་ལ་སོགས་པ་ཕུལ་བས། རྒྱལ་པོའི་ཞལ་ནས། ཁྱོད་བོད་འབངས་རྣམས་དད་པ་ཆེ་ཆུང་ཁྱད་རེ་ཆེ། ལ་ལས་ནི་ནོར་དཔག་མེད་ཕུལ། ལ་ལས་ནི་རེ་རྩུལ་དང་རས་སློག་མིན་པ་མི་འབུལ་ལོ། ཞེས་གསུངས་པས། བོད་འབངས་རྣམས་ན་རེ། དད་པ་ཆེ་ཆུང་ཡོད་པ་མ་ལགས་ཏེ། ཕྱུག་པོ་རྣམས་ལ་འབུལ་རྒྱུ་ཡོད། དབུལ་པོ་རྣམས་ལ་འབུལ་རྒྱུ་མེད་པས་ལན་ཅེས་ཞུས་པས། རྒྱལ་པོའི་ཞལ་ནས། ངའི་མངའ་འོག་འདིར་མི་རྣམས་ལ་ཕྱོགས་ཕྱུག་ཁྱད་འདི་ཙམ་འོང་བ་མ་འོས་གསུངས་ཏེ། ཕྱོགས་ཕྱུག་ལན་གསུམ་སྙོམས་པས། སླར་ཡང་ཕྱུག་པོ་རྣམས་ནི་སྔར་ལྟར་ཕྱུག །དབུལ་པོ་རྣམས་ནི་སྔར་བཞིན་ཕྱོགས་པས། རྒྱལ་པོའི་ཞལ་ནས། ཕྱོགས་ཕྱུག་ལན་གསུམ་སྙོམས་ཀྱང་སྐྱིད་སྡུག་ལ་ཁྱད་འདི་ཙམ་ཡོང་བ་ཅི་ཡིན་གང་གིས་ལན། ཅེས་གསུངས་པས། མཆོད་གནས་རྣམས་ན་རེ། འདི་དག་ནི་སྔོན་གྱི་སྦྱིན་ཤུགས་ཡིན། ཅེས་ཞུས་པས། ལས་རྒྱུ་འབྲས་ལ་རྒྱལ་པོ་ཐུགས་ཡིད་ཆེས་སོ། དེ་ལྟར་རྒྱལ་པོས་སངས་རྒྱས་ཀྱི་བསྟན་པ་དར་ཞིང་རྒྱས་པར་མཛད་དེ། མཆོད་གནས་རྣམས་དང་རབ་ཏུ་བྱུང་བ་རྣམས་ནི་དབུའི་ལ་ཐོད་བཞིན་ཁུར། འཚོ་བ་བླ་ནས་སྦྱོར། ཆབ་སྲིད་ནི་ཕན་པ་དང་བདེ་བས་བསྐྱངས་སོ། བཙུན་མོ་ཕོ་ཡོང་རྒྱལ་མོ་བཙུན་ཟེར་བ་དེ་ཡབ་རྒྱལ་པོའི་ཡུམ་རྒྱ་མོ་ཟའི་སྐྱིབ་ཡིན་པས། ཡབ་ཐུགས་ལ་འཕྲིང་པར་གྱུར་ཏེ། ཡབ་ཟུར་མཁར་དུ་འབྱོན་དུས་སྲས་ལ་གཏད་གཉེར་མཛད་པས་སྲས་ཀྱིས་ཁབ་ཏུ་བཞེས། ཡབ་རྒྱལ་པོ་གྲོངས་དུས་ཕོ་ཡོང་ཟས་རྒྱན་མ་དཀྱིལ་མྱུ་ངན་མ་བྱས་ཟེར་བ་ལ་སྙད་བཏགས་ནས། ཡུམ་ཚེ་ཡོད་ཟ་ཕྲག་དོག་སྐྱེས་ཏེ་གཤེད་མ་བསྐོས་ནས་གསོད་དུ་བཏང་བས། སྲས་རྒྱལ་པོས་བསྐྱབས་པས་ཡུམ་ལོག་ལྟ་སྐྱེས་ཏེ་སྲས་ལ་གསོལ་ངན་དྲངས་ཏེ། སྲས་རྒྱལ་པོ་མུ་ནེ་བཙན་པོ་ལོ་གཅིག་དང་ཟླ་བ་བདུན་ནམ་དགུ་ལ་རྒྱལ་སྲིད་བཟུང་ནས་ཕོ་བྲང་ཡུམ་བུ་བླ་མཁར་དུ་ཞིང་ལ་གཤེགས་སོ།། [28]

牟尼赞普是国王赤松德赞的儿子，于水虎年（762 年）出生于札玛（བྲག་དམར），法王赤松德赞去世之后接管国政，统治北方一切藏地，并以十善法统治一切庶民，为了圆满父王赤松德赞的心愿，同时也是被对一切众生的大悲心所激励，他建立了广大的三藏法轮，增益了广大寺庙，将四大佛塔的华盖与顶端的飞檐用铁索相连，并竖起大旗、大幡，献上无量的供奉。他下令："对于我父王的这些寺庙，你们藏民要献上除牛马武器之外的金、银、玉、珍珠等等的珠宝"，由于国王严格的敕令，一些人献了许多金银珍宝，一些人献了绿松石和绸缎，一些人献了衣物和饰品，一些人献了破烂衣服和布皮等等，国王说："你们这些藏民信仰差别太大了，一些人献无数珍宝，一些人却是非破烂衣袄不献"，藏民们回答："不是因为信仰有大小，而是富人们有可献的财物，穷人们却无财可献"。国王说；"在我的治下不应该出现这样的贫富差别"，于

28 《法王新胜传 · 牟尼赞普传》，ང 函第 6 叶正面至第 11 叶正面，故宫博物院藏书。

是三次平均贫富，之后富人却又像以前一样富有，穷人像之前一样贫穷。国王说："已经三次平均了贫富，为什么在生计上又出现了差别？" 僧众们答："这是因为之前布施的业力不同"。于是国王开始相信因果。如彼，国王使佛教广为流传起来，对于僧众和出家人，也如同携带头巾一样，负担起了僧人的开支，国政也一直饶益安乐。

妃子波雍嘉摩尊（པོ་ཡོང་རྒྱལ་མོ་བཙུན）是父王母亲嘉摩萨（རྒྱ་མོ་ཟ）的转世，父王心中很惦念她，在其往生天界之时，将她托付给了儿子牟尼赞普，牟尼赞普也应允了。据说在父王去世之后，波雍美食不停，妆容不卸，且无有悲伤，赞普母亲蔡邦萨心生妒恨，任命刑吏前去杀之，因国王保护而未果，于是心生邪见，送上了有毒的食物，牟尼赞普持执国政一年又七个月或九个月后，逝于雍布王宫上师城（པོ་བྲང་ཡུམ་བུ་བླ་མ་མཁར）。

（四）忽必烈薛禅汗传

ཆིང་གེའི་རྒྱལ་པོའི་སྲས་བདུན་ཡོད་པ་ལས་བཙུན་མོ་དམ་པའི་སྲས་བཞི་པ་ཐོ་ལོའི་ཞེས་པའི་སྲས་ཤིང་ཕག་ལོ་པ་སའི་དབང་ཕྱུག་ཆེན་པོ་ཧུ་པི་ལིའི་སེ་ཆེན་ལྷུགས་སྐྱེ་ལོར་རྒྱལ་སར་འཁོད་དེ་ཤིང་སྟག་ལ་འཛང་ཡུལ་དམག་གིས་བླངས་པ་སོགས་ལྷུགས་ལུག་གི་བར་དུ་རྒྱ་བོད་ཧོར་གསུམ་སོགས་ལ་མངའ་བསྒྱུར་ནས། པེ་ཅིང་། ཆ་ཏན། ཁུ་ར། ཐུ་ལང་ཐེད་ཅེས་པའི་མཁར་ཆེན་བཞི་བརྩིགས་ཤིང་ས་སྐྱ་འཕགས་པ་བློ་གྲོས་རྒྱལ་མཚན་དང་མཆོད་ཡོན་དུ་གྱུར་ཏེ། རབ་བྱུང་ལྔ་པའི་མེ་སྤྲེལ་བར་དུ་བསྟན་པའི་གདུགས་དཀར་སྲིད་རྩེའི་བར་དུ་བསྒྲེང་ཞིང་རྒྱལ་སྲིད་ཀྱི་ཆར་སྤྲིན་སྟུག་པོས་འཛམ་གླིང་གི་ཁྱོན་ཕལ་ཆེར་ཁེབས་པར་མཛད་པའི་སྙན་གྲགས་ཀྱི་དབྱར་རྔ་འབྲུམ་གྱིས་ས་སྟེང་ཁྱབ་པར་མཛད་པའི་ཞུ་ནས་བློན་འབངས་ཀྱི་དོན་འཛིན་ལ་བྱམས་བརྩེ་བྱ་དགའ་སོགས་ཀྱི་སྦྱིན་བཅུད་གཆྭའི་རྒྱུན་མཚུངས་སྐྱུལ་བས་ཕན་བདེའི་དགའ་སྟོན་གྱི་འབྲས་བུ་བཟང་པོ་རྒྱ་ཆེར་སྨིན་པར་གྱུར་ཏོ།། ཆིང་གེས་རྒྱལ་པོ་ནས་འདི་ཉིད་ཀྱི་བར་ལ་རིམ་གྱིས་ཐོབ་པའི་མི་སྡེ་ནི་སོག་པོ་སྔོན་པོ་མི་ཁྲིམ་བཞི་འབུམ་ལྷག་དང་། རྒྱ་དམར་པོ། བོད་ནག་པོ། སར་ཐ་གོལ་སེར་པོ། སོ་ལོན་གོས་དཀར་པོ་སྟེ། རང་གི་སྡེ་རིགས་མི་ཁ་དོག་ལྔ་དང་ཙུག་ཏེ་བུ་མོ་གཡོན་ཏུ་བྲང་མིག་ཅན་ཁྲི་མགོ་ཅན་ཏེ། གཞན་སྡེ་རིགས་བཞི་དང་། ཡང་དབྱིབས་དང་བྱ་སྤྱོད་གོས་སོགས་གཏན་ནས་མི་འདྲ་བའི་མི་རིགས་བདུན་ཅུ་ལྷག་ཡོད་ཟེར་ལ། ས་ཆ་ཡང་ནུབ་བྱང་ཕྱོགས་ཐོར་གོད་ཀྱི་རྒྱབ་ན་ཡོད་པའི་ཁིན་ཚའམ་སོག་སྐད་དུ་ཁེམ་ཁེམ་ཆེ་ཟེར་བ་དབྱར་ཉི་རིང་པོའི་མཚན་ཤིན་ཏུ་ཐུང་བར་གྲགས་པ་ནས་བཟུང་ཤར་དང་ལྷོའི་གླིང་ཕྲན་གོའི་ལི་མན་ཧུ་དང་རྒྱ་མཚོའི་གླིང་བ་གཞི་བེན་དང་ཟླ་བང་དང་། སི་ཡན་ལོ་དང་། སི་ཡན་སོགས་དང་། ནུབ་ཀྱི་རྒྱ་གར་ཕྱེད་དང་ཁ་ཆེའི་མཐའ་ཚུན་ཆད་དོ། ཆོས་ཀྱི་རྒྱལ་པོ་འདི་ཉིད་ཀྱིས་སྐྱེ་འགྲོ་ཐམས་ཅད་ལ་ཕན་བདེ་མ་ལུས་པ་འབྱུང་བའི་རྩ་བ་སངས་རྒྱས་ཀྱི་བསྟན་པ་རིན་པོ་ཆེ་རྒྱ་ཆེར་སྤེལ་བར་མཛད་ནས་བསྟན་པ་བསྟན་འཛིན་དང་བཅས་པ་ལ་གུས་པས་མཆོད་ཅིང་བསྙེན་བཀུར་བསམ་གྱིས་མི་ཁྱབ་པ་མཛད་ཞེས་གྲགས་

སོ།།[29]

成吉思汗王（ཆིང་གེའི་རྒྱལ་པོ）的七个儿子中，与正妻皇后所生的第四子，名曰托雷（ཐོ་ལོའི），大王忽必烈薛禅汗正是他的儿子。忽必烈生于木猪年（1215年），于铁猴年（1260年）称帝，自木虎年（1254年）率兵攻占绛域（ལྗང་ཡུལ）到铁羊年（1271年）间，他统治管辖汉、藏、蒙等民族，建立了北京（ཏེ་ཙང）、恰罕（ཆ་ཏན）、库热（ཁུ་ར）和图朗提（ཐུ་ལང་ཐིད）四座大城，并与萨迦派的八思巴罗珠坚赞（འཕགས་པ་བློ་གྲོས་རྒྱལ་མཚན）建立了供施关系，到第五饶迥[30]的火猴年（1296年）间，将教法的白伞升至有顶[31]之间，使王政之稠密雨云遮盖了大部分世间，其声名如雷，响彻大地，为大地上的臣民，降下如恒河一般的慈悲与恩惠之雨，并成熟了利乐喜宴之殊胜果。自成吉思汗到忽必烈统治期间，次第统治的百姓有蓝衣蒙古人超过四十万户，红衣服的汉人，黑衣服的藏族人，黄衣服的萨尔塔郭人（སར་ཐ་གོལ），白衣服的索伦人（སོ་ལོན）五大类，其它还有四种民族以及相貌、风俗、衣着完全不同的民族超过七十种。统治的疆域西北方远到吐尔扈特的背部有一个叫金恰（ཁིན་ཆ）蒙古语叫做肯肯恰（ཁེམ་ཁེམ་ཆ）的地方，其地在夏季白昼很长，夜晚很短。东方和南方远至小岛郭里满珠（གོའི་ལི་མན་ཧུ）和海岛西潘（གཞི་བེན）、普旁（ཕུ་བང）、时延罗（སི་ཡན་ལོ）和时延索（སི་ཡན་སོག），西边占有印度一半的领土以及克什米尔边境以内的所有地方。法王忽必烈利乐了一切众生，广大弘扬了珍贵的教法，礼敬佛教与佛教徒，并做了种种不可思议的供奉与侍奉。

综合以上四位法王的传记，可以清楚地勾勒出一位转轮圣王的形象，它反映了佛教徒对于世俗权利的期待，在这个构建出来的本生系统中，乾隆皇帝的前世因缘被追溯到了胜光王，他与佛同一天出生，是佛陀时代佛的重要施主；他又是觉方王，在佛教衰落时期，击败了支持外道的国王，重新振兴了已经衰落的佛教；他是牟尼赞普，藏人的法王，以十善教法统治庶民，他又是忽必烈薛禅汗，是蒙古人的法王，在辽阔的疆域内，弘扬教法，使治下的一切百姓都能享受教法的利乐。对于乾隆皇帝来说，作为文殊菩萨化身的转轮圣王，他从佛陀时代就已经是教法的守护者，又在佛教衰败的时候力挽狂澜，

29 《法王新胜传 · 忽必烈传》，ཉ 函第 2 叶背面至第 5 叶背面，故宫博物院藏书。

30 饶迥（རབ་བྱུང），藏历以 1027 年为起算点，每六十年为一个饶迥。

31 有顶（སྲིད་རྩེ），天名，即色究竟天，因处于有形世界的最高处，故称有顶。

理应受到佛教徒的顶礼膜拜，他前生是藏族人、蒙古人的法王，因此在现世中，无论是作为护持佛教的法王，还是大一统下的封建皇帝，都具有了宗教上和政治上的正当性。

四、小结

《法王新胜传》是六世班禅在热河陛见乾隆皇帝时特为乾隆皇帝所作的本生故事集。这本书通过构建出一套转世体系，使封建皇权结合宗教影响，一定程度上掌握了宗教上的话语权，而宗教也依附着皇权扩大了自己的影响。在这套传记中，乾隆皇帝前世作为护持佛教的国王，作为得道的大成就者，作为噶当派与格鲁派的著名上师，构建出了一个复杂的宗教形象，背后有其深刻的政治考量，也一定程度上反映了乾隆皇帝个人的宗教兴趣，而佛教徒也借助这样一套叙事逻辑，扩大了自己派别的影响。

◆ 李若愚　故宫博物院图书馆馆员

The Tradition of the Garbha-maṇḍala in Tibet and Its Sand Maṇḍala Creation

TANAKA Kimiaki

Abstract: The Ryōkai Maṇḍalas (两界曼荼罗) that were transmitted to Japan from Tang China at the beginning of the ninth century not only constituted the core of Buddhist icons in Japan, but they also had an influence on the entire culture of Japan as well. Of the two Maṇḍalas, sources related to the Vajradhātu (金 刚 界) Maṇḍala are relatively abundant as its original form in India and documentary records and drawings in Nepal and China's Tibet, where the Maṇḍalas were inherited, have been preserved. However, as far as the Garbha (胎藏) Maṇḍala is concerned, there is very little documentation left today as esoteric Buddhism based on the *Vairocanābhisambodhisūtr*a (大日经) waned in India quite early. Still, it is known that the *Vairocanābhisambodhisūtra* was transmitted from India to Tibet during the Tufan (吐蕃) era, and although they are very rare, there are still examples of the Garbha Maṇḍala in Tibet.

In this paper, I will attempt to shed light on the creation of sand Maṇḍalas of the Garbha Mandala in Amdo, making comparisons with the Sino-Japanese tradition of the Garbha Mandala and outlining their characteristics, mainly on the basis of fieldwork undertaken in 2014 and 2015 at Rwa rgya and Bya kyung monasteries.

I. Introduction:

I previously surveyed the tradition and extant examples of the Garbha-maṇḍala in Tibet on the occasion of an international symposium held at the International Research Center for Japanese Studies (国际日本文化研究中心), Kyoto, in 2001[1] (in Japanese) and at the 10th seminar of the International Association for Tibetan Studies held in Oxford in 2003[2] (in English). However, at that time, due to poor road access, I had been unable to visit Rwa rgya (拉加寺) and Bya khyung (夏琼寺) monasteries in Amdo, both of which still create sand maṇḍalas of the Garbha-maṇḍala nearly every year, although I had already acquired several source materials on the Garbha-maṇḍala originating in Bla brang and Rwa rgya monasteries for the restoration of the Tibetan version of the Ryōkai Maṇḍalas that was undertaken between 1994 and 1996 at Toga (利贺) Meditation Museum[3] in Toyama Prefecture, Japan, where I was working as the chief curator. However, the greatly improved road access in Amdo in recent years has made it possible for a foreign scholar like myself to visit and undertake fieldwork at these monasteries.

In this paper, I will attempt to shed light on the creation of sand maṇḍalas of the Garbha-maṇḍala in Amdo, making comparisons with the Sino-Japanese tradition of the Garbha-maṇḍala and outlining their characteristics, mainly on the basis of fieldwork undertaken in 2014 and 2015 at Rwa rgya and Bya khyung monasteries.

II. Rwa rgya Monastery:

Rwa rgya monastery lies in Rgyun mgo county (军功县), Mgo log Tibetan autonomous prefecture (果洛藏族自治州), in Qinghai province. On the opposite shore of the Yellow river is the town of Rgyun-mgo, and it takes 6-7 hours from Xining to Rgyun mgo by bus.

According to the *Yul mgo-logs lo rgyus deb ther padma dkar po'i chun po*,[4] this monastery

1 Tanaka, "Chibetto ni okeru Taizō Dainichi nyorai to Taizō mandara no denshō to sakurei ni tsuite" チベットにおける胎蔵大日如来と胎蔵曼荼羅の伝承と作例について [Materials concerning the Vairocanābhisambodhisūtra (*Dainichikyō*) and the Garbha (Taizō) maṇḍala in Tibet]. In *Seinaru mono no katachi to ba* 聖なるものの形と場 [Figures and places of the sacred], Kyoto: Kokusai Nihon Bunka Kenkyū Sentā 国際日本文化研究センター (International Research Center for Japanese Studies), 2003: 39-52.

2 Tanaka, "On the Tradition of the *Vairocanābhisambodhi-sūtra* and the Garbhamaṇḍala in Tibet." In *Proceedings of the Tenth Seminar of the IATS, 2003. Volume 13: Art in Tibet*. Leiden: Brill, 2011: 193-201.

3 The Toga Meditation Museum 瞑想の郷 is the unique theme park focussed on Tibeto-Nepalese Buddhist art inaugurated by local goverment in Japan. Now this museum is managed by a quasi-public corporation named Toga Furusato Foundation.

4 Don grub dbang rgyal & Nor sde, *Yul mgo logs lo rgyus deb ther padma dkar po'i chun po* 果洛史要 , Zi ling: Tsho sngon mi rigs dpe skrun khang 西宁：青海民族出版社 , 1992.

was established in 1769 by A rig dge bshes, Rgyal mtshan 'od zer. He later entrusted the monastery to Shing bza' paṇḍita, Blo bzang dar rgyas rgya mtsho. Shing bza' paṇḍita enlarged the monastery, and his incarnations, known as Shing bza' rin po che, have been extremely influential lamas not only in this monastery but also among the Dge lugs pas in Amdo.

In March to April 2014, I visited Rwa rgya monastery for the first time. The monastery is said to transmit 17 kinds of sand maṇḍalas. These are: 1. Kāyavākcitta-pariniṣpanna-Kālacakra-maṇḍala, 2. Vairocanābhisambodhi-maṇḍala, 3. 13-deity Vajrabhairava-maṇḍala, 4. Sarvavid-Vairocana-maṇḍala, 5. Ṣoḍaśabindu-maṇḍala, 6. Mahācakra-Vajrapāṇi-maṇḍala, 7. Sitātapatrā-maṇḍala, 8. 13-deity Akṣobhya-maṇḍala, 9. 9-deity Amitāyus-maṇḍala, 10. Hayagrīva (Rta-mgrin yang gsang) maṇḍala, 11. Guhyasamāja-Akṣobhya-maṇḍala, 12. 62-deity Cakrasaṃvara-maṇḍala, 13. 9-deity Hevajra-maṇḍala, 14. Vajradhātu-maṇḍala, 15. Jinasāgara-maṇḍala, 16. Single-deity Vajrabhairava-maṇḍala, and 17. Maṇḍala of *Bhaiṣajyaguru-sūtra* rite.

At the maṇḍala festival (*dkyil 'khor sgrub mchod chen mo*), 15 of the 17 maṇḍalas were created concurrently at the three colleges, the assembly hall (*tshogs chen*), and the Hayagrīva chapel. According to Rev. Dge 'dun bsod pa, the superintendent lama (*dbu mdzad*) of the Medical College (Sman pa gra tshang), the two remaining maṇḍalas (16. Single-deity Vajrabhairava-maṇḍala and 17. Maṇḍala of *Bhaiṣajyaguru sūtra* rite) are created on the occasion of the New Year ceremony (see Table 1).

Table 1 Rwa rgya Monastery's 17 Repertoires of Sand Maṇḍala

			VA	Mitra	Ngor
Kālacakra-college	1 F	1. Kāyavākcitta-pariniṣpanna-Kālacakra-maṇḍala	36		97
	2 F	2. Garbha-maṇḍala			20
Assembly Hall	1 F	3. 13-deity Vajrabhairava-maṇḍala			139
		4. Sarvavid-Vairocana-maṇḍala		23	27
		5. Ṣoḍaśabindu-maṇḍala			127
		6. Mahācakra-Vajrapāṇi-maṇḍala		46	46
		7. Sitātapatrā-maṇḍala		3	
	2 F	8. 13-deity Akṣobhya-maṇḍala		21	(14)
		9. 9-deity Amitāyus-maṇḍala			10
Hayagrīva chapel		10. Rta mgrin yang gsang maṇḍala			

Tantric college	1 F	11. Guhyasamāja-Akṣobhya-maṇḍala	2		137
		12. 62-deity Cakrasaṃvara-maṇḍala	19		138
	2 F	13. 9-deity Hevajra-maṇḍala	5		99
Medical college		14. Vajradhātu-maṇḍala	37	22	
		15. Jinasāgara-maṇḍala		62	
Not created		16. Single-deity Vajrabhairava-maṇḍala			(59)
		17. Maṇḍala of Bhaiṣajyaguru-sūtra rite			

*VA: *Vajrāvalī*; Mitra: Mitrayogin's 108 Maṇḍalas; Ngor: The Ngor Maṇḍalas of Tibet.

It was difficult to investigate the creation of all the sand maṇḍalas at the same time, and so I focused mainly on the Garbha-maṇḍala created on the second floor of the Kālacakra College. However, when I arrived at Rwa rgya in 2014, the sand maṇḍala creation had already started, and I was unable to witness the preliminary practice and the measuring of the maṇḍala by means of a marking thread (*thig gdab pa*), which is important for the study of the iconometry of the maṇḍala.

Therefore, I revisited Rwa rgya in April 2015 and investigated the measuring of the Garbha-maṇḍala and Vajradhātu-maṇḍala because the iconometry of the Guhyasamāja-Akṣobhya-, Vajrabhairava-, and Cakrasaṃvara-maṇḍalas and other maṇḍalas has already been surveyed in several previous studies.[5]

III. Garbha-maṇḍala of Rwa rgya Monastery:

As I have made clear in previous studies,[6] most examples of the Tibetan Garbha-maṇḍala consist of 122 deities. This is about one-third of the deities in the Garbha-maṇḍala of the Sino-Japanese tradition, which depicts about 414 deities. The number and arrangement of the deities of the sand maṇḍala created at Rwa rgya monastery coincide with the norms of the Garbha-maṇḍala in Tibetan Buddhism (Fig. 1).

Vairocanābhisambodhi, the main deity of the maṇḍala, and Śākyamuni, the principal deity

5 Regarding the iconometry of three major maṇḍalas of Dge lugs pa order, see *The Creation of Maṇḍalas*, Tibetan texts detailing the techinques for laying out and executing tantric Buddhist psychocosmograms by Rong tha Blo bzang dam chos rgya mtsho, 3 vols. New Delhi, 1971-73.

6 Tanaka, *Indo Chibetto mandara no kenkyū* インド・チベット曼荼羅の研究 [Studies in the Indo-Tibetan maṇḍala]. Kyoto: Hōzōkan 法藏館 , 1996: 46-65.

Fig.1 Garbha-maṇḍala in Rwa rgya monastery (2014).

of the second square, are depicted in human form, whereas the other deities are all represented by symbols (*samaya-mudrā*).

Generally speaking, in Tibet the four buddhas and four bodhisattvas of the Garbha-maṇḍala are not depicted on the eight lotus petals of the central lotus. However, the Rwa rgya version depicts the four buddhas of the Garbha-maṇḍala on both sides of the maṇḍala gates between the wish-fulfilling trees (*kalpatarus*) sprouting from vases and banners placed on the roof of the maṇḍala pavilion. Their iconography is as follows: Ratnaketu (red) in the east displays the *dhyāna-mudrā*, Saṃkusumitarājendra (yellow) in the south displays the *varada-mudrā*, Amitābha (green) in the west displays the abhaya-mudrā, and Dundubhisvara (blue) in the north displays the *bhūmisparśa-mudrā*. In this case, the mudrās of the four buddhas seem to have been determined in accordance with their body colour and the colour scheme of the courtyard of the maṇḍala.[7]

Deities who do not have any attributes in their hands are represented only by their seats and

7 Regarding the body colour of the four Buddhas and the colour scheme of the courtyard of the Garbha-maṇḍala, see Tanaka, Indo ni okeru mandara no seiritsu to hatten インドにおける曼荼羅の成立と発展 [Genesis and development of the maṇḍala in India]. Tokyo: Shunjūsha 春秋社, 2010: 448-455.

Fig. 2 Thangka of the Garbha-maṇḍala in Bla brang monastery.

circles, whereas the Sino-Japanese Garbha-maṇḍala depicts their hand gestures (mudrā) as their symbols. In the sand maṇḍala of Rwa rgya the twelve *vajradhara*s, attendant deities of Vajrapāṇi who are depicted in the western sector of the first square in the Ngor, Lokesh Chandra, Rossi and Rossi,[8] and Bla brang (Fig. 2) versions, are arranged in the southern sector, namely, in the sector of the Vajra family. This coincides with a thang-ka in the possession of Tateyama Museum (立山

8 Rossi, Anna Maria, and Fabio Rossi, *Tibetan Painted Maṇḍalas*. London: Rossi & Rossi, 1993, plate "Abhisaṃbodhi Vairocana Mandala."

Fig.3 Maṇḍala drawn on cotton cloth at Rwa rgya monastery.

博物館) and a maṇḍala drawn on cotton cloth at Rwa rgya monastery (Fig. 3).

One of the characteristics of the Garbha-maṇḍala of Rwa rgya monastery is its size. Since the exhibition "Mandara no shutsugen to shōmetsu" (Maṇḍala: Now You See, Now You Don't) held at Seibu Museum in 1980, where a Tibetan sand maṇḍala was publicly shown in Japan for the first time, many Tibetan refugees have been invited to Japan to create sand maṇḍalas on the occasion of exhibitions on Tibet or lectures by Tibetan lamas. However, the size of the maṇḍalas created on such occasions is about 1-1.2 m in diameter because the number of people invited and the time for producing the maṇḍala are limited. The sand maṇḍala created at Rwa rgya, on the other hand, is as much as 3.55 m in diameter, which is nearly three times as large as maṇḍalas created by Tibetan refugees invited to Japan. Therefore, the resolution of the sand maṇḍala is very high, and even minute parts can be clearly represented.

Another unique aspect of the Garbha-maṇḍala is its iconometry. According to the commentary on the *Vairocanābhisambodhi-sūtra* by Buddhaguhya, the Garbha-maṇḍala has a threefold structure, and the area of these three squares should be equal. Therefore, the ratio of one side of each of the three squares should be 1:√2: √3. However, it is not possible to calculate square roots such as √2 or √3 by means of a compass and the grid pattern drawn with a marking thread. How to calculate the square root with a grid pattern and compass was an interesting problem for me.[9] However, I noticed that monks belonging to Kālacakra College used a special measuring tape for drawing the inner squares, ignoring the grid pattern of the outer square, which was a little disappointing to me. This may be a convention (*lag len*) of sand maṇḍala creation at this monastery.

IV. Garbha-maṇḍala Created at Bya khyung Monastery:

Bya khyung monastery (夏琼寺) lies in Hualong Hui autonomous county (化隆回族自治县) in Qinghai province. It is famous because Tsong kha pa spent his boyhood here as a novice under his tutor, Don grub rin chen. Unfortunately, no cultural heritage remains since this monastery was destroyed during 1970s.

Eight kinds of sand maṇḍalas are transmitted at this monastery. These are: 1. Guhyasamāja-Akṣobhya-maṇḍala, 2. Cakrasaṃvara-maṇḍala, and 3. Vajrabhairava-maṇḍala in the Tantric College (Rgyud-pa grva-tshang); 4. Kālacakra-maṇḍala, 5. 51-deity Bhaiṣajyaguru-maṇḍala, and 6. Sarvavid-Vairocana-maṇḍala in the Kālacakra College (Dus 'khor grva tshang); and 7. Garbha-maṇḍala and 8. Vajrabhairava-maṇḍala in the Abhisambodhi College (Mngon byang grva tshang).

Among these, the Abhisambodhi College was founded after the Cultural Revolution by Tshe tan Zhabs drung (1911-86), a renowned historian, and the tradition of the Garbha-maṇḍala is said to have been transmitted from Rwa rgya monastery. When I visited Bya khyung in April 2015, the creation of the sand maṇḍalas had not yet started. However, I obtained a photograph of the Garbha-maṇḍala created in 2013 from a temple monk (Fig. 4).

9 Regarding the iconometry of the Garbha-maṇḍala of Rwa rgya, I read a paper on occasion of the conference of the Association for the Study of Buddhist Iconography 密教図像学会 held at National Research Institute for Cultural Properties, Tokyo 東京文化財研究所 in 2015. See Kimiaki TANAKA "The Iconometry and Arrangement of Deities of the Tibetan Garbha-maṇḍala." In *The Mikkyō Zuzō* (密教図像), Vol.35, 2016.

Fig. 4 Garbha-maṇḍala in Bya khyung monastery (2013).

In contrast to the Rwa rgya version, the Bya khyung version represents all the deities as symbols. The four buddhas of the Garbha-maṇḍala are not depicted on the roof of the maṇḍala pavilion. The most puzzling point is that the twelve *vajradhara*s depicted on the west side of the southern sector in the Rwa rgya version and other versions are depicted on the east side of the southern sector, contrary to convention. This is difficult to explain if the tradition of the Garbha-maṇḍala of Bya khyung was, as is generally claimed, transmitted from Rwa rgya monastery in recent years.

V. Conclusion:

In this paper, I have attempted to shed light on the creation of sand maṇḍalas of the Garbha-maṇḍala by making comparisons with the different iconographic versions found in Tibet and outlining their characteristics as found in two monasteries in Amdo, Rwa rgya and Bya khyung. The *Vairocanābhisambodhi-sūtra*, which once flourished on Indian soil, had been neglected by

Indian and western scholars until a couple of decades ago because it fell into decline after the 9th century. I believe that the study of the *Vairocanābhisambodhi-sūtra* and Garbha-maṇḍala in Amdo is of considerable importance not only for gaining a deeper understanding of Tibetan Buddhism, but also for obtaining further insights into the historical development of the maṇḍala in general.

◆ Author: TANAKA Kimiaki, the Nakamura Hajime Eastern Institute, Japan.

Abstracts

尼泊尔上穆斯塘地区桑宗墓地所见苯教施垛仪轨的考古学证据

马克·奥登德弗

（美国加利福尼亚大学人类学与遗产研究系）

在考古发掘中，发现确凿清晰的有关古代仪式方面的证据一向是很困难的。但也有例外，比如我们在尼泊尔穆斯塘北部地区发掘的古代墓葬，其中所出一系列遗物很可能属于所谓的苯教施垛（Mdos rgyab）仪式。公元 5 世纪晚期的桑宗 5 号墓中，我们发现了铁三脚架、铜容器及木杯和竹杯子，这一套器物与民族志描述的有关苯教施垛仪式中所用的道具惊人地相似。本文解释了何为苯教的施垛仪式，并且依据桑宗 5 号墓的墓葬背景和出土的人工制品，可认为至少在公元 5 世纪苯教已见于穆斯塘北部。

羊距骨：西藏最古老的博具和占卜工具的考古学和民族史初探

约翰·文森特·贝勒扎
（美国弗吉尼亚大学）

本文旨在通过考古学和民族史的证据，对藏族文化中流行的一种物件——“羊距骨”做综合性考察。首先提出了鉴别墓葬中那些具有文化意义羊距骨的标准，并比较了欧亚大陆其他地区同类实例。本文特别关注到一件西藏的红铜合金的羊距骨，这为讨论该类物品在高原古代文化中的意义提供了佐证。文本还讨论了羊距骨在藏族博具、占卜、计数及其他仪式、观念中的作用。最后，本文聚焦羊距骨的跨文化意义，尝试说明羊距骨能够帮助我们进一步理解史前晚期（约公元前1200年至公元600年）及历史时期欧亚大陆跨文化交流的一些面貌。

Re-examination of Materials about the Communications between Nepal and China in the Early Tang Dynasty

Wang Bangwei
(Peking University)

The Bod-Balpo Ancient Road has a long history, which can be traced back to the Paleolithic Age on the basis of archaeological discoveries. As for the history of the Bod-Balpo Ancient Road, we can distinguish three periods, namely, pre-, during, and post-Tang dynasty to the Qing dynasty. In the specific case of the Bod-Balpo Ancient Road, we need to consider the situation of East Asia, South Asia and even Central Asia at that time, the chronological order of the literary records and the recent archaeological discoveries. In the meantime, although many researchers have noticed and quoted the literary records on the Bod-Balpo Ancient Road, there are still some problems that require further studies. In addition, we also should pay attention to the relationship between the Buddhist monks and diplomatic envoys and merchants, they always traveled together at that time. In fact, the routes taken by Buddhist monks coincide with those taken by commerce.

在河西走廊和西藏发现的不空之影响

尤利·霍赫洛夫
（英国独立学者）

本文分析了莫高窟和榆林窟被认为是受到吐蕃影响的早期藏传佛教艺术遗存。与此观点相反，本文认为这些图像实际上是受到了南印度艺术的影响，尤其是泰米尔纳德帕拉瓦王国艺术的影响，这与8世纪上半叶来自帕拉瓦王国的著名佛教大师金刚智在中国的传法密切相关，更与不空8世纪中叶在河西的活动有关。这些图像属于金刚智所创造的一种独特艺术传统，他也是一位伟大的画家。吐蕃统治时期的艺术只是吐蕃占领河西以前已经存在的艺术和宗教传统的继续延续而已。不仅如此，吐蕃控制河西走廊使得吐蕃能够移植当时当地流行的宗教和艺术潮流。因此，吐蕃将佛教作为国教正是基于不空在唐代所提出的以佛法护国的模式，本文支持这一理论。

A Preliminary Survey on *Mthing shog* Manuscripts

Zhu Lishuang
(Center for Dunhuang Studies, Lanzhou University)

Mthing shog, translated as blue-black paper 蓝 黑 纸 in Tibetan-Chinese dictionaries, is a kind of colored paper that we find in Tibetan culture. Its production covers three steps: 1) several layers of papers are laminated with a wheat paste; 2) a specially made coloring material is applied to the surface of the paper; and 3) the paper is burnished with a *gzi* bead or a smooth piece of conch shell or other smooth and hard precious stones. The recipes and substances of making coloring materials for *mthing shog* vary. For instance, one formula uses black ink, which is made from soot (*sre nag*) or burnt resinous pine wood (*sgron shing*), which is mixed with yak and/or sheep brains; one formula uses a mixture consisting of black vitriol (*nag mtshur*), euphorbia (*thar nu*), borax (*tsa la*), wheat beer (*gro chang*), and myrobalan (*a ru ra*); one formula uses a solution made with ground white cowry shell (*'gron bu*), ground cardamom (*dzā ti*) and myrobalan juice; one formula uses indigo (*rams*).

Judging from literary sources and extant objects, the expression *mthing shog* derives from *shug bu mthing ga* of the Tibetan dynastic period. It is *mthing shog* that was used for writing royal edicts. Beginning from the 10th century, *mthing shog* is most often used to write Buddhist sutras. The most prized manuscripts frequently use gold ink or a combination of gold and silver ink. The main purpose of preparing *mthing shog* manuscripts is for devotional purposes. These are deposited in shrines and monasteries and prepared for the accumulation of merit; they are not intended for circulation.

Chinese scholars often term the black-blue paper of Tibetan cultural tradition as 瓷/磁青纸, "porcelain green paper," an indigo-dyed paper in Chinese culture. However, as mentioned above, there are many different materials that are used to make *mthing shog*. *Mthing shog* includes indigo-dyed paper, but they are not identical. The gold or/and silver manuscripts produced in China proper, especially those in the Ming and Qing courts, may be written on indigo-dyed paper or *mthing shog*. As for gold or/and silver manuscripts from the Tibetan cultural area, the situation is more complicated, and it seems that not all gold or/and silver texts are written on *mthing shog*.

An Interpretation of the Mural of Lce btsun Shes rab 'byung gnas in Zhwa lu Monastery

Jia Yuping

(Collage of Art and Design, Chengdu University)

This paper discusses the mural depicting Lce bstun Shes rab 'byung gnas (the 11th century founder of Zhwa lu) in the Sgo gsum ma lha khang of Zhwa lu monastery. The history of the monastery and the Lce clan from the 11th to the 14th century are fully presented through the images and inscriptions in a series of murals. Combining the literature on the genealogies of Zhwa lu and related Tibetan sources, this paper discusses some stories about Zhwa lu that were hitherto not well known. These include aspects of its religious background and its connections with the Indian subcontinent, as well as its contact with western Tibet during the period of the second diffusion of Buddhism. Its governance through a combination of politics and religion makes Zhwa lu one of the earliest monasteries that was under the control of a family-owned theocratic system.

On the Mural Painting of Buddha's life in the Corridor of the Assembly Hall on the First Floor of Zhwa lu Monastery

Meng Yu

(School of Chinese Classics, Renmin University of China)

The 101st mural painting in the corridor of the Assembly Hall on the first floor of Zhwa lu Monastery is concerned with the biography of the Buddha, from his birth to nirvana. Twenty significant scenes of the Buddha's life were chosen and depicted in this mural. This essay provides a detailed discussion of each scene and concludes that the 101st mural painting is based on the *Lalitavistara* and other sources. The life of the Buddha is a popular subject in Buddhist art and literature. It can be found in many texts, besides the one in *Skyes rabs brgya ba*. In addition to texts, the illustrations of the Buddha's life can also be found in other parts of Tibet. This essay also briefly compares the stories of the Buddha's life in the *Skyes rabs brgya ba* and other literary sources in Tibetan, and its representation in Zhwa lu and other places. A conclusion is drawn that, prior to the sixteenth century, the textual and pictorial representations of Buddha's life in Tibet share obvious similarities.

桑噶地区赤洛纳特寺观音崇拜的艺术史证据

林瑞宾

（美国西北大学）

自 19 世纪以来，赤洛纳特寺（Triloknāth Mandir）就一直吸引着宗教史、人类学、艺术史和建筑各领域学者的兴趣。该寺位于喜马偕尔邦钱德拉巴嘎河谷的屯德村（藏语称“热帕”村），属于西喜马拉雅佛教文化圈。竹巴噶举派喇嘛达仓热巴（1574-1651 年）于 17 世纪时到过这里，在其所撰朝圣行纪中称该地为“乌苌那”，引起了图齐的关注。赤洛纳特寺诱人之处部分缘于以下现象，即现在该地居民将寺中的白色大理石造像视为湿婆神并加以供奉，而来自拉胡尔、桑噶及其他地区的佛教信徒则认为这是一尊佛教造像。近年来，一位佛教僧人和一位印度教祭师被委派至该寺以协助不同宗教的朝圣者。寺中另一独特之处是该寺建筑为通常见于北印度婆罗门教建筑的西柯罗高塔，寺内却供奉佛教雕塑，造像材质为白色大理石，在喜马拉雅地区佛教造像中极为罕见。关于该寺的很多问题都观点不一，如寺院的创建时间，这尊造像何时被安置在寺中，寺院建筑最初是否为印度教寺院而在后来容纳了一尊佛像，抑或建寺伊始就是佛教寺院？暂且遑顾上述众多未决之疑问，本文拟集中探讨这尊造像的图像问题，善趣观音（Sugatiśaṃdārśana Lokeśvara）及其与克什米尔的联系，相邻的桑噶地区的图像推测应系模仿今赤洛纳特寺白色大理石造像。大部分桑噶地区的造像所属时期均相对较晚，因此本研究对赤洛纳特寺白色大理石像的断代、以及此像何时取代了另一尊较早的灰色小石像诸问题也将提供一些依据。

Research on the Seals Granted by the Ming Dynasty to Tibet

Li Shuai

(Post-Doctor, Department of Archaeology, Sichuan University)

The types of seals granted by the Ming dynasty to Tibetan individuals include at least four types: religious — title seals, knighthood seals, official seals and stamp seals. The difference of these seals depends on the social status of the grantees. The type of seal and the motivation of granting them reflected the flexibility and diversity of Ming policies towards Tibet. The seals did not only function as political symbols, they also had practical functions in Tibet. They were used to announce local official statements, to handle local affairs, etc. Some of the seals continued to be in use until well into the Qing dynasty and thus form important evidence that their recipients maintained their political status and were able to influence the governance of Tibet.

Research on the Official Seals of the Chieftain (*Tusi*) in the Tibetan Region of Sichuan Province in the Qing Dynasty

Liu Sha

(Sichuan Museum)

Based on the literary sources, this article investigates seventeen seals of the chieftains (*tusi*, 土司) of the Tibetan region of Sichuan Province in the Qing Dynasty in terms of their nature, characteristics, origin, how they were awarded and how they functioned. This paper considers that the official seals used by the chieftains were mainly granted by the central government of the Qing Dynasty. According to the official seal system of the Qing court, the texture, shape, size, impression and inscription of these seals have special provisions. As political tokens, these official seals played a multifaceted role in local society aside from having practical functions. They were highly valued by the chieftains over generations. Through comparison, it was found that the official seals used by the chieftains in the Sichuan Tibetan areas were quite different from those that were in use in Central Tibet. This was no doubt owed to the differences in their administration. The study of the official seals of the chieftains serves to further explore the policies and characteristics of the Qing Dynasty's governance of the border areas.

The Imperial Kapala Drums of the Qianlong Emperor

Lin Huan

(The Palace Museum, Beijing)

This paper studies the *kapala* drums (*ḍamaru*) that are found in collection of the Palace Museum. They belong to the Qianlong period of the Qing dynasty. The *ḍamaru* drums were mainly made of human skull caps, ivory, jade or wood and are also called "hand drum" or "tambourine," and they belong to the inventory of musical instruments or ritual instruments. The drums in the Palace collection mostly came from the Tibetan areas in the form as tribute to the Qing court. Based on archival sources and extant objects, we know that the Qianlong Emperor had asked the court workshops partly to change these drums and also ordered the court workshops in Suzhou to imitate these with different materials. The extant drums show different influences from Tibetan, Han Chinese and Mongolian culture. They reflected the Qianlong Emperor's aesthetic taste. These drums were decorated with turquoise, coral, beeswax and tridacna, etc. and thus became luxury objects. However, the shape of the drums and their packaging were not overly modified, and maintained the simple nature of the artifact itself. These drums also demonstrate that under the "great unification" pattern, the mature handicraft skills of the border areas could be transplanted to the court (and even to Suzhou). These skills were quickly mastered and reached a very high standard.

Fa Wang Xin Sheng Zhuan —— Stories of Qianlong Emperor's Incarnations

Li Ruoyu

(The Palace Museum, Beijing)

The Palace Museum collection, no. Zong 23584, contains a book that is titled *Fawang xinsheng zhuan* 法王新胜传. It was composed by the 6th Panchen Lama Blo bzang dpal ldan ye shes (1738-1780) in 1780 when he visited Rehe for the celebration of the Qianlong Emperor's birthday. It contains eleven stories of the Qianlong Emperor's previous lives thereby creating a system of the emperor's reincarnations. In this system, the Qianlong Emperor's earlier incarnations included kings who protected Buddhism, siddhas and great gurus of the Bka' gdams pa and Dge lugs pa schools. This paper studies the date and background when this book was produced. It also includes translations of parts of the stories for the first time in the hope of achieving a better understanding of the history of this period and this kind of Tibetan text.

西藏的胎藏界曼荼罗传统及其彩砂曼荼罗制作

田中公明

（日本中村元东方研究所）

“两界曼荼罗”于9世纪初自唐传入日本，不仅构建了日本佛教造像的核心体系，并对整个日本文化产生了深远影响。在这两类曼荼罗中，与“金刚界曼荼罗”相关的遗存较为丰富，其原型出自印度，尼泊尔及西藏继承了的印度的曼荼罗传统，并有大量文献记录和绘画保存至今。然而，留存下来的“胎藏界曼荼罗”相关文献却非常少，其原因在于基于《大日经》的密教体系在古印度很早就已衰亡。此外,《大日经》在吐蕃时期自印度传入西藏，迄今仍有一些胎藏界曼荼罗的实例得以留存，尽管这类遗存极为稀少。此前，本人曾于2001年在日本京都日本文化国际研究中心举行的一次国际学术讨论会，及2003年于牛津举行的第10届国际藏学会上，就西藏的胎藏界曼荼罗传统及相关遗存发表过演讲。但当时限于交通条件，我未能亲自考察位于安多的拉加寺、夏琼寺，这两座寺院至今仍几乎每年都要制作胎藏界曼荼罗的彩砂坛城；尽管1994-1996年间当我担任富山市瑜伽禅修博物馆的首席讲师时，藉馆内复原藏传佛教两界曼荼罗之机，就已经获得了一些源自拉卜楞寺、拉加寺的胎藏界曼荼罗资料。近年来，由于安多地区交通大为改善，使我这样的国外学者得以至上述寺院实地考察。本文主要在笔者于2014、2015年田野考察的基础上完成，拟通过对安多寺院中胎藏界曼荼罗彩砂坛城的制作进行初步介绍，并与唐密—东密传统的胎藏界曼荼罗相比较，进而概括总结其特点。

Journal of Tibetology (Vol.21)

Edited by

Center for Tibetan Studies of Sichuan University
Chengdu, China

ISBN 978-7-5211-0206-2
First Published in December 2019
China Tibetology Publishing House
Beijing, China

图书在版编目(CIP)数据

藏学学刊 . 第 21 辑 / 四川大学中国藏学研究所编 .
—北京：中国藏学出版社， 2019.12
ISBN 978-7-5211-0206-2

Ⅰ . ①藏… Ⅱ . ①四… Ⅲ . ①藏学－文集 Ⅳ . ① K281.4-53

中国版本图书馆 CIP 数据核字（2019）第 289412 号

藏学学刊〔**第 21 辑**〕　四川大学中国藏学研究所 主编

责任编辑　张荣德
藏文审校　顿珠次仁
装帧设计　翟跃飞
出版发行　中国藏学出版社
印　　刷　中国电影出版社印刷厂
版　　次　2019 年 12 月第 1 版第 1 次印刷
开　　本　787 毫米 ×1092 毫米　1/16
字　　数　370 千字
印　　张　20.5
定　　价　88.00 元
书　　号　ISBN 978-7-5211-0206-2 / K · 576

图书如有质量问题，请与本社联系
E-mail: dfhw64892902@126.com 电话: 010-64892902
版权所有 侵权必究

《藏学学刊》稿约

《藏学学刊》（བོད་རིག་པའི་དུས་དེབ། *Journal of Tibetology*）系中国教育部普通高等学校人文社会科学重点研究基地四川大学中国藏学研究所主办的藏学类专业性学术刊物，CSSCI（2014–2018）来源集刊，创刊于2004年，旨在搭建藏学研究的学术交流平台。从2014年开始，本刊由年刊改为半年刊，接受中、英文稿件，设有论文、书评、译文等栏目，热忱欢迎国内外藏学研究者惠赐稿件。来稿时请注意以下事项：

1. 来稿请注明字数并提供作者简介，包括姓名、出生年月、性别、民族、籍贯、职称、学位、工作单位、联系方式和主要研究方向等，其中姓名和工作单位名称请提供正确的英文译名。

2. 来稿必须为原创性作品，此前未经公开发表。严禁抄袭、剽窃和一稿多投，如有发现，将永不刊用该作者来稿。

3. 为保证文稿的准确性，电子版来稿须同时提供word和pdf两种文档格式并遵循本刊用稿规范（详见本所网页）。来稿字数不限，提倡言简意赅，以一万字左右为宜。

4. 本刊每期收稿截止日期为每年六月三十日和十二月三十日。该日期以后收到的稿件将纳入下一期的编辑工作。

5. 本刊取舍稿件惟以学术为标尺，并实行2–3名专家匿名审稿制度，根据专家审稿意见决定稿件取舍。本刊在尊重原作的前提下，有权对拟刊用稿件作必要的删改并告知作者，作者如果不同意对文稿作文字性修改或适当删节，请在来稿时予以说明。

6. 本刊所刊文章均为作者个人观点，不代表编辑部意见，文责由作者自负。

7. 本刊已加入期刊数字化网络系统，作者若无此意愿，请在来稿时注明，否则视为默许。

8. 稿件请直接投寄本刊编辑部。自寄稿之日起，若二个月内未接到用稿通知，可自行处理。来稿除图版原件外，一律不退稿，敬请作者谅解。

9. 本刊对刊用文稿将支付作者稿酬，并赠送样刊五册。

10. 本刊热诚欢迎国内外学者或编辑部与本刊建立资料互赠交流关系。

地　　址：中国四川省成都市望江路29号

四川大学中国藏学研究所《藏学学刊》编辑部

邮　　编：610064

电子邮件：zangxuexuekan@163.com

电话／传真：+86-28-8541 2567

网　　址：http://www.zangx.com

Call for Contributions

Founded in 2004, the *Journal of Tibetology* (བོད་རིག་པའི་དུས་དེབ། 藏学学刊) is a peer-reviewed bilingual scholarly journal dedicated to publishing papers in the field of Tibetan Studies. Featuring articles and reviews in either Chinese or English, the journal is published biannually by the Center for Tibetan Studies of Sichuan University, Chengdu, PRC. The *Journal of Tibetology* welcomes the submission of academic and unpublished (and original) work, including the Chinese translation of foreign research and serious, critical reviews of books or review articles, in any area of research that deals with the Tibetan cultural area.

Essential Guidelines:

1. The manuscript should contain information on the total number of words/characters and author's details, including the following information: (1) full name and institutional affiliation; (2) academic title; (3) contact information, (4) the primary field of research.
2. The *Journal of Tibetology* has a zero-tolerance plagiarism policy.
3. Essays and reviews should be submitted electronically in Microsoft Word file and PDF format, using Unicode, to zangxuexuekan@163.com and conform to the style sheet of the *Journal of Tibetology* that is found at the website of the institute. If this is not done, they will automatically be not considered for publication. There is no limit on the length of the manuscript, but we strongly encourage the manuscript to be concise with approximately 10,000 words in English or Chinese.
4. The deadline for the submission of articles and reviews is June 30 of each year. Articles and reviews received and accepted for publication after this date will be considered for the next issue.
5. The *Journal of Tibetology* uses a double-blind review process. Each manuscript is sent to two or three referees for double-blind peer review. Based on their recommendations, the editor then decides whether the manuscript will be accepted as is, whether it needs to be revised, or whether it will be rejected.
6. The views and opinions expressed in the articles and reviews are those of the author alone and do not reflect the views or opinions of the editor(s) or the editorial board. The author is responsible for his/her own views.
7. The journal is already part of the digital network of Chinese journals. If any author does not want to have his or her article published online, please note this upon submitting the manuscript. Otherwise, the editor will take it as tacitly granting permission to do so.
8. The manuscript should be directly submitted to the editor. If one has not received a notice of acceptance for publication within two months since the day the manuscript was submitted, it is within one's discretion to submit the manuscript elsewhere for publication. Excepting the originals of maps, charts or photographs the editor will not return the manuscript to the author.
9. The journal will pay remuneration to the author and send five copies of the issue of the journal in which his or her article appears.
10. Scholars or editorial boards in China and abroad are warmly welcomed to establish a growing network of exchanging copies of journals with the editor of the *Journal of Tibetology*.

Correspondence should be addressed to:
Dr. Zhang Changhong
Center for Tibetan Studies of Sichuan University
Chengdu, Sichuan Province
P.R. China
610064
Email : zangxuexuekan@163.com
Tel/Fax: +86-28-8541 2567
Website: http://www.zangx.com